JAY JACKSON (1905–1954) was a prolific artist and cartoonist whose work appeared for many years in the Black newspaper *The Chicago Defender*, among numerous other publications. Before he began his cartooning career, he hammered spikes for a railroad, labored in a steel mill, started a short-lived sign-painting business, and even had a brief career as an amateur boxer. In the late 1940s, Jackson moved with his family from Chicago to Los Angeles, where he resided for the remainder of his life.

JEET HEER is a comics critic and the national affairs correspondent for *The Nation*. He is the author of *In Love with Art: Françoise Mouly's Adventures in Comics with Art Spiegelman* and *Sweet Lechery: Reviews, Essays & Profiles*. He divides his time between Toronto and Regina, Canada.

Bungleton GREEN And The Mystic Commandos

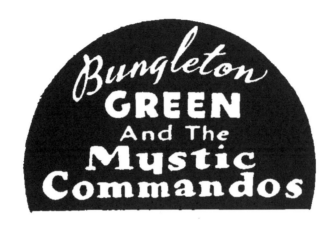

BY JAY JACKSON

INTRODUCTION BY JEET HEER

NEW YORK REVIEW COMICS

THIS IS A NEW YORK REVIEW COMIC
PUBLISHED BY THE NEW YORK REVIEW OF BOOKS
435 Hudson Street, New York, NY 10014
www.nyrb.com/comics
Introduction copyright 2022 © Jeet Heer

A catalog record for this book is available from The Library of Congress.

New York Review Comics would like to thank Dan Nadel for his
significant role in the creation of this book.

ISBN: 978-1-68137-665-3

Printed in South Korea

10 9 8 7 6 5 4 3 2 1

CONTENTS

COMMANDO RAIDS AGAINST RACISM:
Jay Jackson's Audacious Comics

By Jeet Heer

In June 1942, Harold Gray's nationally syndicated comic strip *Little Orphan Annie* made a singular contribution to the war effort: the titular heroine formed a group called the Junior Commandos, a club for boys and girls to fight fascism. The logic behind the Junior Commandos was that because America was in a total war, kids had to pitch in, too. Some of their adventures were fanciful, such as foiling a Nazi submarine attack off the East Coast. Other Junior Commando actions reflected the actual ways total war had transformed everyday American life: starting vegetable gardens, rationing, buying war bonds, and recycling. The concept of the Junior Commandos took off in real life too, with many actual kids' organizations mimicking the good citizenship promoted in the strip.

The Junior Commandos also mirrored the way the war was unsettling gender hierarchies—Annie as a girl in charge (aided by a war widow) — as well as racial ones. A Sunday page that ran on August 2nd featured a young Black boy named George, who helps the Junior Commandos find an old train engine discarded in a quarry, the wartime recycling equivalent of a gold mine. George is deferential and isn't even sure he can be a commando. Annie responds, "You're an American! We're all loyal Americans... It's our fight—yours, George. Angelo's... Fritz's... Marie's... mine!" The use of Italian and German names underscored that this conflict was, at least on the European front, an ideological war, not an ethnic or racial one. To drive home the message of national unity in wartime, Annie makes George a sergeant.

Gray was a right-wing Republican with a Lincolnian streak. This story appeared at a moment when the American army was segregated. It could easily be read as a critique of that segregation, although as one that was cautiously framed. George is shown as smart and capable but also mildly obsequious, literally doffing his cap in front of Annie. The strip produced a polarized response. Many Black readers were delighted. Benzell Graham, an 18-year-old sophomore at the University of California who would later write children's books, was enthusiastic. In a fan letter, she wrote, "We negroes, as all other faithful Americans, are doing our best to help win this war. It encourages us to know that our efforts are appreciated." Other Black readers objected that George was too much of an Uncle Tom. But Ralph B. Chandler, the white editor of the *Mobile Press Register*, wrote a strong letter of objection, saying that some of his readers were upset over "mixing a negro character in with white children." To Chandler's relief and the dismay of many Black readers, George only appeared once in *Little Orphan Annie*.

Gray wasn't the only cartoonist who thought the idea of a commando unit could usefully help integrate children into the war effort. Joe Simon and Jack Kirby, fresh from their success in creating Captain America, launched two more wartime hits: *The Newsboy Legion* (first running in *Star-Spangled #7*, April 1942) and *The Boy Commandos* (debuting in *Detective Comics #64*, June 1942). The Newsboy Legion were a rag-tag gang of white slum boys, saved from the lure of crime by a superhero mentor called The Guardian. The Boy Commandos took the same idea and applied it to the war effort, with a multi-national teenage gang of Nazi fighters that included a Brooklyn boy, a London Cockney lad, a French *garçon*, and a Dutch *jongen*. The politics of The *Newsboy Legion* and *Boy Commandos* series was broadly popular-front, with stories insisting that fighting fascism required a reenergized New Deal at home and international alliances abroad (making nods in a few episodes to the contribution of the Soviet Union). When Jack Kirby revived *The Newsboy Legion* in the 1970s for DC comics, he made amends for the notable racial exclusion by giving the new incarnation of the gang a Black member.

If the idea of child commandos was given a conservative (although multiracial) form by Gray and a New Deal liberal form by Simon and Kirby, it was given a fearlessly radical form by Jay Jackson in late 1942. In the pages of the *Chicago Defender*, Jackson rebooted the long-running strip *Bungleton Green*, which had been predominately a vehicle for comedy and burlesque adventure, into a full-blown science-fiction epic, *Bungleton Green and the Mystic Commandos*. Going beyond pleas for national unity or even the demand for economic reform that appeared in other stories of child commandos, Jackson offered breakneck time-travel adventures that hopped back into the past and leapt into the future to show that the battle against Nazism was merely one phase of a war against racism that was older than America itself. In one particularly breathtaking sequence, Jackson imagined a utopian United States of America of the year 2044, where racism had been definitively defeated and the country served as a model of multiracial democracy.

Jackson was almost certainly aware of Gray's Junior Commando storyline and very likely had an acquaintance with Simon and Kirby's work in The *Newsboy Legion* and *Boy Commandos*. It was not just that *Little Orphan Annie* was one of the most popular comic strips of the time but also that it was distributed by the Chicago Tribune New York News Syndicate. Jackson was a Chicago resident and the *Defender*, the city's Black newspaper, kept a close eye on what the largest-selling daily in the city was publishing. The story of George had been praised by civil rights groups, including the Chicago Urban League.

Simon and Kirby's comics also likely had an influence on Jackson's work in ways beyond their kids-organization storylines. In 1940, during his jack-of-all-trades career as a commercial artist, Jackson dabbled in the then-burgeoning field of comic books, drawing the adventures of *Blond Garth* (a kind of Tarzan knock-off) for *Colossus Comics #1*. Jackson's energetic and breakneck art in *Bungleton Green and the Mystic Commandos* had more in common with the headlong dynamism of Jack Kirby's comic book work that was revolutionizing the field, than the more stately, classical art common in newspaper strips like *Prince Valiant* or *Flash Gordon*. A story in which Bungleton Green becomes a superhero (in fact, very likely the first Black superhero) also demonstrates a close study of comic books.

Yet if Jay Jackson owed a debt to *Little Orphan Annie*, The *Newsboy Legion*, the *Boy Commandos* and other comics, the creator of *Bungleton Green and the Mystic Commandos* was also much more daring than anything being done by other adventure cartoonists of the 1940s. Jackson's boldness is inseparable from his audience. *Little Orphan Annie* and the *Boy Commandos* were addressed to a primarily white audience. Gray's unwillingness to ever again be as directly anti-racist as he was in the George sequence is surely a mark of the sharp limits of what he thought his audience would accept.

Jackson felt no such constraint. His work emerged from the specific way he was able to fuse together his own experience as a Black person in America with the shared narrative power of comics and pulp fiction. The result of this fusion was an explosive comic strip featuring politically energized stories that were unique in their time.

Jay Jackson was born in Oberlin, Ohio, in 1905, the first boy in a family that already had three girls. Oberlin was a pivotal city in the history of abolitionism, a hotbed of anti-slavery sentiment in the nineteenth century that was a crucial node in the underground railroad and home of a college famed for admitting Black students as early as 1835. The Oberlin roots surely explain Jackson's immersion in African-American history, which shows up in panels honoring Black heroes that accompanied many of the *Bungleton Green and the Mystic Commandos* pages, as well as the extensive time-travel story about the battle over slavery during the American revolution.

Jackson's family were middle-class but, as was common among the Black petit bourgeois, precariously so. Jackson's father worked as a gallery photographer. In a charming autobiographical essay published in *Fantastic Adventures* in 1941, Jackson wrote about driving spikes for the railroad at age thirteen and later working in a steel mill. But these stories emphasized how difficult he found manual labor. He attended Ohio Wesleyan University for one year (where he met his first wife, Adaline Smith, whom he married in 1925). During college he drove a mail truck at night to support himself. He also took up boxing and, while he would later dismiss his abilities and brief career, he maintained a love of the sport.

After leaving college, Jackson started a sign-painting business in Pittsburgh. This led to a position as a shop foreman for a theater chain. Then he was hit by a string of personal tragedies. "Everything was swell until the old man with the scythe caught up with my life and struck swiftly, viciously—my father, my first child—my wife … leaving me with an infant daughter [named Carrie Lou] and not the vaguest idea how to fold a diaper," Jackson recalled. "I was twenty-two."

He recounted a period of being a lost soul: "The next scene comes on like an Orson Welles film set, crazy pictures at crazy angles … loneliness, bitterness, sullenness, strange hotels and soulless rooms, moonshine whiskey, bathtub gin, despair." (The allusion to Welles, made in an essay published the same year *Citizen Kane* was released, suggests that like fellow adventure cartoonists such as Milton Caniff and Will Eisner, Jackson was paying attention to experiments in visual storytelling in cinema.

In 1928, he moved to Chicago to be closer to his sister, Mabel, and pulled himself out of his slough of despair. Working hard was one salve. He was always a productive commercial artist and honed his skills by taking classes at Chicago's Art Institute. Aside from painting theater signs, he also painted murals for the Old Mexico exhibit at the Century of Progress International Exposition in 1933-34.

Unlike white artists like Gray and Kirby, Jackson never had the luxury of being able to specialize. Gray in particular benefited from the fact that syndication allowed him to reap a large income from one strip appearing in many newspapers. No such path was available for a Black cartoonist unless they passed as white, like George Herriman, the creator of *Krazy Kat*. The color line in newspaper syndication wasn't broken until 1940, when King Features accepted *Cuties*, a syndicated panel strip by E. Simms Campbell. At that point, Jackson had already been locked into the African-American newspaper market for roughly fifteen years, although he'd made freelance forays outside of it.

Throughout his career as a commercial artist, Jackson took numerous gigs as a magazine illustrator, a newspaper political and strip cartoonist, a poster artist, and an advertising illustrator. Jackson had freelanced since the late 1920s for the *Chicago Defender* and *Abbott's Monthly* (both owned by Robert Sengstacke Abbott). In 1934 he took a staff job at the *Defender*, although even after that point he continued a busy freelance career, including providing cartoons for other African-American newspapers such as the *New York Amsterdam News*.

It was at the *Defender* that Jackson met Eleanor Poston, who worked in the circulation department and was also an artist. They married in 1935. In his *Fantastic Adventures* autobiographical essay, Jackson provided this window into his domestic life: "I have my studio in our little suburban home where my wife models for me, in between her own enthusiasm for dress design." Poston also helped Jackson with the art and writing of the many comic strips he worked on.

Just prior to his marriage, Jackson took over the *Bungleton Green* comic strip, a mainstay at the *Defender*. The comic strip had been created in 1920 by Leslie Rogers (it would eventually be taken over by other hands and last until 1964, making it the longest-running strip to run in an African-American newspaper). The strip belonged to the popular early-twentieth-century comic-strip genre of the sporting life strip, which celebrated lower-middle-class n'e-er-do wells who quickly gained and lost fortunes. Bungleton Green was a Black counterpart to such white wastrels as Barney Google, Moon Mullins and Andy Gump. Not surprisingly, Rogers would regularly dine with Sidney Smith, creator of *The Gumps*. (Harold Gray got his start as an assistant for Smith, who was a friend and mentor as well as an employer. So it's possible that Gray tagged along to Smith's meetings with Rogers.)

This type of boisterous comedy flourished in the 1920s but soon found competition from more melodramatic adventure strips, such as *Little Orphan Annie* (created in 1924), *Buck Rogers* (1929) and *Dick Tracy* (1931). As the type of humor found in *Bungleton Green* fell out of fashion, the strip changed hands. Henry Brown took it over from 1929 to 1934. The reins fell to Jackson in 1934, who would continue working on it till his death in 1954. Jackson's major innovation was to shift *Bungleton Green* into the action-adventure genre. This happened gradually, with the early adventures still having a burlesque feel to them. The character design of Bungleton, who was extremely short with a long pipe nose, worked against him becoming a hero.

But Jackson had a strong instinct for melodrama and adventure, as can be seen in the other comic strips he worked on, such as *Tisha Mingo* (a soap opera about a Black woman trying to succeed as an actress in New York), *Speed Jaxon* (about a Black secret agent who works for the UN and encounters an advanced secret civilization), and *Adventures of Bill* (about a boxer, perhaps echoing Jackson's college experiences of the sport).

The 1942 introduction of the Mystic Commandos allowed Jackson to make a break. Bungleton was still around, but he was a mentor to a group of young boys attracted to a life of crime. This was the formula for the popular *Dead End Kids* movie series, which Joe Simon and Jack Kirby had already adapted to comics in *The Newsboy Legion*. Bungleton Green became a secondary character, seeming almost to shrink in size from episode to episode, as the Mystic Commandos took charge.

Jackson's magpie career as a freelancer energized his creativity. Starting in 1938, he started illustrating pulp magazines for the Chicago -based publishing firm Ziff Davis (*Amazing, Weird Tales, Fantastic Adven-*

tures). He became well-versed in the tropes of fantasy and science fiction, which now drove the plots of *Bungleton Green*. His foray into comic books, drawing the adventures of jungle adventurer Blond Garth, also helped. The pulps were an ambiguous demi-monde for Black writers and artists. Unquestionably, there were racists in powerful positions in that world: notably the recently deceased horror writer H.P. Lovecraft and John W. Campbell, the editor of the influential *Astounding Science Fiction*, who would one day write editorials defending slavery and also reject a Samuel R. Delany novel for featuring a Black leading character. In 1941, *Astounding* serialized Robert A. Heinlein's Yellow Peril novel *Sixth Column*, whose racist plot of an "Asiatic" conquest of the United States was supplied by Campbell. During the years Jay Jackson worked on *Bungleton Green*, both the pulps and comics (although often created by artists and writers of diverse backgrounds) featured by convention WASP heroes like Heinlein's Lazarus Long, Jerry Siegel and Joe Shuster's Superman (a.k.a. Clark Kent) or Bob Kane and Bill Finger's Batman (a.k.a. Bruce Wayne).

But still, precisely because the pulps and the comics were at the lowest ring of the publishing world, they provided a precarious opening for a few Black artists. These included not just Jackson, but also Matt Baker and E. C. Stoner, as well as many more descended from Eastern and Southern Europe immigrants. It's undeniable that the pulps offered Jackson not just freelance work but also a set of useful science-fiction tropes (time travel, hidden kingdoms) that the cartoonist repurposed to create pioneering Afro-futurist stories which imagined an inhabitable and indeed utopian future for Black people.

The glamor-girl art Jackson did on *Tisha Mingo* would find another outlet in the beautiful women now populating *Bungleton Green*. Even the poster work Jackson did for the U.S. Treasury Department promoting war bonds would find echoes in the wartime propaganda that runs through his comic strips.

But if Jackson was a propagandist, he was a subtle one. Throughout *Bungleton Green and the Mystic Commandos*, he offers a critical support of the war: America has to win, but defeating fascism would only be meaningful if racism were eradicated. Fascism, he repeatedly stresses, has roots in racism and could have an afterlife in future racist regimes. Within his science-fiction allegories, Jackson pressed upon issues that still remain pertinent (the use of the filibuster in the Senate as a hurdle to racial progress appears in one storyline). In a fantastic narrative of an anti-racist America confronting a society of green-skinned men who oppress whites, Jackson didn't just create a clever topsy-turvy scenario. He also anticipated the postwar reality that a need to improve America's global reputation would create an opening for the civil rights movement. The sequence was perhaps influenced by George Schuyler's 1931 novel *Black No More*, a satire that also played with the theme of race reversal. Throughout Jackson's work, his satire is impudent, scathingly sardonic, and audaciously bitter.

Bungleton Green and the Mystic Commandos is a remarkable achievement. There's no other satirical or adventure comic strip of the era that was quite as far-reaching in its challenge to conventional thought. It deserves to be revived and Jackson's larger body of work will, one hopes, also be reprinted in the future.

ertained at a reception Tuesday......JULIUS ADAMS, former naging editor of the Chicago Defender, now with the Amsterdam ws in New York, welcomed a chance to cover the GOP meet, ause it gave him a chance to let friends see his wifie and two ngsters......That was JIMMIE (Harlem cafe) ALLISON throw- that champagne party for those visitors from Boston........ ASH! One in the party will be his bride, but he'll deny it...... RLIE (Bethel Church) DICKIE became a bride Sunday.

* * *

Vith T. BONE WALKER, the guitar playing blues singer return- to CHARLIE GLENN'S Rhumboogie, the spot has taken on new despite the intense heat......New show premiers at the DELISA day night and is titled "Yankee Doodle Hayride"......SADIE RISTMAS is now Mrs. McKinley Williams......MARY (Eight lock Girls) DEDRICK is saving her cash to skip to New York. ASH! Ask FRED (bartender) VAUGHN to tell you the name of chick who threw that glass at him and why......Wonder why MA FRANKLIN doesn't come back to Chicago?......HILLIARD ite Masters) HOGAN is having so much fun in Los Angeles, he decided to make it his home.

* * *

GEORGE V. HILL, stationed at Fort Lawton, Wash., has been omoted to corporal and MILTON J. FARQUHAR has been pro- ted to technician fifth grade. . . . FLASH! Parkway Ballroom is ebrating its 4th ANNIVERSARY with a cabaret party Saturday, ly 29.

SQUARE'S steak house dropped Evanna Waterford Cotton as nist and then CUT prices......BILL SOMMERFORD who has en in boot training up at Great Lakes, comes in Monday on his st leave......JEAN BLANCHET, the bar maid at 411, has an eresting story to tell you about somebody she met in Washington. d who was the cat SADIE GUYLER had dinner with at the 63rd eet spot t'other day?......JOE HIGGINS, the one time star bas- ball player at Wendell Phillips, now somewhere in Africa, sends e to ANN WHITE and BERTHA ROBINSON......Which reminds that HENRY (Money) RANSOM is back after 18 months in Africa.

* * *

JOHN WILLIAMS had a little family quarrel with his wife ANNA ile he was drunk and she chased him into the Wabash avenue tion......UP TO DATERS will entertain summer visitors at a ort danc at the Parkway Sunday afternoon......That night, the AU BRUMMELS are crowning "Miss High School Grad"........ KIE FITZHUGH will skip to Washington, D. C., next week to see at fly young thing?......RAYMOND PENDARIUS and JOHN PSON will be the tip top mixologists at the Grand Terrace which ens this week......FREDDIE GUYNARD, former secretary of ampion JOE LOUIS was in town telling everybody about his new tel in Detroit......IRENE HARRISON was called to Cincinnati cause of serious illness of her mama.....

* * *

Here are some G.I.s who can stand some mail: Pvt. ROBERT I. ACK, APO 980, c-o Postmaster, Seattle, Wash.; S.-Sgt. LLEWEL- N (Neiser Bros., Inc.) DANIEL, APO 93, c-o Postmaster, San ancisco, Calif.; T.-Sgt. DANIEL H. OSBORNE, Navy 337, c-o FPO, n Francisco, Calif.; Cpl. J. O. STEELE, APO 709, c-o Postmaster, n Francisco Calif.; Cpl. MILTON McGEE, APO 20-A, c-o Post- ster, Shreveport, La.; Cpl. P. BURNS, 20621508, APO 502, c-o Post- ster, San Francisco, Calif.; Pfc. ROBERT L. TRAMMELL, 34712651, O 115, c-o Postmaster New York, N. Y.; Sgt. WILLARD O. AUGH, 36393832, APO 928, c-o- Postmaster, San Francisco, Calif.; JOSEPH COOPER, 36794013, APO 511, c-o Postmaster, New rk, N. Y.; Pfc. ALBERT "AL" ROBERTS, APO 9768, c-o Post- ster, New York, N. Y.; Sgt. JAMES D. KELLUM, 36795677, APO , c-o Postmaster, New York, N. Y.

* * *

Add these names to your list of tip top bartenders of the week: ADY-O of the DuSable; REX EDWARDS and BOB HENLEY of 's......PLATO BIBBS showed the fellas he was a good fellow esday when he banqueted them at Rose Eat shop........The HITTIER (Chicago Defender) SENGSTACKES had an arrival from Stork......EDWINA HARLESTON will be on her way to Dixie en you read this and when she returns three weeks later, she will EDWINA GREEN......And so the new bartender at the 308 b is CHARLES GRAY........The Don Juans picked HELEN YD "Miss Sweetheart Grad" and JESSIE MAE CRAWFORD is iss Undergrad"......They are congratulating ED HARRIS as d bartender and SAM WALDER as manager of the Hurricane.

* * *

ZEPHRONIA HOLLOWAY is seeing the sights in Los Angeles..... T BARNES, who is now DOT SIMMONS, is vacationing in Mexico d may remain on the west coast until hubby returns from the uthwest Pacific....What happened between MERCEDES SOUTH d that 47th street bartender?......IDA GANTT OWENS is making e to hubby who is now with the tank destroyers in Ft. Huachuca, iz......and so the LEFT FIELDER of the American Giants base- ll team got a nice bob on the head Sunday, all because he KISSED oman near the dressing room......DR. JAMES (Mayor of Bronze- le) SCOTT returns Sunday after a vacation in New York and East......Because he whipped his wife and took two pot shots STERLING SLAUGHTER, poor DANIEL HOLLOWELL will have take a 60-day vacation in California, out at 26th street....... ARRY FIELDS and CHARLEY COLE of the Pershing Lounge; NNIE SKOLLER of the CIRCLE INN and MINNIE HORTON of Midway Inn, have been busy all week giving the glad hand- ake to GOP delegates.

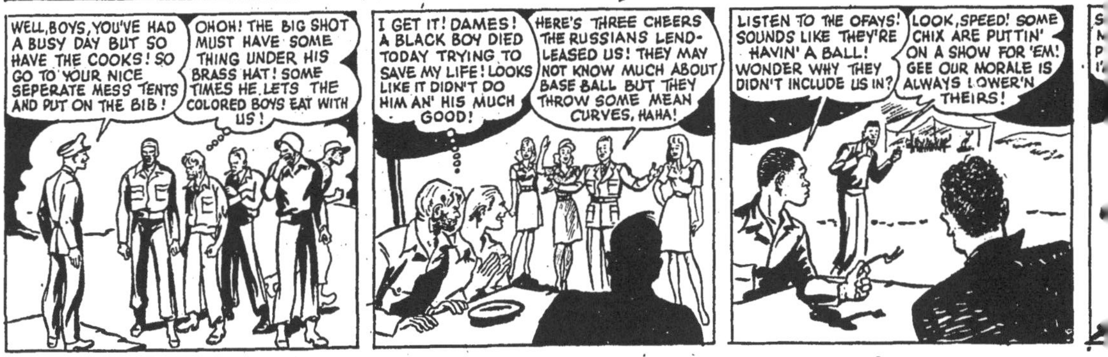

WELL, BOYS, YOU'VE HAD A BUSY DAY BUT SO HAVE THE COOKS! SO GO TO YOUR NICE SEPERATE MESS TENTS AND PUT ON THE BIB!
OHOH! THE BIG SHOT MUST HAVE SOME THING UNDER HIS BRASS HAT! SOME TIMES HE LETS THE COLORED BOYS EAT WITH US!
I GET IT! DAMES! A BLACK BOY DIED TODAY TRYING TO SAVE MY LIFE! LOOKS LIKE IT DIDN'T DO HIM AN' HIS MUCH GOOD!
HERE'S THREE CHEERS THE RUSSIANS LEND-LEASED US! THEY MAY NOT KNOW MUCH ABOUT BASE BALL BUT THEY THROW SOME MEAN CURVES, HAHA!
LISTEN TO THE OFAYS! SOUNDS LIKE THEY'RE HAVIN' A BALL! WONDER WHY THEY DIDN'T INCLUDE US IN?
LOOK, SPEED! SOME CHIX ARE PUTTIN' ON A SHOW FOR 'EM! GEE OUR MORALE IS ALWAYS LOWER'N THEIRS!

PRINCE WHIPPLE

February 1943 – July 1943

Sweetheart

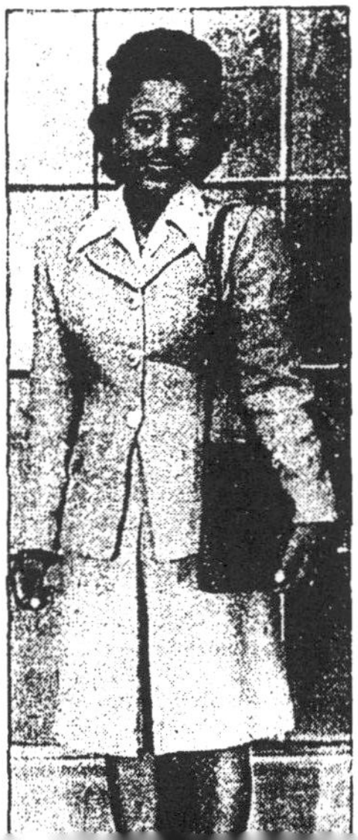

See Harlem's Interracial Hospital As Successful

By RAMONA LOWE
(Defender New York Bureau)

NEW YORK — When Sydenham Hospital was converted into an interracial hospital last December, controversy raged in Harlem.

There were those who said it would become a jim crow institution. Others thought that if any money was to be given in Harlem for hospital facilities, it should be given to the Edgecombe Sanitarium. The Sanitarium was described as a "boarding house with a sign out in front." It had no elevator nor oxygen tent, but it was all Harlem could boast of in the way of a private hospital.

A community hospital was sorely needed.

It was needed so that a patient could have the care of his private doctor and yet have the advantage of hospital facilities. It was needed so that Harlem's 175 doctors could have a workshop outside of Harlem Hospital, which is a municipal hospital rendering only basic care and offering none of the refinements that private hospitals afford.

Most of the babies delivered in the community were delivered by

Sydnham had a current debt of $60,000 in bills and mortgage. Located in what was fast becoming a Negro slum area, its white patients had fallen off. It was willing therefore to organize an interracial staff and trustee board if its debt could be paid off.

It was a sound business offer and the two million dollar plant was taken over for $100,000. Twelve trustees were elected, six of them Negro. To the medical staff, 23 Negro doctors were added.

The only voluntary interracial hospital in the country it now has Negroes on the nursing staff, in the technical department and on the clerical staff.

The experiment is considered a success by Benjamin Roth, president of the hospital. And it inspired the New York County Medical Society to pass a resolution in April calling on voluntary hospitals to open their doors to Negroes.

"Now it is the moral obligation of the Harlem community to keep it going," one doctor said. "Unfortunately we have developed a community that in 20 years has no

Waiter Marks His 50 Years Of Work By Buying Bonds

RICHMOND, Va.—(ANP)—Fifty years of service at the internationally known Commonwealth club here was marked last week by William Rush, popular headwaiter, by a purchase of $1,000 worth of war bonds.

Rush, who wears five golden stars on his sleeve indicating 10 years each, is said to be as popular for his recitation of Lee's farewell address as for his unusual recipes. He includes Lady Astor and other famous personages among his friends.

The famous headwaiter boasts that he has had the honor to see and serve about four or five generations of the Virginia gentry here, and made a revelation about the changing tide of things at the club.

"I'll tell you how it's changed though, in these 50 years," he remarked. "Long time ago, the gentlemen played poker and there'd be a kitty attached. Well, after the game, the waiters participated in the kitty. But these days they play this new fangled bridge. No kitty. No participation."

ASK LYNN CASE REARGUMENT

2 More C Soldier

U.S. ARME NEW CALE more Chicago area have bee command in their performan revealed this we The men, both dell Phillips hig Arthur L. Gill

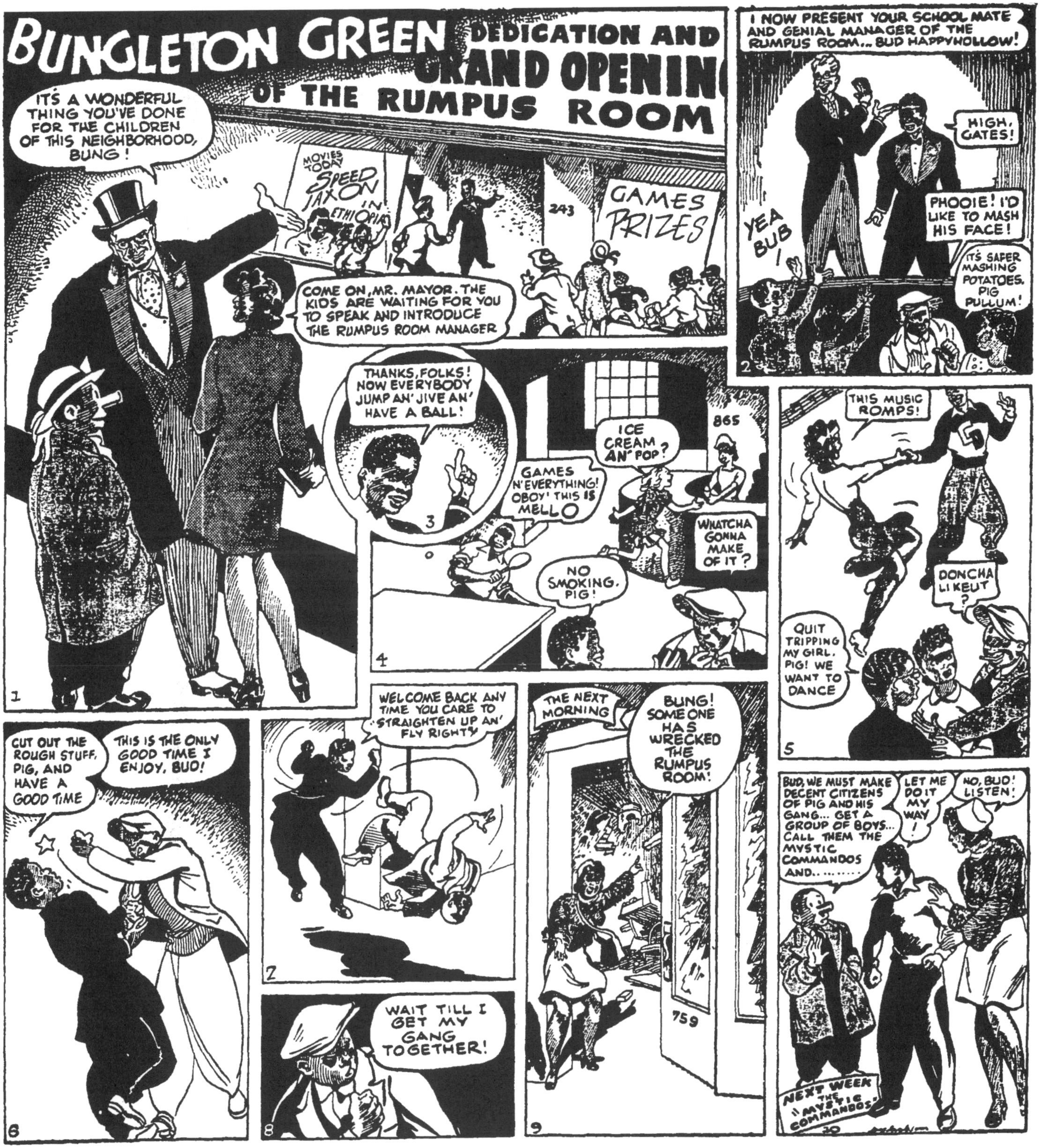
BUNGLETON GREEN
DEDICATION AND GRAND OPENING OF THE RUMPUS ROOM
IT'S A WONDERFUL THING YOU'VE DONE FOR THE CHILDREN OF THIS NEIGHBORHOOD, BUNG!
MOVIES TODAY SPEED JAXON IN ETHIOPIA
GAMES PRIZES
COME ON, MR. MAYOR. THE KIDS ARE WAITING FOR YOU TO SPEAK AND INTRODUCE THE RUMPUS ROOM MANAGER
I NOW PRESENT YOUR SCHOOL MATE AND GENIAL MANAGER OF THE RUMPUS ROOM... BUD HAPPYHOLLOW!
HIGH, GATES!
YEA BUB!
PHOOIE! I'D LIKE TO MASH HIS FACE!
IT'S SAFER MASHING POTATOES, PIG PULLUM!
THANKS, FOLKS! NOW EVERYBODY JUMP AN' JIVE AN' HAVE A BALL!
GAMES N' EVERYTHING! OBOY! THIS IS MELLO
ICE CREAM AN' POP?
NO SMOKING, PIG!
WHATCHA GONNA MAKE OF IT?
THIS MUSIC ROMPS!
DONCHA LIKEUT?
QUIT TRIPPING MY GIRL, PIG! WE WANT TO DANCE
CUT OUT THE ROUGH STUFF, PIG, AND HAVE A GOOD TIME
THIS IS THE ONLY GOOD TIME I ENJOY, BUD!
WELCOME BACK ANY TIME YOU CARE TO 'STRAIGHTEN UP AN' FLY RIGHT'!
WAIT TILL I GET MY GANG TOGETHER!
THE NEXT MORNING
BUNG! SOME ONE HAS WRECKED THE RUMPUS ROOM!
BUD, WE MUST MAKE DECENT CITIZENS OF PIG AND HIS GANG... GET A GROUP OF BOYS... CALL THEM THE MYSTIC COMMANDOS AND.........
LET ME DO IT MY WAY!
NO, BUD! LISTEN!
NEXT WEEK THE "MYSTIC COMMANDOS"

NOVEMEBER 28, 1942

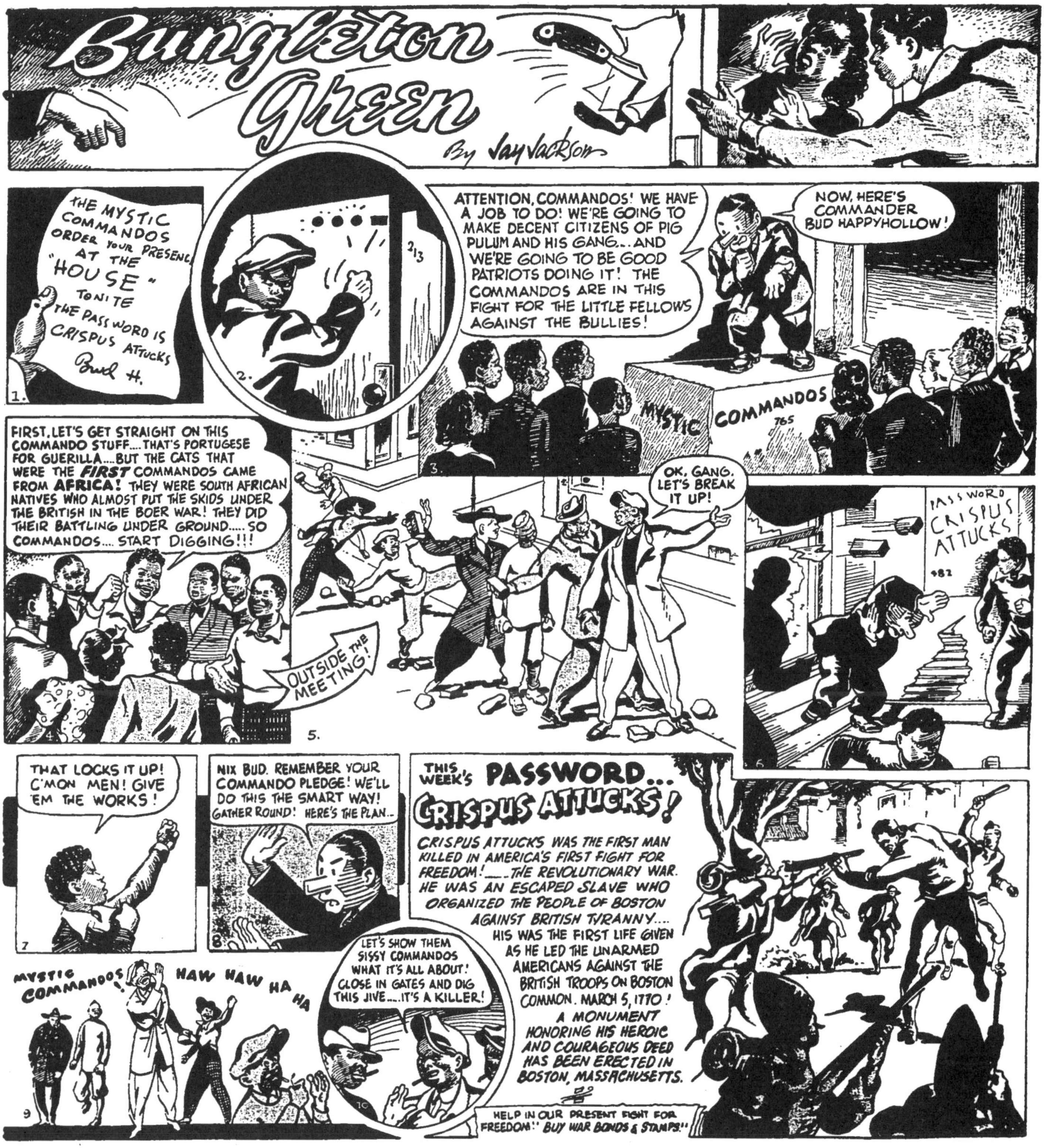
Bungleton Green
By Jay Jackson
THE MYSTIC COMMANDOS ORDER YOUR PRESENCE AT THE "HOUSE" TONITE THE PASSWORD IS CRISPUS ATTUCKS Bud H.
ATTENTION, COMMANDOS! WE HAVE A JOB TO DO! WE'RE GOING TO MAKE DECENT CITIZENS OF PIG PULUM AND HIS GANG...AND WE'RE GOING TO BE GOOD PATRIOTS DOING IT! THE COMMANDOS ARE IN THIS FIGHT FOR THE LITTLE FELLOWS AGAINST THE BULLIES!
NOW, HERE'S COMMANDER BUD HAPPYHOLLOW!
MYSTIC COMMANDOS
FIRST, LET'S GET STRAIGHT ON THIS COMMANDO STUFF....THAT'S PORTUGESE FOR GUERILLA....BUT THE CATS THAT WERE THE FIRST COMMANDOS CAME FROM AFRICA! THEY WERE SOUTH AFRICAN NATIVES WHO ALMOST PUT THE SKIDS UNDER THE BRITISH IN THE BOER WAR! THEY DID THEIR BATTLING UNDER GROUND..... SO COMMANDOS.... START DIGGING!!!
OUTSIDE THE MEETING!
OK, GANG. LET'S BREAK IT UP!
PASSWORD CRISPUS ATTUCKS
THAT LOCKS IT UP! C'MON MEN! GIVE 'EM THE WORKS!
NIX BUD. REMEMBER YOUR COMMANDO PLEDGE! WE'LL DO THIS THE SMART WAY! GATHER ROUND! HERE'S THE PLAN...
MYSTIC COMMANDOS! HAW HAW HA HA
LET'S SHOW THEM SISSY COMMANDOS WHAT IT'S ALL ABOUT! CLOSE IN GATES AND DIG THIS JIVE....IT'S A KILLER!
THIS WEEK'S PASSWORD... CRISPUS ATTUCKS!
CRISPUS ATTUCKS WAS THE FIRST MAN KILLED IN AMERICA'S FIRST FIGHT FOR FREEDOM!___THE REVOLUTIONARY WAR. HE WAS AN ESCAPED SLAVE WHO ORGANIZED THE PEOPLE OF BOSTON AGAINST BRITISH TYRANNY.... HIS WAS THE FIRST LIFE GIVEN AS HE LED THE UNARMED AMERICANS AGAINST THE BRITISH TROOPS ON BOSTON COMMON. MARCH 5, 1770! A MONUMENT HONORING HIS HEROIC AND COURAGEOUS DEED HAS BEEN ERECTED IN BOSTON, MASSACHUSETTS.
HELP IN OUR PRESENT FIGHT FOR FREEDOM!" BUY WAR BONDS & STAMPS!"

DECEMBER 5, 1942

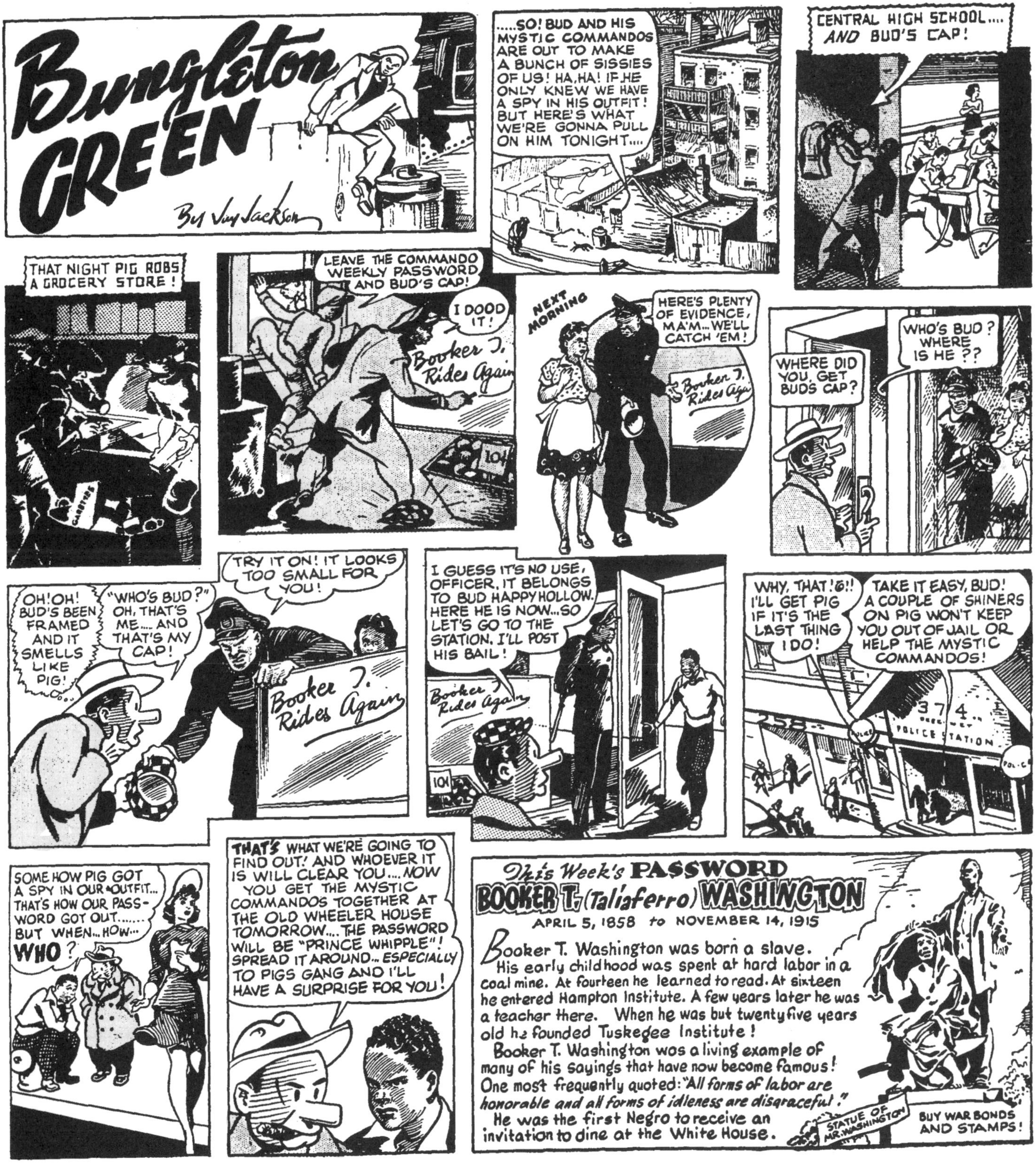
Bungleton Green
By Jay Jackson
.....SO! BUD AND HIS MYSTIC COMMANDOS ARE OUT TO MAKE A BUNCH OF SISSIES OF US! HA,HA! IF HE ONLY KNEW WE HAVE A SPY IN HIS OUTFIT! BUT HERE'S WHAT WE'RE GONNA PULL ON HIM TONIGHT....
CENTRAL HIGH SCHOOL.... AND BUD'S CAP!
THAT NIGHT PIG ROBS A GROCERY STORE!
LEAVE THE COMMANDO WEEKLY PASSWORD AND BUD'S CAP!
I DOOD IT!
Booker T. Rides Again
NEXT MORNING
HERE'S PLENTY OF EVIDENCE, MA'M... WE'LL CATCH 'EM!
Booker T. Rides Again
WHO'S BUD? WHERE IS HE??
WHERE DID YOU GET BUD'S CAP?
OH! OH! BUD'S BEEN FRAMED AND IT SMELLS LIKE PIG!
"WHO'S BUD?" OH, THAT'S ME.... AND THAT'S MY CAP!
TRY IT ON! IT LOOKS TOO SMALL FOR YOU!
Booker T. Rides Again
I GUESS IT'S NO USE, OFFICER, IT BELONGS TO BUD HAPPYHOLLOW. HERE HE IS NOW...SO LET'S GO TO THE STATION. I'LL POST HIS BAIL!
Booker T. Rides Again
WHY, THAT! I'LL GET PIG IF IT'S THE LAST THING I DO!
TAKE IT EASY, BUD! A COUPLE OF SHINERS ON PIG WON'T KEEP YOU OUT OF JAIL OR HELP THE MYSTIC COMMANDOS!
POLICE STATION
SOME HOW PIG GOT A SPY IN OUR OUTFIT... THAT'S HOW OUR PASSWORD GOT OUT....... BUT WHEN... HOW... WHO?
THAT'S WHAT WE'RE GOING TO FIND OUT! AND WHOEVER IT IS WILL CLEAR YOU.... NOW YOU GET THE MYSTIC COMMANDOS TOGETHER AT THE OLD WHEELER HOUSE TOMORROW.... THE PASSWORD WILL BE "PRINCE WHIPPLE"! SPREAD IT AROUND... ESPECIALLY TO PIGS GANG AND I'LL HAVE A SURPRISE FOR YOU!
This Week's PASSWORD
BOOKER T. (Taliaferro) WASHINGTON
APRIL 5, 1858 to NOVEMBER 14, 1915
Booker T. Washington was born a slave.
His early childhood was spent at hard labor in a coal mine. At fourteen he learned to read. At sixteen he entered Hampton Institute. A few years later he was a teacher there. When he was but twenty five years old he founded Tuskegee Institute!
Booker T. Washington was a living example of many of his sayings that have now become famous! One most frequently quoted: "All forms of labor are honorable and all forms of idleness are disgraceful."
He was the first Negro to receive an invitation to dine at the White House.
STATUE OF MR. WASHINGTON
BUY WAR BONDS AND STAMPS!

DECEMBER 12, 1942

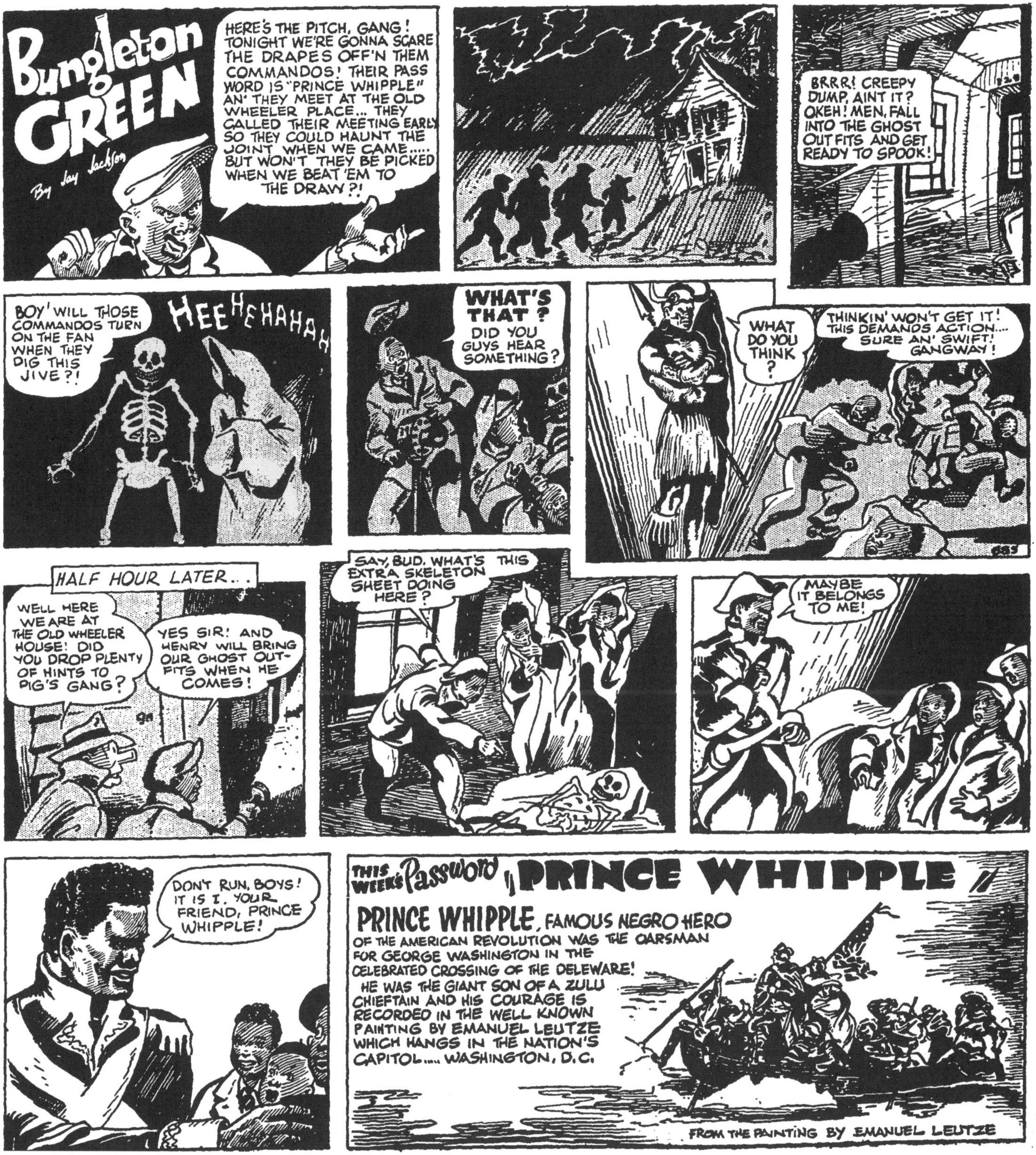
Bungleton GREEN
By Jay Jackson
HERE'S THE PITCH, GANG! TONIGHT WE'RE GONNA SCARE THE DRAPES OFF'N THEM COMMANDOS! THEIR PASS WORD IS "PRINCE WHIPPLE" AN' THEY MEET AT THE OLD WHEELER PLACE... THEY CALLED THEIR MEETING EARLY SO THEY COULD HAUNT THE JOINT WHEN WE CAME..... BUT WON'T THEY BE PICKED WHEN WE BEAT 'EM TO THE DRAW?!
BRRR! CREEPY DUMP, AINT IT? OKEH! MEN, FALL INTO THE GHOST OUTFITS AND GET READY TO SPOOK!
BOY! WILL THOSE COMMANDOS TURN ON THE FAN WHEN THEY DIG THIS JIVE?!
HEE HEHAHAH
WHAT'S THAT? DID YOU GUYS HEAR SOMETHING?
WHAT DO YOU THINK?
THINKIN' WON'T GET IT! THIS DEMANDS ACTION.... SURE AN' SWIFT! GANGWAY!
HALF HOUR LATER...
WELL HERE WE ARE AT THE OLD WHEELER HOUSE: DID YOU DROP PLENTY OF HINTS TO PIG'S GANG?
YES SIR! AND HENRY WILL BRING OUR GHOST OUTFITS WHEN HE COMES!
SAY, BUD, WHAT'S THIS EXTRA SKELETON SHEET DOING HERE?
MAYBE IT BELONGS TO ME!
DON'T RUN, BOYS! IT IS I, YOUR FRIEND, PRINCE WHIPPLE!
THIS WEEK'S Password "PRINCE WHIPPLE"
PRINCE WHIPPLE, FAMOUS NEGRO HERO OF THE AMERICAN REVOLUTION WAS THE OARSMAN FOR GEORGE WASHINGTON IN THE CELEBRATED CROSSING OF THE DELEWARE! HE WAS THE GIANT SON OF A ZULU CHIEFTAIN AND HIS COURAGE IS RECORDED IN THE WELL KNOWN PAINTING BY EMANUEL LEUTZE WHICH HANGS IN THE NATION'S CAPITOL.... WASHINGTON, D.C.
FROM THE PAINTING BY EMANUEL LEUTZE

DECEMBER 19, 1942

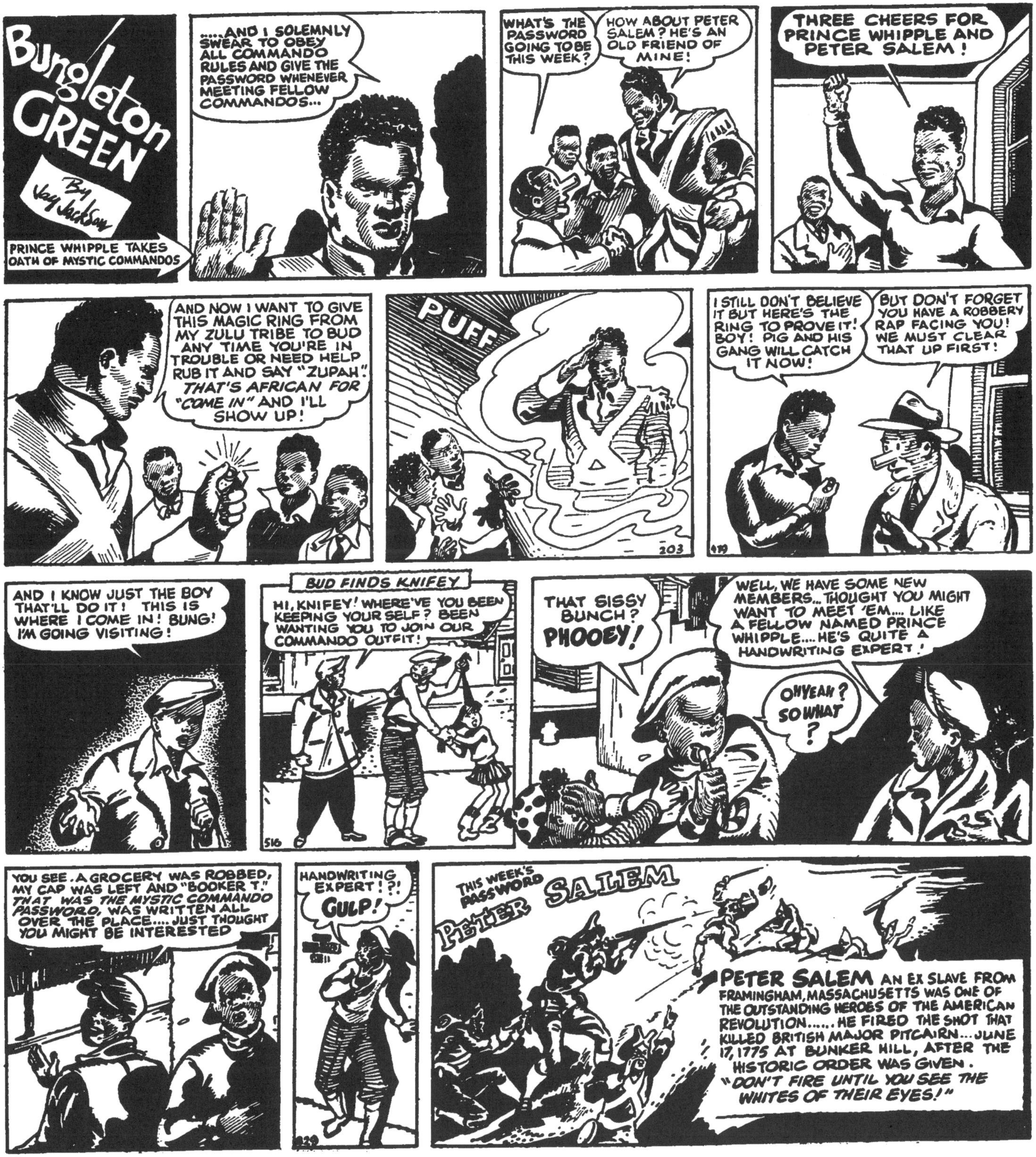

Bungleton Green
By Jay Jackson
PRINCE WHIPPLE TAKES OATH OF MYSTIC COMMANDOS
.....AND I SOLEMNLY SWEAR TO OBEY ALL COMMANDO RULES AND GIVE THE PASSWORD WHENEVER MEETING FELLOW COMMANDOS...
WHAT'S THE PASSWORD GOING TO BE THIS WEEK?
HOW ABOUT PETER SALEM? HE'S AN OLD FRIEND OF MINE!
THREE CHEERS FOR PRINCE WHIPPLE AND PETER SALEM!
AND NOW I WANT TO GIVE THIS MAGIC RING FROM MY ZULU TRIBE TO BUD ANY TIME YOU'RE IN TROUBLE OR NEED HELP RUB IT AND SAY "ZUPAH". THAT'S AFRICAN FOR "COME IN" AND I'LL SHOW UP!
PUFF
I STILL DON'T BELIEVE IT BUT HERE'S THE RING TO PROVE IT! BOY! PIG AND HIS GANG WILL CATCH IT NOW!
BUT DON'T FORGET YOU HAVE A ROBBERY RAP FACING YOU! WE MUST CLEAR THAT UP FIRST!
AND I KNOW JUST THE BOY THAT'LL DO IT! THIS IS WHERE I COME IN! BUNG! I'M GOING VISITING!
BUD FINDS KNIFEY
HI, KNIFEY! WHERE'VE YOU BEEN KEEPING YOUR SELF? BEEN WANTING YOU TO JOIN OUR COMMANDO OUTFIT!
THAT SISSY BUNCH? PHOOEY!
WELL, WE HAVE SOME NEW MEMBERS... THOUGHT YOU MIGHT WANT TO MEET 'EM.... LIKE A FELLOW NAMED PRINCE WHIPPLE.... HE'S QUITE A HANDWRITING EXPERT!
OH YEAH? SO WHAT?
YOU SEE. A GROCERY WAS ROBBED, MY CAP WAS LEFT AND "BOOKER T." THAT WAS THE MYSTIC COMMANDO PASSWORD, WAS WRITTEN ALL OVER THE PLACE.... JUST THOUGHT YOU MIGHT BE INTERESTED
HANDWRITING EXPERT!?!
GULP!
THIS WEEK'S PASSWORD
PETER SALEM
PETER SALEM AN EX SLAVE FROM FRAMINGHAM, MASSACHUSETTS WAS ONE OF THE OUTSTANDING HEROES OF THE AMERICAN REVOLUTION...... HE FIRED THE SHOT THAT KILLED BRITISH MAJOR PITCAIRN... JUNE 17, 1775 AT BUNKER HILL, AFTER THE HISTORIC ORDER WAS GIVEN. "DON'T FIRE UNTIL YOU SEE THE WHITES OF THEIR EYES!"

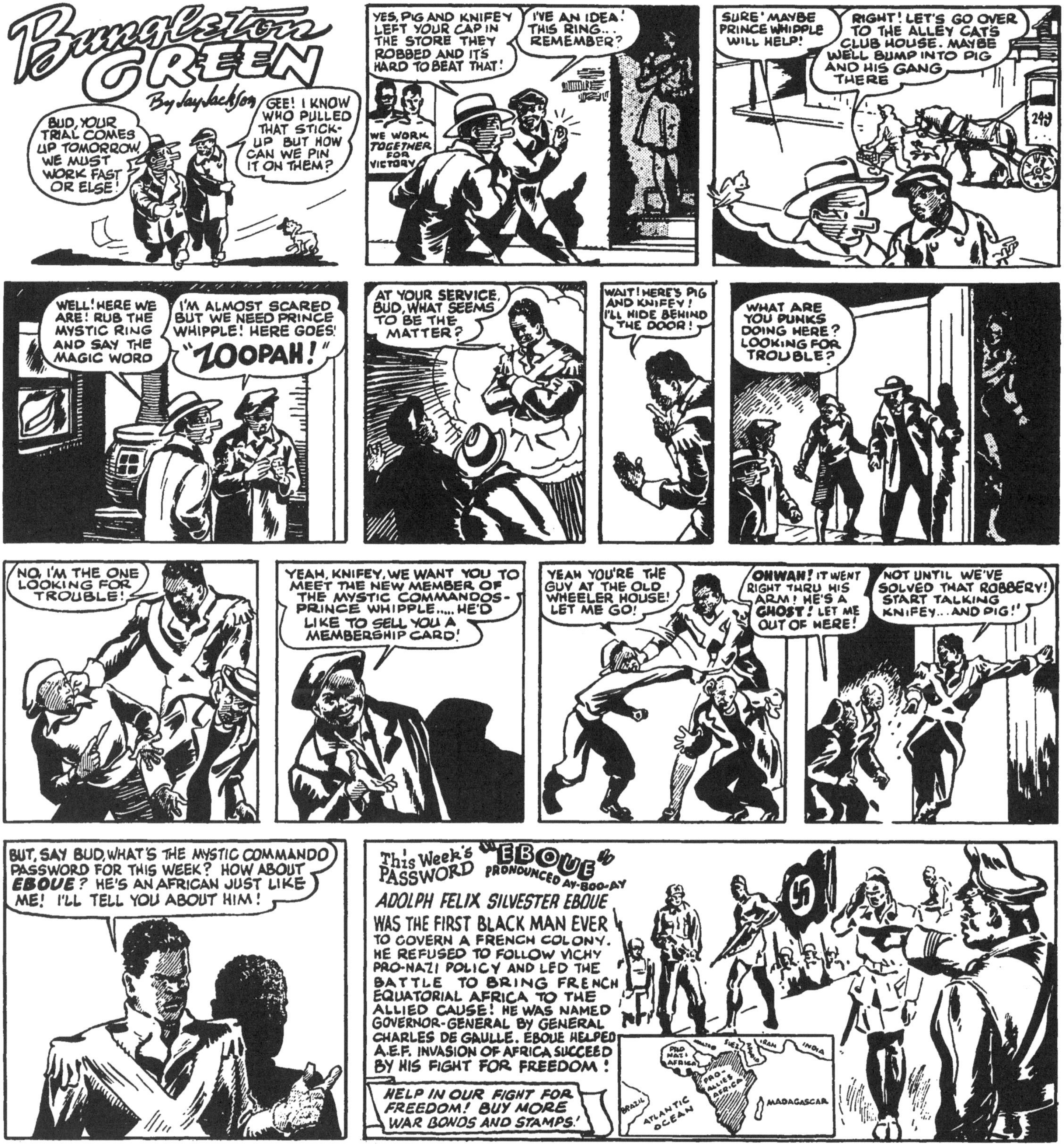
Bungleton GREEN
By Jay Jackson
BUD, YOUR TRIAL COMES UP TOMORROW, WE MUST WORK FAST OR ELSE!
GEE! I KNOW WHO PULLED THAT STICK-UP BUT HOW CAN WE PIN IT ON THEM?
YES, PIG AND KNIFEY LEFT YOUR CAP IN THE STORE THEY ROBBED AND IT'S HARD TO BEAT THAT!
I'VE AN IDEA! THIS RING... REMEMBER?
WE WORK TOGETHER FOR VICTORY
SURE! MAYBE PRINCE WHIPPLE WILL HELP!
RIGHT! LET'S GO OVER TO THE ALLEY CAT'S CLUB HOUSE. MAYBE WE'LL BUMP INTO PIG AND HIS GANG THERE
WELL! HERE WE ARE! RUB THE MYSTIC RING AND SAY THE MAGIC WORD
I'M ALMOST SCARED BUT WE NEED PRINCE WHIPPLE! HERE GOES! "ZOOPAH!"
AT YOUR SERVICE, BUD, WHAT SEEMS TO BE THE MATTER?
WAIT! HERE'S PIG AND KNIFEY! I'LL HIDE BEHIND THE DOOR!
WHAT ARE YOU PUNKS DOING HERE? LOOKING FOR TROUBLE?
NO, I'M THE ONE LOOKING FOR TROUBLE!
YEAH, KNIFEY, WE WANT YOU TO MEET THE NEW MEMBER OF THE MYSTIC COMMANDOS-PRINCE WHIPPLE..... HE'D LIKE TO SELL YOU A MEMBERSHIP CARD!
YEAH YOU'RE THE GUY AT THE OLD WHEELER HOUSE! LET ME GO!
OHWAH! IT WENT RIGHT THRU HIS ARM! HE'S A GHOST! LET ME OUT OF HERE!
NOT UNTIL WE'VE SOLVED THAT ROBBERY! START TALKING KNIFEY... AND PIG!"
BUT, SAY BUD, WHAT'S THE MYSTIC COMMANDO PASSWORD FOR THIS WEEK? HOW ABOUT EBOUE? HE'S AN AFRICAN JUST LIKE ME! I'LL TELL YOU ABOUT HIM!
This Week's PASSWORD "EBOUE" PRONOUNCED AY-BOO-AY
ADOLPH FELIX SILVESTER EBOUE WAS THE FIRST BLACK MAN EVER TO GOVERN A FRENCH COLONY. HE REFUSED TO FOLLOW VICHY PRO-NAZI POLICY AND LED THE BATTLE TO BRING FRENCH EQUATORIAL AFRICA TO THE ALLIED CAUSE! HE WAS NAMED GOVERNOR-GENERAL BY GENERAL CHARLES DE GAULLE. EBOUE HELPED A.E.F. INVASION OF AFRICA SUCCEED BY HIS FIGHT FOR FREEDOM!
HELP IN OUR FIGHT FOR FREEDOM! BUY MORE WAR BONDS AND STAMPS!
PRO NAZI AFRICA
SUEZ
IRAN
INDIA
PRO-ALLIES AFRICA
BRAZIL
ATLANTIC OCEAN
MADAGASCAR

JANUARY 2, 1943

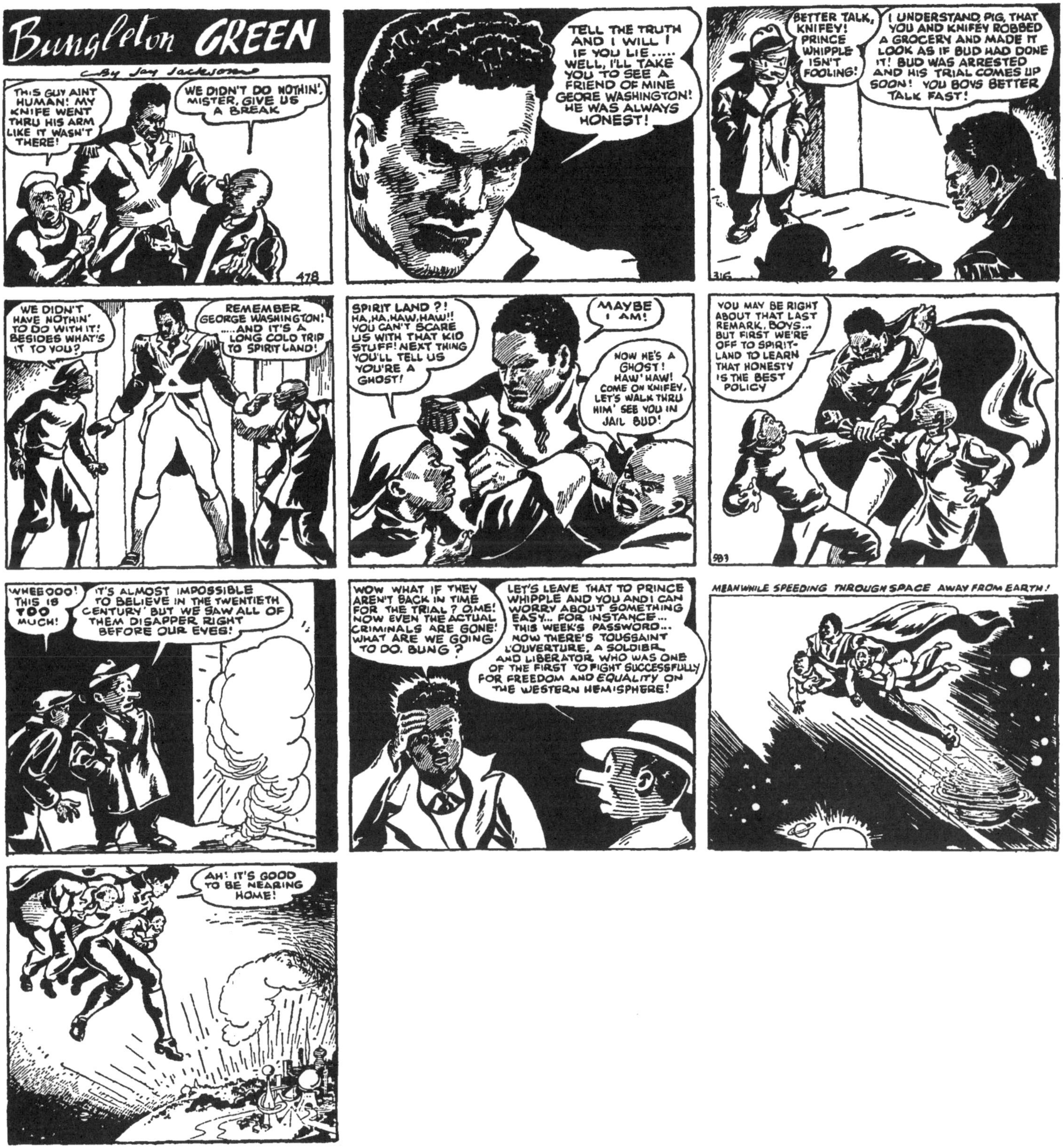
Bungleton GREEN
By Jay Jackson
THIS GUY AINT HUMAN! MY KNIFE WENT THRU HIS ARM LIKE IT WASN'T THERE!
WE DIDN'T DO NOTHIN', MISTER, GIVE US A BREAK
TELL THE TRUTH AND I WILL! IF YOU LIE..... WELL, I'LL TAKE YOU TO SEE A FRIEND OF MINE GEORE WASHINGTON! HE WAS ALWAYS HONEST!
BETTER TALK, KNIFEY! PRINCE WHIPPLE ISN'T FOOLING!
I UNDERSTAND, PIG, THAT YOU AND KNIFEY ROBBED A GROCERY AND MADE IT LOOK AS IF BUD HAD DONE IT! BUD WAS ARRESTED AND HIS TRIAL COMES UP SOON! YOU BOYS BETTER TALK FAST!
WE DIDN'T HAVE NOTHIN' TO DO WITH IT! BESIDES WHAT'S IT TO YOU?
REMEMBER GEORGE WASHINGTON! .....AND IT'S A LONG COLD TRIP TO SPIRIT LAND!
SPIRIT LAND?! HA, HA, HAW, HAW!! YOU CAN'T SCARE US WITH THAT KID STUFF! NEXT THING YOU'LL TELL US YOU'RE A GHOST!
MAYBE I AM!
NOW HE'S A GHOST! HAW' HAW! COME ON KNIFEY, LET'S WALK THRU HIM' SEE YOU IN JAIL BUD!
YOU MAY BE RIGHT ABOUT THAT LAST REMARK, BOYS... BUT FIRST WE'RE OFF TO SPIRIT-LAND TO LEARN THAT HONESTY IS THE BEST POLICY
WHEEOOO! THIS IS TOO MUCH!
IT'S ALMOST IMPOSSIBLE TO BELIEVE IN THE TWENTIETH CENTURY' BUT WE SAW ALL OF THEM DISAPPER RIGHT BEFORE OUR EYES!
WOW WHAT IF THEY AREN'T BACK IN TIME FOR THE TRIAL? O.ME! NOW EVEN THE ACTUAL CRIMINALS ARE GONE! WHAT ARE WE GOING TO DO, BUNG?
LET'S LEAVE THAT TO PRINCE WHIPPLE AND YOU AND I CAN WORRY ABOUT SOMETHING EASY... FOR INSTANCE... THIS WEEK'S PASSWORD... NOW THERE'S TOUSSAINT L'OUVERTURE, A SOLDIER AND LIBERATOR WHO WAS ONE OF THE FIRST TO FIGHT SUCCESSFULLY FOR FREEDOM AND EQUALITY ON THE WESTERN HEMISPHERE!
MEANWHILE SPEEDING THROUGH SPACE AWAY FROM EARTH!
AH! IT'S GOOD TO BE NEARING HOME!

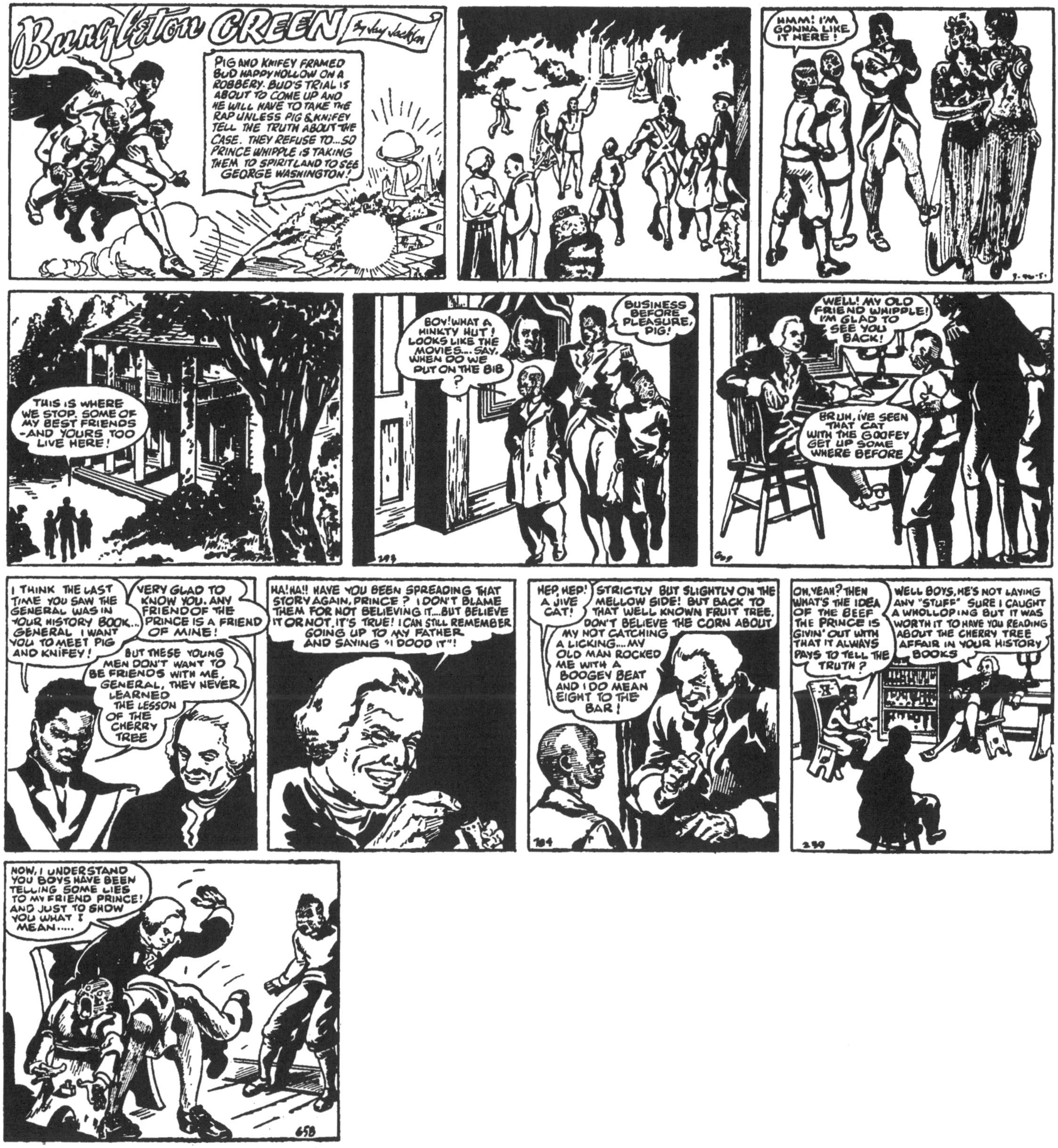
Bungleton GREEN
By Jay Jackson
PIG AND KNIFEY FRAMED BUD HAPPYHOLLOW ON A ROBBERY. BUD'S TRIAL IS ABOUT TO COME UP AND HE WILL HAVE TO TAKE THE RAP UNLESS PIG & KNIFEY TELL THE TRUTH ABOUT THE CASE. THEY REFUSE TO...SO PRINCE WHIPPLE IS TAKING THEM TO SPIRITLAND TO SEE GEORGE WASHINGTON!
HMM! I'M GONNA LIKE IT HERE!
THIS IS WHERE WE STOP. SOME OF MY BEST FRIENDS -AND YOURS TOO LIVE HERE!
BOY! WHAT A MINKTY HUT! LOOKS LIKE THE MOVIES.... SAY, WHEN DO WE PUT ON THE BIB?
BUSINESS BEFORE PLEASURE, PIG!
WELL! MY OLD FRIEND WHIPPLE! I'M GLAD TO SEE YOU BACK!
BRUH, I'VE SEEN THAT CAT WITH THE GOOFEY GET UP SOME WHERE BEFORE
I THINK THE LAST TIME YOU SAW THE GENERAL WAS IN YOUR HISTORY BOOK... GENERAL I WANT YOU TO MEET PIG AND KNIFEY!
VERY GLAD TO KNOW YOU. ANY FRIEND OF THE PRINCE IS A FRIEND OF MINE!
BUT THESE YOUNG MEN DON'T WANT TO BE FRIENDS WITH ME, GENERAL, THEY NEVER LEARNED THE LESSON OF THE CHERRY TREE
HA! HA!! HAVE YOU BEEN SPREADING THAT STORY AGAIN, PRINCE? I DON'T BLAME THEM FOR NOT BELIEVING IT....BUT BELIEVE IT OR NOT, IT'S TRUE! I CAN STILL REMEMBER GOING UP TO MY FATHER AND SAYING "I DOOD IT"!
HEP, HEP! A JIVE CAT!
STRICTLY BUT SLIGHTLY ON THE MELLOW SIDE! BUT BACK TO THAT WELL KNOWN FRUIT TREE. DON'T BELIEVE THE CORN ABOUT MY NOT CATCHING A LICKING....MY OLD MAN ROCKED ME WITH A BOOGEY BEAT AND I DO MEAN EIGHT TO THE BAR!
OH, YEAH? THEN WHAT'S THE IDEA OF THE BEEF THE PRINCE IS GIVIN' OUT WITH THAT IT ALWAYS PAYS TO TELL THE TRUTH?
WELL BOYS, HE'S NOT LAYING ANY "STUFF" SURE I CAUGHT A WHOLLOPING BUT IT WAS WORTH IT TO HAVE YOU READING ABOUT THE CHERRY TREE AFFAIR IN YOUR HISTORY BOOKS
NOW, I UNDERSTAND YOU BOYS HAVE BEEN TELLING SOME LIES TO MY FRIEND PRINCE! AND JUST TO SHOW YOU WHAT I MEAN.....

JANUARY 16, 1943

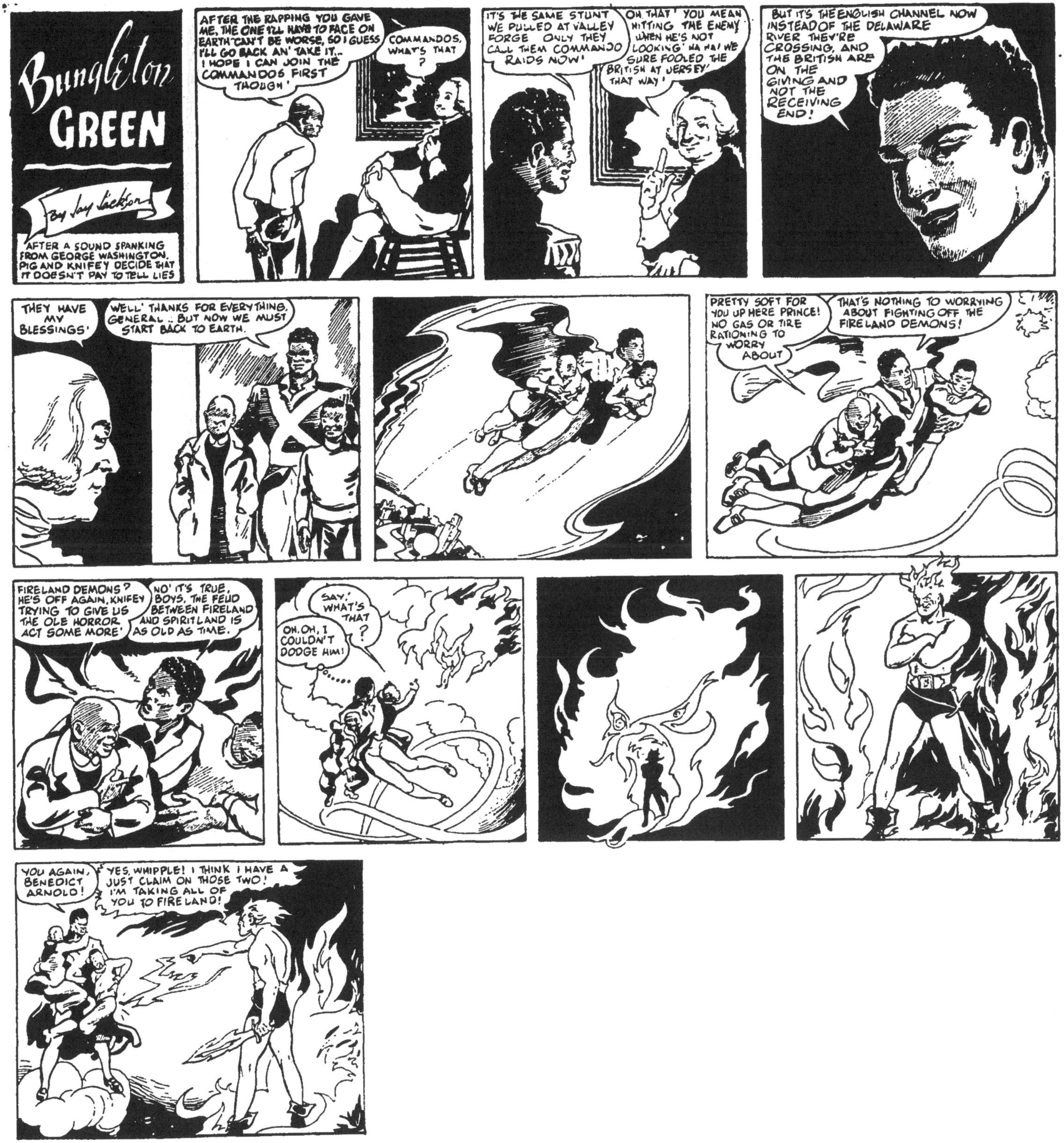

Bungleton GREEN
By Jay Jackson
AFTER A SOUND SPANKING FROM GEORGE WASHINGTON, PIG AND KNIFEY DECIDE THAT IT DOESN'T PAY TO TELL LIES
AFTER THE RAPPING YOU GAVE ME, THE ONE I'LL HAVE TO FACE ON EARTH CAN'T BE WORSE, SO I GUESS I'LL GO BACK AN' TAKE IT... I HOPE I CAN JOIN THE COMMANDOS FIRST THOUGH!
COMMANDOS, WHAT'S THAT ?
IT'S THE SAME STUNT WE PULLED AT VALLEY FORGE ONLY THEY CALL THEM COMMANDO RAIDS NOW!
OH THAT! YOU MEAN HITTING THE ENEMY WHEN HE'S NOT LOOKING! HA HA! WE SURE FOOLED THE BRITISH AT JERSEY THAT WAY!
BUT IT'S THE ENGLISH CHANNEL NOW INSTEAD OF THE DELAWARE RIVER THEY'RE CROSSING, AND THE BRITISH ARE ON THE GIVING AND NOT THE RECEIVING END!
THEY HAVE MY BLESSINGS!
WELL! THANKS FOR EVERYTHING, GENERAL.. BUT NOW WE MUST START BACK TO EARTH.
PRETTY SOFT FOR YOU UP HERE PRINCE! NO GAS OR TIRE RATIONING TO WORRY ABOUT
THAT'S NOTHING TO WORRYING ABOUT FIGHTING OFF THE FIRELAND DEMONS!
FIRELAND DEMONS? HE'S OFF AGAIN, KNIFEY TRYING TO GIVE US THE OLE HORROR ACT SOME MORE!
NO! IT'S TRUE, BOYS, THE FEUD BETWEEN FIRELAND AND SPIRITLAND IS AS OLD AS TIME.
SAY! WHAT'S THAT ?
OH, OH, I COULDN'T DODGE HIM!
YOU AGAIN, BENEDICT ARNOLD!
YES, WHIPPLE! I THINK I HAVE A JUST CLAIM ON THOSE TWO! I'M TAKING ALL OF YOU TO FIRELAND!

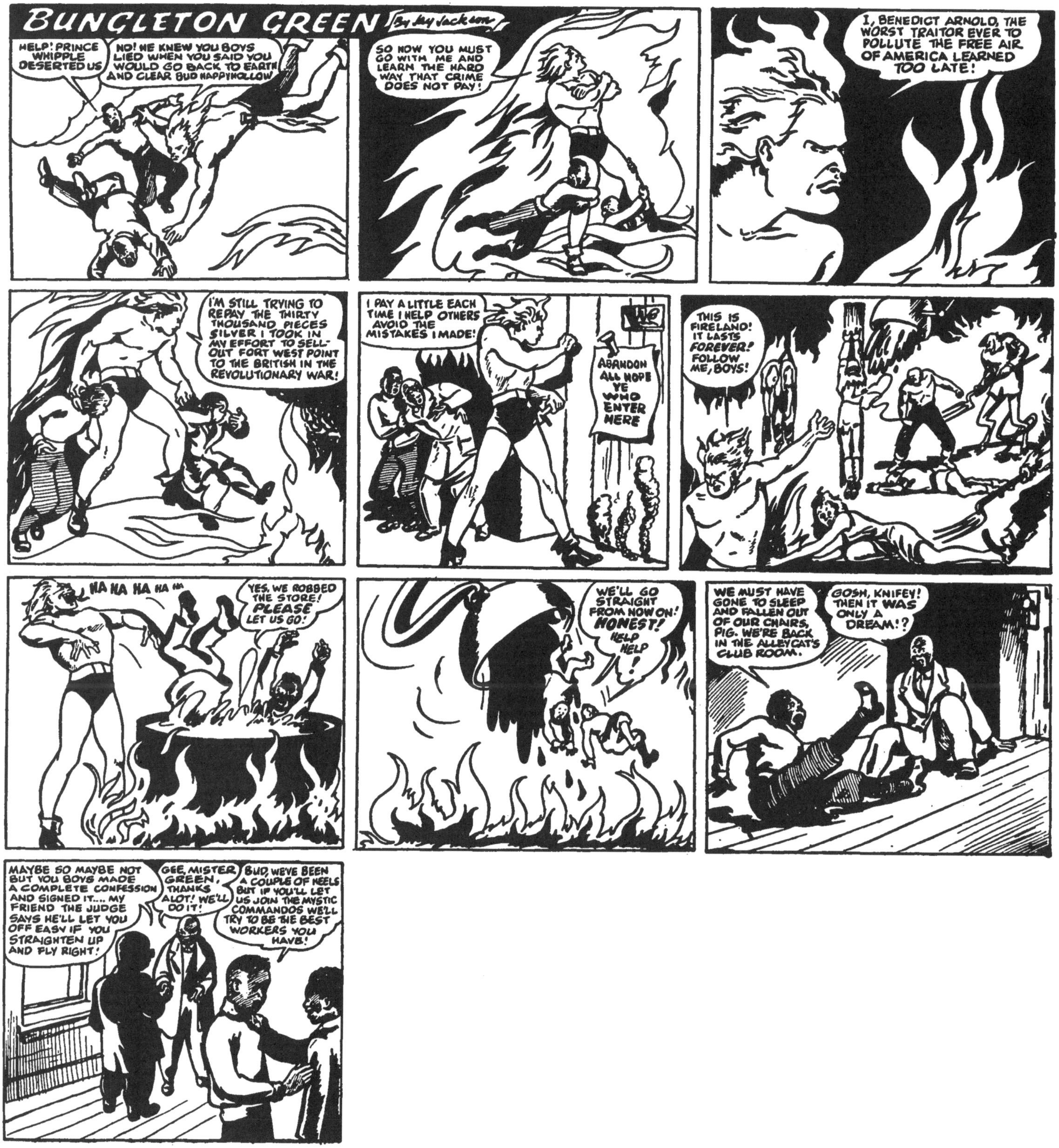
BUNGLETON GREEN
By Jay Jackson
HELP! PRINCE WHIPPLE DESERTED US
NO! HE KNEW YOU BOYS LIED WHEN YOU SAID YOU WOULD GO BACK TO EARTH AND CLEAR BUD HAPPYHOLLOW
SO NOW YOU MUST GO WITH ME AND LEARN THE HARD WAY THAT CRIME DOES NOT PAY!
I, BENEDICT ARNOLD, THE WORST TRAITOR EVER TO POLLUTE THE FREE AIR OF AMERICA LEARNED TOO LATE!
I'M STILL TRYING TO REPAY THE THIRTY THOUSAND PIECES SILVER I TOOK IN MY EFFORT TO SELL-OUT FORT WEST POINT TO THE BRITISH IN THE REVOLUTIONARY WAR!
I PAY A LITTLE EACH TIME I HELP OTHERS AVOID THE MISTAKES I MADE!
ABANDON ALL HOPE YE WHO ENTER HERE
THIS IS FIRELAND! IT LASTS FOREVER! FOLLOW ME, BOYS!
HA HA HA HA HA
YES, WE ROBBED THE STORE! PLEASE LET US GO!
WE'LL GO STRAIGHT FROM NOW ON! HONEST!
HELP HELP
WE MUST HAVE GONE TO SLEEP AND FALLEN OUT OF OUR CHAIRS, PIG. WE'RE BACK IN THE ALLEYCAT'S CLUB ROOM.
GOSH, KNIFEY! THEN IT WAS ONLY A DREAM!?
MAYBE SO MAYBE NOT BUT YOU BOYS MADE A COMPLETE CONFESSION AND SIGNED IT.... MY FRIEND THE JUDGE SAYS HE'LL LET YOU OFF EASY IF YOU STRAIGHTEN UP AND FLY RIGHT!
GEE, MISTER GREEN, THANKS ALOT! WE'LL DO IT!
BUD, WEVE BEEN A COUPLE OF HEELS BUT IF YOU'LL LET US JOIN THE MYSTIC COMMANDOS WE'LL TRY TO BE THE BEST WORKERS YOU HAVE!

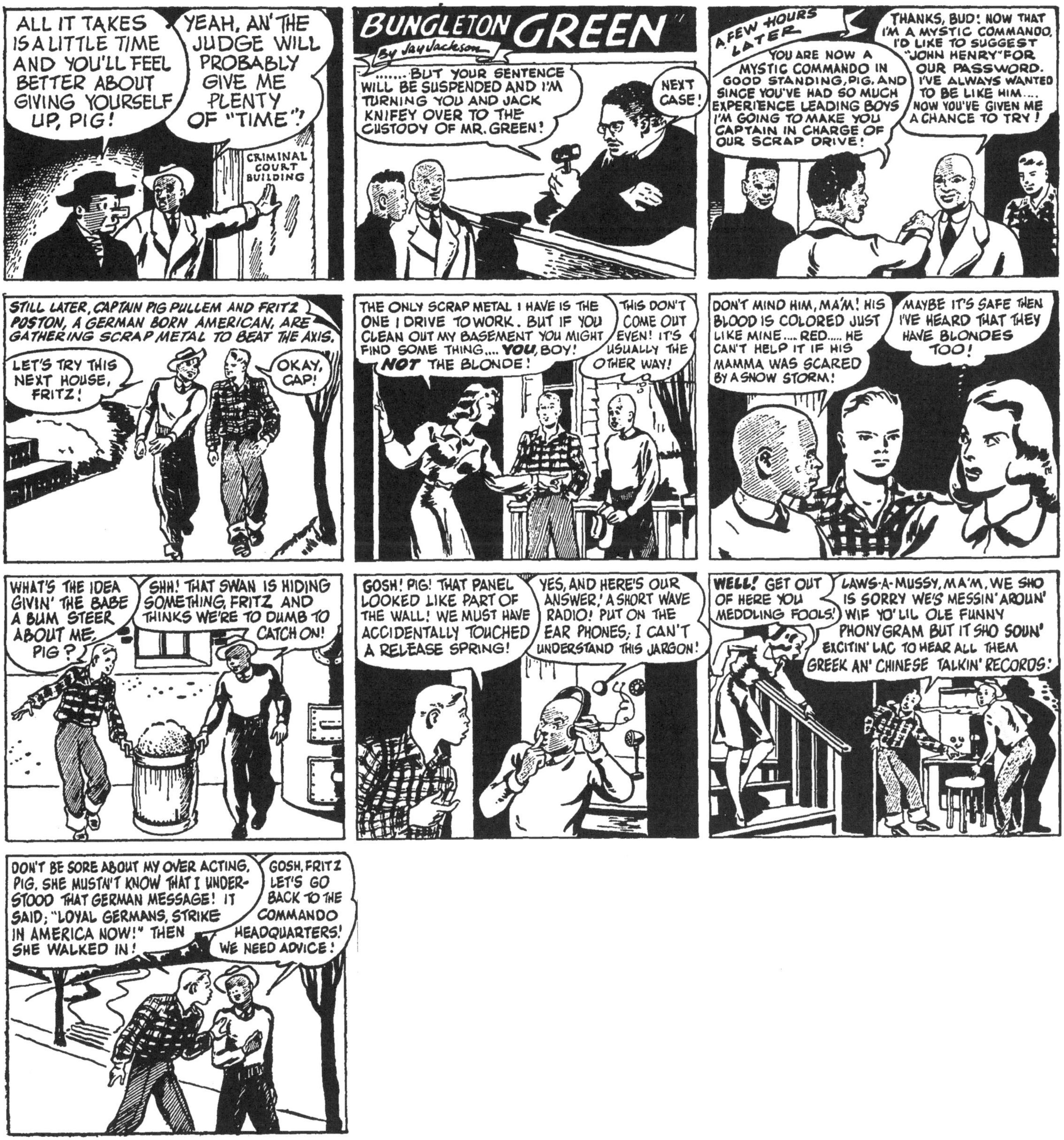
ALL IT TAKES IS A LITTLE TIME AND YOU'LL FEEL BETTER ABOUT GIVING YOURSELF UP, PIG!
YEAH, AN' THE JUDGE WILL PROBABLY GIVE ME PLENTY OF "TIME"!
CRIMINAL COURT BUILDING
BUNGLETON GREEN
By Jay Jackson
......BUT YOUR SENTENCE WILL BE SUSPENDED AND I'M TURNING YOU AND JACK KNIFEY OVER TO THE CUSTODY OF MR. GREEN!
NEXT CASE!
A FEW HOURS LATER
YOU ARE NOW A MYSTIC COMMANDO IN GOOD STANDING, PIG. AND SINCE YOU'VE HAD SO MUCH EXPERIENCE LEADING BOYS I'M GOING TO MAKE YOU CAPTAIN IN CHARGE OF OUR SCRAP DRIVE!
THANKS, BUD! NOW THAT I'M A MYSTIC COMMANDO, I'D LIKE TO SUGGEST "JOHN HENRY" FOR OUR PASSWORD. I'VE ALWAYS WANTED TO BE LIKE HIM.... NOW YOU'VE GIVEN ME A CHANCE TO TRY!
STILL LATER, CAPTAIN PIG PULLEM AND FRITZ POSTON, A GERMAN BORN AMERICAN, ARE GATHERING SCRAP METAL TO BEAT THE AXIS.
LET'S TRY THIS NEXT HOUSE, FRITZ!
OKAY, CAP!
THE ONLY SCRAP METAL I HAVE IS THE ONE I DRIVE TO WORK. BUT IF YOU CLEAN OUT MY BASEMENT YOU MIGHT FIND SOME THING.... YOU, BOY! NOT THE BLONDE!
THIS DON'T COME OUT EVEN! IT'S USUALLY THE OTHER WAY!
DON'T MIND HIM, MA'M! HIS BLOOD IS COLORED JUST LIKE MINE.... RED..... HE CAN'T HELP IT IF HIS MAMMA WAS SCARED BY A SNOW STORM!
MAYBE IT'S SAFE THEN I'VE HEARD THAT THEY HAVE BLONDES TOO!
WHAT'S THE IDEA GIVIN' THE BABE A BUM STEER ABOUT ME, PIG?
SHH! THAT SWAN IS HIDING SOMETHING, FRITZ AND THINKS WE'RE TO DUMB TO CATCH ON!
GOSH! PIG! THAT PANEL LOOKED LIKE PART OF THE WALL! WE MUST HAVE ACCIDENTALLY TOUCHED A RELEASE SPRING!
YES, AND HERE'S OUR ANSWER, A SHORT WAVE RADIO! PUT ON THE EAR PHONES; I CAN'T UNDERSTAND THIS JARGON!
WELL! GET OUT OF HERE YOU MEDDLING FOOLS!
LAWS-A-MUSSY, MA'M, WE SHO IS SORRY WE'S MESSIN' AROUN' WIF YO' LIL OLE FUNNY PHONYGRAM BUT IT SHO SOUN' EXCITIN' LAC TO HEAR ALL THEM GREEK AN' CHINESE TALKIN' RECORDS!
DON'T BE SORE ABOUT MY OVER ACTING, PIG. SHE MUSTN'T KNOW THAT I UNDERSTOOD THAT GERMAN MESSAGE! IT SAID; "LOYAL GERMANS, STRIKE IN AMERICA NOW!" THEN SHE WALKED IN!
GOSH, FRITZ LET'S GO BACK TO THE COMMANDO HEADQUARTERS! WE NEED ADVICE!

FEBRUARY 6, 1943

A LOT OF THINGS AH
WANT CHANGED!

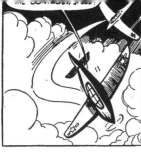

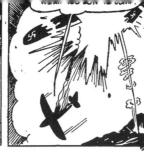

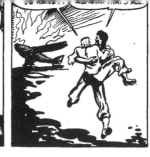

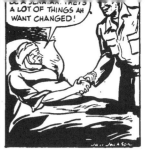

THE MONOCLE

February 1943 – July 1943

band mix-up and unless things
e BAD.... That was ADRIONNO
for words in that outfit at Sun-

he Chicago Defender BUD BIL-
Regal theatre SATURDAY, Dec.
and ERSKINE HAWKINS and
whirlwind stage show..... FREE
ers.

*

boogie Friday night was Mayor
hich has nothing to do with a
n a well known minister and
th street. . . . Hand an orchid
test cocktail party of the month
go Defender Christmas Basket
. Incidentally, EDNA WILLIS,
r hubby to Uncle Sam for the

*

VELL is better after that attack
ETTIE GEORGE SPEEDY whose
Sunday night. . . . WILLIAM
a baseball bat by JESSE BING-
. . . Who is the guy EHRLEAN
t least twice a week? . . . WAC
n the city recruiting. . . . Lieut.
up her WAC job, is now on the

*

d to meet when he was on big
will shake your hand at the
MB is still the top bartender at
egal) BLEWITT was the happiest
pent a few days here with wifie.
UGHN planning to go to Vicks-
gie cafe? . . . LUCILLE CUN-
a policeman on the hand. . . .
LLMAN and FLORENCE COLE
ng dinner. . . MARY PHILLIPS
onyas are improving after that

*

McMINN back from South Dakota
pheasants. . . . Here's a FLASH!
n bartender who said he couldn't
dn't call him, got his papers the
hat ERNESTINE WINSTON and
Saturday. . . . Cpl. MALCOLM
p Forrest, Tenn., most any day.
oo many drinks at the "Boogie"
. . SOPHRONIA HOLLOWAY
VE YOUNG WOMEN of Pilgrim
at Oakwood Village Friday.

*

G and hubby have come to the
has a warm spot in her heart
TERSON in town on furlough
s. . . . BOB (Chicago Defender)
nner at home and New Year's
ddy, HARRY (Defender) SMITH
hearsing his marching steps for
first of the year. . . . Lieut.
preparing to keep his date at
Staff Sgt. WILLIS ARMSTEAD
issus were ringsiders at the Up
. . . CARRIE MAE GLENN is
ostoffice) JOYNES had to leave
bedside of stricken father.

RMAN
ologer

d free in this column only when a
th your QUESTION YOUR FULL
DRESS. For private reply send 25c
ASTROLOGY READING and receive
any THREE QUESTIONS Address
AN (the astrologer) care of THE
AVE., CHICAGO, ILL.

Judge what you should and should
not do.

* * *

E. N.—Dear Professor Herman:
t has been sometime since I wrote
you. As you know I am a regular
customer of yours, or should I say
friend? For you have proven your-
self to be more than a friend.
When I needed help and was unable to obtain any financial assist-
ance, you did not hesitate to come
to my rescue . . . giving your
valuable time and advice, just to
help me. I shall never forget what
you have done, that is why I am
again coming to you for help. May
God bless you and your wonderful
work.

* * *

C. S.—What is the most deadly
poison? Why don't men like me?
Will I ever go to the man I care
for?

Ans.: Only one question is answered in the column, because of the limited amount of space. If you write in for a private reply I shall be more than glad to aid you in solving your problems.

* * *

E. E.—Dear Sir: I am a constant
reader of your column and find it

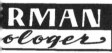

Poll Tax Ban In Soldiers Vote Bill Irks Congress

WASHINGTON. — (ANP) — Inferring that the next presidential elections might easily be set aside if congress relies upon the war powers bill to pass the soldier-vote bill, debate on which opened in the senate last week, opponents of the poll tax waiver undertook a subtle attempt to get that portion of the Green-Lucas measure eliminated..

Few doubted, however, that the measure would fail of passage since its express provisions without a constitutional amendment."

Sen James O. Eastland (D) of Mississippi followed him and said that, "the measure is unconstitutional and its enactment will certainly cast grave doubt on the validity of the next presidential election, and upon the election of senators and representatives."

It was Sen. Millard Tydings (D) of Maryland who raised the poll

Major Randall Promoted; Now A Lieut. Colonel

Major Oscar Randall, prominent Chicagoan and a former member of the 184th Field Artillery, has been promoted to lieutenant colonel it was learned this week.

Colonel Randall is now an executive officer assigned to the 366th Infantry, Camp Atterbury, Ind. He was formerly assigned to Camp Devens, Mass. In civilian life, Col. Randall was an instructor in mathematics at DuSable high school.

vote bill for similar reasons. The difference, as he saw it, was one

Urban League Challenges AFL Race Boycott Claim

NEW YORK.—The National Urban League this week announced a forthcoming conference between league staff members and high-ranking officials of the American Federation of Labor.

The conference was agreed to by William Green, AFL president, after an exchange of correspondence between himself and Lester B. Granger, executive secretary of the Urban League. Granger challenged a statement made by Green at the recent AFL convention held in Bos-

initiative in promoting Negro members in AFL unions and referred to the nation's workers' education program which was directly responsible for the induction of "more than 10,000 Negro workers " in both AFL and CIO unions.

Subsequent correspondence established an agreement that in the near future Granger, together with Julius A. Thomas, director of the department of industrial relations, and other national and local Urban League secretaries, will meet at

such employee his wage
to the time of such disc
lay-off.

(2) Not later than
regular pay day after an
quits his employment, s
ployer shall pay such
his wages in full to the
such quitting, unless
ployee shall have given
previous notice of his
to leave, in which case
ployer shall pay such em
full to the time of such
at the time of such quitt

(3) Whenever a strik
the employer shall at
regular pay day follow
strike pay the striking
their wages in full to
such employees ceased
If less than five days
between such strike and
day, the employer shall
striking employees not l
five days after such strik
option of the employer,
to such striking employ
be made through the De
of Labor. Whenever pa
to be made, notices an
such manner of paymen
posted at the regular
business of the employer
sition easily accessible t
ployees.

(4) If because of abse
the place of payment
ployee is not paid within
specified above, he shall
at any time thereafter on
or he shall, if he so den
paid by mail, less the a
of transmission.

When the office of any
from which payment to
is made is out of this
because of this fact paym
not be made at the time
herein, such employer
allowed such additional
making payments as se
sonable under all the circ
es but in no case shall s
tional time for making
as seems reasonable unde
circumstances but in no
such additional time ex
days.

2. Any employer or a
of an employer, who, b
to pay wages and being
duty to pay, wilfully
pay as provided in Sec
this Act, or falsely d
amount or validity there
the same is due, with
secure for himself or o
son any underpayment
indebtedness or with
annoy, harass, oppress
delay or defraud the
whom such indebtedness
who fails to post the
required by Section 4 of
is guilty of a misdemean
conviction thereof shall
not less than twenty-fiv
($25.00) and not more
hundred dollars ($200.00

YOUR Mone

By WALTER L. I
Insurance Broker

Ques.: What coverage by title insurance for real estate?

Ans.: Insurer guarantee of the date of policy, the good, marketable and free of liens, encumbrances and defects except those stated in the policy. Insurer's liability is limited to the amount stated in the policy but the guarantee is forever. In addition, the insurer agrees to defend the insured in eve

Walte

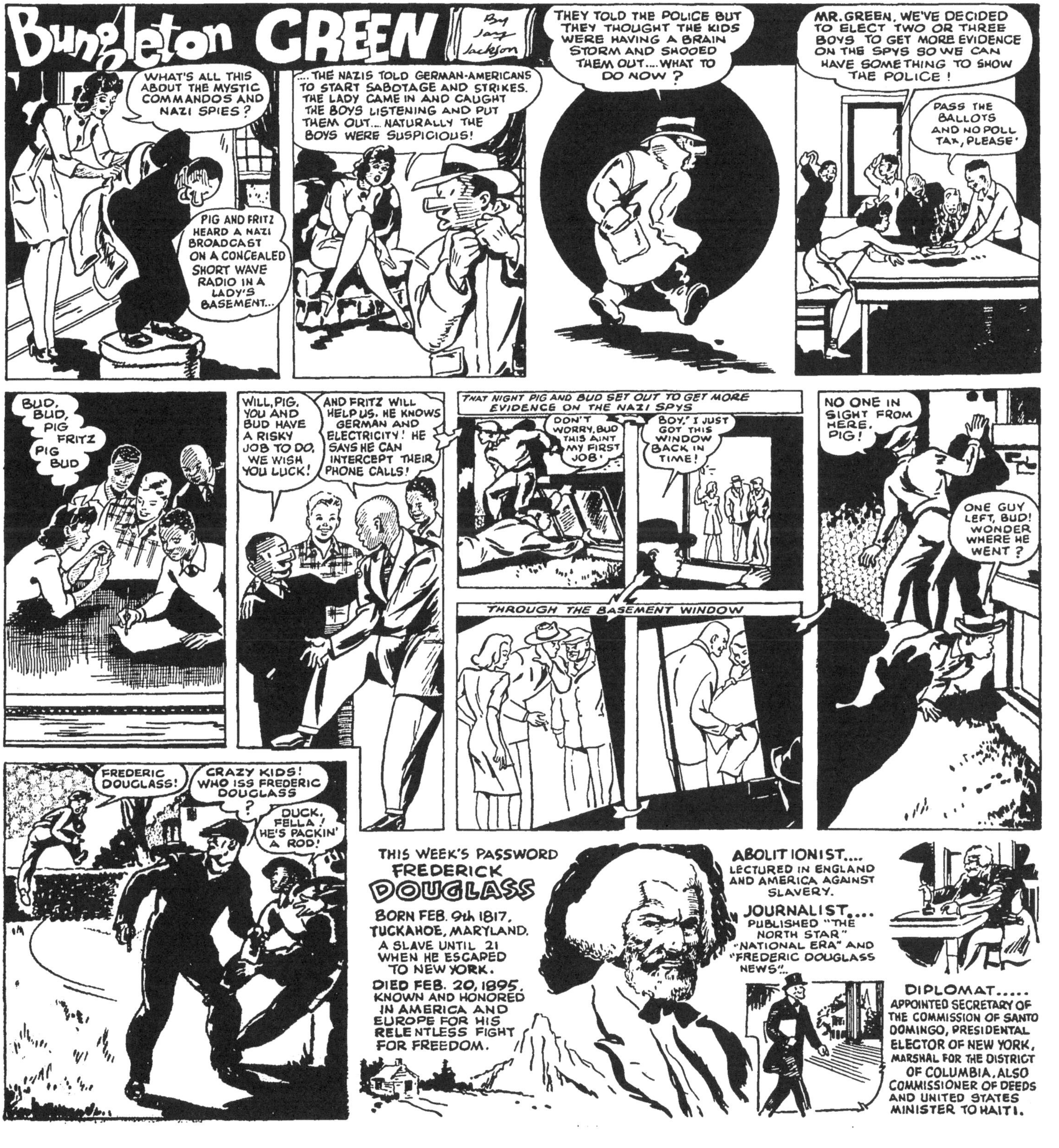
Bungleton GREEN
By Jay Jackson
WHAT'S ALL THIS ABOUT THE MYSTIC COMMANDOS AND NAZI SPIES?
PIG AND FRITZ HEARD A NAZI BROADCAST ON A CONCEALED SHORT WAVE RADIO IN A LADY'S BASEMENT...
....THE NAZIS TOLD GERMAN-AMERICANS TO START SABOTAGE AND STRIKES. THE LADY CAME IN AND CAUGHT THE BOYS LISTENING AND PUT THEM OUT... NATURALLY THE BOYS WERE SUSPICIOUS!
THEY TOLD THE POLICE BUT THEY THOUGHT THE KIDS WERE HAVING A BRAIN STORM AND SHOOED THEM OUT.... WHAT TO DO NOW ?
MR. GREEN, WE'VE DECIDED TO ELECT TWO OR THREE BOYS TO GET MORE EVIDENCE ON THE SPYS SO WE CAN HAVE SOMETHING TO SHOW THE POLICE !
PASS THE BALLOTS AND NO POLL TAX, PLEASE'
BUD, BUD, PIG FRITZ PIG BUD
WILL, PIG, YOU AND BUD HAVE A RISKY JOB TO DO. WE WISH YOU LUCK!
AND FRITZ WILL HELP US. HE KNOWS GERMAN AND ELECTRICITY! HE SAYS HE CAN INTERCEPT THEIR PHONE CALLS!
THAT NIGHT PIG AND BUD SET OUT TO GET MORE EVIDENCE ON THE NAZI SPYS
DON'T WORRY, BUD THIS AINT MY FIRST JOB'
BOY,' I JUST GOT THIS WINDOW BACK IN TIME!
THROUGH THE BASEMENT WINDOW
NO ONE IN SIGHT FROM HERE, PIG!
ONE GUY LEFT, BUD! WONDER WHERE HE WENT ?
FREDERIC DOUGLASS!
CRAZY KIDS! WHO ISS FREDERIC DOUGLASS ?
DUCK, FELLA! HE'S PACKIN' A ROD!
THIS WEEK'S PASSWORD
FREDERICK DOUGLASS
BORN FEB. 9th 1817, TUCKAHOE, MARYLAND.
A SLAVE UNTIL 21 WHEN HE ESCAPED TO NEW YORK.
DIED FEB. 20, 1895. KNOWN AND HONORED IN AMERICA AND EUROPE FOR HIS RELENTLESS FIGHT FOR FREEDOM.
ABOLITIONIST.... LECTURED IN ENGLAND AND AMERICA AGAINST SLAVERY.
JOURNALIST.... PUBLISHED "THE NORTH STAR" "NATIONAL ERA" AND "FREDERIC DOUGLASS NEWS"...
DIPLOMAT..... APPOINTED SECRETARY OF THE COMMISSION OF SANTO DOMINGO, PRESIDENTAL ELECTOR OF NEW YORK, MARSHAL FOR THE DISTRICT OF COLUMBIA. ALSO COMMISSIONER OF DEEDS AND UNITED STATES MINISTER TO HAITI.

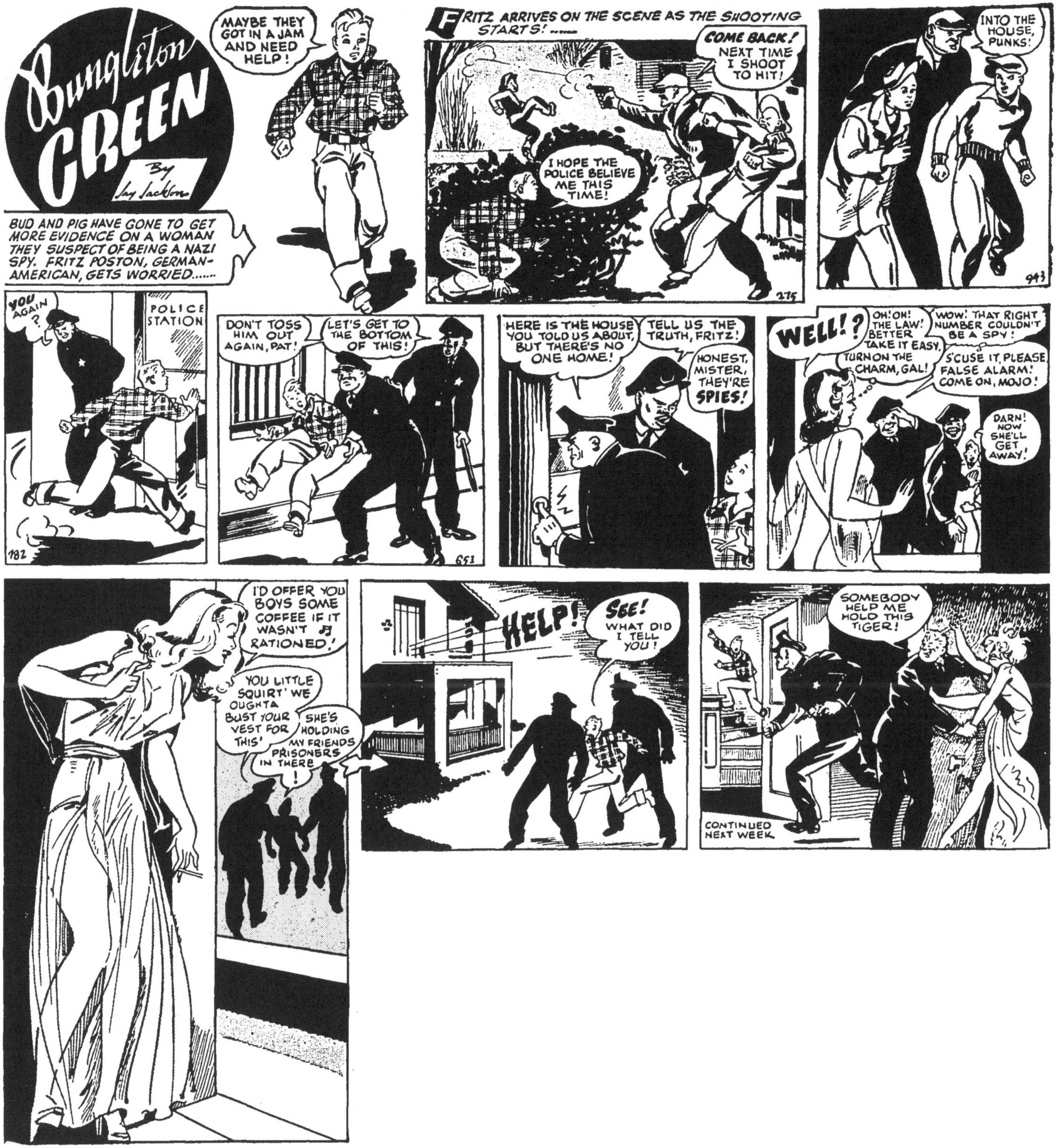
Bungleton GREEN
By Jay Jackson
BUD AND PIG HAVE GONE TO GET MORE EVIDENCE ON A WOMAN THEY SUSPECT OF BEING A NAZI SPY. FRITZ POSTON, GERMAN-AMERICAN, GETS WORRIED......
MAYBE THEY GOT IN A JAM AND NEED HELP!
FRITZ ARRIVES ON THE SCENE AS THE SHOOTING STARTS! .....
COME BACK! NEXT TIME I SHOOT TO HIT!
I HOPE THE POLICE BELIEVE ME THIS TIME!
INTO THE HOUSE, PUNKS!
YOU AGAIN ?
POLICE STATION
DON'T TOSS HIM OUT AGAIN, PAT!
LET'S GET TO THE BOTTOM OF THIS!
HERE IS THE HOUSE YOU TOLD US ABOUT, BUT THERE'S NO ONE HOME!
TELL US THE TRUTH, FRITZ!
HONEST, MISTER, THEY'RE SPIES!
WELL!?
OH! OH! THE LAW! BETTER TAKE IT EASY. TURN ON THE CHARM, GAL!
WOW! THAT RIGHT NUMBER COULDN'T BE A SPY!
S'CUSE IT, PLEASE. FALSE ALARM! COME ON, MOJO!
DARN! NOW SHE'LL GET AWAY!
I'D OFFER YOU BOYS SOME COFFEE IF IT WASN'T RATIONED!
YOU LITTLE SQUIRT! WE OUGHTA BUST YOUR VEST FOR THIS!
SHE'S HOLDING MY FRIENDS PRISONERS IN THERE !
HELP!
SEE! WHAT DID I TELL YOU!
SOMEBODY HELP ME HOLD THIS TIGER!
CONTINUED NEXT WEEK

FEBRUARY 20, 1943

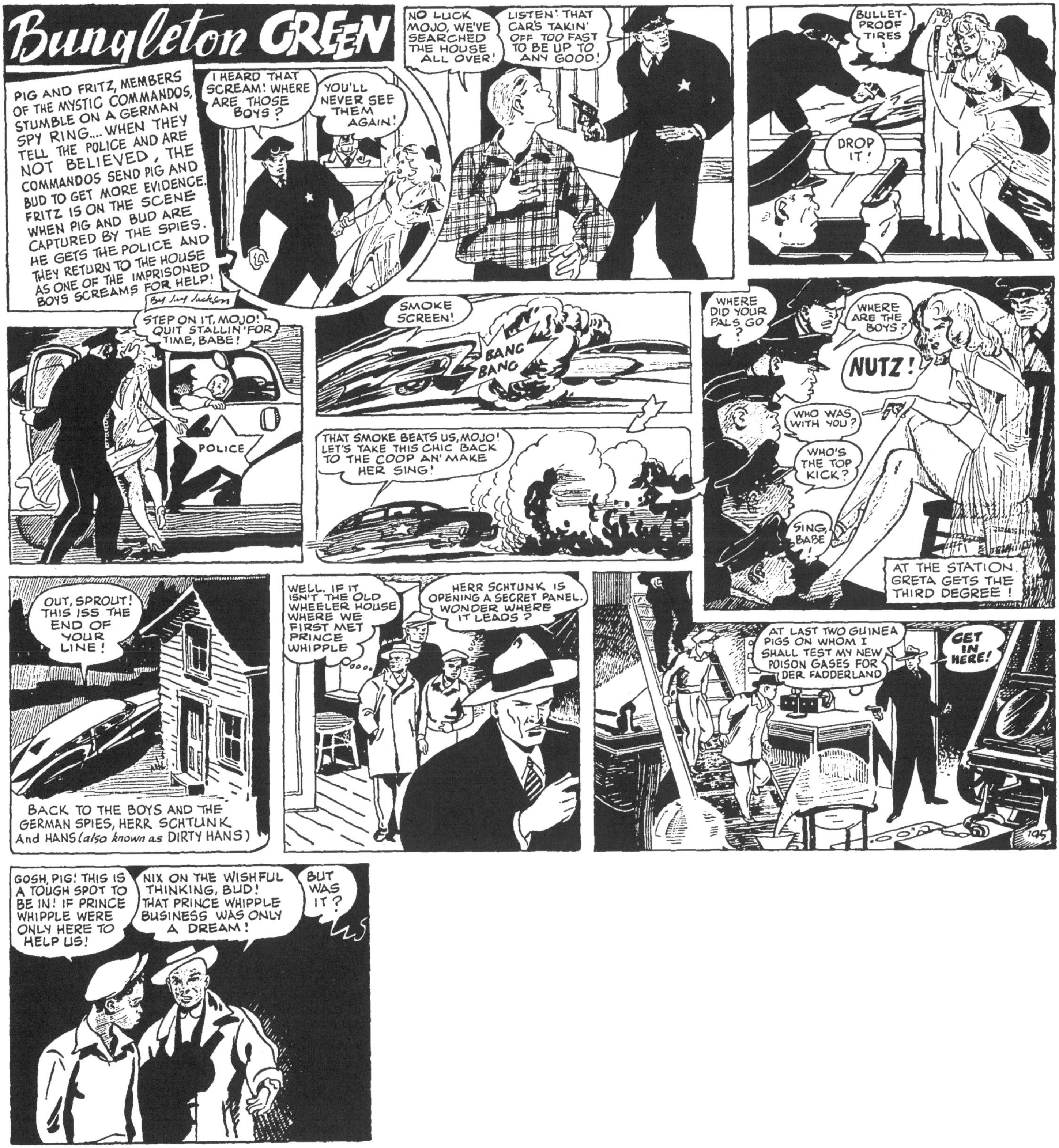
Bungleton GREEN
PIG AND FRITZ, MEMBERS OF THE MYSTIC COMMANDOS, STUMBLE ON A GERMAN SPY RING.... WHEN THEY TELL THE POLICE AND ARE NOT BELIEVED, THE COMMANDOS SEND PIG AND BUD TO GET MORE EVIDENCE. FRITZ IS ON THE SCENE WHEN PIG AND BUD ARE CAPTURED BY THE SPIES. HE GETS THE POLICE AND THEY RETURN TO THE HOUSE AS ONE OF THE IMPRISONED BOYS SCREAMS FOR HELP!
I HEARD THAT SCREAM! WHERE ARE THOSE BOYS?
YOU'LL NEVER SEE THEM AGAIN!
NO LUCK MOJO, WE'VE SEARCHED THE HOUSE ALL OVER!
LISTEN! THAT CAR'S TAKIN' OFF TOO FAST TO BE UP TO ANY GOOD!
BULLET-PROOF TIRES!
DROP IT!
STEP ON IT, MOJO! QUIT STALLIN' FOR TIME, BABE!
POLICE
SMOKE SCREEN!
BANG BANG
THAT SMOKE BEATS US, MOJO! LET'S TAKE THIS CHIC BACK TO THE COOP AN' MAKE HER SING!
WHERE DID YOUR PALS GO?
WHERE ARE THE BOYS?
NUTZ!
WHO WAS WITH YOU?
WHO'S THE TOP KICK?
SING, BABE!
AT THE STATION, GRETA GETS THE THIRD DEGREE!
OUT, SPROUT! THIS ISS THE END OF YOUR LINE!
BACK TO THE BOYS AND THE GERMAN SPIES, HERR SCHTUNK And HANS (also known as DIRTY HANS)
WELL, IF IT ISN'T THE OLD WHEELER HOUSE WHERE WE FIRST MET PRINCE WHIPPLE
HERR SCHTUNK IS OPENING A SECRET PANEL. WONDER WHERE IT LEADS?
AT LAST TWO GUINEA PIGS ON WHOM I SHALL TEST MY NEW POISON GASES FOR DER FADDERLAND
GET IN HERE!
GOSH, PIG! THIS IS A TOUGH SPOT TO BE IN! IF PRINCE WHIPPLE WERE ONLY HERE TO HELP US!
NIX ON THE WISHFUL THINKING, BUD! THAT PRINCE WHIPPLE BUSINESS WAS ONLY A DREAM!
BUT WAS IT?

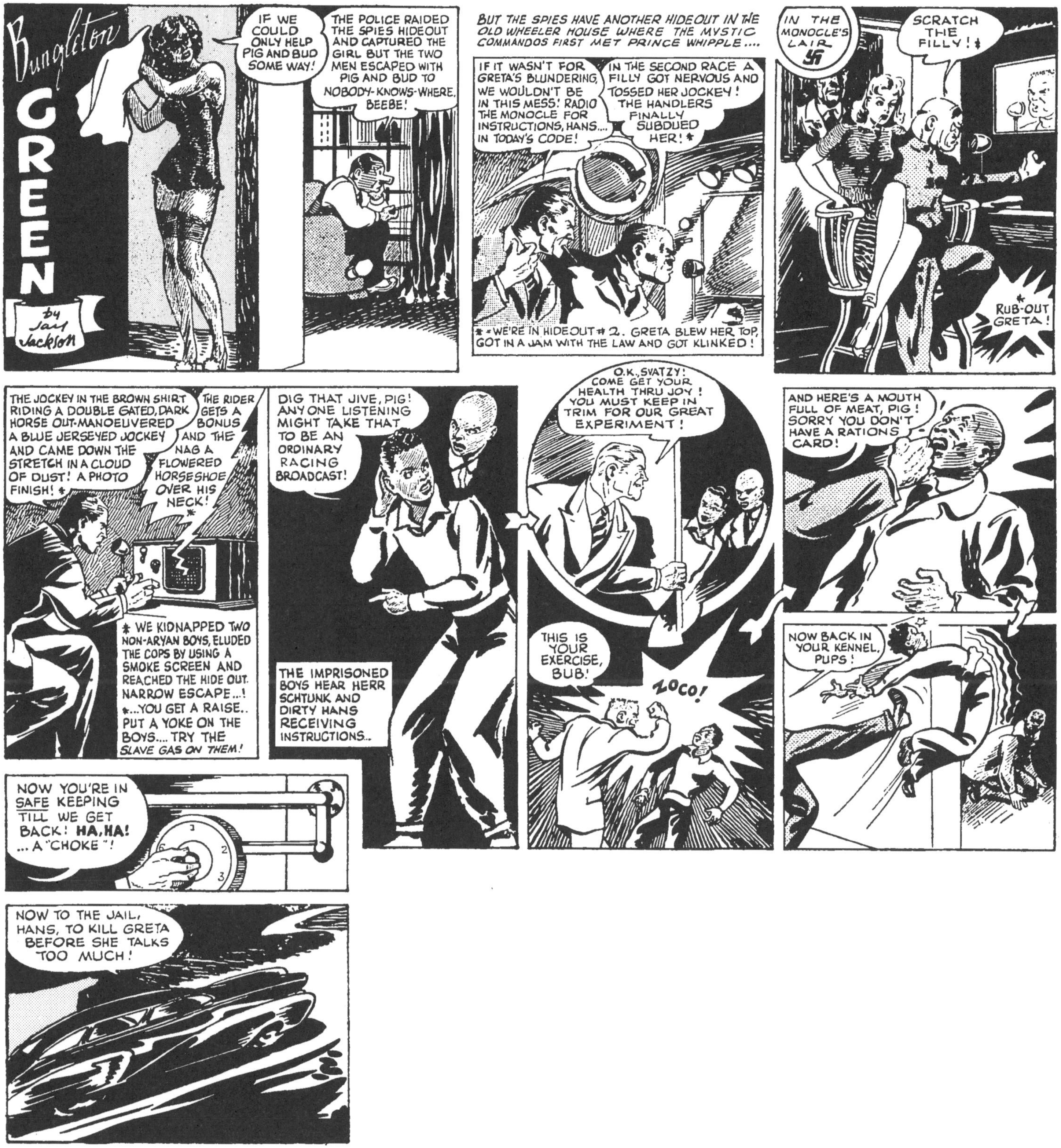
Bungleton GREEN
by Jay Jackson
IF WE COULD ONLY HELP PIG AND BUD SOME WAY!
THE POLICE RAIDED THE SPIES HIDEOUT AND CAPTURED THE GIRL BUT THE TWO MEN ESCAPED WITH PIG AND BUD TO NOBODY-KNOWS-WHERE, BEEBE!
BUT THE SPIES HAVE ANOTHER HIDEOUT IN THE OLD WHEELER HOUSE WHERE THE MYSTIC COMMANDOS FIRST MET PRINCE WHIPPLE....
IF IT WASN'T FOR GRETA'S BLUNDERING, WE WOULDN'T BE IN THIS MESS! RADIO THE MONOCLE FOR INSTRUCTIONS, HANS.... IN TODAY'S CODE!
IN THE SECOND RACE A FILLY GOT NERVOUS AND TOSSED HER JOCKEY! THE HANDLERS FINALLY SUBDUED HER! *
*=WE'RE IN HIDEOUT # 2. GRETA BLEW HER TOP, GOT IN A JAM WITH THE LAW AND GOT KLINKED!
IN THE MONOCLE'S LAIR
SCRATCH THE FILLY! $
$ RUB-OUT GRETA!
THE JOCKEY IN THE BROWN SHIRT RIDING A DOUBLE GATED, DARK HORSE OUT-MANOEUVERED A BLUE JERSEYED JOCKEY AND CAME DOWN THE STRETCH IN A CLOUD OF DUST! A PHOTO FINISH! *
THE RIDER GETS A BONUS AND THE NAG A FLOWERED HORSESHOE OVER HIS NECK! *
* WE KIDNAPPED TWO NON-ARYAN BOYS, ELUDED THE COPS BY USING A SMOKE SCREEN AND REACHED THE HIDE OUT. NARROW ESCAPE...! *...YOU GET A RAISE.. PUT A YOKE ON THE BOYS.... TRY THE SLAVE GAS ON THEM!
DIG THAT JIVE, PIG! ANYONE LISTENING MIGHT TAKE THAT TO BE AN ORDINARY RACING BROADCAST!
THE IMPRISONED BOYS HEAR HERR SCHTUNK AND DIRTY HANS RECEIVING INSTRUCTIONS..
O.K., SVATZY! COME GET YOUR HEALTH THRU JOY! YOU MUST KEEP IN TRIM FOR OUR GREAT EXPERIMENT!
THIS IS YOUR EXERCISE, BUB!
ZOCO!
AND HERE'S A MOUTH FULL OF MEAT, PIG! SORRY YOU DON'T HAVE A RATIONS CARD!
NOW BACK IN YOUR KENNEL, PUPS!
NOW YOU'RE IN SAFE KEEPING TILL WE GET BACK! HA,HA! ... A "CHOKE"!
NOW TO THE JAIL, HANS, TO KILL GRETA BEFORE SHE TALKS TOO MUCH!

MARCH 6, 1943

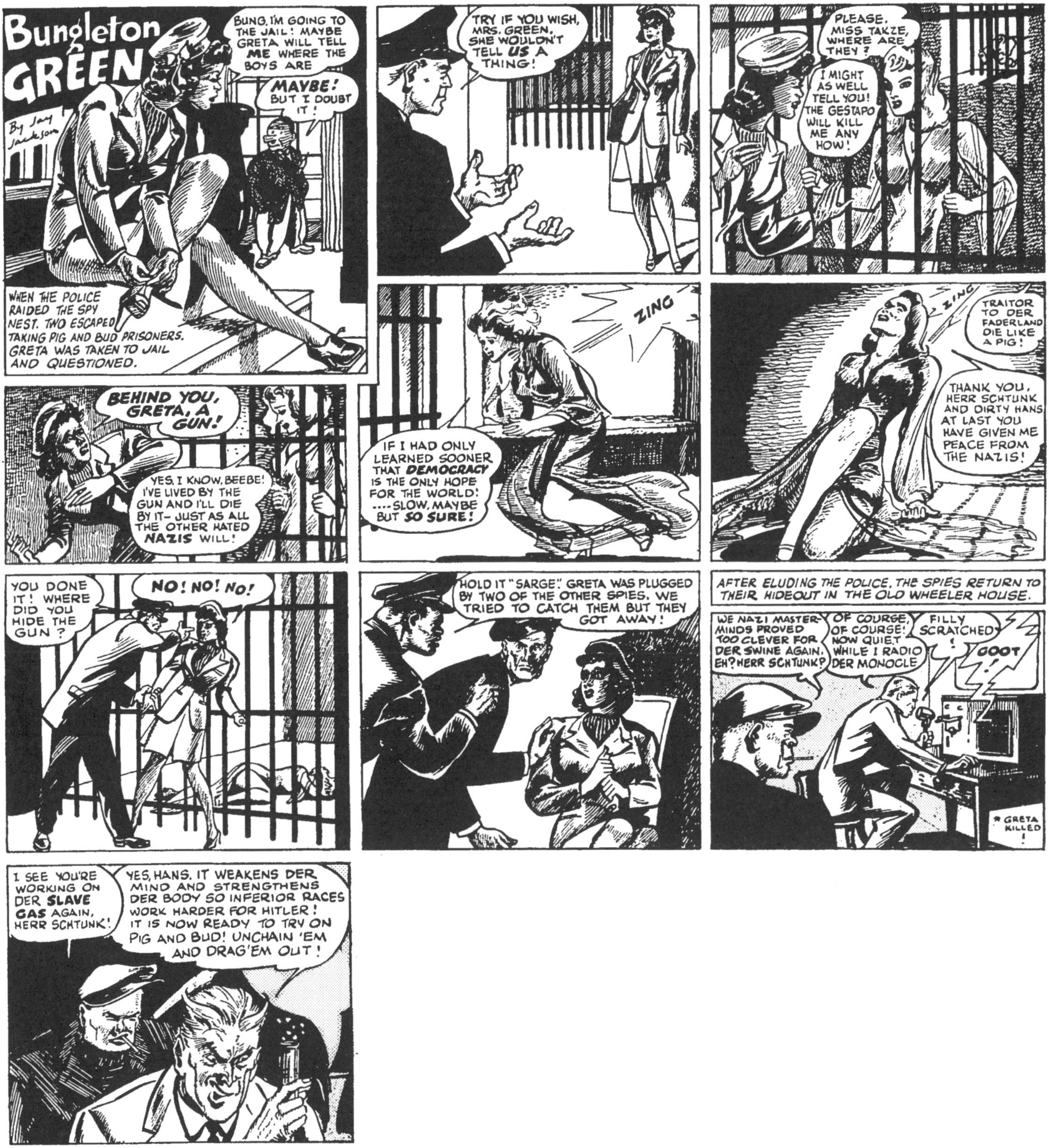

Bungleton GREEN
By Jay Jackson
BUNG, I'M GOING TO THE JAIL: MAYBE GRETA WILL TELL **ME** WHERE THE BOYS ARE
MAYBE! BUT I DOUBT IT!
WHEN THE POLICE RAIDED THE SPY NEST, TWO ESCAPED TAKING PIG AND BUD PRISONERS. GRETA WAS TAKEN TO JAIL AND QUESTIONED.
TRY IF YOU WISH, MRS. GREEN, SHE WOULDN'T TELL **US** A THING!
PLEASE, MISS TAKZE, WHERE ARE THEY?
I MIGHT AS WELL TELL YOU! THE GESTAPO WILL KILL ME ANY HOW!
BEHIND YOU, GRETA, A GUN!
YES, I KNOW, BEEBE! I'VE LIVED BY THE GUN AND I'LL DIE BY IT- JUST AS ALL THE OTHER HATED **NAZIS** WILL!
ZING
IF I HAD ONLY LEARNED SOONER THAT **DEMOCRACY** IS THE ONLY HOPE FOR THE WORLD! ....SLOW, MAYBE BUT **SO SURE!**
ZING
TRAITOR TO DER FADERLAND DIE LIKE A PIG!
THANK YOU, HERR SCHTUNK AND DIRTY HANS AT LAST YOU HAVE GIVEN ME PEACE FROM THE NAZIS!
YOU DONE IT! WHERE DID YOU HIDE THE GUN?
NO! NO! NO!
HOLD IT "SARGE". GRETA WAS PLUGGED BY TWO OF THE OTHER SPIES. WE TRIED TO CATCH THEM BUT THEY GOT AWAY!
AFTER ELUDING THE POLICE, THE SPIES RETURN TO THEIR HIDEOUT IN THE OLD WHEELER HOUSE.
WE NAZI MASTER-MINDS PROVED TOO CLEVER FOR **DER SWINE** AGAIN, EH? HERR SCHTUNK?
OF COURSE, OF COURSE! NOW QUIET WHILE I RADIO DER MONOCLE
FILLY SCRATCHED!
GOOT!
* GRETA KILLED!
I SEE YOU'RE WORKING ON DER **SLAVE GAS** AGAIN, HERR SCHTUNK!
YES, HANS, IT WEAKENS DER MIND AND STRENGTHENS DER BODY SO INFERIOR RACES WORK HARDER FOR HITLER! IT IS NOW READY TO TRY ON PIG AND BUD! UNCHAIN 'EM AND DRAG'EM OUT!

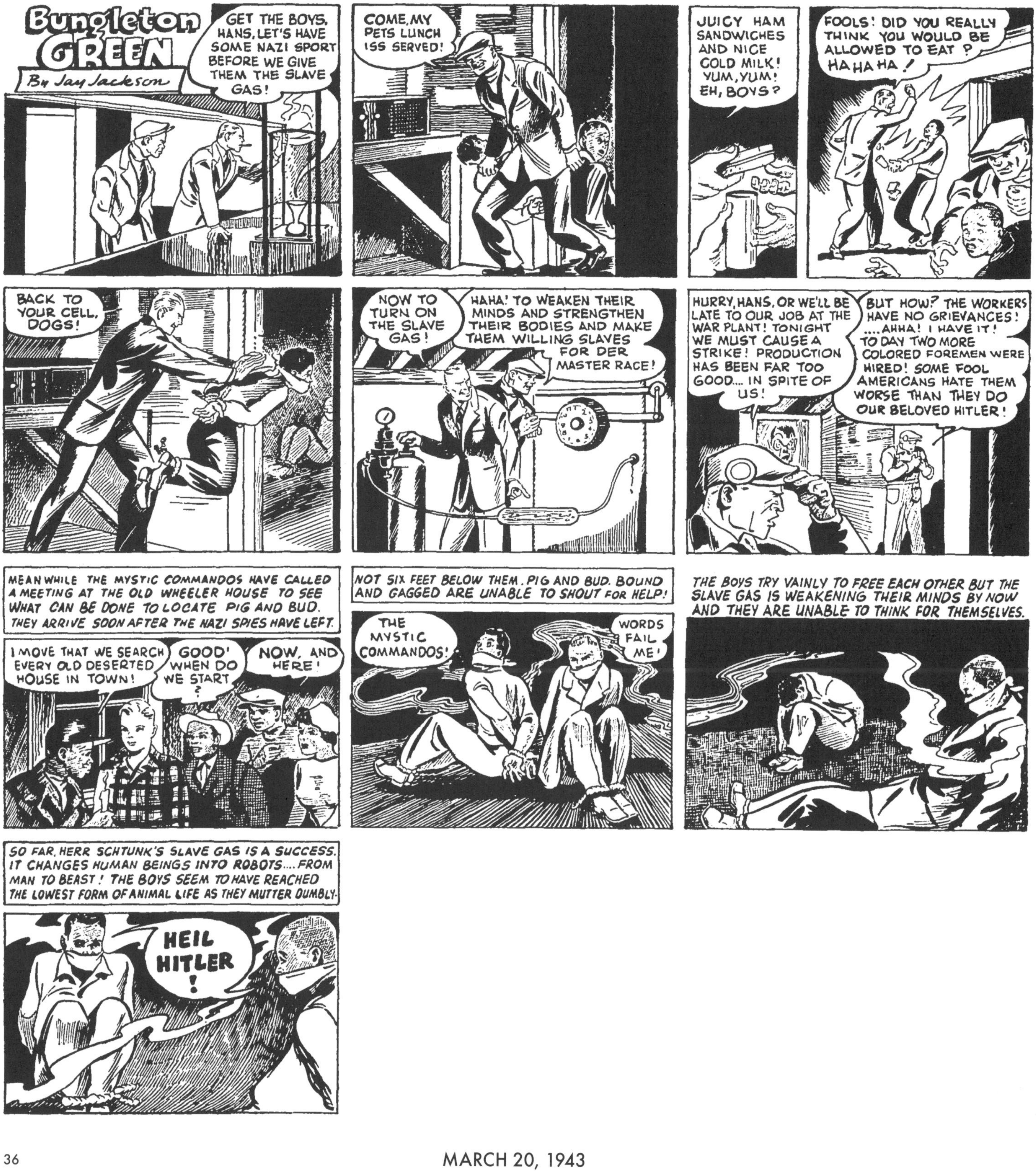
Bungleton GREEN
By Jay Jackson
GET THE BOYS, HANS, LET'S HAVE SOME NAZI SPORT BEFORE WE GIVE THEM THE SLAVE GAS!
COME, MY PETS LUNCH ISS SERVED!
JUICY HAM SANDWICHES AND NICE COLD MILK! YUM, YUM! EH, BOYS?
FOOLS! DID YOU REALLY THINK YOU WOULD BE ALLOWED TO EAT? HA HA HA!
BACK TO YOUR CELL, DOGS!
NOW TO TURN ON THE SLAVE GAS!
HAHA! TO WEAKEN THEIR MINDS AND STRENGTHEN THEIR BODIES AND MAKE THEM WILLING SLAVES FOR DER MASTER RACE!
HURRY, HANS, OR WE'LL BE LATE TO OUR JOB AT THE WAR PLANT! TONIGHT WE MUST CAUSE A STRIKE! PRODUCTION HAS BEEN FAR TOO GOOD.... IN SPITE OF US!
BUT HOW? THE WORKERS HAVE NO GRIEVANCES! ....AHHA! I HAVE IT! TO DAY TWO MORE COLORED FOREMEN WERE HIRED! SOME FOOL AMERICANS HATE THEM WORSE THAN THEY DO OUR BELOVED HITLER!
MEANWHILE THE MYSTIC COMMANDOS HAVE CALLED A MEETING AT THE OLD WHEELER HOUSE TO SEE WHAT CAN BE DONE TO LOCATE PIG AND BUD. THEY ARRIVE SOON AFTER THE NAZI SPIES HAVE LEFT.
I MOVE THAT WE SEARCH EVERY OLD DESERTED HOUSE IN TOWN!
GOOD! WHEN DO WE START?
NOW, AND HERE!
NOT SIX FEET BELOW THEM. PIG AND BUD. BOUND AND GAGGED ARE UNABLE TO SHOUT FOR HELP!
THE MYSTIC COMMANDOS!
WORDS FAIL ME!
THE BOYS TRY VAINLY TO FREE EACH OTHER BUT THE SLAVE GAS IS WEAKENING THEIR MINDS BY NOW AND THEY ARE UNABLE TO THINK FOR THEMSELVES.
SO FAR, HERR SCHTUNK'S SLAVE GAS IS A SUCCESS. IT CHANGES HUMAN BEINGS INTO ROBOTS.... FROM MAN TO BEAST! THE BOYS SEEM TO HAVE REACHED THE LOWEST FORM OF ANIMAL LIFE AS THEY MUTTER DUMBLY.
HEIL HITLER!

MARCH 20, 1943

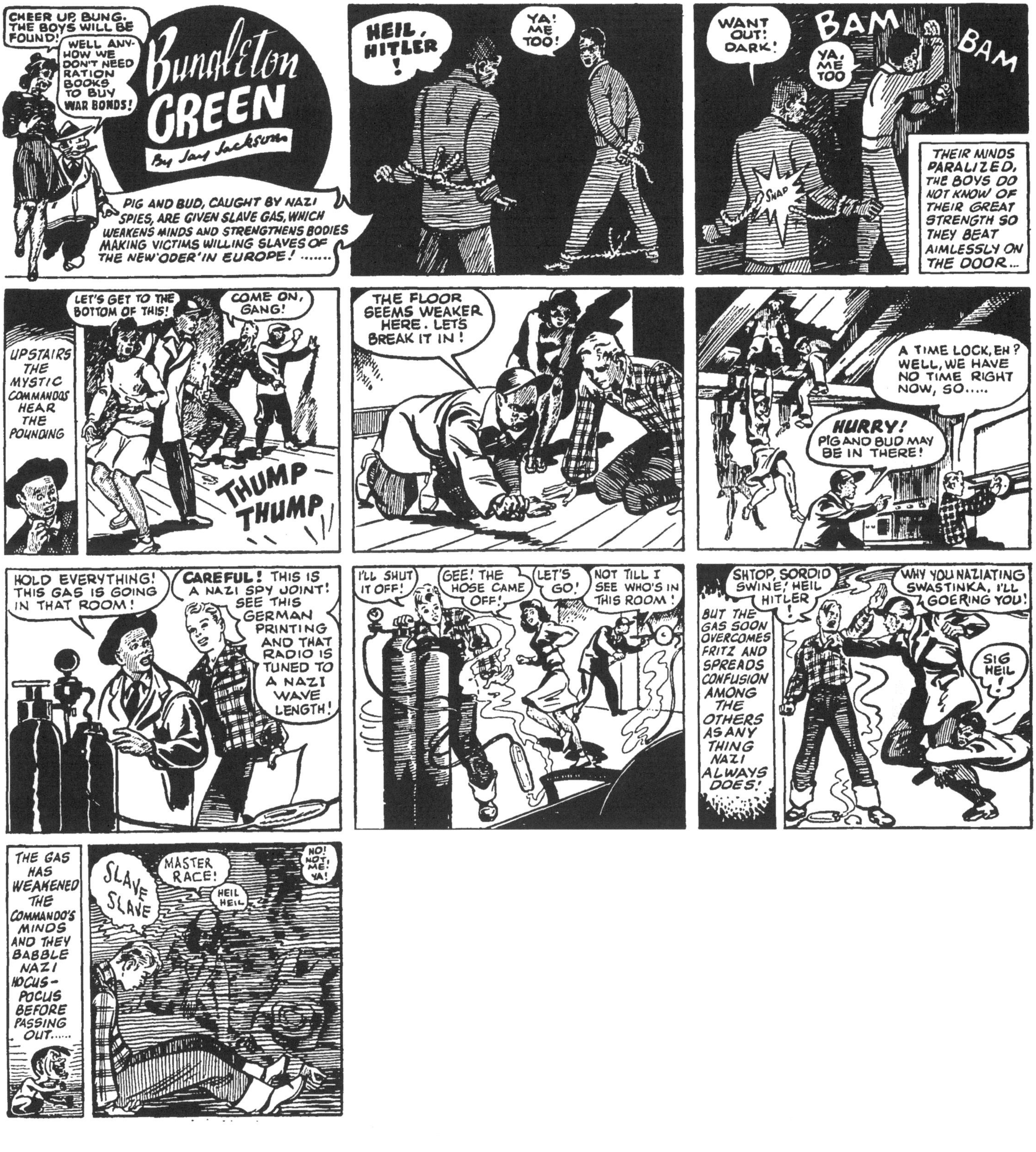
CHEER UP, BUNG. THE BOYS WILL BE FOUND!
WELL ANY-HOW WE DON'T NEED RATION BOOKS TO BUY WAR BONDS!
Bungleton GREEN
By Jay Jackson
PIG AND BUD, CAUGHT BY NAZI SPIES, ARE GIVEN SLAVE GAS, WHICH WEAKENS MINDS AND STRENGTHENS BODIES MAKING VICTIMS WILLING SLAVES OF THE NEW 'ODER' IN EUROPE! ....
HEIL, HITLER!
YA! ME TOO!
WANT OUT! DARK!
BAM
YA, ME TOO
BAM
SNAP
THEIR MINDS PARALIZED, THE BOYS DO NOT KNOW OF THEIR GREAT STRENGTH SO THEY BEAT AIMLESSLY ON THE DOOR...
UPSTAIRS THE MYSTIC COMMANDOS HEAR THE POUNDING
LET'S GET TO THE BOTTOM OF THIS!
COME ON, GANG!
THUMP THUMP
THE FLOOR SEEMS WEAKER HERE. LETS BREAK IT IN!
A TIME LOCK, EH? WELL, WE HAVE NO TIME RIGHT NOW, SO.....
HURRY! PIG AND BUD MAY BE IN THERE!
HOLD EVERYTHING! THIS GAS IS GOING IN THAT ROOM!
CAREFUL! THIS IS A NAZI SPY JOINT! SEE THIS GERMAN PRINTING AND THAT RADIO IS TUNED TO A NAZI WAVE LENGTH!
I'LL SHUT IT OFF!
GEE! THE HOSE CAME OFF!
LET'S GO!
NOT TILL I SEE WHO'S IN THIS ROOM!
SHTOP, SORDID SWINE, HEIL HITLER!
WHY YOU NAZIATING SWASTINKA, I'LL GOERING YOU!
BUT THE GAS SOON OVERCOMES FRITZ AND SPREADS CONFUSION AMONG THE OTHERS AS ANY THING NAZI ALWAYS DOES!
SIG HEIL!
THE GAS HAS WEAKENED THE COMMANDO'S MINDS AND THEY BABBLE NAZI HOCUS-POCUS BEFORE PASSING OUT......
SLAVE SLAVE
MASTER RACE!
HEIL HEIL
NO! NOT ME! YA!

MARCH 27, 1943

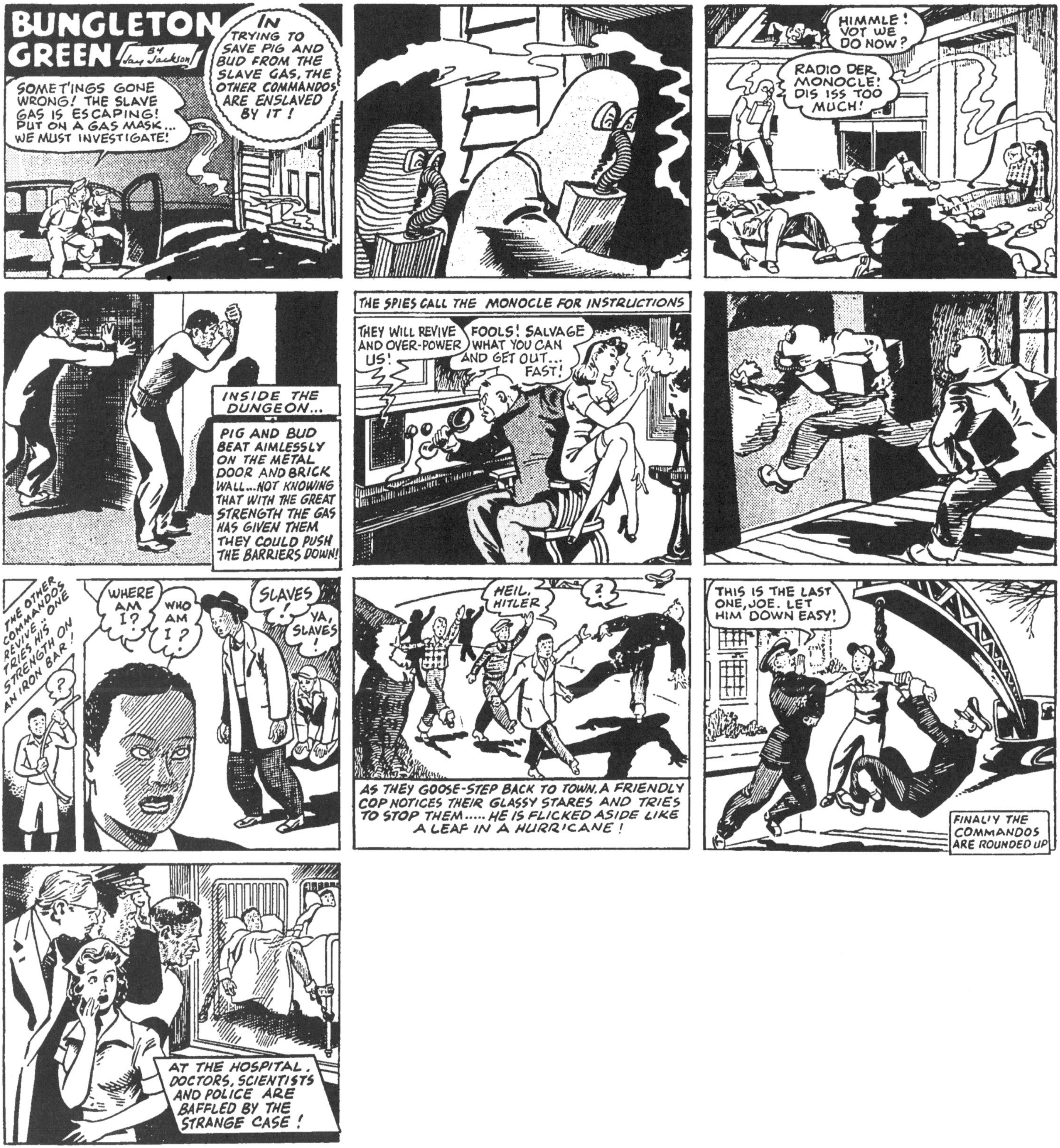

BUNGLETON GREEN
BY Jay Jackson
IN TRYING TO SAVE PIG AND BUD FROM THE SLAVE GAS, THE OTHER COMMANDOS ARE ENSLAVED BY IT!
SOMET'INGS GONE WRONG! THE SLAVE GAS IS ESCAPING! PUT ON A GAS MASK... WE MUST INVESTIGATE!
HIMMLE! VOT WE DO NOW?
RADIO DER MONOCLE! DIS ISS TOO MUCH!
INSIDE THE DUNGEON...
PIG AND BUD BEAT AIMLESSLY ON THE METAL DOOR AND BRICK WALL...NOT KNOWING THAT WITH THE GREAT STRENGTH THE GAS HAS GIVEN THEM THEY COULD PUSH THE BARRIERS DOWN!
THE SPIES CALL THE MONOCLE FOR INSTRUCTIONS
THEY WILL REVIVE AND OVER-POWER US!
FOOLS! SALVAGE WHAT YOU CAN AND GET OUT... FAST!
THE OTHER COMMANDOS REVIVE... ONE TRIES HIS STRENGTH ON AN IRON BAR!
?
WHERE AM I?
WHO AM I?
SLAVES!
YA, SLAVES!
HEIL, HITLER
?
AS THEY GOOSE-STEP BACK TO TOWN, A FRIENDLY COP NOTICES THEIR GLASSY STARES AND TRIES TO STOP THEM..... HE IS FLICKED ASIDE LIKE A LEAF IN A HURRICANE!
THIS IS THE LAST ONE, JOE. LET HIM DOWN EASY!
FINALLY THE COMMANDOS ARE ROUNDED UP
AT THE HOSPITAL, DOCTORS, SCIENTISTS AND POLICE ARE BAFFLED BY THE STRANGE CASE!

APRIL 3, 1943

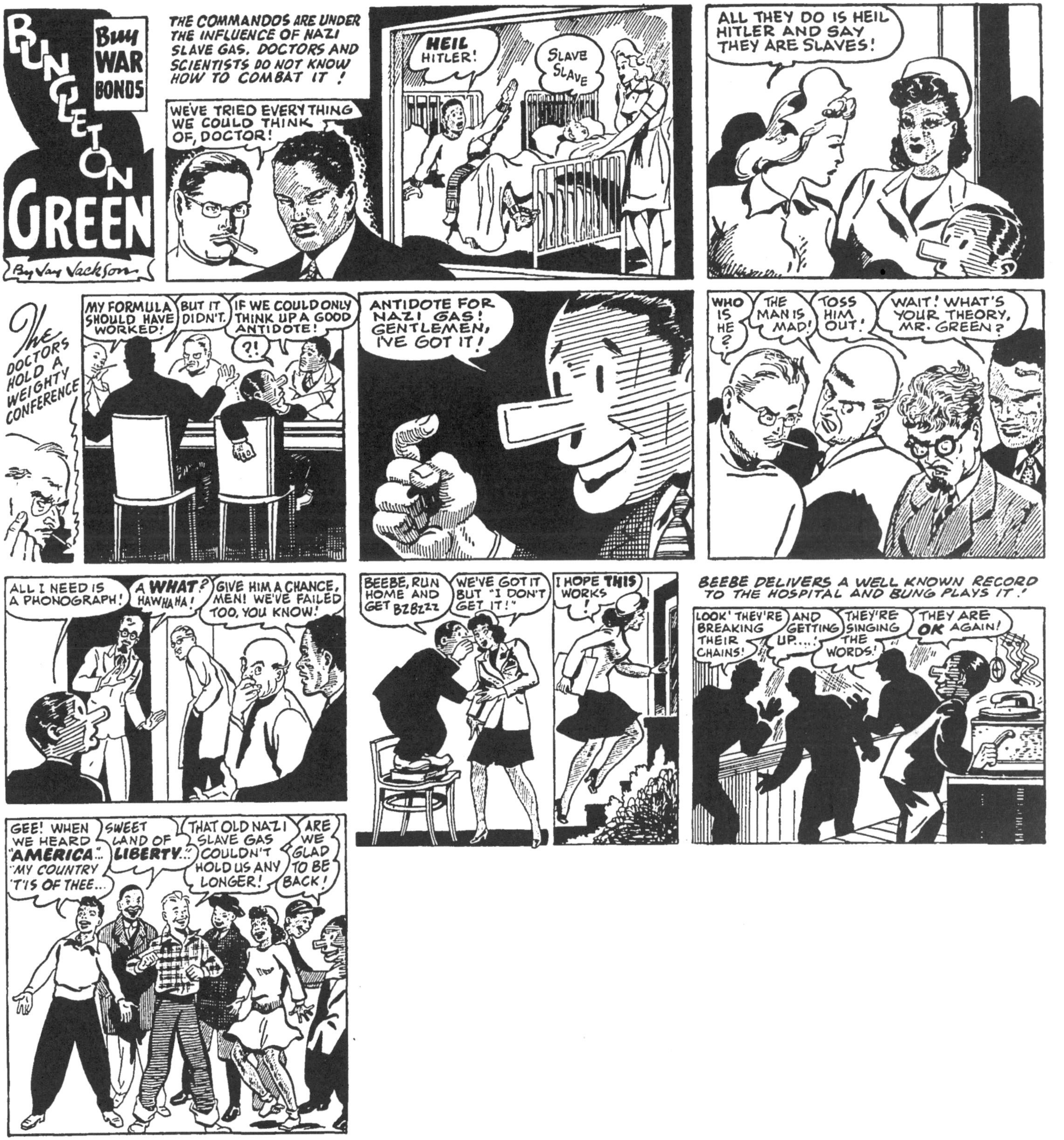
BUNGLETON GREEN
Buy WAR BONDS
By Jay Jackson
THE COMMANDOS ARE UNDER THE INFLUENCE OF NAZI SLAVE GAS. DOCTORS AND SCIENTISTS DO NOT KNOW HOW TO COMBAT IT!
WE'VE TRIED EVERYTHING WE COULD THINK OF, DOCTOR!
HEIL HITLER!
SLAVE SLAVE
ALL THEY DO IS HEIL HITLER AND SAY THEY ARE SLAVES!
The DOCTORS HOLD A WEIGHTY CONFERENCE
MY FORMULA SHOULD HAVE WORKED!
BUT IT DIDN'T.
IF WE COULD ONLY THINK UP A GOOD ANTIDOTE!
?!
ANTIDOTE FOR NAZI GAS! GENTLEMEN, I'VE GOT IT!
WHO IS HE?
THE MAN IS MAD!
TOSS HIM OUT!
WAIT! WHAT'S YOUR THEORY, MR. GREEN?
ALL I NEED IS A PHONOGRAPH!
A WHAT? HAWHAHA!
GIVE HIM A CHANCE, MEN! WE'VE FAILED TOO, YOU KNOW!
BEEBE, RUN HOME AND GET BZBZZZ
WE'VE GOT IT BUT "I DON'T GET IT!"
I HOPE THIS WORKS!
BEEBE DELIVERS A WELL KNOWN RECORD TO THE HOSPITAL AND BUNG PLAYS IT!
LOOK! THEY'RE BREAKING THEIR CHAINS!
AND GETTING UP....!
THEY'RE SINGING THE WORDS!
THEY ARE OK AGAIN!
GEE! WHEN WE HEARD "AMERICA"... "MY COUNTRY 'T'IS OF THEE...
SWEET LAND OF LIBERTY..."
THAT OLD NAZI SLAVE GAS COULDN'T HOLD US ANY LONGER!
ARE WE GLAD TO BE BACK!

APRIL 10, 1943

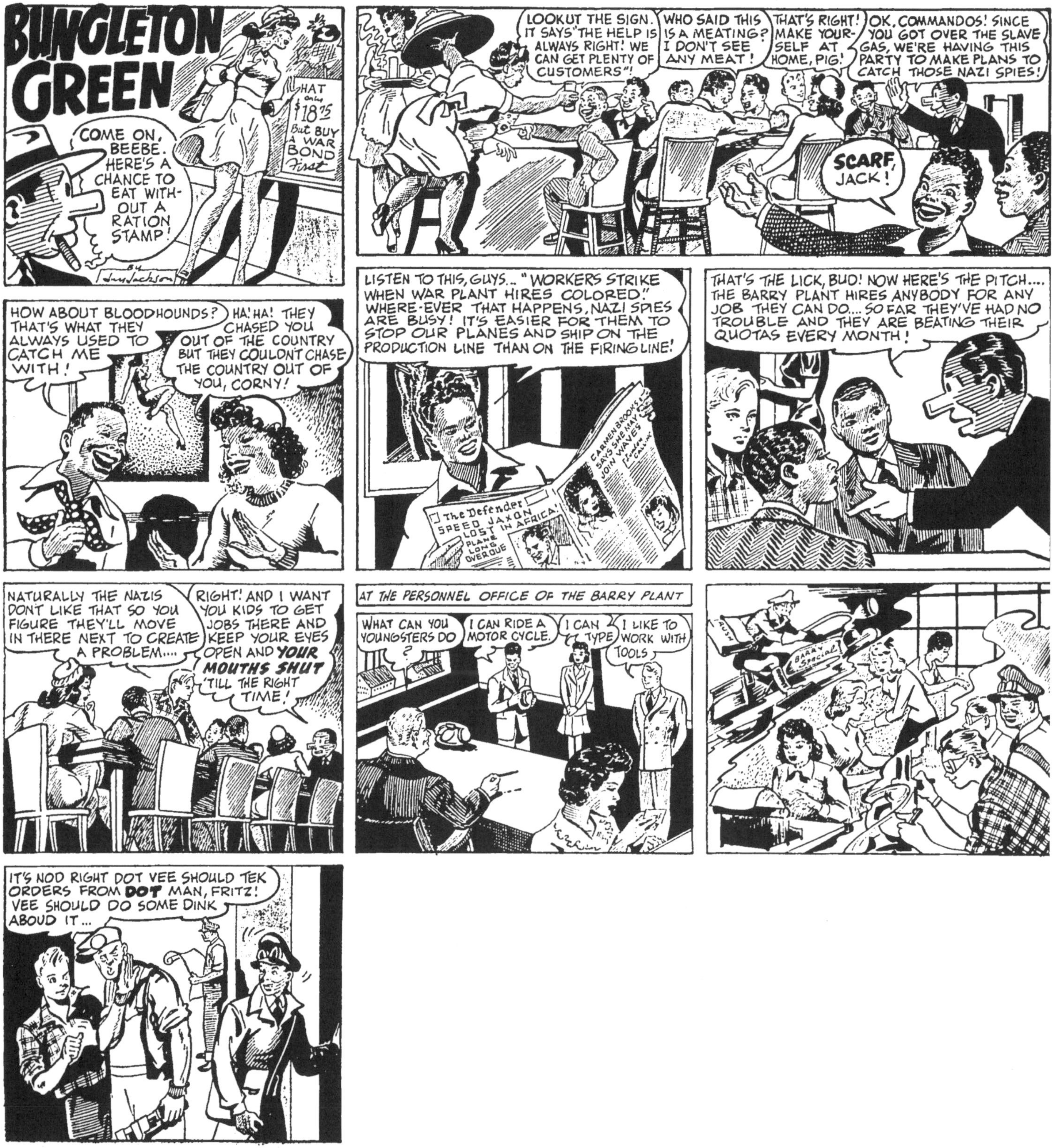
BUNGLETON GREEN
COME ON, BEEBE. HERE'S A CHANCE TO EAT WITH-OUT A RATION STAMP!
HAT only $18.75 But BUY A WAR BOND First
LOOKUT THE SIGN. IT SAYS "THE HELP IS ALWAYS RIGHT! WE CAN GET PLENTY OF CUSTOMERS"!
WHO SAID THIS IS A MEATING? I DON'T SEE ANY MEAT!
THAT'S RIGHT! MAKE YOUR-SELF AT HOME, PIG!
OK, COMMANDOS! SINCE YOU GOT OVER THE SLAVE GAS, WE'RE HAVING THIS PARTY TO MAKE PLANS TO CATCH THOSE NAZI SPIES!
SCARF, JACK!
HOW ABOUT BLOODHOUNDS? THAT'S WHAT THEY ALWAYS USED TO CATCH ME WITH!
HA! HA! THEY CHASED YOU OUT OF THE COUNTRY BUT THEY COULDN'T CHASE THE COUNTRY OUT OF YOU, CORNY!
LISTEN TO THIS, GUYS... "WORKERS STRIKE WHEN WAR PLANT HIRES COLORED." WHERE-EVER THAT HAPPENS, NAZI SPIES ARE BUSY! IT'S EASIER FOR THEM TO STOP OUR PLANES AND SHIP ON THE PRODUCTION LINE THAN ON THE FIRING LINE!
The Defender
SPEED JAXON LOST IN AFRICA!
PLANE LONG OVERDUE
CARMEN BROOKS SAYS SHE MAY JOIN WAVES
THAT'S THE LICK, BUD! NOW HERE'S THE PITCH.... THE BARRY PLANT HIRES ANYBODY FOR ANY JOB THEY CAN DO.... SO FAR THEY'VE HAD NO TROUBLE AND THEY ARE BEATING THEIR QUOTAS EVERY MONTH!
NATURALLY THE NAZIS DONT LIKE THAT SO YOU FIGURE THEY'LL MOVE IN THERE NEXT TO CREATE A PROBLEM....
RIGHT! AND I WANT YOU KIDS TO GET JOBS THERE AND KEEP YOUR EYES OPEN AND YOUR MOUTHS SHUT 'TILL THE RIGHT TIME!
AT THE PERSONNEL OFFICE OF THE BARRY PLANT
WHAT CAN YOU YOUNGSTERS DO?
I CAN RIDE A MOTOR CYCLE.
I CAN TYPE
I LIKE TO WORK WITH TOOLS
BARRY Special
IT'S NOD RIGHT DOT VEE SHOULD TEK ORDERS FROM DOT MAN, FRITZ! VEE SHOULD DO SOME DINK ABOUD IT...

APRIL 17, 1943

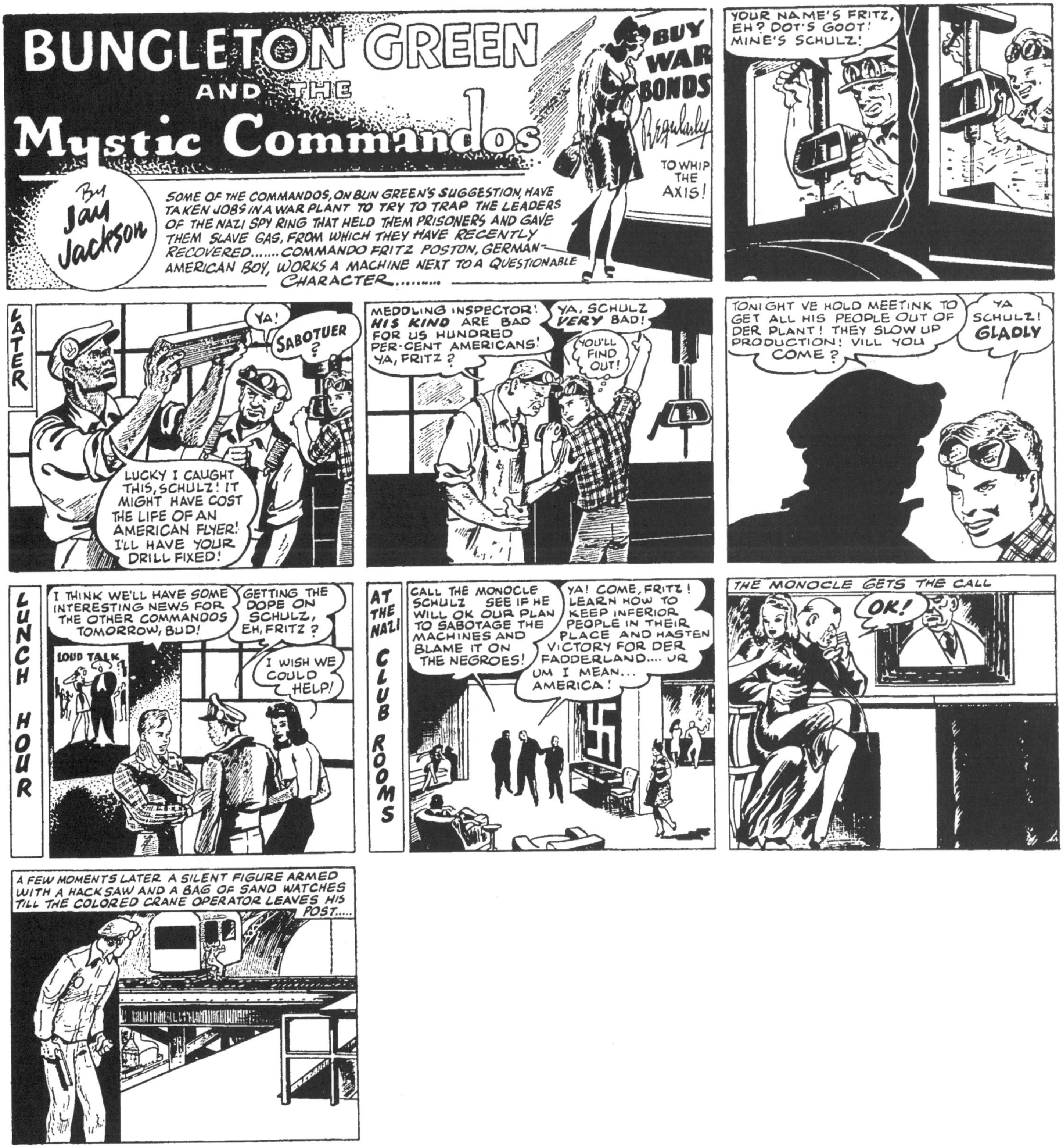
BUNGLETON GREEN
AND THE
Mystic Commandos
By Jay Jackson
SOME OF THE COMMANDOS, ON BUN GREEN'S SUGGESTION, HAVE TAKEN JOBS IN A WAR PLANT TO TRY TO TRAP THE LEADERS OF THE NAZI SPY RING THAT HELD THEM PRISONERS AND GAVE THEM SLAVE GAS, FROM WHICH THEY HAVE RECENTLY RECOVERED....... COMMANDO FRITZ POSTON, GERMAN-AMERICAN BOY, WORKS A MACHINE NEXT TO A QUESTIONABLE CHARACTER.........
BUY WAR BONDS Regularly TO WHIP THE AXIS!
YOUR NAME'S FRITZ, EH? DOT'S GOOT! MINE'S SCHULZ!
LATER
YA!
SABOTUER ?
LUCKY I CAUGHT THIS, SCHULZ! IT MIGHT HAVE COST THE LIFE OF AN AMERICAN FLYER! I'LL HAVE YOUR DRILL FIXED!
MEDDLING INSPECTOR! HIS KIND ARE BAD FOR US HUNDRED PER-CENT AMERICANS! YA, FRITZ ?
YA, SCHULZ VERY BAD!
YOU'LL FIND OUT!
TONIGHT VE HOLD MEETINK TO GET ALL HIS PEOPLE OUT OF DER PLANT! THEY SLOW UP PRODUCTION! VILL YOU COME ?
YA SCHULZ! GLADLY
LUNCH HOUR
I THINK WE'LL HAVE SOME INTERESTING NEWS FOR THE OTHER COMMANDOS TOMORROW, BUD!
GETTING THE DOPE ON SCHULZ, EH, FRITZ ?
I WISH WE COULD HELP!
LOUD TALK
AT THE NAZI CLUB ROOMS
CALL THE MONOCLE SCHULZ SEE IF HE WILL OK OUR PLAN TO SABOTAGE THE MACHINES AND BLAME IT ON THE NEGROES!
YA! COME, FRITZ! LEARN HOW TO KEEP INFERIOR PEOPLE IN THEIR PLACE AND HASTEN VICTORY FOR DER FADDERLAND.... UR UM I MEAN... AMERICA!
THE MONOCLE GETS THE CALL
OK!
A FEW MOMENTS LATER A SILENT FIGURE ARMED WITH A HACK SAW AND A BAG OF SAND WATCHES TILL THE COLORED CRANE OPERATOR LEAVES HIS POST.....

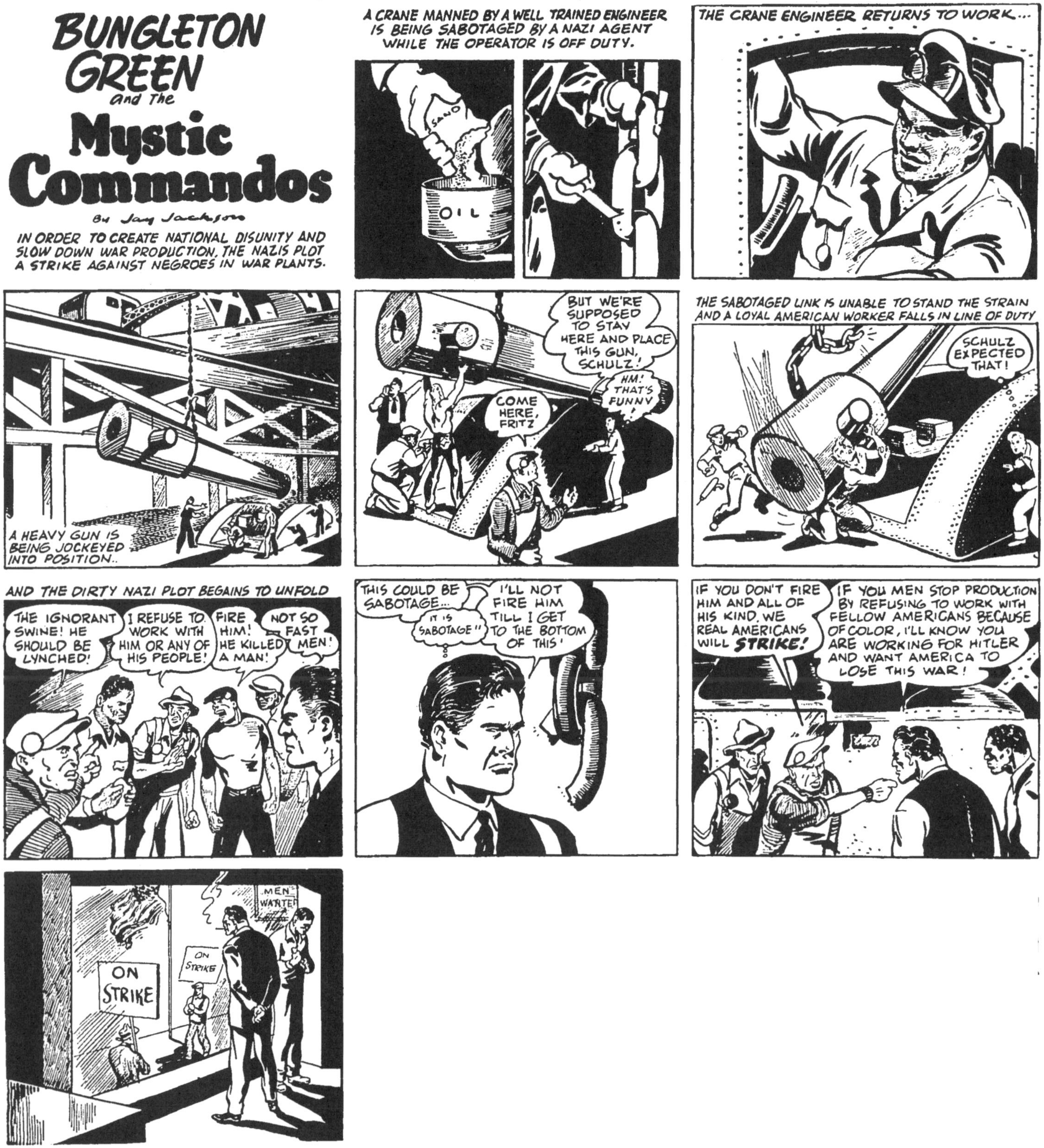
BUNGLETON GREEN and The Mystic Commandos
By Jay Jackson
IN ORDER TO CREATE NATIONAL DISUNITY AND SLOW DOWN WAR PRODUCTION, THE NAZIS PLOT A STRIKE AGAINST NEGROES IN WAR PLANTS.
A CRANE MANNED BY A WELL TRAINED ENGINEER IS BEING SABOTAGED BY A NAZI AGENT WHILE THE OPERATOR IS OFF DUTY.
SAND
OIL
THE CRANE ENGINEER RETURNS TO WORK...
A HEAVY GUN IS BEING JOCKEYED INTO POSITION..
BUT WE'RE SUPPOSED TO STAY HERE AND PLACE THIS GUN, SCHULZ!
HM! THAT'S FUNNY!
COME HERE, FRITZ
THE SABOTAGED LINK IS UNABLE TO STAND THE STRAIN AND A LOYAL AMERICAN WORKER FALLS IN LINE OF DUTY
SCHULZ EXPECTED THAT!
AND THE DIRTY NAZI PLOT BEGAINS TO UNFOLD
THE IGNORANT SWINE! HE SHOULD BE LYNCHED!
I REFUSE TO WORK WITH HIM OR ANY OF HIS PEOPLE!
FIRE HIM! HE KILLED A MAN!
NOT SO FAST MEN!
THIS COULD BE SABOTAGE...
IT IS SABOTAGE"
I'LL NOT FIRE HIM TILL I GET TO THE BOTTOM OF THIS'
IF YOU DON'T FIRE HIM AND ALL OF HIS KIND, WE REAL AMERICANS WILL STRIKE!
IF YOU MEN STOP PRODUCTION BY REFUSING TO WORK WITH FELLOW AMERICANS BECAUSE OF COLOR, I'LL KNOW YOU ARE WORKING FOR HITLER AND WANT AMERICA TO LOSE THIS WAR!
ON STRIKE
ON STRIKE

MAY 1, 1943

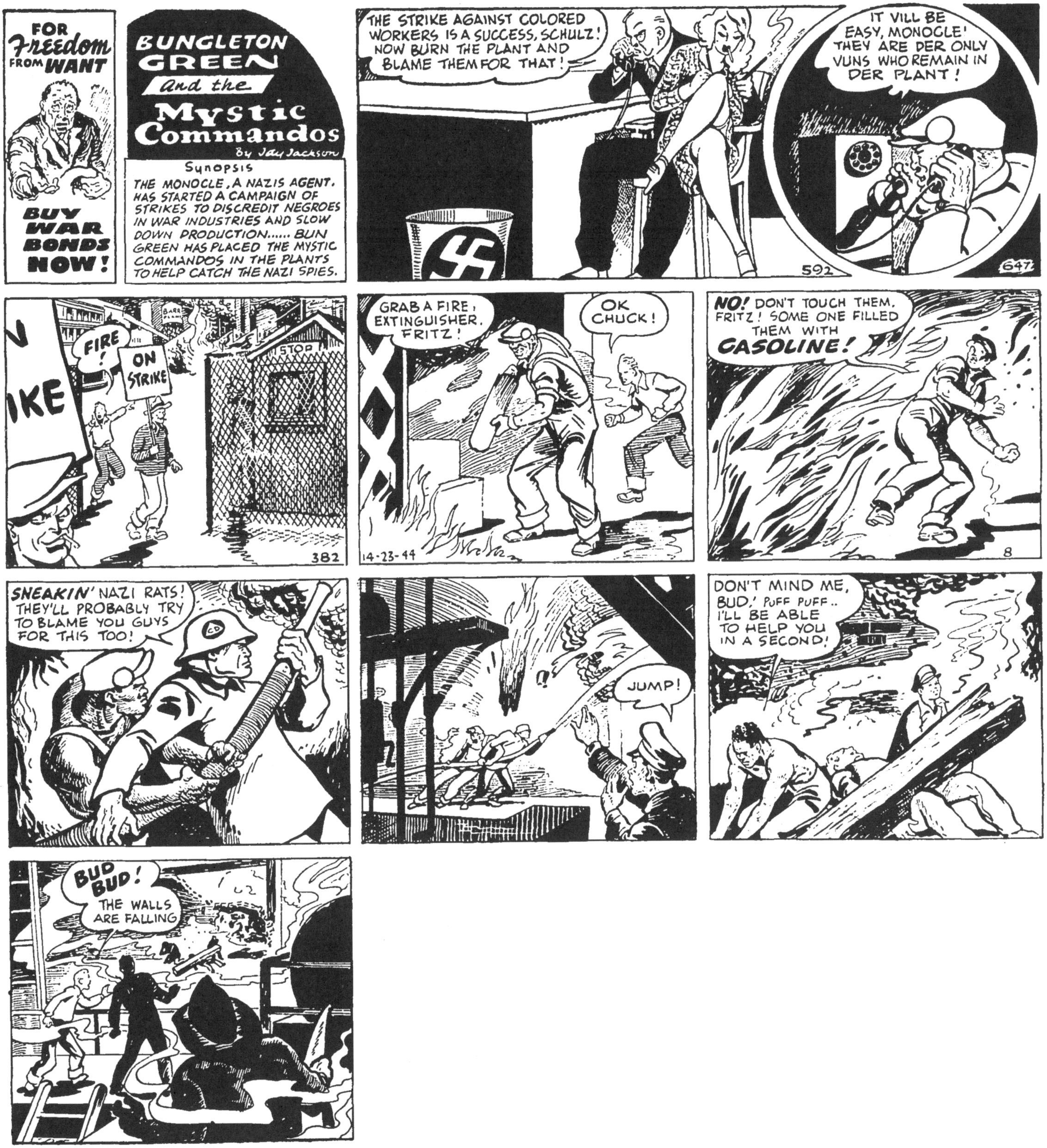

FOR Freedom FROM WANT
BUY WAR BONDS NOW!
BUNGLETON GREEN and the Mystic Commandos
By Jay Jackson
Synopsis
THE MONOCLE, A NAZIS AGENT, HAS STARTED A CAMPAIGN OF STRIKES TO DISCREDIT NEGROES IN WAR INDUSTRIES AND SLOW DOWN PRODUCTION...... BUN GREEN HAS PLACED THE MYSTIC COMMANDOS IN THE PLANTS TO HELP CATCH THE NAZI SPIES.
THE STRIKE AGAINST COLORED WORKERS IS A SUCCESS, SCHULZ! NOW BURN THE PLANT AND BLAME THEM FOR THAT!
IT VILL BE EASY, MONOCLE! THEY ARE DER ONLY VUNS WHO REMAIN IN DER PLANT!
FIRE!
ON STRIKE
STOP
GRAB A FIRE EXTINGUISHER, FRITZ!
OK CHUCK!
NO! DON'T TOUCH THEM, FRITZ! SOME ONE FILLED THEM WITH GASOLINE!
SNEAKIN' NAZI RATS! THEY'LL PROBABLY TRY TO BLAME YOU GUYS FOR THIS TOO!
JUMP!
DON'T MIND ME, BUD! PUFF PUFF.. I'LL BE ABLE TO HELP YOU IN A SECOND!
BUD BUD! THE WALLS ARE FALLING

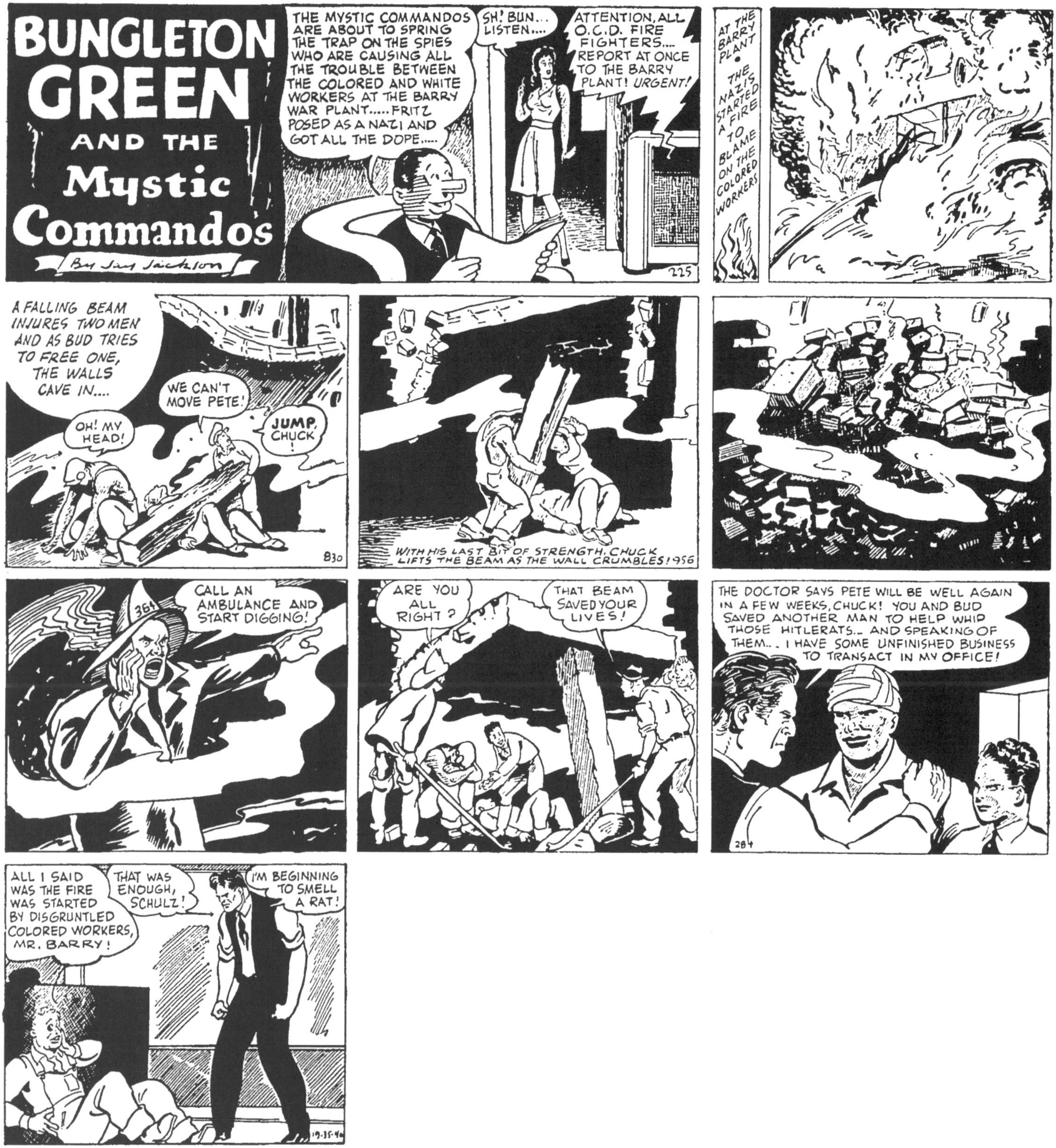
BUNGLETON GREEN AND THE Mystic Commandos
By Jay Jackson
THE MYSTIC COMMANDOS ARE ABOUT TO SPRING THE TRAP ON THE SPIES WHO ARE CAUSING ALL THE TROUBLE BETWEEN THE COLORED AND WHITE WORKERS AT THE BARRY WAR PLANT.....FRITZ POSED AS A NAZI AND GOT ALL THE DOPE.....
SH! BUN... LISTEN....
ATTENTION, ALL O.C.D. FIRE FIGHTERS.... REPORT AT ONCE TO THE BARRY PLANT! URGENT!
AT THE BARRY PLANT • THE NAZIS STARTED A FIRE TO BLAME ON THE COLORED WORKERS
A FALLING BEAM INJURES TWO MEN AND AS BUD TRIES TO FREE ONE, THE WALLS CAVE IN....
WE CAN'T MOVE PETE!
OH! MY HEAD!
JUMP, CHUCK!
WITH HIS LAST BIT OF STRENGTH, CHUCK LIFTS THE BEAM AS THE WALL CRUMBLES!
CALL AN AMBULANCE AND START DIGGING!
ARE YOU ALL RIGHT?
THAT BEAM SAVED YOUR LIVES!
THE DOCTOR SAYS PETE WILL BE WELL AGAIN IN A FEW WEEKS, CHUCK! YOU AND BUD SAVED ANOTHER MAN TO HELP WHIP THOSE HITLERATS.. AND SPEAKING OF THEM.. I HAVE SOME UNFINISHED BUSINESS TO TRANSACT IN MY OFFICE!
ALL I SAID WAS THE FIRE WAS STARTED BY DISGRUNTLED COLORED WORKERS, MR. BARRY!
THAT WAS ENOUGH, SCHULZ!
I'M BEGINNING TO SMELL A RAT!

MAY 15, 1943

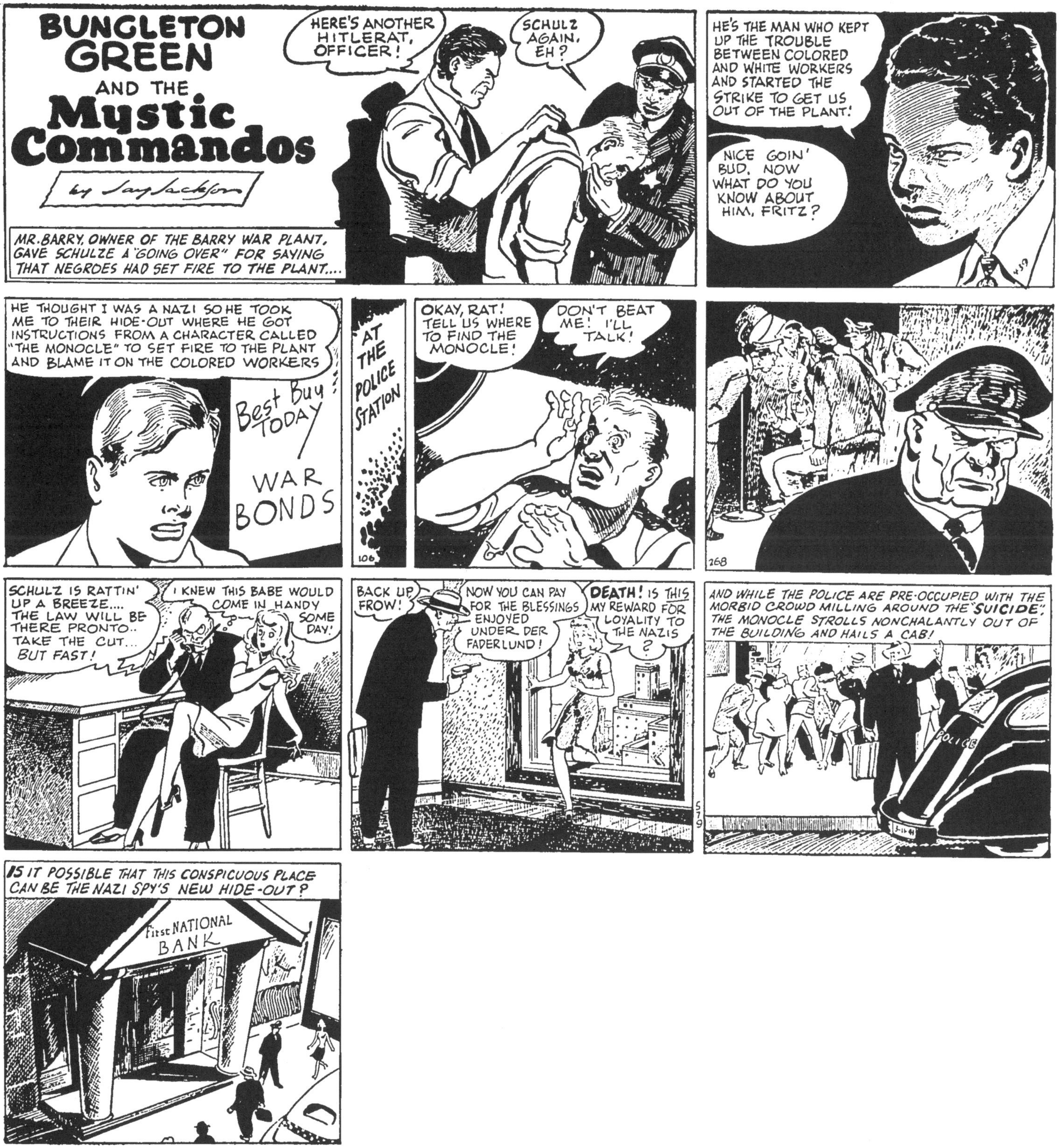
BUNGLETON GREEN AND THE Mystic Commandos
by Jay Jackson
MR. BARRY, OWNER OF THE BARRY WAR PLANT, GAVE SCHULZE A "GOING OVER" FOR SAYING THAT NEGROES HAD SET FIRE TO THE PLANT....
HERE'S ANOTHER HITLERAT, OFFICER!
SCHULZ AGAIN, EH?
HE'S THE MAN WHO KEPT UP THE TROUBLE BETWEEN COLORED AND WHITE WORKERS AND STARTED THE STRIKE TO GET US OUT OF THE PLANT!
NICE GOIN' BUD. NOW WHAT DO YOU KNOW ABOUT HIM, FRITZ?
HE THOUGHT I WAS A NAZI SO HE TOOK ME TO THEIR HIDE-OUT WHERE HE GOT INSTRUCTIONS FROM A CHARACTER CALLED "THE MONOCLE" TO SET FIRE TO THE PLANT AND BLAME IT ON THE COLORED WORKERS
Best Buy TODAY
WAR BONDS
AT THE POLICE STATION
OKAY, RAT! TELL US WHERE TO FIND THE MONOCLE!
DON'T BEAT ME! I'LL TALK!
SCHULZ IS RATTIN' UP A BREEZE.... THE LAW WILL BE THERE PRONTO.. TAKE THE CUT... BUT FAST!
I KNEW THIS BABE WOULD COME IN HANDY SOME DAY!
BACK UP FROW!
NOW YOU CAN PAY FOR THE BLESSINGS ENJOYED UNDER DER FADERLUND!
DEATH! IS THIS MY REWARD FOR LOYALITY TO THE NAZIS ?
AND WHILE THE POLICE ARE PRE-OCCUPIED WITH THE MORBID CROWD MILLING AROUND THE "SUICIDE", THE MONOCLE STROLLS NONCHALANTLY OUT OF THE BUILDING AND HAILS A CAB!
POLICE
IS IT POSSIBLE THAT THIS CONSPICUOUS PLACE CAN BE THE NAZI SPY'S NEW HIDE-OUT?
First NATIONAL BANK

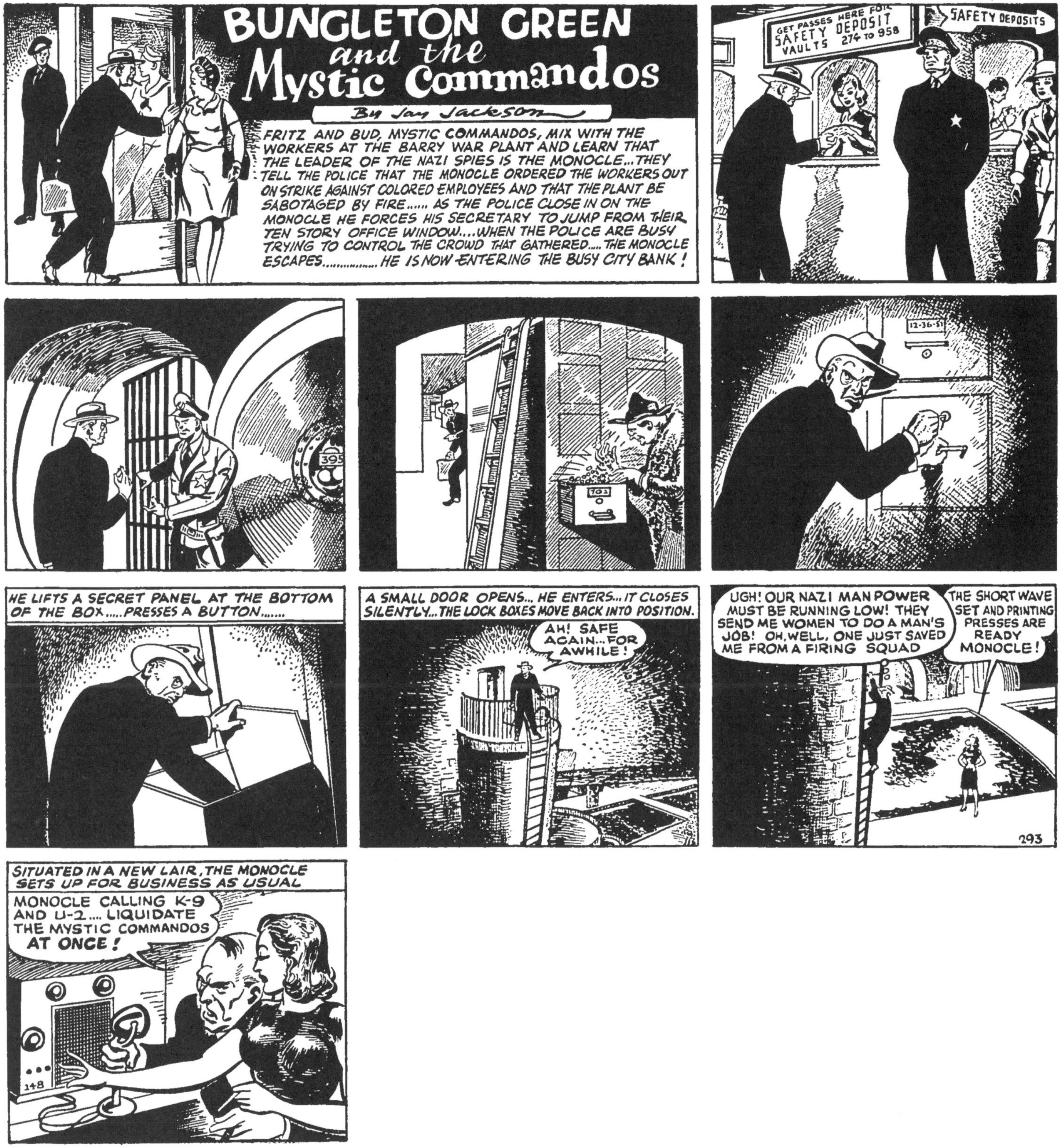

BUNGLETON GREEN
and the
Mystic Commandos
By Jay Jackson
FRITZ AND BUD, MYSTIC COMMANDOS, MIX WITH THE WORKERS AT THE BARRY WAR PLANT AND LEARN THAT THE LEADER OF THE NAZI SPIES IS THE MONOCLE... THEY TELL THE POLICE THAT THE MONOCLE ORDERED THE WORKERS OUT ON STRIKE AGAINST COLORED EMPLOYEES AND THAT THE PLANT BE SABOTAGED BY FIRE...... AS THE POLICE CLOSE IN ON THE MONOCLE HE FORCES HIS SECRETARY TO JUMP FROM THEIR TEN STORY OFFICE WINDOW.... WHEN THE POLICE ARE BUSY TRYING TO CONTROL THE CROWD THAT GATHERED..... THE MONOCLE ESCAPES............... HE IS NOW ENTERING THE BUSY CITY BANK!
GET PASSES HERE FOR SAFETY DEPOSIT VAULTS 274 TO 958
SAFETY DEPOSITS
HE LIFTS A SECRET PANEL AT THE BOTTOM OF THE BOX..... PRESSES A BUTTON.......
A SMALL DOOR OPENS... HE ENTERS... IT CLOSES SILENTLY... THE LOCK BOXES MOVE BACK INTO POSITION.
AH! SAFE AGAIN... FOR AWHILE!
UGH! OUR NAZI MAN POWER MUST BE RUNNING LOW! THEY SEND ME WOMEN TO DO A MAN'S JOB! OH, WELL, ONE JUST SAVED ME FROM A FIRING SQUAD
THE SHORT WAVE SET AND PRINTING PRESSES ARE READY MONOCLE!
293
SITUATED IN A NEW LAIR, THE MONOCLE SETS UP FOR BUSINESS AS USUAL
MONOCLE CALLING K-9 AND U-2.... LIQUIDATE THE MYSTIC COMMANDOS AT ONCE!
148

MAY 29, 1943

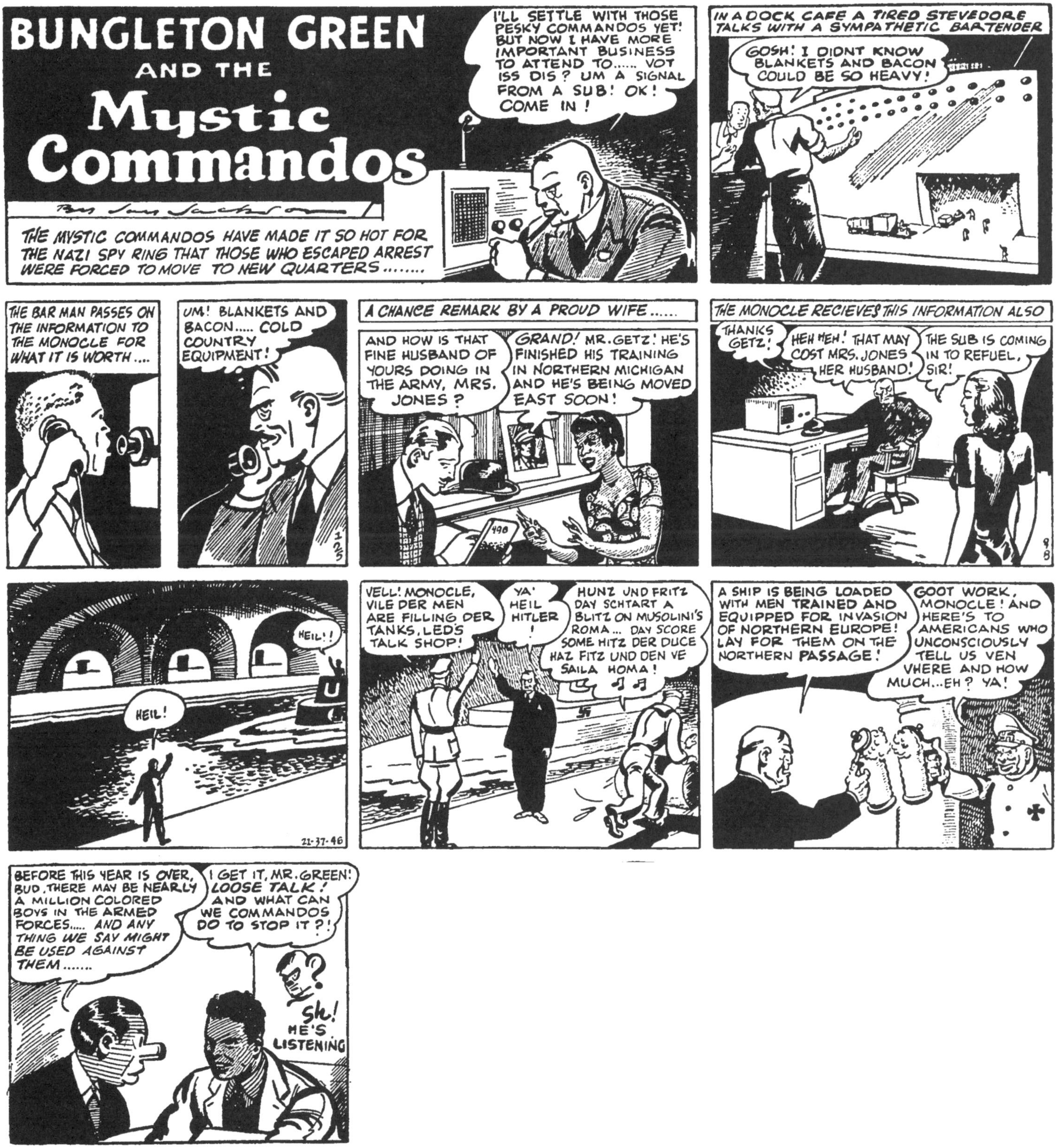
BUNGLETON GREEN
AND THE
Mystic Commandos
THE MYSTIC COMMANDOS HAVE MADE IT SO HOT FOR THE NAZI SPY RING THAT THOSE WHO ESCAPED ARREST WERE FORCED TO MOVE TO NEW QUARTERS........
I'LL SETTLE WITH THOSE PESKY COMMANDOS YET! BUT NOW I HAVE MORE IMPORTANT BUSINESS TO ATTEND TO...... VOT ISS DIS? UM A SIGNAL FROM A SUB! OK! COME IN!
IN A DOCK CAFE A TIRED STEVEDORE TALKS WITH A SYMPATHETIC BARTENDER
GOSH! I DIDNT KNOW BLANKETS AND BACON COULD BE SO HEAVY!
THE BAR MAN PASSES ON THE INFORMATION TO THE MONOCLE FOR WHAT IT IS WORTH....
UM! BLANKETS AND BACON..... COLD COUNTRY EQUIPMENT!
A CHANCE REMARK BY A PROUD WIFE......
AND HOW IS THAT FINE HUSBAND OF YOURS DOING IN THE ARMY, MRS. JONES?
GRAND! MR. GETZ! HE'S FINISHED HIS TRAINING IN NORTHERN MICHIGAN AND HE'S BEING MOVED EAST SOON!
THE MONOCLE RECIEVES THIS INFORMATION ALSO
THANKS GETZ!
HEH HEH! THAT MAY COST MRS. JONES HER HUSBAND!
THE SUB IS COMING IN TO REFUEL, SIR!
HEIL!!
HEIL!
21-37-46
VELL! MONOCLE, VILE DER MEN ARE FILLING DER TANKS, LED'S TALK SHOP!
YA' HEIL HITLER!
HUNZ UND FRITZ DAY SCHTART A BLITZ ON MUSOLINI'S ROMA... DAY SCORE SOME HITZ DER DUCE HAZ FITZ UND DEN VE SAILA HOMA!
A SHIP IS BEING LOADED WITH MEN TRAINED AND EQUIPPED FOR INVASION OF NORTHERN EUROPE! LAY FOR THEM ON THE NORTHERN PASSAGE!
GOOT WORK, MONOCLE! AND HERE'S TO AMERICANS WHO UNCONSCIOUSLY TELL US VEN VHERE AND HOW MUCH...EH? YA!
BEFORE THIS YEAR IS OVER, BUD, THERE MAY BE NEARLY A MILLION COLORED BOYS IN THE ARMED FORCES..... AND ANY THING WE SAY MIGHT BE USED AGAINST THEM.......
I GET IT, MR. GREEN! LOOSE TALK! AND WHAT CAN WE COMMANDOS DO TO STOP IT?!
SH! HE'S LISTENING

JUNE 5, 1943

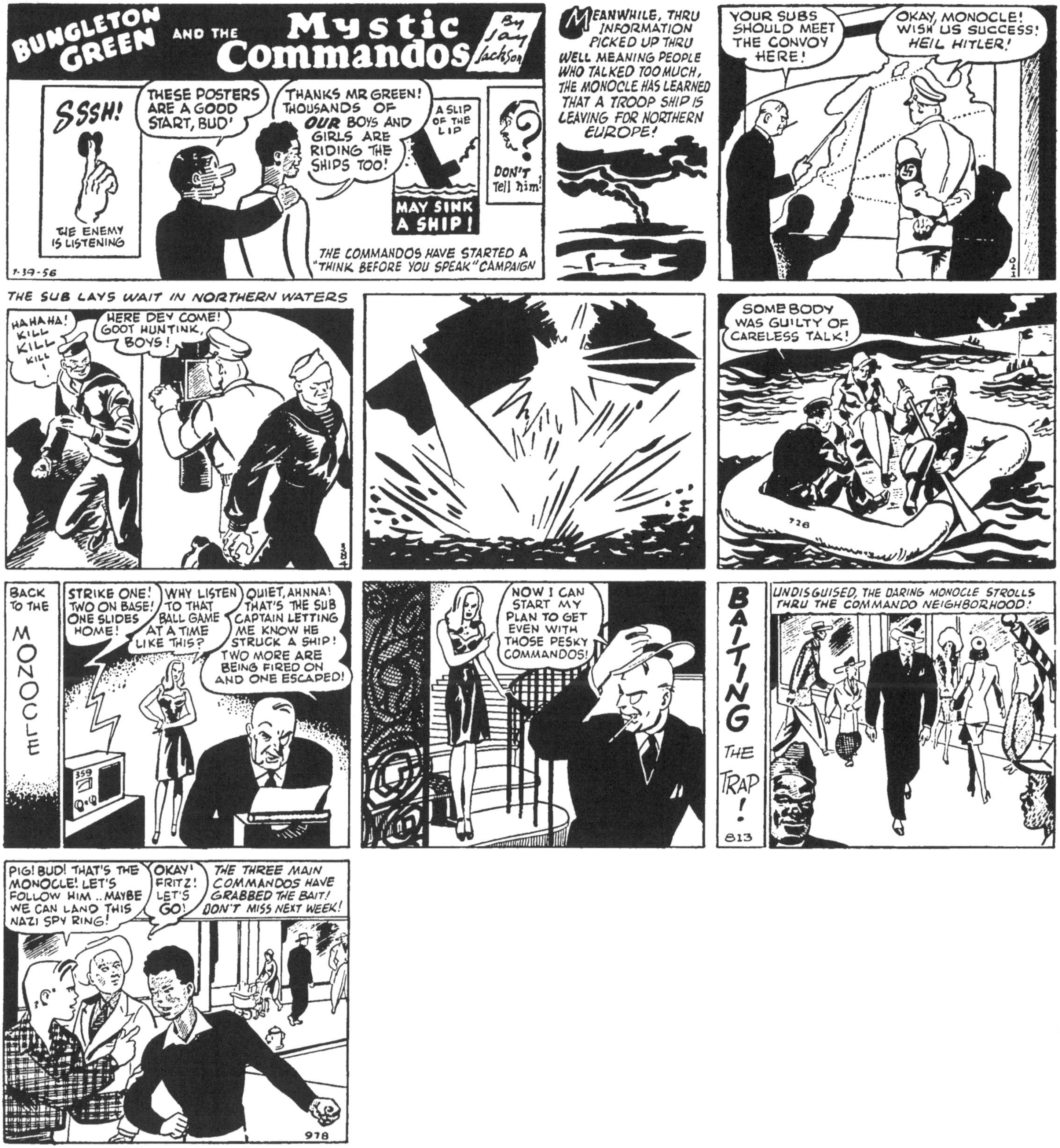
BUNGLETON GREEN AND THE Mystic Commandos
By Jay Jackson
SSSH!
THE ENEMY IS LISTENING
THESE POSTERS ARE A GOOD START, BUD'
THANKS MR GREEN! THOUSANDS OF OUR BOYS AND GIRLS ARE RIDING THE SHIPS TOO!
A SLIP OF THE LIP
MAY SINK A SHIP!
DON'T Tell him!
THE COMMANDOS HAVE STARTED A "THINK BEFORE YOU SPEAK" CAMPAIGN
MEANWHILE, THRU INFORMATION PICKED UP THRU WELL MEANING PEOPLE WHO TALKED TOO MUCH, THE MONOCLE HAS LEARNED THAT A TROOP SHIP IS LEAVING FOR NORTHERN EUROPE!
YOUR SUBS SHOULD MEET THE CONVOY HERE!
OKAY, MONOCLE! WISH US SUCCESS! HEIL HITLER!
THE SUB LAYS WAIT IN NORTHERN WATERS
HAHAHA! KILL KILL KILL!
HERE DEY COME! GOOT HUNTINK, BOYS!
SOMEBODY WAS GUILTY OF CARELESS TALK!
BACK TO THE MONOCLE
STRIKE ONE! TWO ON BASE! ONE SLIDES HOME!
WHY LISTEN TO THAT BALL GAME AT A TIME LIKE THIS?
QUIET, AHNNA! THAT'S THE SUB CAPTAIN LETTING ME KNOW HE STRUCK A SHIP! TWO MORE ARE BEING FIRED ON AND ONE ESCAPED!
NOW I CAN START MY PLAN TO GET EVEN WITH THOSE PESKY COMMANDOS!
BAITING THE TRAP!
UNDISGUISED, THE DARING MONOCLE STROLLS THRU THE COMMANDO NEIGHBORHOOD!
PIG! BUD! THAT'S THE MONOCLE! LET'S FOLLOW HIM .. MAYBE WE CAN LAND THIS NAZI SPY RING!
OKAY! FRITZ! LET'S GO!
THE THREE MAIN COMMANDOS HAVE GRABBED THE BAIT! DON'T MISS NEXT WEEK!

JUNE 12, 1943

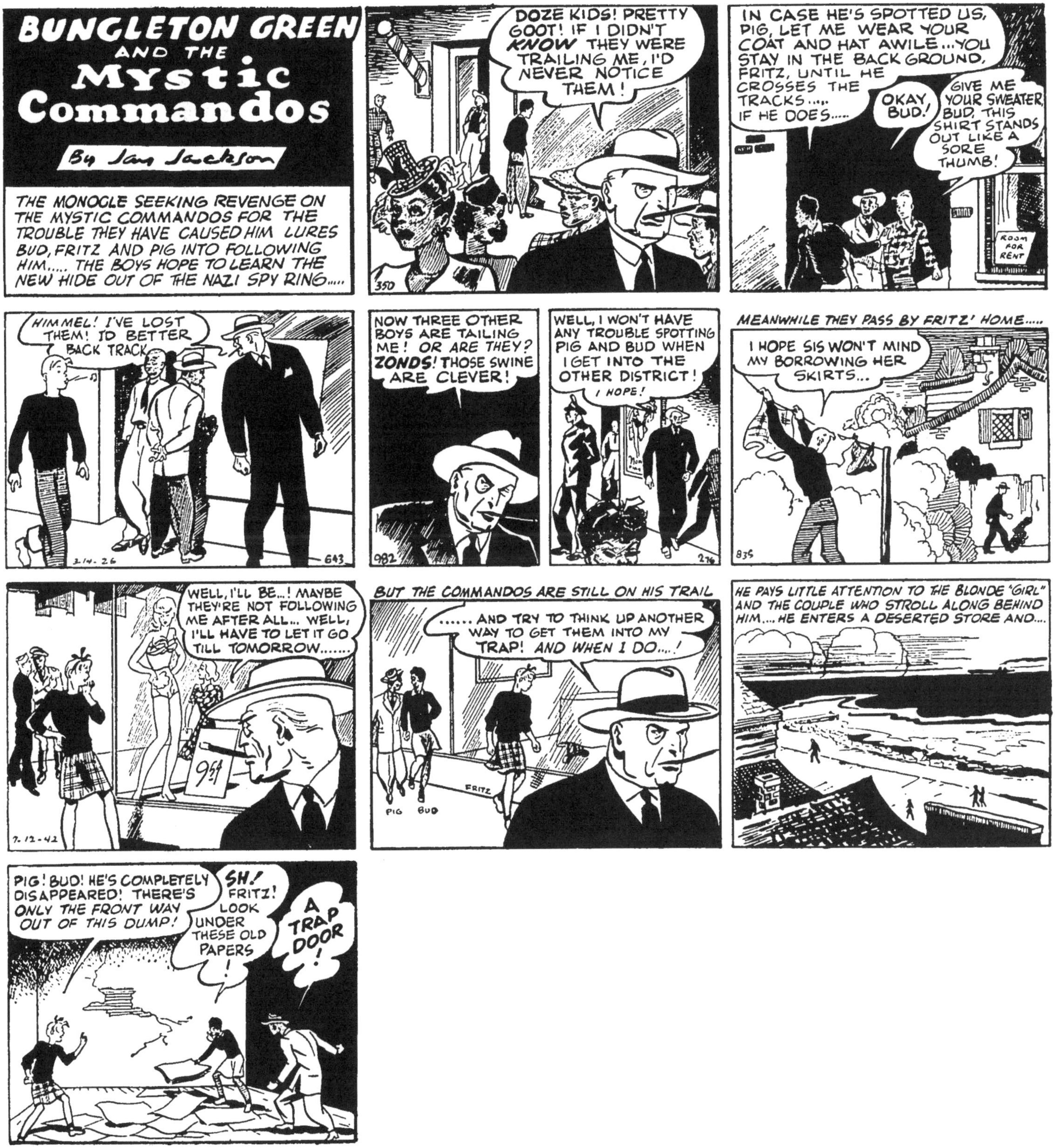
BUNGLETON GREEN
AND THE
Mystic Commandos
By Jay Jackson
THE MONOCLE SEEKING REVENGE ON THE MYSTIC COMMANDOS FOR THE TROUBLE THEY HAVE CAUSED HIM LURES BUD, FRITZ AND PIG INTO FOLLOWING HIM..... THE BOYS HOPE TO LEARN THE NEW HIDE OUT OF THE NAZI SPY RING.....
DOZE KIDS! PRETTY GOOT! IF I DIDN'T KNOW THEY WERE TRAILING ME, I'D NEVER NOTICE THEM!
IN CASE HE'S SPOTTED US, PIG, LET ME WEAR YOUR COAT AND HAT AWILE...YOU STAY IN THE BACK GROUND, FRITZ, UNTIL HE CROSSES THE TRACKS..... IF HE DOES.....
OKAY, BUD!
GIVE ME YOUR SWEATER, BUD, THIS SHIRT STANDS OUT LIKE A SORE THUMB!
ROOM FOR RENT
HIMMEL! I'VE LOST THEM! I'D BETTER BACK TRACK
NOW THREE OTHER BOYS ARE TAILING ME! OR ARE THEY? ZONDS! THOSE SWINE ARE CLEVER!
WELL, I WON'T HAVE ANY TROUBLE SPOTTING PIG AND BUD WHEN I GET INTO THE OTHER DISTRICT!
I HOPE!
MEANWHILE THEY PASS BY FRITZ' HOME.....
I HOPE SIS WON'T MIND MY BORROWING HER SKIRTS...
WELL, I'LL BE...! MAYBE THEY'RE NOT FOLLOWING ME AFTER ALL... WELL, I'LL HAVE TO LET IT GO TILL TOMORROW.......
BUT THE COMMANDOS ARE STILL ON HIS TRAIL
......AND TRY TO THINK UP ANOTHER WAY TO GET THEM INTO MY TRAP! AND WHEN I DO....!
PIG
BUD
FRITZ
HE PAYS LITTLE ATTENTION TO THE BLONDE "GIRL" AND THE COUPLE WHO STROLL ALONG BEHIND HIM.... HE ENTERS A DESERTED STORE AND....
PIG! BUD! HE'S COMPLETELY DISAPPEARED! THERE'S ONLY THE FRONT WAY OUT OF THIS DUMP!
SH! FRITZ! LOOK UNDER THESE OLD PAPERS!
A TRAP DOOR!

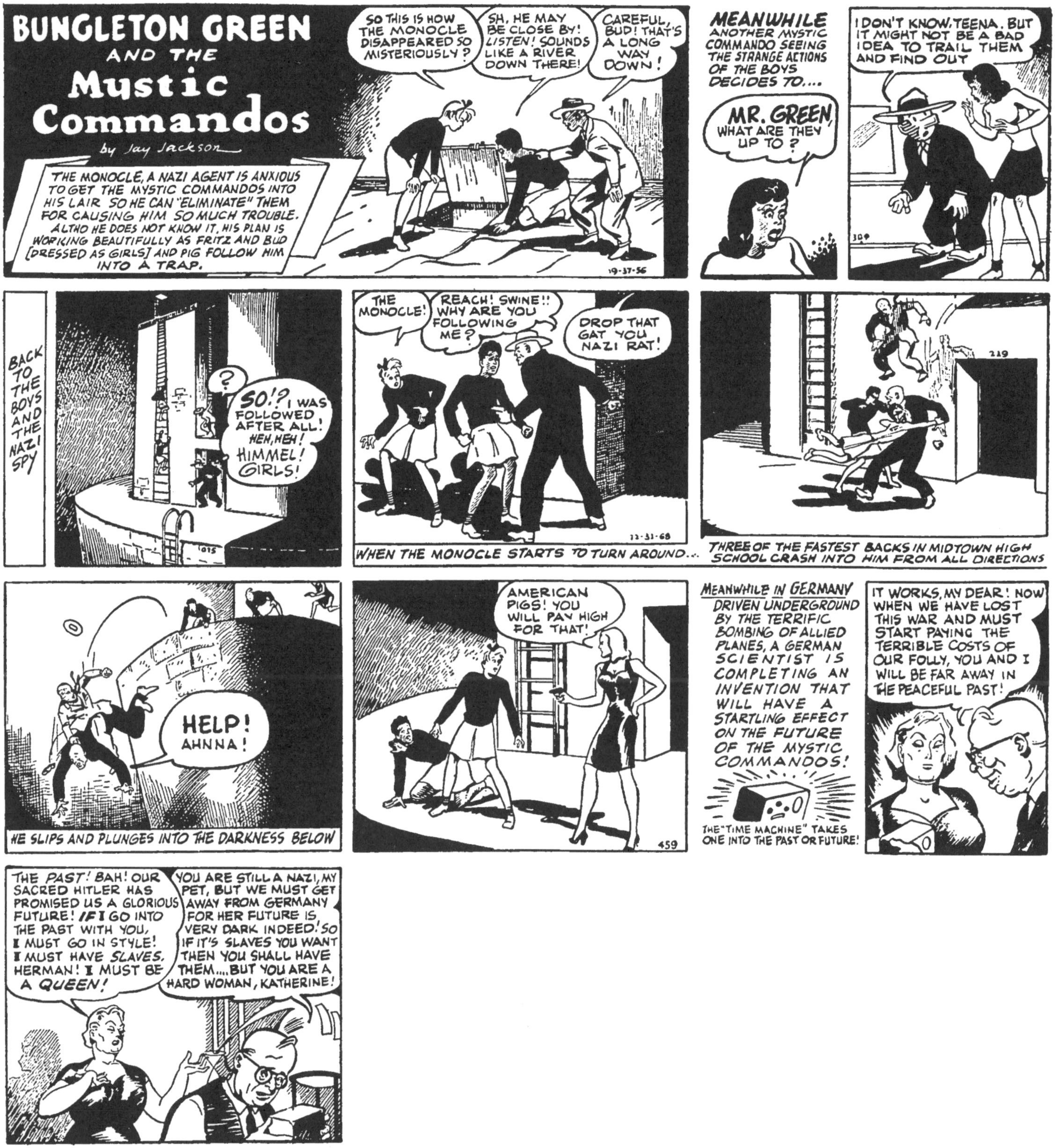
BUNGLETON GREEN AND THE Mystic Commandos
by Jay Jackson
THE MONOCLE, A NAZI AGENT IS ANXIOUS TO GET THE MYSTIC COMMANDOS INTO HIS LAIR SO HE CAN "ELIMINATE" THEM FOR CAUSING HIM SO MUCH TROUBLE. ALTHO HE DOES NOT KNOW IT, HIS PLAN IS WORKING BEAUTIFULLY AS FRITZ AND BUD [DRESSED AS GIRLS] AND PIG FOLLOW HIM INTO A TRAP.
SO THIS IS HOW THE MONOCLE DISAPPEARED SO MISTERIOUSLY?
SH, HE MAY BE CLOSE BY! LISTEN! SOUNDS LIKE A RIVER DOWN THERE!
CAREFUL, BUD! THAT'S A LONG WAY DOWN!
MEANWHILE ANOTHER MYSTIC COMMANDO SEEING THE STRANGE ACTIONS OF THE BOYS DECIDES TO....
MR. GREEN, WHAT ARE THEY UP TO?
I DON'T KNOW, TEENA. BUT IT MIGHT NOT BE A BAD IDEA TO TRAIL THEM AND FIND OUT
BACK TO THE BOYS AND THE NAZI SPY
?
SO!? I WAS FOLLOWED AFTER ALL! HEH, HEH! HIMMEL! GIRLS!
THE MONOCLE!
REACH! SWINE!! WHY ARE YOU FOLLOWING ME?
DROP THAT GAT YOU NAZI RAT!
WHEN THE MONOCLE STARTS TO TURN AROUND...
THREE OF THE FASTEST BACKS IN MIDTOWN HIGH SCHOOL CRASH INTO HIM FROM ALL DIRECTIONS
HELP! AHNNA!
HE SLIPS AND PLUNGES INTO THE DARKNESS BELOW
AMERICAN PIGS! YOU WILL PAY HIGH FOR THAT!
MEANWHILE IN GERMANY DRIVEN UNDERGROUND BY THE TERRIFIC BOMBING OF ALLIED PLANES, A GERMAN SCIENTIST IS COMPLETING AN INVENTION THAT WILL HAVE A STARTLING EFFECT ON THE FUTURE OF THE MYSTIC COMMANDOS!
THE "TIME MACHINE" TAKES ONE INTO THE PAST OR FUTURE!
IT WORKS, MY DEAR! NOW WHEN WE HAVE LOST THIS WAR AND MUST START PAYING THE TERRIBLE COSTS OF OUR FOLLY, YOU AND I WILL BE FAR AWAY IN THE PEACEFUL PAST!
THE PAST! BAH! OUR SACRED HITLER HAS PROMISED US A GLORIOUS FUTURE! IF I GO INTO THE PAST WITH YOU, I MUST GO IN STYLE! I MUST HAVE SLAVES, HERMAN! I MUST BE A QUEEN!
YOU ARE STILL A NAZI, MY PET, BUT WE MUST GET AWAY FROM GERMANY FOR HER FUTURE IS VERY DARK INDEED! SO IF IT'S SLAVES YOU WANT THEN YOU SHALL HAVE THEM.... BUT YOU ARE A HARD WOMAN, KATHERINE!

JUNE 26, 1943

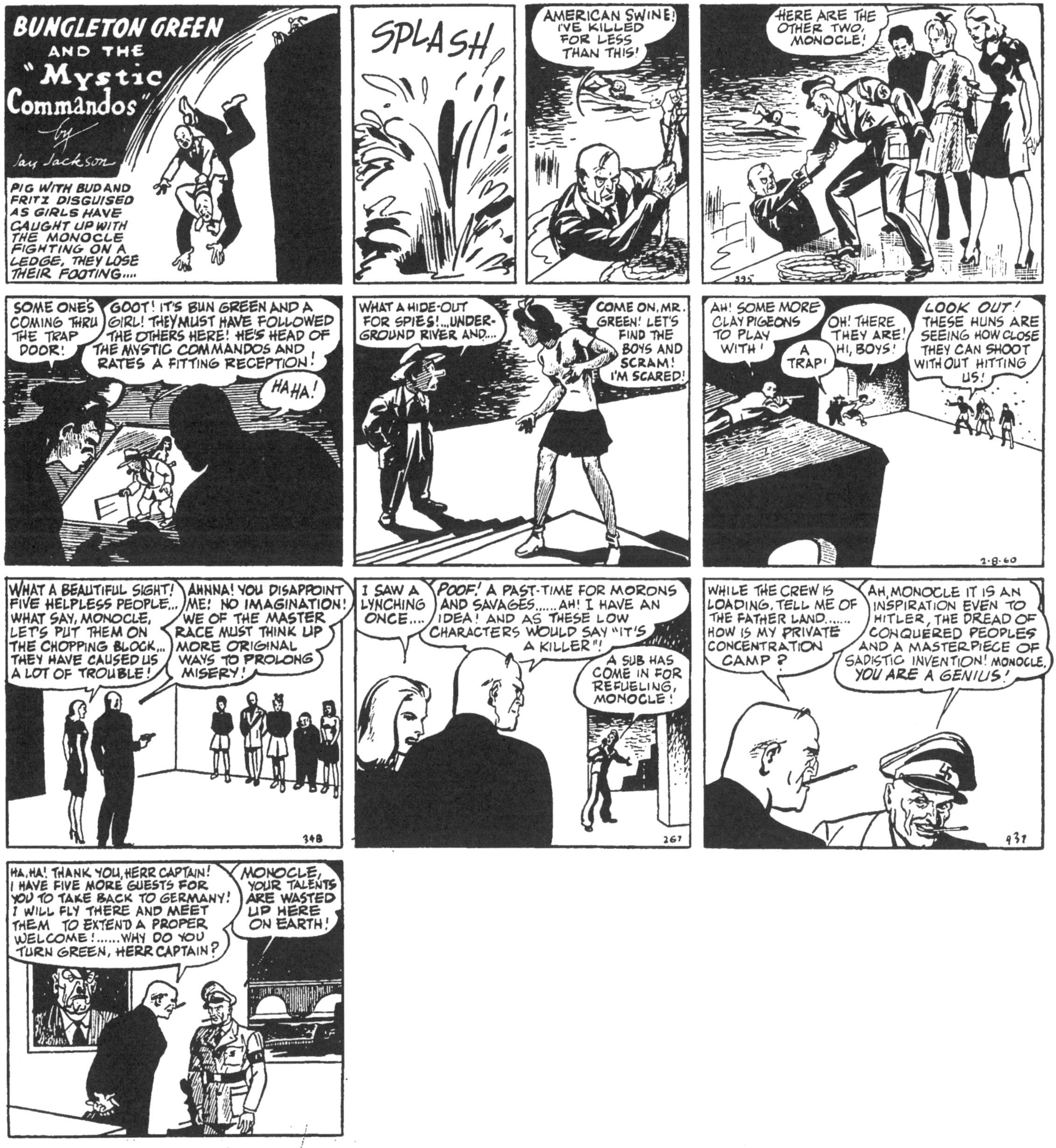
BUNGLETON GREEN AND THE "Mystic Commandos"
by Jay Jackson
PIG WITH BUD AND FRITZ DISGUISED AS GIRLS HAVE CAUGHT UP WITH THE MONOCLE FIGHTING ON A LEDGE, THEY LOSE THEIR FOOTING....
SPLASH
AMERICAN SWINE! I'VE KILLED FOR LESS THAN THIS!
HERE ARE THE OTHER TWO, MONOCLE!
SOME ONES COMING THRU THE TRAP DOOR!
GOOT! IT'S BUN GREEN AND A GIRL! THEY MUST HAVE FOLLOWED THE OTHERS HERE! HE'S HEAD OF THE MYSTIC COMMANDOS AND RATES A FITTING RECEPTION!
HA HA!
WHAT A HIDE-OUT FOR SPIES!...UNDERGROUND RIVER AND....
COME ON, MR. GREEN! LET'S FIND THE BOYS AND SCRAM! I'M SCARED!
AH! SOME MORE CLAY PIGEONS TO PLAY WITH!
A TRAP!
OH! THERE THEY ARE! HI, BOYS!
LOOK OUT! THESE HUNS ARE SEEING HOW CLOSE THEY CAN SHOOT WITHOUT HITTING US!
WHAT A BEAUTIFUL SIGHT! FIVE HELPLESS PEOPLE... WHAT SAY, MONOCLE, LET'S PUT THEM ON THE CHOPPING BLOCK... THEY HAVE CAUSED US A LOT OF TROUBLE!
AHNNA! YOU DISAPPOINT ME! NO IMAGINATION! WE OF THE MASTER RACE MUST THINK UP MORE ORIGINAL WAYS TO PROLONG MISERY!
I SAW A LYNCHING ONCE....
POOF! A PAST-TIME FOR MORONS AND SAVAGES......AH! I HAVE AN IDEA! AND AS THESE LOW CHARACTERS WOULD SAY "IT'S A KILLER"!
A SUB HAS COME IN FOR REFUELING, MONOCLE!
WHILE THE CREW IS LOADING, TELL ME OF THE FATHER LAND....... HOW IS MY PRIVATE CONCENTRATION CAMP?
AH, MONOCLE IT IS AN INSPIRATION EVEN TO HITLER, THE DREAD OF CONQUERED PEOPLES AND A MASTERPIECE OF SADISTIC INVENTION! MONOCLE, YOU ARE A GENIUS!
HA, HA! THANK YOU, HERR CAPTAIN! I HAVE FIVE MORE GUESTS FOR YOU TO TAKE BACK TO GERMANY! I WILL FLY THERE AND MEET THEM TO EXTEND A PROPER WELCOME!......WHY DO YOU TURN GREEN, HERR CAPTAIN?
MONOCLE, YOUR TALENTS ARE WASTED UP HERE ON EARTH!

YBODY
GOES
AGON COMES
NOSEY

to the Chicago Defender
'O VICTORY parade and
g. . . . Yes, we expected
lors and WACs, but the
the picnic in Washington
. FLASH! Of course you
ver to UNCLE SAM the
highest purchasers were
e company, $25,000; Su-
25,000 and Netcher's Bos-

GRETCHER JOHNSON
tlantic City, Washington,
LDIERS asking for mail
t. ROBERT BLAKE, Sgt.
EN TOWBRIDGE, 813th
d, Calif.; Pvt. HOMER
A.P.O. 709, Care of Post-
OBERT CALDWELL, No.
as, La.; T.-Sgt. ROBERT
-Sgt. JAMES DENHAM,
th AAA, Camp Stewart,
d Service Unit, Section 2,
BERT KNOX, A.P.O. 93,
Cpl. FRANK S. WHITE,
LES (I'm From Chicago)
Stewart, Ga.; Cpl. JOHN
l Field, Ga.; Somewhere
511, Care of Postmaster,
AN, A.P.O. 511, Care of
ES A. WEST, A.P.O. 759,

might double back and
h reminds us that CAR-
ach fun with GENE (cafe
oled back and now CAR-
. . . Husbands are funny
TURN home and anyway
wife. Is this clear?
himself a new chic out
njoying the hot sun down
A certain Forty-seventh
ED by state officials and
front page story in this
y. . . . If you've missed
. . . . SOLDIERS and
arkway ballroom Friday
club dance so says the
. . . They cremated Dr.
actor last week. . . . .
rst taste of Dixie. . . .
about LOIS JAMES and
EN CUNNINGHAM and
hat little trip down to

SONNY WILSON'S farm
JOHN BANKS, not the
tion fluid while despond-
in the Psychopathic hos-
NES is in St. Louis for a
e Steel Workers Stream-
the war. . . . MARY
ne on her birthday with
ENE HARPER is honey-
MITH. . . . Get a load
team of Tondelayo and
baby girl and the daddy
wn to see the sights is
. . . The FREEMAN
oy shopping. . . . HIL-
Sam's uniform. . . . .
, has given up the stage
Sgt. THOMAS SHANKS,
e home with wifie next

er boy friend ROBERT
LEN AMOS was caught
end, CARRIE BROOMS
hospital a few minutes
D did not bring his wife
?

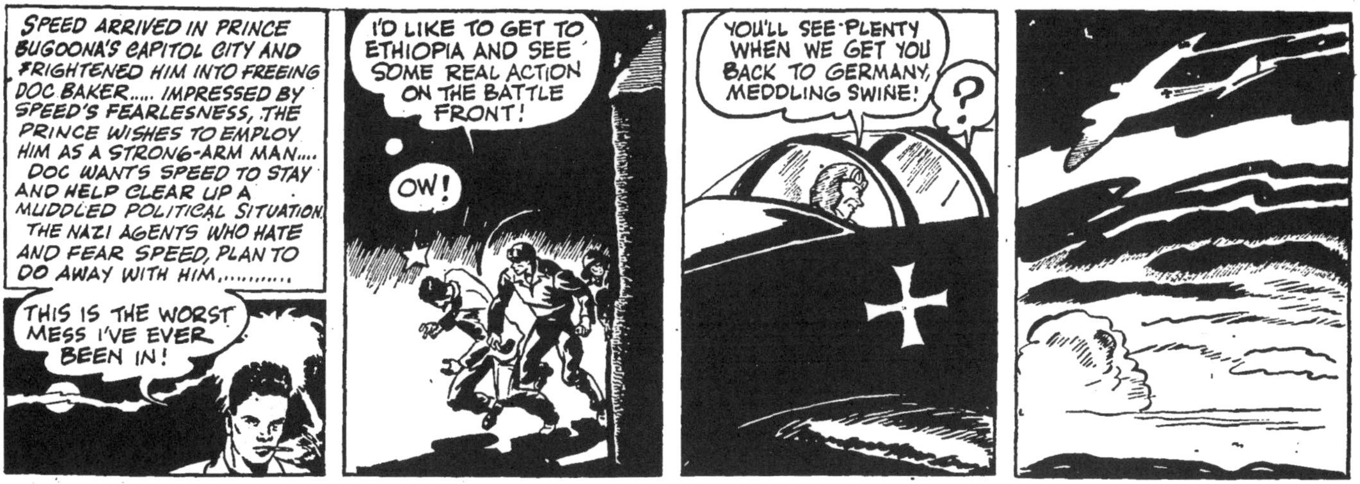

SPEED ARRIVED IN PRINCE BUGOONA'S CAPITOL CITY AND FRIGHTENED HIM INTO FREEING DOC BAKER..... IMPRESSED BY SPEED'S FEARLESSNESS, THE PRINCE WISHES TO EMPLOY HIM AS A STRONG-ARM MAN.... DOC WANT'S SPEED TO STAY AND HELP CLEAR UP A MUDDLED POLITICAL SITUATION. THE NAZI AGENTS WHO HATE AND FEAR SPEED, PLAN TO DO AWAY WITH HIM............
THIS IS THE WORST MESS I'VE EVER BEEN IN!
I'D LIKE TO GET TO ETHIOPIA AND SEE SOME REAL ACTION ON THE BATTLE FRONT!
OW!
YOU'LL SEE PLENTY WHEN WE GET YOU BACK TO GERMANY, MEDDLING SWINE!
?

THE SCIENTIST

MARCH 1944 – DECEMBER 1944

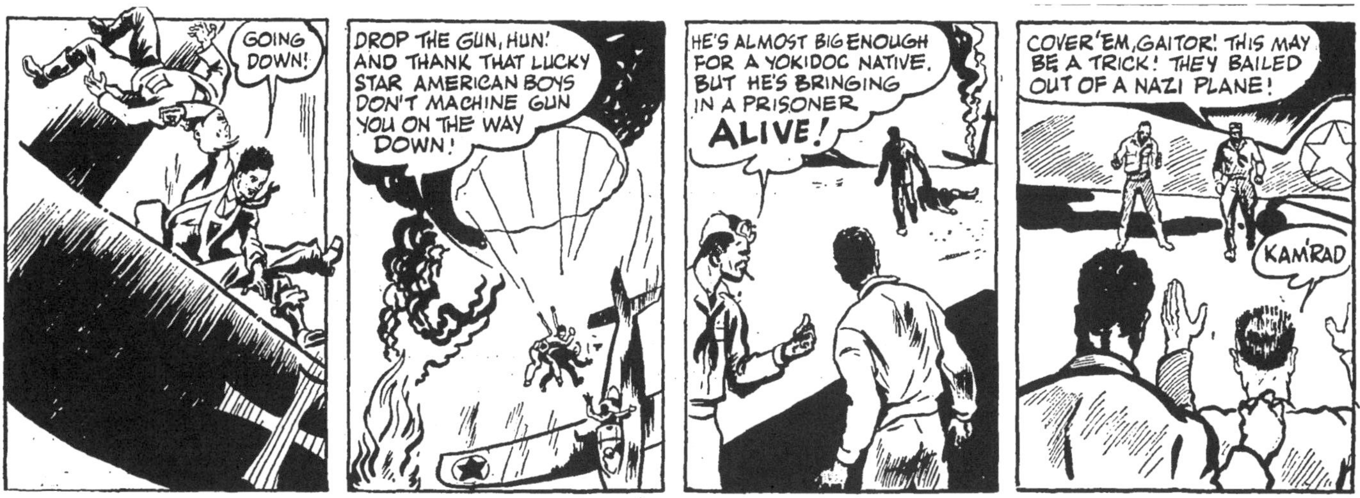

GOING DOWN!
DROP THE GUN, HUN! AND THANK THAT LUCKY STAR AMERICAN BOYS DON'T MACHINE GUN YOU ON THE WAY DOWN!
HE'S ALMOST BIG ENOUGH FOR A YOKIDOC NATIVE. BUT HE'S BRINGING IN A PRISONER ALIVE!
COVER 'EM, GAITOR! THIS MAY BE A TRICK! THEY BAILED OUT OF A NAZI PLANE!
KAM'RAD

Follow The Adventures Of Speed Jaxon And Bungleton Green Every Week In The Chicago Defender

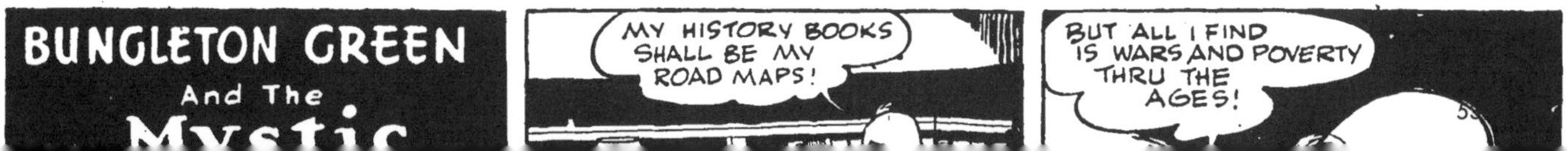

BUNGLETON GREEN
And The
MY HISTORY BOOKS SHALL BE MY ROAD MAPS!
BUT ALL I FIND IS WARS AND POVERTY THRU THE AGES!

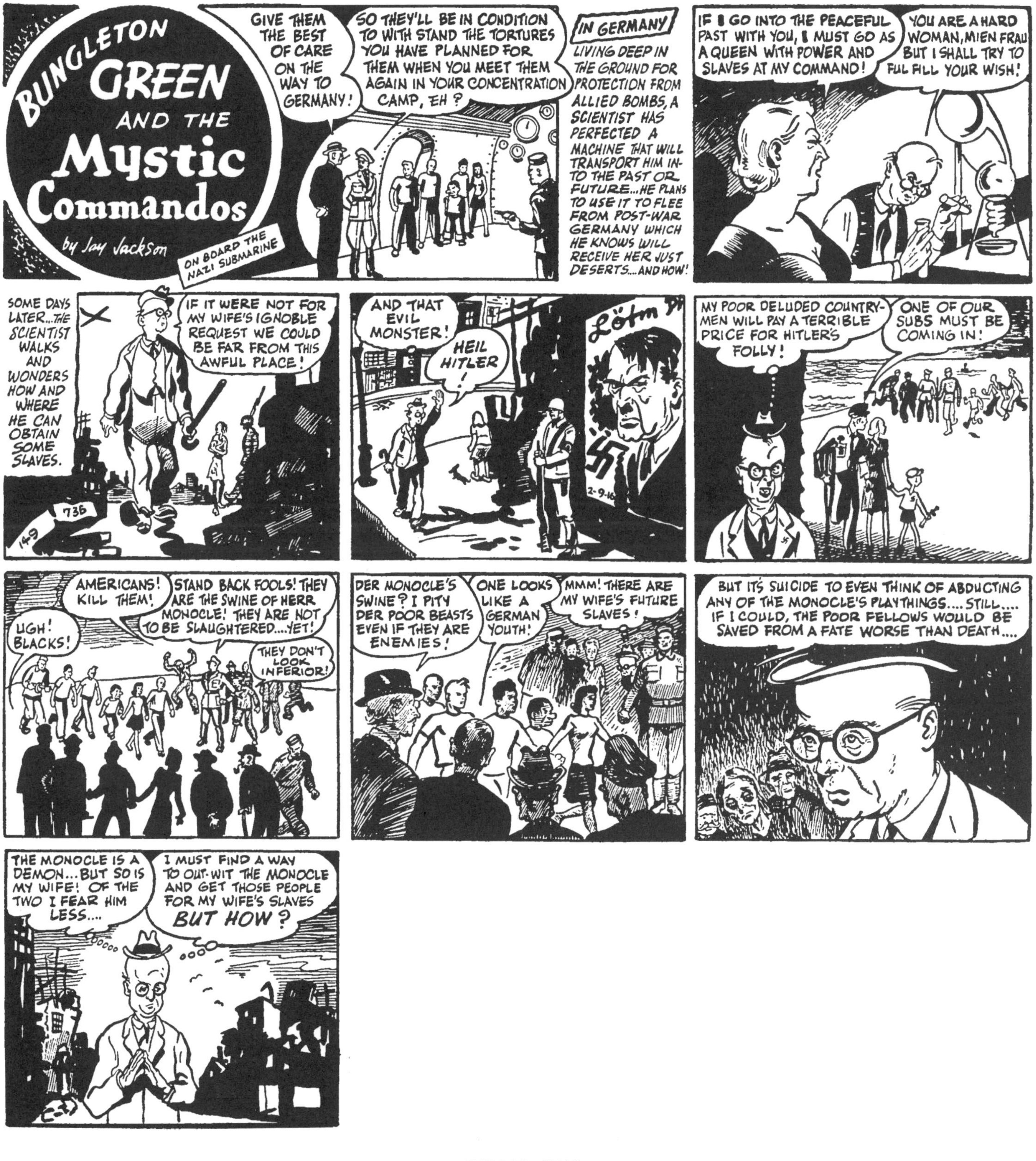
BUNGLETON GREEN AND THE Mystic Commandos
by Jay Jackson
ON BOARD THE NAZI SUBMARINE
GIVE THEM THE BEST OF CARE ON THE WAY TO GERMANY!
SO THEY'LL BE IN CONDITION TO WITH STAND THE TORTURES YOU HAVE PLANNED FOR THEM WHEN YOU MEET THEM AGAIN IN YOUR CONCENTRATION CAMP, EH?
IN GERMANY
LIVING DEEP IN THE GROUND FOR PROTECTION FROM ALLIED BOMBS, A SCIENTIST HAS PERFECTED A MACHINE THAT WILL TRANSPORT HIM INTO THE PAST OR FUTURE...HE PLANS TO USE IT TO FLEE FROM POST-WAR GERMANY WHICH HE KNOWS WILL RECEIVE HER JUST DESERTS...AND HOW!
IF I GO INTO THE PEACEFUL PAST WITH YOU, I MUST GO AS A QUEEN WITH POWER AND SLAVES AT MY COMMAND!
YOU ARE A HARD WOMAN, MIEN FRAU BUT I SHALL TRY TO FUL FILL YOUR WISH!
SOME DAYS LATER...THE SCIENTIST WALKS AND WONDERS HOW AND WHERE HE CAN OBTAIN SOME SLAVES.
IF IT WERE NOT FOR MY WIFE'S IGNOBLE REQUEST WE COULD BE FAR FROM THIS AWFUL PLACE!
736
149
AND THAT EVIL MONSTER!
HEIL HITLER!
2-9-16
MY POOR DELUDED COUNTRYMEN WILL PAY A TERRIBLE PRICE FOR HITLER'S FOLLY!
ONE OF OUR SUBS MUST BE COMING IN!
UGH! BLACKS!
AMERICANS! KILL THEM!
STAND BACK FOOLS! THEY ARE THE SWINE OF HERR MONOCLE! THEY ARE NOT TO BE SLAUGHTERED....YET!
THEY DON'T LOOK INFERIOR!
DER MONOCLE'S SWINE? I PITY DER POOR BEASTS EVEN IF THEY ARE ENEMIES!
ONE LOOKS LIKE A GERMAN YOUTH!
MMM! THERE ARE MY WIFE'S FUTURE SLAVES!
BUT IT'S SUICIDE TO EVEN THINK OF ABDUCTING ANY OF THE MONOCLE'S PLAYTHINGS.... STILL.... IF I COULD, THE POOR FELLOWS WOULD BE SAVED FROM A FATE WORSE THAN DEATH....
THE MONOCLE IS A DEMON... BUT SO IS MY WIFE! OF THE TWO I FEAR HIM LESS....
I MUST FIND A WAY TO OUT-WIT THE MONOCLE AND GET THOSE PEOPLE FOR MY WIFE'S SLAVES BUT HOW?

JULY 10, 1943

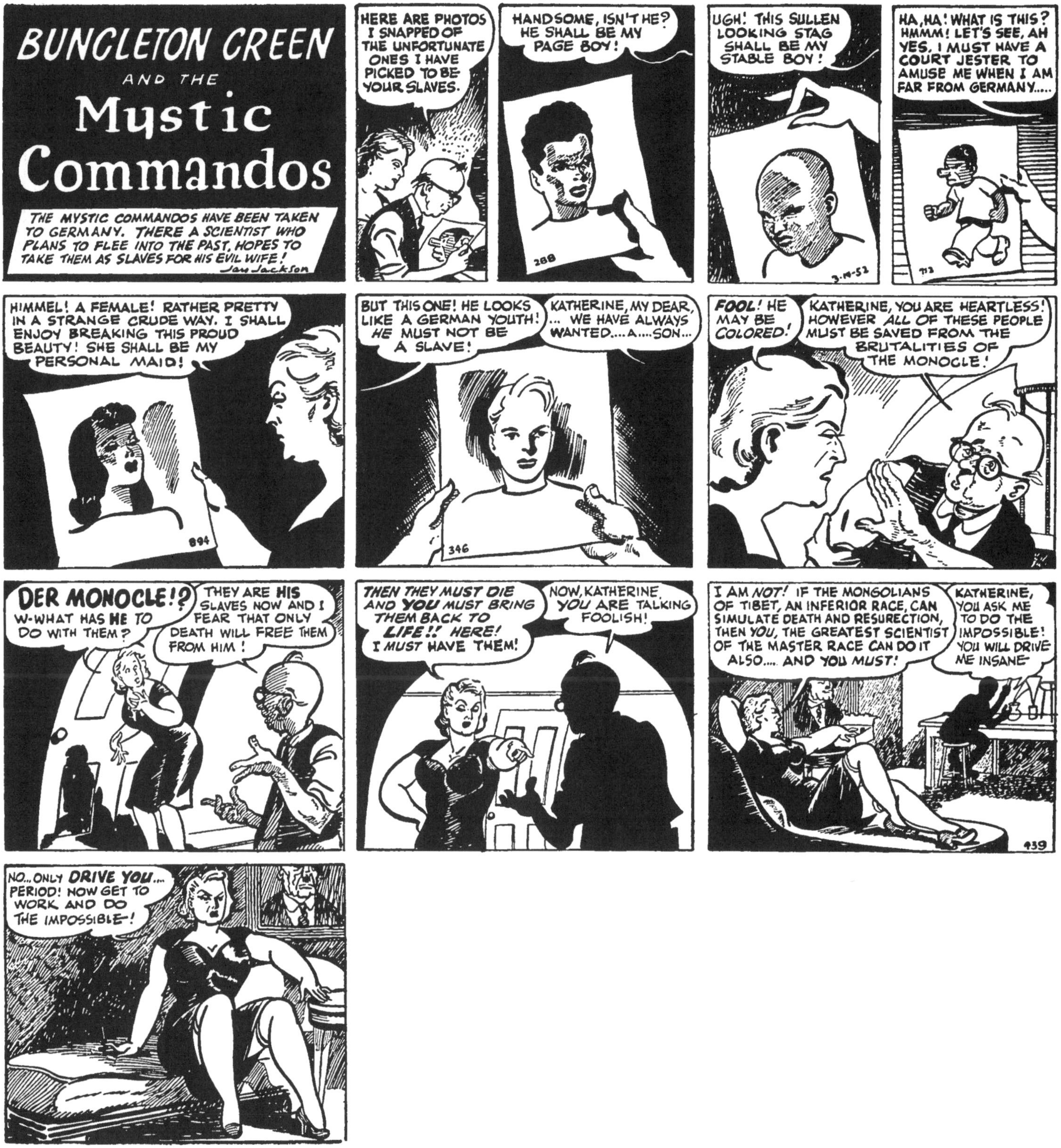

BUNGLETON GREEN AND THE Mystic Commandos
THE MYSTIC COMMANDOS HAVE BEEN TAKEN TO GERMANY. THERE A SCIENTIST WHO PLANS TO FLEE INTO THE PAST, HOPES TO TAKE THEM AS SLAVES FOR HIS EVIL WIFE!
Jay Jackson
HERE ARE PHOTOS I SNAPPED OF THE UNFORTUNATE ONES I HAVE PICKED TO BE YOUR SLAVES.
HANDSOME, ISN'T HE? HE SHALL BE MY PAGE BOY!
UGH! THIS SULLEN LOOKING STAG SHALL BE MY STABLE BOY!
HA, HA! WHAT IS THIS? HMMM! LET'S SEE, AH YES, I MUST HAVE A COURT JESTER TO AMUSE ME WHEN I AM FAR FROM GERMANY.....
HIMMEL! A FEMALE! RATHER PRETTY IN A STRANGE CRUDE WAY. I SHALL ENJOY BREAKING THIS PROUD BEAUTY! SHE SHALL BE MY PERSONAL MAID!
BUT THIS ONE! HE LOOKS LIKE A GERMAN YOUTH! HE MUST NOT BE A SLAVE!
KATHERINE, MY DEAR, ... WE HAVE ALWAYS WANTED.... A.... SON...
FOOL! HE MAY BE COLORED!
KATHERINE, YOU ARE HEARTLESS! HOWEVER ALL OF THESE PEOPLE MUST BE SAVED FROM THE BRUTALITIES OF THE MONOCLE!
DER MONOCLE!? W-WHAT HAS HE TO DO WITH THEM?
THEY ARE HIS SLAVES NOW AND I FEAR THAT ONLY DEATH WILL FREE THEM FROM HIM!
THEN THEY MUST DIE AND YOU MUST BRING THEM BACK TO LIFE!! HERE! I MUST HAVE THEM!
NOW, KATHERINE, YOU ARE TALKING FOOLISH!
I AM NOT! IF THE MONGOLIANS OF TIBET, AN INFERIOR RACE, CAN SIMULATE DEATH AND RESURECTION, THEN YOU, THE GREATEST SCIENTIST OF THE MASTER RACE CAN DO IT ALSO.... AND YOU MUST!
KATHERINE, YOU ASK ME TO DO THE IMPOSSIBLE! YOU WILL DRIVE ME INSANE
NO... ONLY DRIVE YOU... PERIOD! NOW GET TO WORK AND DO THE IMPOSSIBLE!

JULY 17, 1943

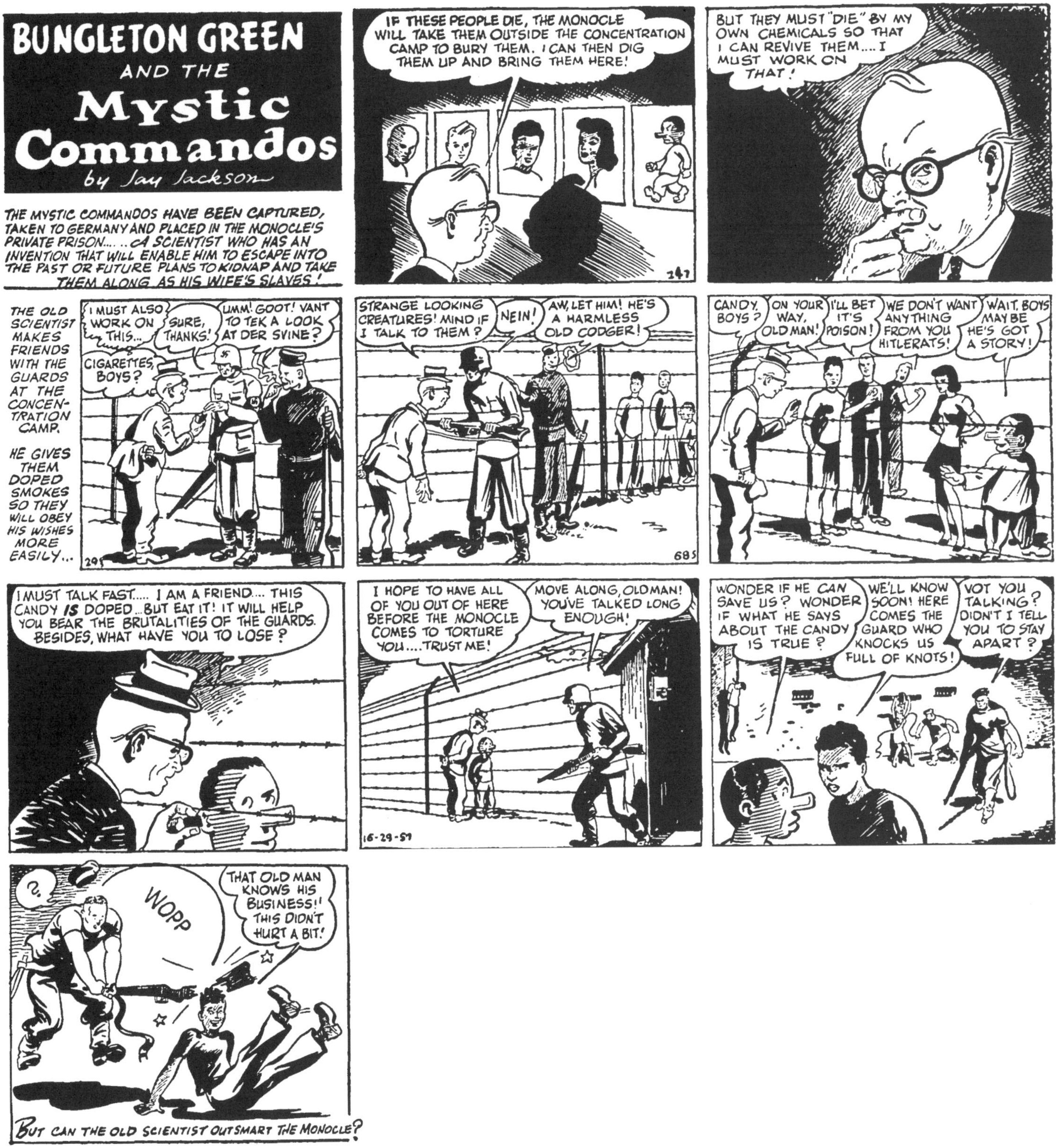
BUNGLETON GREEN AND THE Mystic Commandos
by Jay Jackson
THE MYSTIC COMMANDOS HAVE BEEN CAPTURED, TAKEN TO GERMANY AND PLACED IN THE MONOCLE'S PRIVATE PRISON... ...A SCIENTIST WHO HAS AN INVENTION THAT WILL ENABLE HIM TO ESCAPE INTO THE PAST OR FUTURE PLANS TO KIDNAP AND TAKE THEM ALONG AS HIS WIFE'S SLAVES!
IF THESE PEOPLE DIE, THE MONOCLE WILL TAKE THEM OUTSIDE THE CONCENTRATION CAMP TO BURY THEM. I CAN THEN DIG THEM UP AND BRING THEM HERE!
BUT THEY MUST "DIE" BY MY OWN CHEMICALS SO THAT I CAN REVIVE THEM.... I MUST WORK ON THAT!
THE OLD SCIENTIST MAKES FRIENDS WITH THE GUARDS AT THE CONCENTRATION CAMP.
HE GIVES THEM DOPED SMOKES SO THEY WILL OBEY HIS WISHES MORE EASILY...
I MUST ALSO WORK ON THIS...
CIGARETTES, BOYS?
SURE, THANKS!
UMM! GOOT! VANT TO TEK A LOOK AT DER SVINE?
STRANGE LOOKING CREATURES! MIND IF I TALK TO THEM?
NEIN!
AW, LET HIM! HE'S A HARMLESS OLD CODGER!
CANDY, BOYS?
ON YOUR WAY, OLD MAN!
I'LL BET IT'S POISON!
WE DON'T WANT ANYTHING FROM YOU HITLERATS!
WAIT, BOYS MAYBE HE'S GOT A STORY!
I MUST TALK FAST..... I AM A FRIEND.... THIS CANDY IS DOPED... BUT EAT IT! IT WILL HELP YOU BEAR THE BRUTALITIES OF THE GUARDS. BESIDES, WHAT HAVE YOU TO LOSE?
I HOPE TO HAVE ALL OF YOU OUT OF HERE BEFORE THE MONOCLE COMES TO TORTURE YOU.... TRUST ME!
MOVE ALONG, OLD MAN! YOU'VE TALKED LONG ENOUGH!
WONDER IF HE CAN SAVE US? WONDER IF WHAT HE SAYS ABOUT THE CANDY IS TRUE?
WE'LL KNOW SOON! HERE COMES THE GUARD WHO KNOCKS US FULL OF KNOTS!
VOT YOU TALKING? DIDN'T I TELL YOU TO STAY APART?
?
WOPP
THAT OLD MAN KNOWS HIS BUSINESS!! THIS DIDN'T HURT A BIT!
BUT CAN THE OLD SCIENTIST OUTSMART THE MONOCLE?

JULY 24, 1943

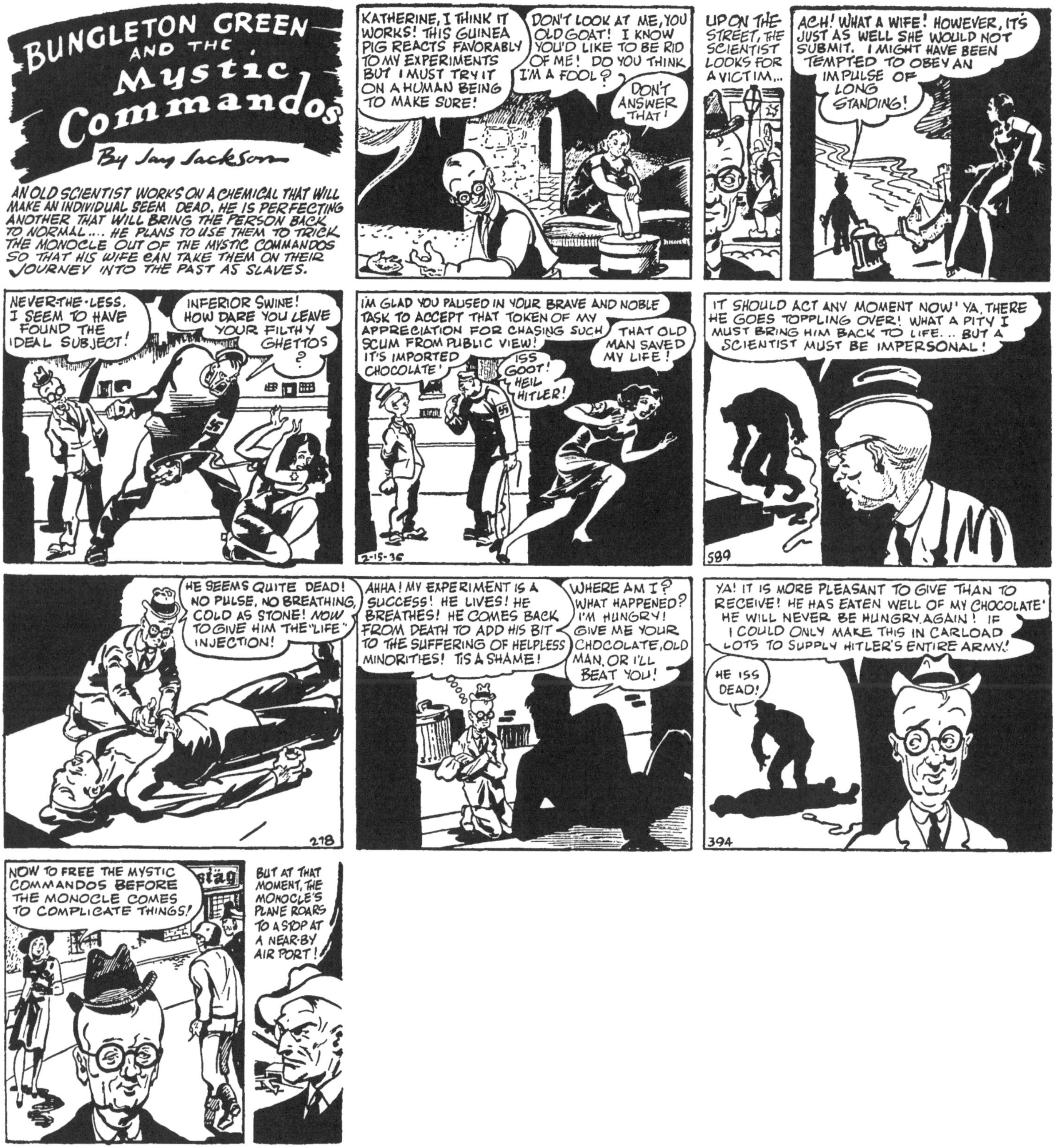
BUNGLETON GREEN AND THE Mystic Commandos
By Jay Jackson
AN OLD SCIENTIST WORKS ON A CHEMICAL THAT WILL MAKE AN INDIVIDUAL SEEM DEAD. HE IS PERFECTING ANOTHER THAT WILL BRING THE PERSON BACK TO NORMAL.... HE PLANS TO USE THEM TO TRICK THE MONOCLE OUT OF THE MYSTIC COMMANDOS SO THAT HIS WIFE CAN TAKE THEM ON THEIR JOURNEY INTO THE PAST AS SLAVES.
KATHERINE, I THINK IT WORKS! THIS GUINEA PIG REACTS FAVORABLY TO MY EXPERIMENTS BUT I MUST TRY IT ON A HUMAN BEING TO MAKE SURE!
DON'T LOOK AT ME, YOU OLD GOAT! I KNOW YOU'D LIKE TO BE RID OF ME! DO YOU THINK I'M A FOOL?
DON'T ANSWER THAT!
UP ON THE STREET, THE SCIENTIST LOOKS FOR A VICTIM...
ACH! WHAT A WIFE! HOWEVER, IT'S JUST AS WELL SHE WOULD NOT SUBMIT. I MIGHT HAVE BEEN TEMPTED TO OBEY AN IMPULSE OF LONG STANDING!
NEVER-THE-LESS, I SEEM TO HAVE FOUND THE IDEAL SUBJECT!
INFERIOR SWINE! HOW DARE YOU LEAVE YOUR FILTHY GHETTOS?
I'M GLAD YOU PAUSED IN YOUR BRAVE AND NOBLE TASK TO ACCEPT THAT TOKEN OF MY APPRECIATION FOR CHASING SUCH SCUM FROM PUBLIC VIEW! IT'S IMPORTED CHOCOLATE!
ISS GOOT! HEIL HITLER!
THAT OLD MAN SAVED MY LIFE!
2-15-36
IT SHOULD ACT ANY MOMENT NOW! YA, THERE HE GOES TOPPLING OVER! WHAT A PITY I MUST BRING HIM BACK TO LIFE... BUT A SCIENTIST MUST BE IMPERSONAL!
589
HE SEEMS QUITE DEAD! NO PULSE, NO BREATHING, COLD AS STONE! NOW TO GIVE HIM THE "LIFE" INJECTION!
278
AHHA! MY EXPERIMENT IS A SUCCESS! HE LIVES! HE BREATHES! HE COMES BACK FROM DEATH TO ADD HIS BIT TO THE SUFFERING OF HELPLESS MINORITIES! TIS A SHAME!
WHERE AM I? WHAT HAPPENED? I'M HUNGRY! GIVE ME YOUR CHOCOLATE, OLD MAN, OR I'LL BEAT YOU!
YA! IT IS MORE PLEASANT TO GIVE THAN TO RECEIVE! HE HAS EATEN WELL OF MY CHOCOLATE! HE WILL NEVER BE HUNGRY AGAIN! IF I COULD ONLY MAKE THIS IN CARLOAD LOTS TO SUPPLY HITLER'S ENTIRE ARMY!
HE ISS DEAD!
394
NOW TO FREE THE MYSTIC COMMANDOS BEFORE THE MONOCLE COMES TO COMPLICATE THINGS!
BUT AT THAT MOMENT, THE MONOCLE'S PLANE ROARS TO A STOP AT A NEAR-BY AIR PORT!

JULY 31, 1943

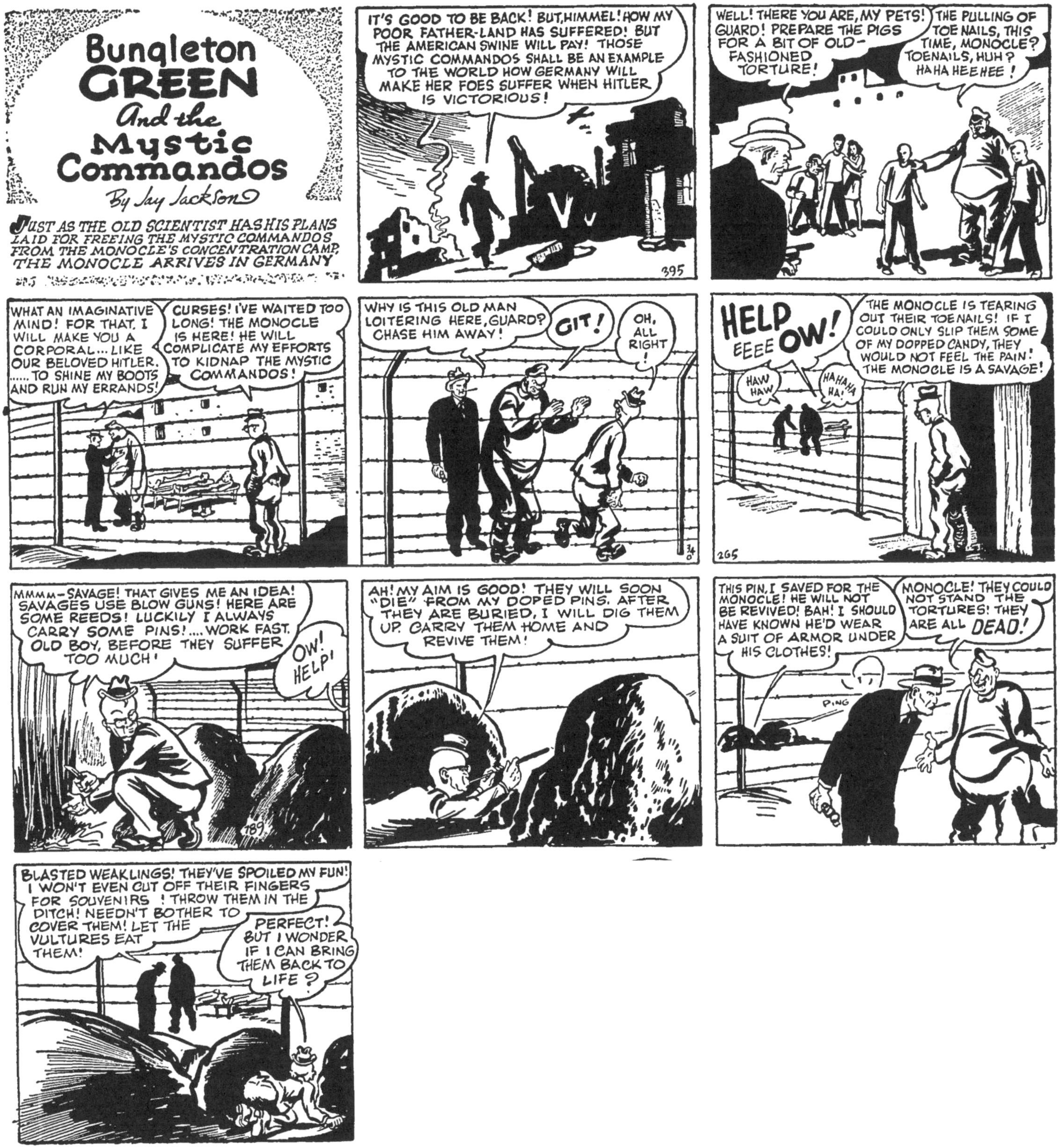
Bungleton GREEN And the Mystic Commandos
By Jay Jackson
JUST AS THE OLD SCIENTIST HAS HIS PLANS LAID FOR FREEING THE MYSTIC COMMANDOS FROM THE MONOCLE'S CONCENTRATION CAMP, THE MONOCLE ARRIVES IN GERMANY
IT'S GOOD TO BE BACK! BUT, HIMMEL! HOW MY POOR FATHER-LAND HAS SUFFERED! BUT THE AMERICAN SWINE WILL PAY! THOSE MYSTIC COMMANDOS SHALL BE AN EXAMPLE TO THE WORLD HOW GERMANY WILL MAKE HER FOES SUFFER WHEN HITLER IS VICTORIOUS!
WELL! THERE YOU ARE, MY PETS! GUARD! PREPARE THE PIGS FOR A BIT OF OLD-FASHIONED TORTURE!
THE PULLING OF TOE NAILS, THIS TIME, MONOCLE? TOENAILS, HUH? HAHA HEEHEE!
WHAT AN IMAGINATIVE MIND! FOR THAT, I WILL MAKE YOU A CORPORAL... LIKE OUR BELOVED HITLER. ......TO SHINE MY BOOTS AND RUN MY ERRANDS!
CURSES! I'VE WAITED TOO LONG! THE MONOCLE IS HERE! HE WILL COMPLICATE MY EFFORTS TO KIDNAP THE MYSTIC COMMANDOS!
WHY IS THIS OLD MAN LOITERING HERE, GUARD? CHASE HIM AWAY!
GIT!
OH, ALL RIGHT!
HELP
EEEE OW!
HAW HAW
HAHAHA HA!
THE MONOCLE IS TEARING OUT THEIR TOENAILS! IF I COULD ONLY SLIP THEM SOME OF MY DOPPED CANDY, THEY WOULD NOT FEEL THE PAIN! THE MONOCLE IS A SAVAGE!
MMMM-SAVAGE! THAT GIVES ME AN IDEA! SAVAGES USE BLOW GUNS! HERE ARE SOME REEDS! LUCKILY I ALWAYS CARRY SOME PINS! .... WORK FAST, OLD BOY, BEFORE THEY SUFFER TOO MUCH!
OW! HELP!
AH! MY AIM IS GOOD! THEY WILL SOON "DIE" FROM MY DOPED PINS. AFTER THEY ARE BURIED, I WILL DIG THEM UP, CARRY THEM HOME AND REVIVE THEM!
THIS PIN, I SAVED FOR THE MONOCLE! HE WILL NOT BE REVIVED! BAH! I SHOULD HAVE KNOWN HE'D WEAR A SUIT OF ARMOR UNDER HIS CLOTHES!
PING
MONOCLE! THEY COULD NOT STAND THE TORTURES! THEY ARE ALL DEAD!
BLASTED WEAKLINGS! THEY'VE SPOILED MY FUN! I WON'T EVEN CUT OFF THEIR FINGERS FOR SOUVENIRS! THROW THEM IN THE DITCH! NEEDN'T BOTHER TO COVER THEM! LET THE VULTURES EAT THEM!
PERFECT! BUT I WONDER IF I CAN BRING THEM BACK TO LIFE?

AUGUST 7, 1943

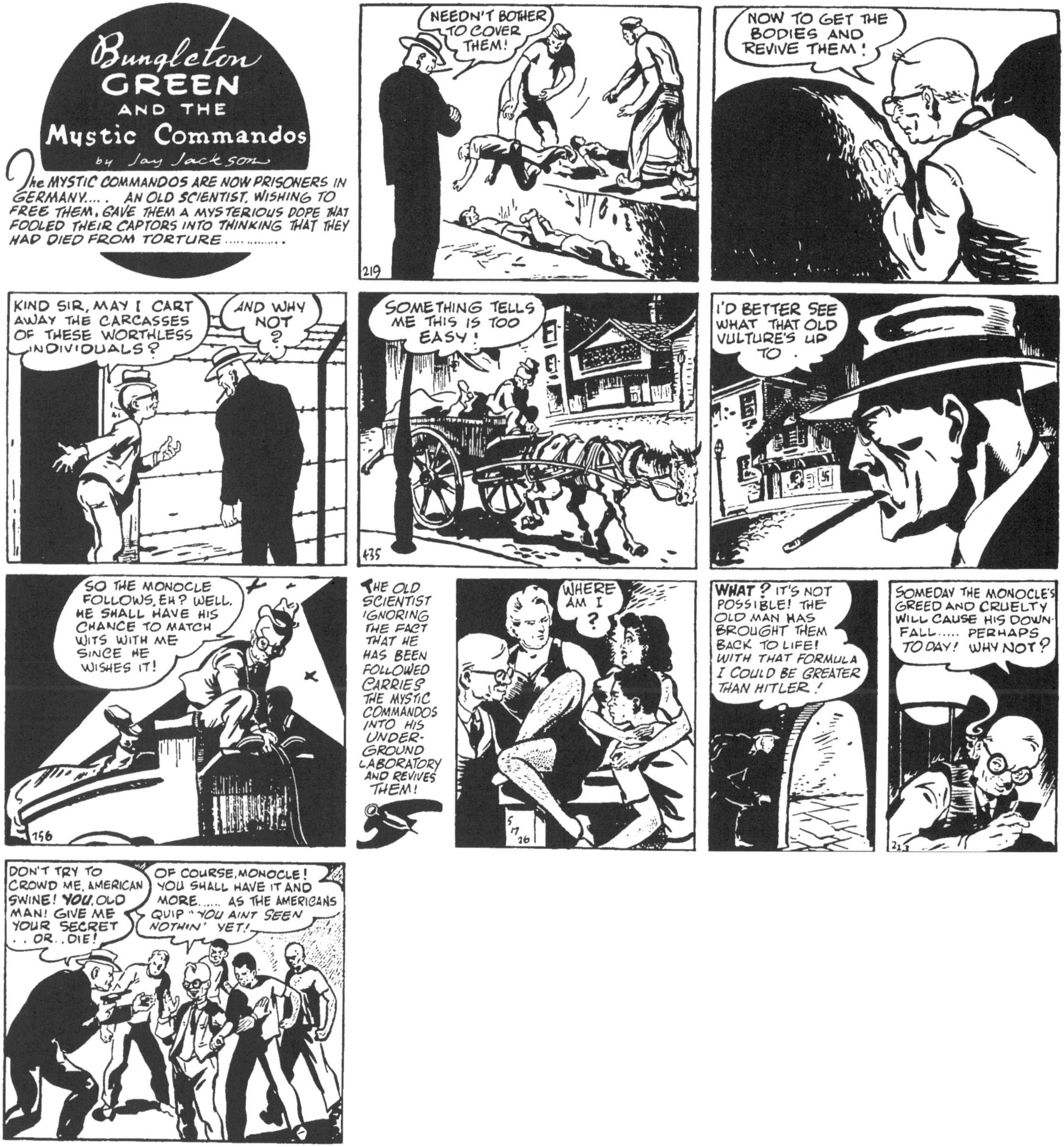
Bungleton GREEN AND THE Mystic Commandos
by Jay Jackson
The MYSTIC COMMANDOS ARE NOW PRISONERS IN GERMANY.... AN OLD SCIENTIST, WISHING TO FREE THEM, GAVE THEM A MYSTERIOUS DOPE THAT FOOLED THEIR CAPTORS INTO THINKING THAT THEY HAD DIED FROM TORTURE ....
NEEDN'T BOTHER TO COVER THEM!
NOW TO GET THE BODIES AND REVIVE THEM!
KIND SIR, MAY I CART AWAY THE CARCASSES OF THESE WORTHLESS INDIVIDUALS?
AND WHY NOT?
SOMETHING TELLS ME THIS IS TOO EASY!
I'D BETTER SEE WHAT THAT OLD VULTURE'S UP TO.
SO THE MONOCLE FOLLOWS, EH? WELL, HE SHALL HAVE HIS CHANCE TO MATCH WITS WITH ME SINCE HE WISHES IT!
THE OLD SCIENTIST IGNORING THE FACT THAT HE HAS BEEN FOLLOWED CARRIES THE MYSTIC COMMANDOS INTO HIS UNDERGROUND LABORATORY AND REVIVES THEM!
WHERE AM I?
WHAT? IT'S NOT POSSIBLE! THE OLD MAN HAS BROUGHT THEM BACK TO LIFE! WITH THAT FORMULA I COULD BE GREATER THAN HITLER!
SOMEDAY THE MONOCLE'S GREED AND CRUELTY WILL CAUSE HIS DOWNFALL..... PERHAPS TODAY! WHY NOT?
DON'T TRY TO CROWD ME, AMERICAN SWINE! YOU, OLD MAN! GIVE ME YOUR SECRET . . OR . . DIE!
OF COURSE, MONOCLE! YOU SHALL HAVE IT AND MORE...... AS THE AMERICANS QUIP "YOU AINT SEEN NOTHIN' YET!"

AUGUST 14, 1943

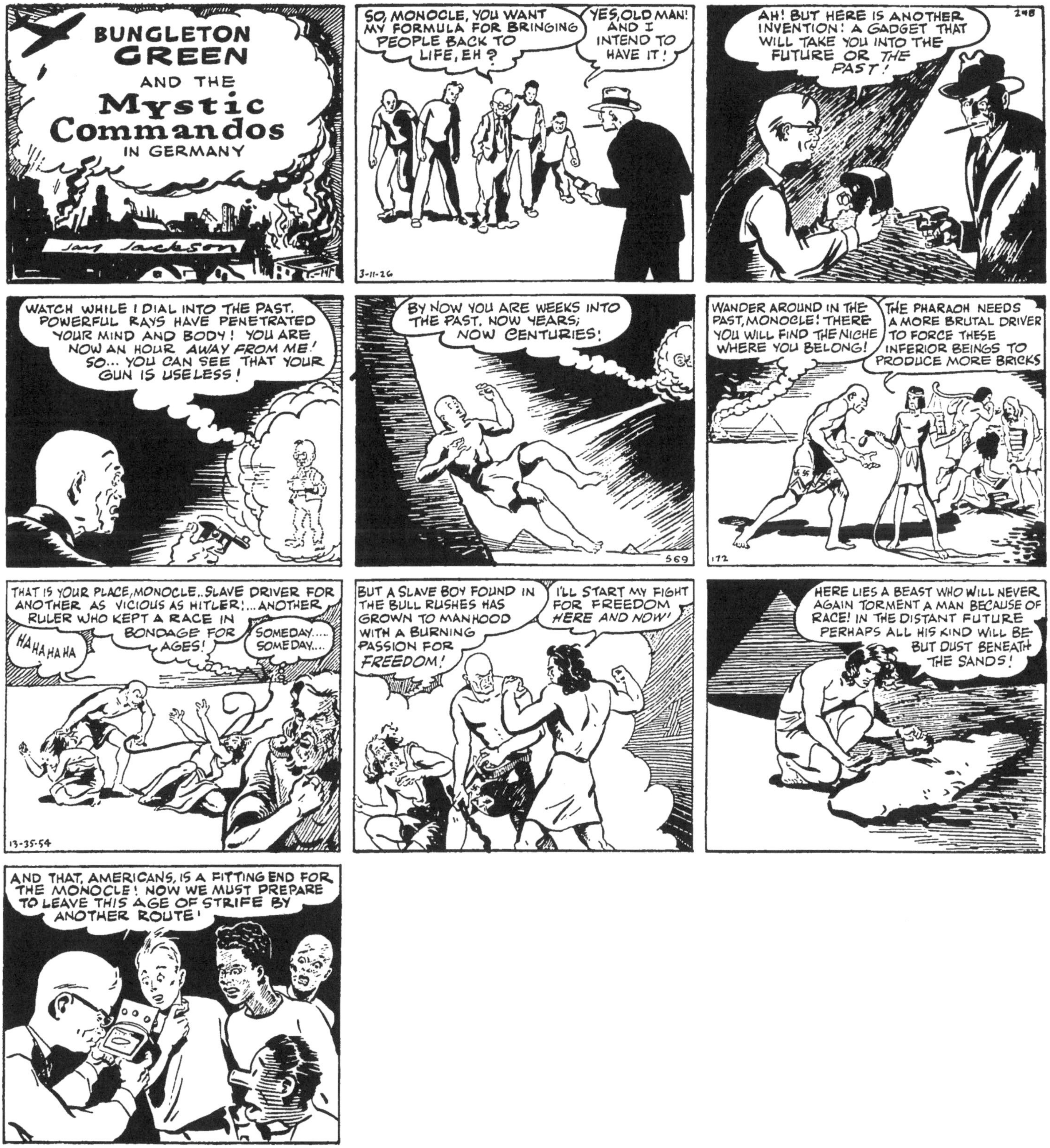
BUNGLETON GREEN
AND THE
Mystic Commandos
IN GERMANY
Jay Jackson
SO, MONOCLE, YOU WANT MY FORMULA FOR BRINGING PEOPLE BACK TO LIFE, EH?
YES, OLD MAN! AND I INTEND TO HAVE IT!
AH! BUT HERE IS ANOTHER INVENTION: A GADGET THAT WILL TAKE YOU INTO THE FUTURE OR THE PAST!
WATCH WHILE I DIAL INTO THE PAST. POWERFUL RAYS HAVE PENETRATED YOUR MIND AND BODY! YOU ARE NOW AN HOUR AWAY FROM ME! SO... YOU CAN SEE THAT YOUR GUN IS USELESS!
BY NOW YOU ARE WEEKS INTO THE PAST. NOW YEARS; NOW CENTURIES!
WANDER AROUND IN THE PAST, MONOCLE! THERE YOU WILL FIND THE NICHE WHERE YOU BELONG!
THE PHARAOH NEEDS A MORE BRUTAL DRIVER TO FORCE THESE INFERIOR BEINGS TO PRODUCE MORE BRICKS
THAT IS YOUR PLACE, MONOCLE.. SLAVE DRIVER FOR ANOTHER AS VICIOUS AS HITLER!... ANOTHER RULER WHO KEPT A RACE IN BONDAGE FOR AGES!
HA HA HA HA
SOMEDAY..... SOMEDAY....
BUT A SLAVE BOY FOUND IN THE BULL RUSHES HAS GROWN TO MANHOOD WITH A BURNING PASSION FOR FREEDOM!
I'LL START MY FIGHT FOR FREEDOM HERE AND NOW!
HERE LIES A BEAST WHO WILL NEVER AGAIN TORMENT A MAN BECAUSE OF RACE! IN THE DISTANT FUTURE PERHAPS ALL HIS KIND WILL BE BUT DUST BENEATH THE SANDS!
AND THAT, AMERICANS, IS A FITTING END FOR THE MONOCLE! NOW WE MUST PREPARE TO LEAVE THIS AGE OF STRIFE BY ANOTHER ROUTE!

AUGUST 21, 1943

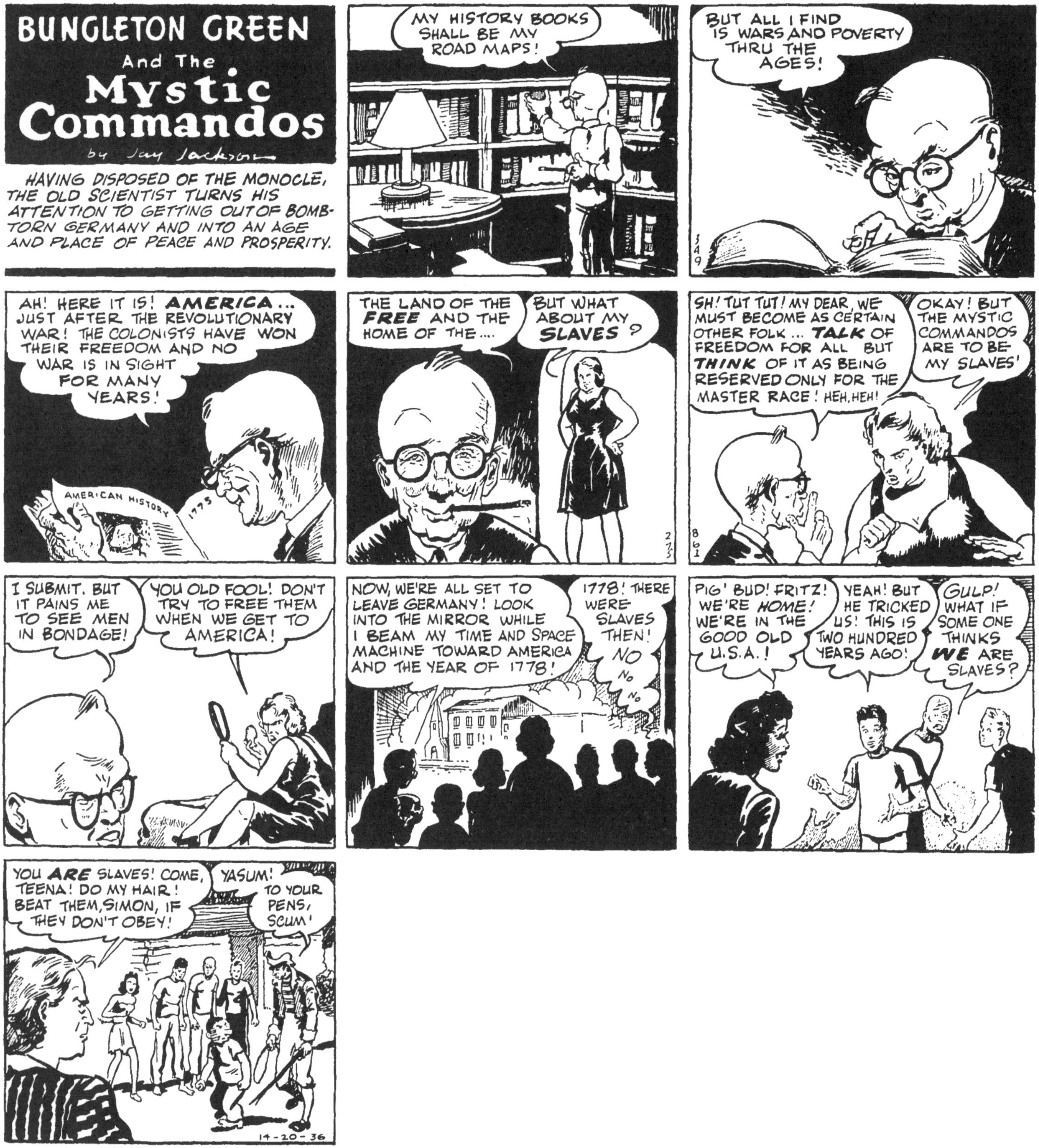
BUNGLETON GREEN
And The
Mystic Commandos
by Jay Jackson
HAVING DISPOSED OF THE MONOCLE, THE OLD SCIENTIST TURNS HIS ATTENTION TO GETTING OUT OF BOMB-TORN GERMANY AND INTO AN AGE AND PLACE OF PEACE AND PROSPERITY.
MY HISTORY BOOKS SHALL BE MY ROAD MAPS!
BUT ALL I FIND IS WARS AND POVERTY THRU THE AGES!
AH! HERE IT IS! AMERICA... JUST AFTER THE REVOLUTIONARY WAR! THE COLONISTS HAVE WON THEIR FREEDOM AND NO WAR IS IN SIGHT FOR MANY YEARS!
AMERICAN HISTORY 1775
THE LAND OF THE FREE AND THE HOME OF THE....
BUT WHAT ABOUT MY SLAVES ?
SH! TUT TUT! MY DEAR, WE MUST BECOME AS CERTAIN OTHER FOLK ... TALK OF FREEDOM FOR ALL BUT THINK OF IT AS BEING RESERVED ONLY FOR THE MASTER RACE! HEH, HEH!
OKAY! BUT THE MYSTIC COMMANDOS ARE TO BE MY SLAVES'
I SUBMIT. BUT IT PAINS ME TO SEE MEN IN BONDAGE!
YOU OLD FOOL! DON'T TRY TO FREE THEM WHEN WE GET TO AMERICA!
NOW, WE'RE ALL SET TO LEAVE GERMANY! LOOK INTO THE MIRROR WHILE I BEAM MY TIME AND SPACE MACHINE TOWARD AMERICA AND THE YEAR OF 1778!
1778! THERE WERE SLAVES THEN! NO No No
PIG! BUD! FRITZ! WE'RE HOME! WE'RE IN THE GOOD OLD U.S.A.!
YEAH! BUT HE TRICKED US! THIS IS TWO HUNDRED YEARS AGO!
GULP! WHAT IF SOME ONE THINKS WE ARE SLAVES?
YOU ARE SLAVES! COME, TEENA! DO MY HAIR! BEAT THEM, SIMON, IF THEY DON'T OBEY!
YASUM!
TO YOUR PENS, SCUM'
14-20-36

AUGUST 28, 1943

THE CHICAGO DEFENDER, Saturday, February 26, 1944

ERYBODY GOES When THE WAGON Comes — Ole Nosey

that the Lenten season is being observed, there is every cation that social activities everywhere will be slowed up. For the next forty days those of us on the home front will re serious thought to the church. . . . The past week, how- aw a rush of parties and dances, given with the hope of under the wire" before Ash Wednesday.

* * *

y of lovelies were in Chicago over the week end for the Boule of the Alpha Kappa Alphas. . . . The sessions were Bethesda Baptist church with banquet in the community Saturday evening. . . . Kappa Alpha Psi scholarship dance Pershing ballroom Saturday night gave the visitors a chance how many men are missing in Chicago's fraternity ranks. LL GRAHAM, personal manager of MARVA LOUIS, in town everybody how lovely his protege is and that she heads eenwich Village at a reported salary of a grand a week some- April.

* * *

can mark down the names of JUANITA HODGES and JOHN ER as heading for the middle aisle sooner than you expect. ou get the idea from the way they made eyes at each other their stay in the city. Both are from Louisville, Ky. . . . RICHARD (Dick) JONES has been transferred to Camp

* * *

RI O'BRYANT, now a specialist A, second class, passed the city last week en route to the west coast and when rns he may "have 'em." . . . BILL (Mayor of 58th street) got his farewell party from the Olde Tymers Sunday. . . . to the army Feb. 28. . . . . MUSETTE BROOKS FLEM- spending her cash in Florida and plans to stop in New Or- route to the Windy City. . . . Pvt. SIMON J. MARTIN p Gordon, Ga., visited wifie LOUIS here during a short . . . . Little DOC (Chiropodist) JOYNER is enjoying the and baths in Hot Springs and promises to be at the fence he nags run at Oaklawn Monday, Feb. 28. . . . Rev. J. C. back from Hot Springs looking the picture of health. . . . TA (Don's Den) KNOX skipped to Los Angeles to see hubby, t. JOHN KNOX Jr., who is in the hospital recovering from ation. . . . When you read this IRENE HANCOCK will be west coast. . . . No truth to the rumor that BENJO JOHN- ll see the horses run at Hot Springs.

* * *

what liquor will do to some people....Take the case of R WILKENS, who was having so much fun Saturday night 00 at a 63rd street tavern....He flashed his roll and bought s a drink and everybody had a good time until WILKENS the invitation of the boys to "catch a little air."...Once the boys proceeded to ROB poor WILKENS of his cash.... ILKENS was pretty sore aside from being plenty high.... rned to the tavern and exclaimed loudly, "You guys thought re smart, I got $250 in my shoes that you didn't get!".... make a long story short, when WILKENS left the tavern e, the boys took his shoes and the $250....FLASH! FLASH! owners had better be careful because government men are lookout for some of this BAD whiskey you're selling.....

* * *

e on WILLIE HOWARD for hitting his wife over the head wrench just because they couldn't settle that argument.... (Winsome Misses) COWAN who has taken up a singing kips to New York soon....Despondent because hubby had for the navy CLARA WILLIAMS took poison Tuesday night. think that was silly....DAVID (Foxes) MINOR leaves for Lakes Tuesday where he will begin his boot training.... E DAVIS had too many drinks and decided to fight..... ldn't find anyone who would accept his challenge, so he up to a plate glass window and knocked it out with his LASH! Mr. Davis is in the jail house now.

* * *

(drug cashier) FONZA'S hubby took her wedding and nent rings and threw them in the fire, but t'other day she rting two fine sparklers....Wonder if hubby bought these other cat....New show at the Club DeLisa is titled, "SWEET- PARADE" and is a honey....FRANK (Red Moon) GROSS Pvt. Gross....Those smiles you see "CHINK" LAWRENCE these days are due to his wife ESTHER'S arrival in the m Pittsburgh, Pa....Chicago Unicorns are dancing at the ttox club Saturday night.

* * *

STINIA (manicurist) BYRD back from sunny California. too sweet for words....and that outfit ANNA OVERBEY Sunday was the last word.....FREIDA MURRAY is all because hubby, PVT. EUGENE MURRAY, is in town from Field, Fla.

* * *

s this about SUSIE TYLER and JANET of the Brass Rail in love with the same guy, who is none other than THEO- ..Wonder why did BOB CRAWFORD'S wife pull him off at that 47th street tavern t'other night?...Now that DUCKY the 'Boogie BILL HILLMAN and FRED VAUGHN are tak- honors as bartenders....The boys along 61st street say that ED JOYNER is the personality girl at the Red Moon..... SIA SHELBY got tired of living Friday and tried to commit but failed....She is still so sick at the county hospital.

rof. HERMAN
he Astrologer

Your questions will be answered free in this column only when a of this feature is enclosed with your QUESTION, YOUR FULL BIRTHDATE and CORRECT ADDRESS. For private reply send 25c) and stamped envelope for my ASTROLOGY READING and receive n mail my FREE OPINIONS on any THREE QUESTIONS. Address munications to PROF. HERMAN (the astrologer) care of THE GO DEFENDER, 3435 INDIANA AVE., CHICAGO, ILL.

SILVER THREADS

outward individual grows e inner-self should grow with knowledge and un- ng. It is a very sad thing the years advance folks expand in proportion to periences.

en hear that we are as old el, and if we are forty but thirty, we have evidently od care of ourselves and to retain some of our

for I do not vision them as being lost or stolen.

* * *

I.M. Dear Prof. Herman: I have enjoyed your column in the Chicago Defender, very much. I would like for you to please answer my question. Is this man really in love with me?

Ans.: Concentrating upon your question, I find that this young man is deeply in love with you.

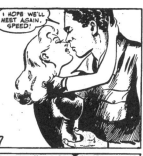

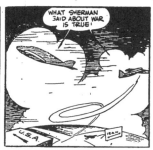

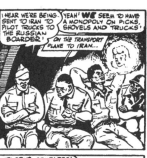

SPEED JAXON
By Jay Jackson
MINTA, POSING AS A NAZI SPY, HAS HAD SPEED RELEASED FROM A NAZI PRISON. HOWEVER HER TRICK IS DISCOVERED BEFORE REACHING THE AMERICAN LINES BUT SPEED OVER-POWERS THE GERMAN ESCORT AND TAKES THEM PRISONERS... HE AND MINTA ARE HIGHLY COMMENDED AND.....
I'M BEING SENT BACK TO THE STATES ON FURLOUGH.... BUT I'D RATHER GO WITH YOU!
MINTA, YOU'VE BEEN AN ANGEL! I WISH YOU COULD! BUT IRAN IS GOING TO BE A PRETTY HOT SPOT I THINK!
I HOPE WE'LL MEET AGAIN, SPEED!
WHAT SHERMAN SAID ABOUT WAR IS TRUE!
U.S.A.
IRAN
I HEAR WE'RE BEING SENT TO IRAN TO PILOT TRUCKS TO THE RUSSIAN BOARDER!
YEAH! WE SEEM TO HAVE A MONOPOLY ON PICKS, SHOVELS AND TRUCKS!
ON THE TRANSPORT PLANE TO IRAN...
QUIT BEEFIN'! HOW ABOUT OUR BOYS BOMBING THE HEIL OUT OF THE HITLERATS OVER ITALY?
THEY'RE LIKE THE MOTTO ON OUR SILVER DOLLAR- "OUT OF MANY ONE!"
COLORED PEOPLE GET THE SAME CORNY DEAL THE WORLD OVER! OH!OH! LOOKUT, SLIM! WHO IS HE?
WELCOME, COMRADES! I'M GENERAL GEORGEZ WASHINGTONSKI SVOSKI OF THE RUSSIAN ARMY!

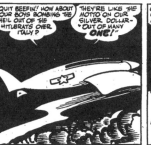

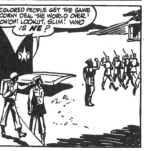

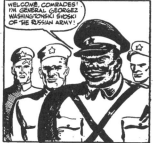

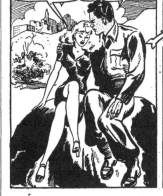

1778

SEPTEMBER 1943 – DECEMBER 1943

Britain Told Negroes Hold Balance Of Power In U.S.

By GEORGE PADMORE
(Defender London Correspondent)

LONDON—(Censored)— "Spectators see more of the game than the players." This truism applies as much to politics as to sport. At the present time the British people are following political trends in the United States with an objectivity that American participators are denied. The forthcoming presidential election is of vital concern to Britishers who have been made to realize by their political leaders that the future of world peace and security may well depend upon the next occupant of the White House.

Generally speaking, President Roosevelt is the best known and most popular figure in American public life, not only because of high office he occupies, but because he has proved himself a loyal friend of this country in its darkest hour.

Wendell Willkie, however, is also well known in Britain and exceedingly popular among progressive elements for his outspoken attitude on foreign affairs and the colonial question.

troversy concerning votes for soldiers, the Observer remarks that "Southern Democrats are particularly anxious to prevent the southern Negro soldiers voting. Some Republicans say, however, that many soldiers would vote Republican, hoping that the new administration would not want policing of the world, so that they could go home sooner. They also say that no President has ever been popular in the army. Lincoln was almost defeated by his soldiers."

At the present moment soldiers in this European theatre of operations are not particularly concerned with the opening of the second front against Hitler's western fortress, for this is a matter of life and death. The struggle will be grim and they have no illusions. Casualties will be high. Thousands who lead the assault will not be alive to vote in November should the right to do so be extended them.

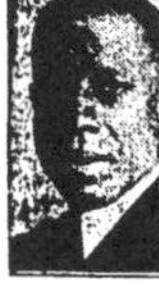

Negro Troops Now

YOUR Money

By WALTER L. LOWE
Insurance Broker

Ques.: What is the wisest investment plan now?

Ans.: Under the present conditions, even if one is inclined to believe that prices will go higher, it is still quite a task to decide which is a sound investment policy to follow at this time. Even if an expert analyst gives an opinion on the matter, he would have to be conservative. Should he be otherwise he would most certainly expose some trusting person to financial disaster.

Walter Lowe

On the other hand should an analyst give conservative advice he would instinctively become very, very cautious. Briefly, the wisest investment plan at present is conservativeness, caution and above all

Tough Arms Unit Starts Bombs On Way To Japs

By FLETCHER P. MARTIN
(Representing Negro Newspaper Pool)

ADVANCED SOUTH PACIFIC BASE—(Via Airmail)—When two-thousand pounds of hurtling missles of steel and powder smash enemy installations on Bougainville, it is a safe wager that these flying fragmentations of death were handled by a Negro ordnance unit.

It is safe to add that when Mitchells and Liberators, pregnant with block-busters, hover above Rabaul, strong brown hands are they which shoved the bombs up through the bomb bays before the ships took flight.

Somewhere in the bosom of the Solomons, hidden from the bespectacled eyes of enemy reconnaissance is a potent and formidable ammunition area, acres long, acres wide. Guarding the handling each fuse, each bomb, is a unit of Negro specialists in ordnance. The exact amount of destruction there is confidential information, but confidentially, there is enough to blow the citizens of Tokyo to the land of

as a soldier and athlete specializing in boxing, baseball and track.

Little technical information can be given about this outfit because of the confidential nature of the work and of its potent importance in the pursuit of allied aims in the Pacific. But its mission is an essential part of what gains are made here. When Bougainville and Rabaul feel the earth tremor, these men are unquestionably guilty of having a hand in it.

One important item of major interest explained by Sgt. Hypps and the commanding officer—98 per cent of the unit are to receive shortly Good Conduct medals awarded by the army. This is the largest percentage in the South Pacific.

Church Leaders Set Racial Mee

NEW YORK.—The National Co ference of Church Leaders, an inte racial, interdenominational mov ment composed of churchmen fro 12 different national denominatio will hold its sixth annual meeti at Antioch College, Yellow Spring Ohio, April 13-14, according to D George E. Haynes, executive sec tary of the Department of Race R lations of the Federal Council Churches and secretary of the co ference.

The purpose of the conferen according to Dr. Haynes, is to e able national and state chur leaders to share their thoughts a clarify their views as a basis f action on racial issues which a of mutual concern to them and their churches. Specific measu which can be undertaken churches to improve race relatio will be discussed.

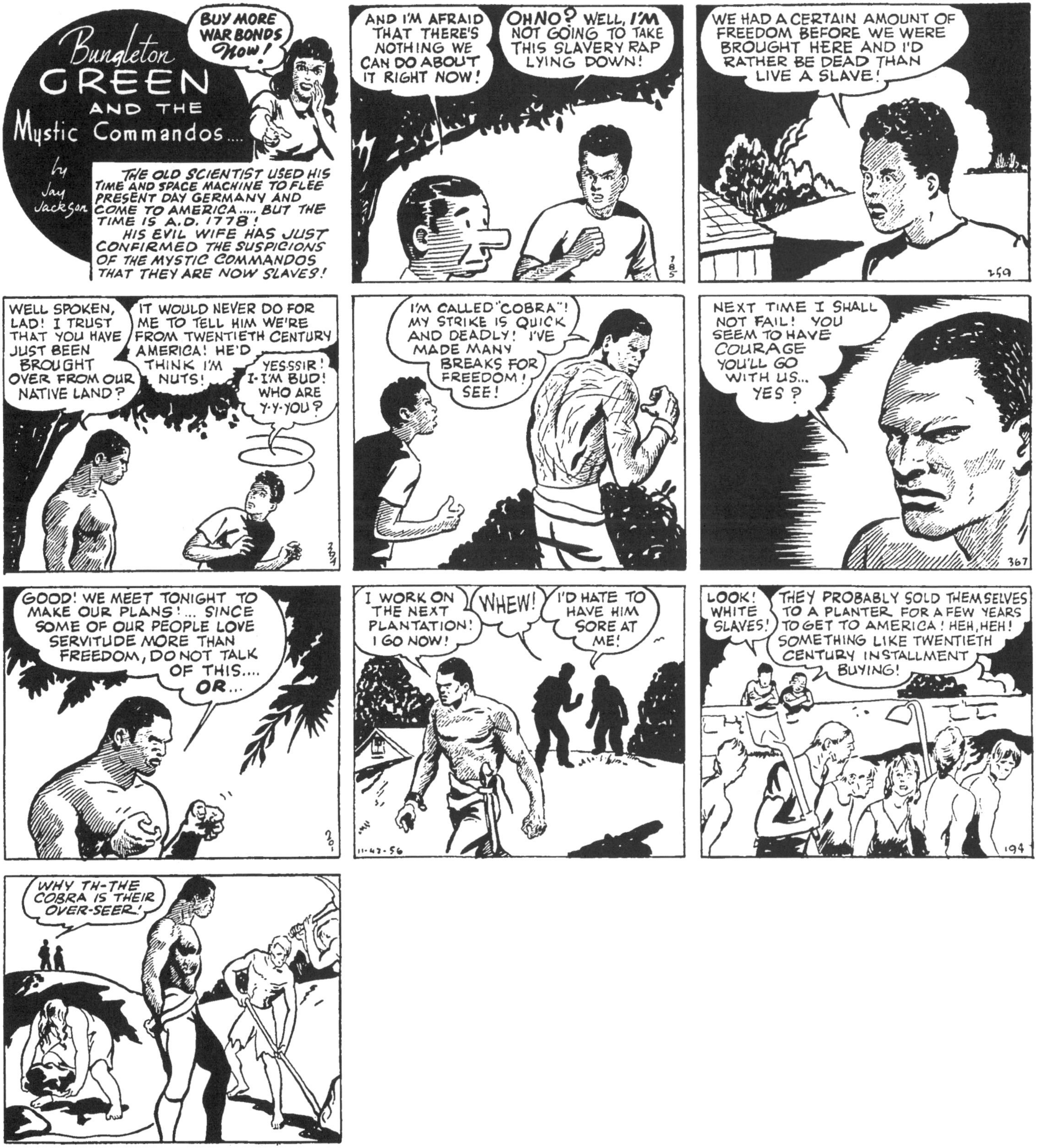
BUY MORE WAR BONDS Now!
Bungleton GREEN AND THE Mystic Commandos....
by Jay Jackson
THE OLD SCIENTIST USED HIS TIME AND SPACE MACHINE TO FLEE PRESENT DAY GERMANY AND COME TO AMERICA..... BUT THE TIME IS A.D. 1778!
HIS EVIL WIFE HAS JUST CONFIRMED THE SUSPICIONS OF THE MYSTIC COMMANDOS THAT THEY ARE NOW SLAVES!
AND I'M AFRAID THAT THERE'S NOTHING WE CAN DO ABOUT IT RIGHT NOW!
OH NO? WELL, I'M NOT GOING TO TAKE THIS SLAVERY RAP LYING DOWN!
WE HAD A CERTAIN AMOUNT OF FREEDOM BEFORE WE WERE BROUGHT HERE AND I'D RATHER BE DEAD THAN LIVE A SLAVE!
WELL SPOKEN, LAD! I TRUST THAT YOU HAVE JUST BEEN BROUGHT OVER FROM OUR NATIVE LAND?
IT WOULD NEVER DO FOR ME TO TELL HIM WE'RE FROM TWENTIETH CENTURY AMERICA! HE'D THINK I'M NUTS!
YES-SSIR! I-I'M BUD! WHO ARE Y-Y-YOU?
I'M CALLED "COBRA"! MY STRIKE IS QUICK AND DEADLY! I'VE MADE MANY BREAKS FOR FREEDOM! SEE!
NEXT TIME I SHALL NOT FAIL! YOU SEEM TO HAVE COURAGE YOU'LL GO WITH US... YES?
GOOD! WE MEET TONIGHT TO MAKE OUR PLANS!... SINCE SOME OF OUR PEOPLE LOVE SERVITUDE MORE THAN FREEDOM, DO NOT TALK OF THIS.... OR...
I WORK ON THE NEXT PLANTATION! I GO NOW!
WHEW!
I'D HATE TO HAVE HIM SORE AT ME!
LOOK! WHITE SLAVES!
THEY PROBABLY SOLD THEMSELVES TO A PLANTER FOR A FEW YEARS TO GET TO AMERICA! HEH, HEH! SOMETHING LIKE TWENTIETH CENTURY INSTALLMENT BUYING!
WHY TH-THE COBRA IS THEIR OVER-SEER!

SEPTEMBER 4, 1943

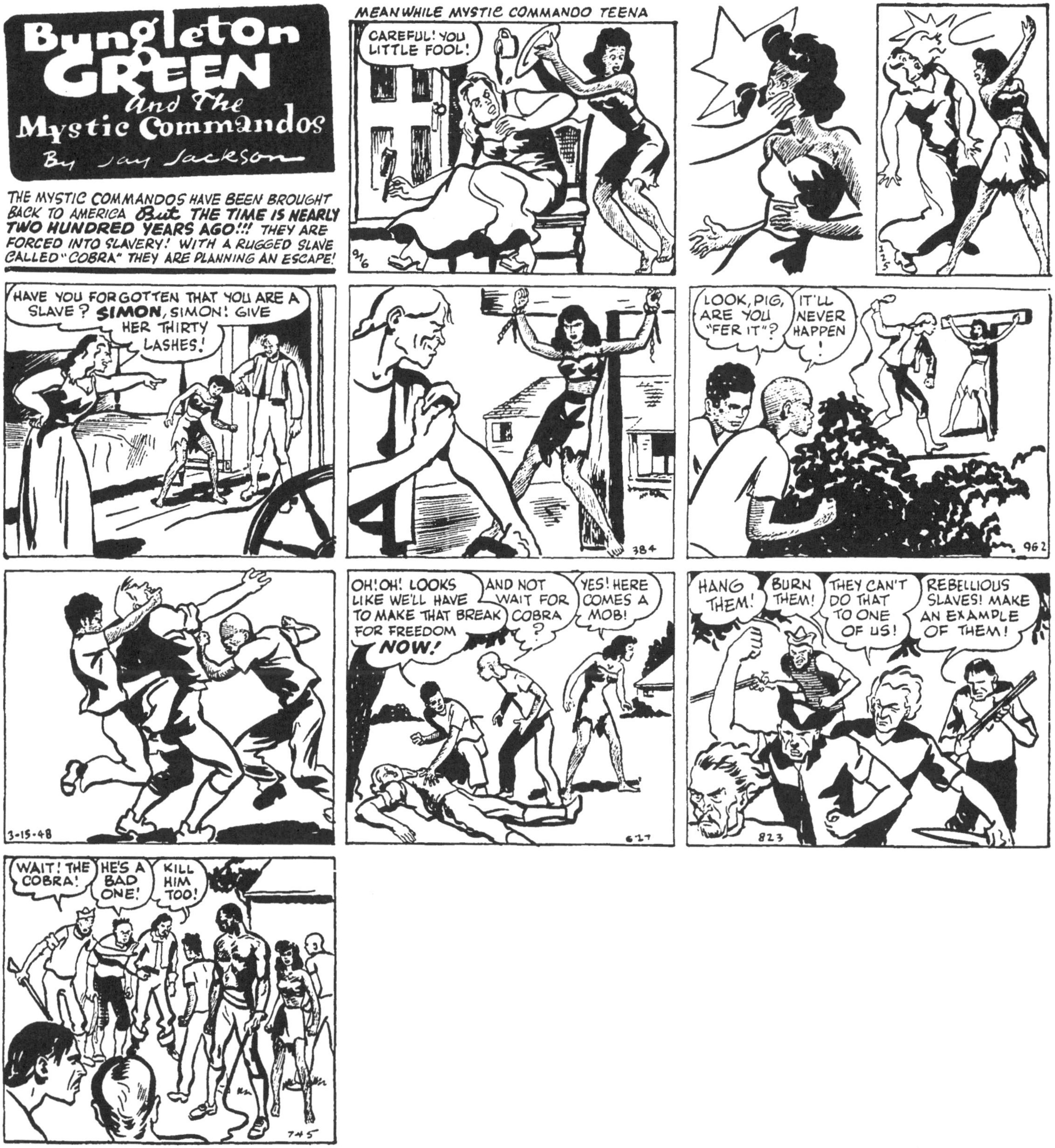
Bungleton Green and The Mystic Commandos
By Jay Jackson
THE MYSTIC COMMANDOS HAVE BEEN BROUGHT BACK TO AMERICA But THE TIME IS NEARLY TWO HUNDRED YEARS AGO!!! THEY ARE FORCED INTO SLAVERY! WITH A RUGGED SLAVE CALLED "COBRA" THEY ARE PLANNING AN ESCAPE!
MEANWHILE MYSTIC COMMANDO TEENA
CAREFUL! YOU LITTLE FOOL!
HAVE YOU FORGOTTEN THAT YOU ARE A SLAVE? SIMON, SIMON! GIVE HER THIRTY LASHES!
LOOK, PIG, ARE YOU "FER IT"?
IT'LL NEVER HAPPEN!
OH! OH! LOOKS LIKE WE'LL HAVE TO MAKE THAT BREAK FOR FREEDOM NOW!
AND NOT WAIT FOR COBRA?
YES! HERE COMES A MOB!
HANG THEM!
BURN THEM!
THEY CAN'T DO THAT TO ONE OF US!
REBELLIOUS SLAVES! MAKE AN EXAMPLE OF THEM!
WAIT! THE COBRA!
HE'S A BAD ONE!
KILL HIM TOO!

SEPTEMBER 11, 1943

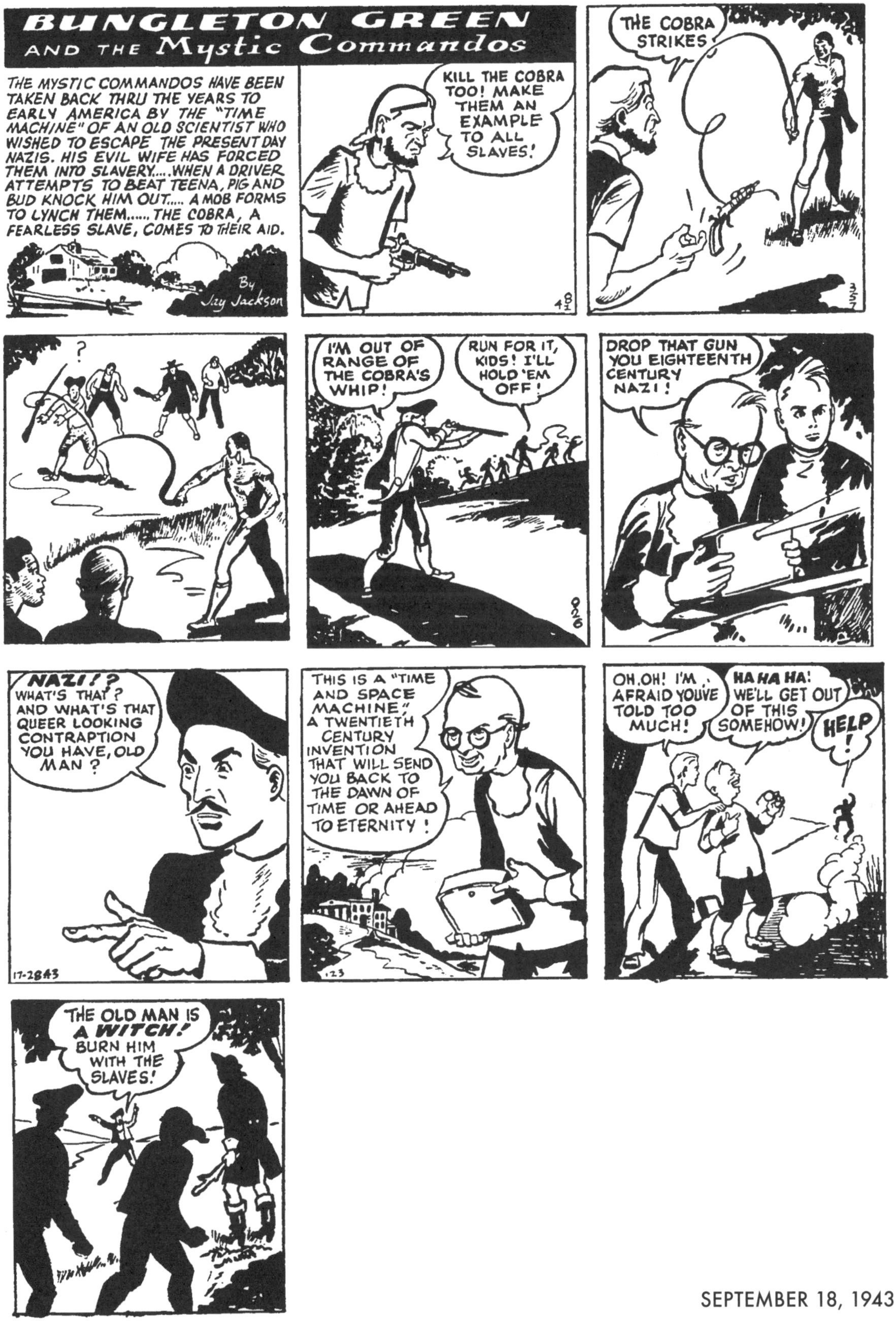
BUNGLETON GREEN
AND THE Mystic Commandos
THE MYSTIC COMMANDOS HAVE BEEN TAKEN BACK THRU THE YEARS TO EARLY AMERICA BY THE "TIME MACHINE" OF AN OLD SCIENTIST WHO WISHED TO ESCAPE THE PRESENT DAY NAZIS. HIS EVIL WIFE HAS FORCED THEM INTO SLAVERY.....WHEN A DRIVER ATTEMPTS TO BEAT TEENA, PIG AND BUD KNOCK HIM OUT..... A MOB FORMS TO LYNCH THEM......THE COBRA, A FEARLESS SLAVE, COMES TO THEIR AID.
By Jay Jackson
KILL THE COBRA TOO! MAKE THEM AN EXAMPLE TO ALL SLAVES!
THE COBRA STRIKES
?
I'M OUT OF RANGE OF THE COBRA'S WHIP!
RUN FOR IT, KIDS! I'LL HOLD 'EM OFF!
DROP THAT GUN YOU EIGHTEENTH CENTURY NAZI!
NAZI!? WHAT'S THAT? AND WHAT'S THAT QUEER LOOKING CONTRAPTION YOU HAVE, OLD MAN?
THIS IS A "TIME AND SPACE MACHINE," A TWENTIETH CENTURY INVENTION THAT WILL SEND YOU BACK TO THE DAWN OF TIME OR AHEAD TO ETERNITY!
OH, OH! I'M AFRAID YOU'VE TOLD TOO MUCH!
HA HA HA! WE'LL GET OUT OF THIS SOMEHOW!
HELP!
THE OLD MAN IS A WITCH! BURN HIM WITH THE SLAVES!
17-2843

SEPTEMBER 18, 1943

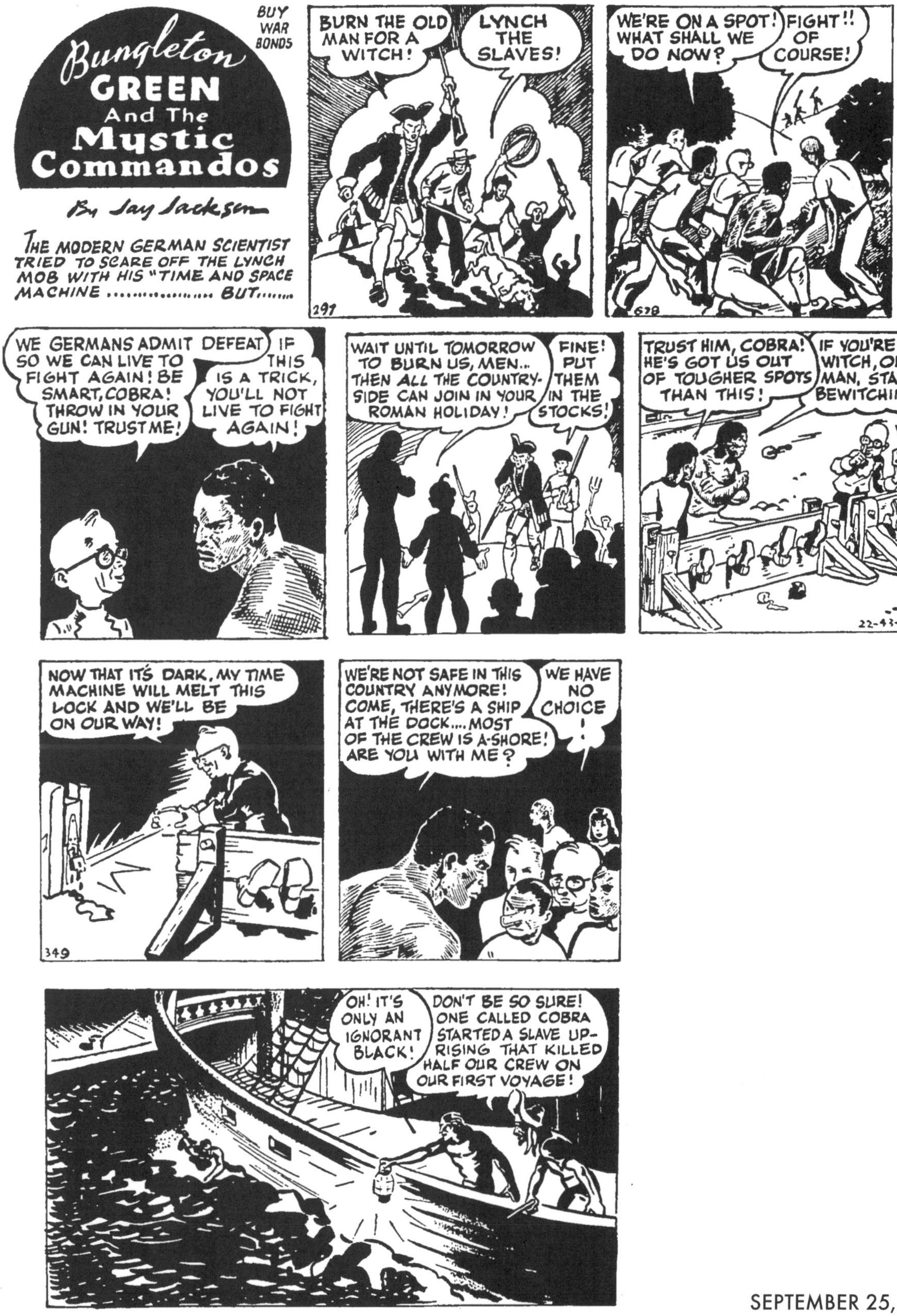
BUY WAR BONDS
Bungleton GREEN And The Mystic Commandos
By Jay Jackson
THE MODERN GERMAN SCIENTIST TRIED TO SCARE OFF THE LYNCH MOB WITH HIS "TIME AND SPACE MACHINE .... BUT.......
BURN THE OLD MAN FOR A WITCH!
LYNCH THE SLAVES!
WE'RE ON A SPOT! WHAT SHALL WE DO NOW?
FIGHT!! OF COURSE!
WE GERMANS ADMIT DEFEAT SO WE CAN LIVE TO FIGHT AGAIN! BE SMART, COBRA! THROW IN YOUR GUN! TRUST ME!
IF THIS IS A TRICK, YOU'LL NOT LIVE TO FIGHT AGAIN!
WAIT UNTIL TOMORROW TO BURN US, MEN.. THEN ALL THE COUNTRY-SIDE CAN JOIN IN YOUR ROMAN HOLIDAY!
FINE! PUT THEM IN THE STOCKS!
TRUST HIM, COBRA! HE'S GOT US OUT OF TOUGHER SPOTS THAN THIS!
IF YOU'RE A WITCH, OLD MAN, START BEWITCHING!
NOW THAT IT'S DARK, MY TIME MACHINE WILL MELT THIS LOCK AND WE'LL BE ON OUR WAY!
WE'RE NOT SAFE IN THIS COUNTRY ANYMORE! COME, THERE'S A SHIP AT THE DOCK.... MOST OF THE CREW IS A-SHORE! ARE YOU WITH ME?
WE HAVE NO CHOICE!
OH! IT'S ONLY AN IGNORANT BLACK!
DON'T BE SO SURE! ONE CALLED COBRA STARTED A SLAVE UP-RISING THAT KILLED HALF OUR CREW ON OUR FIRST VOYAGE!

SEPTEMBER 25, 1943

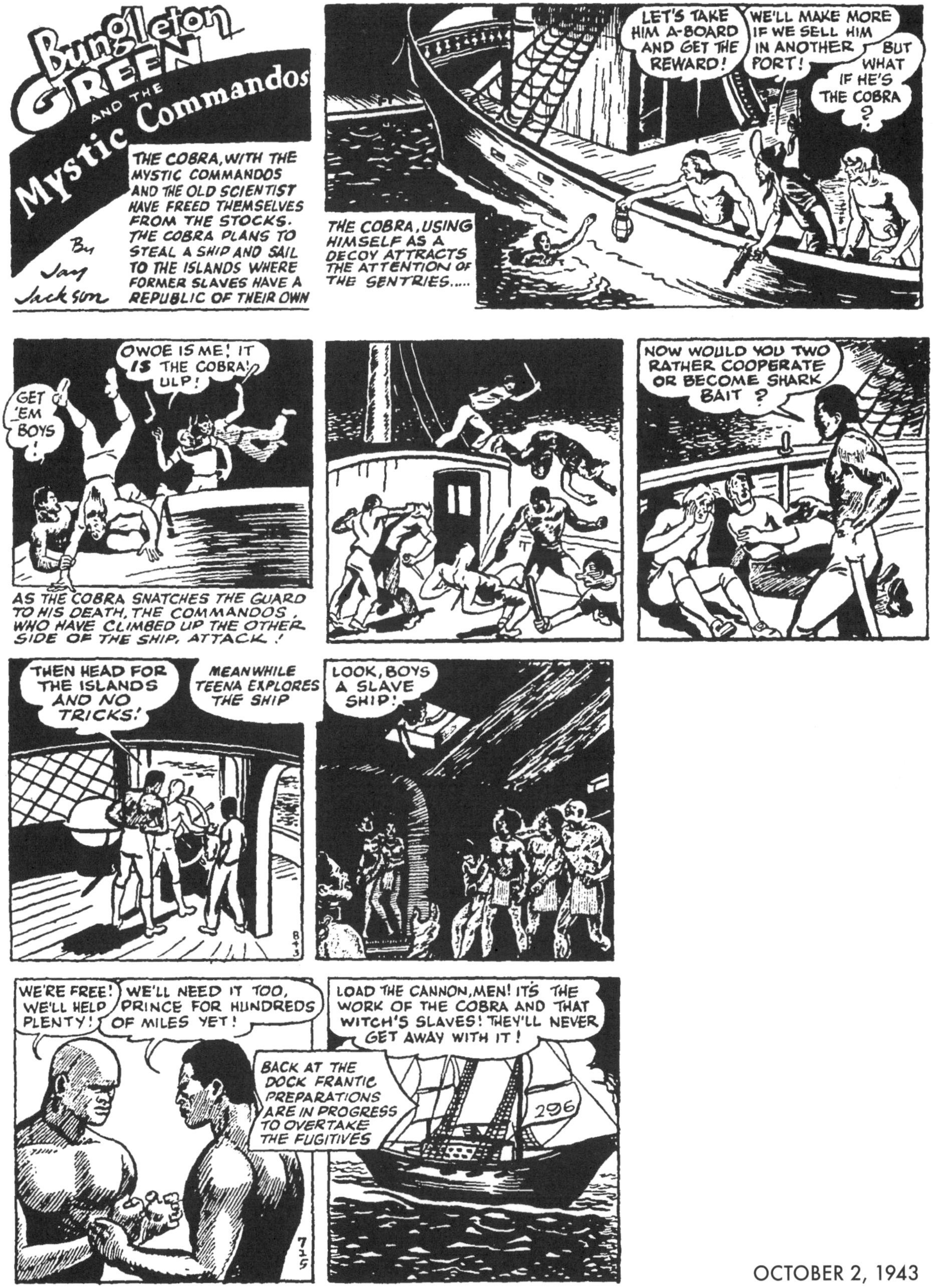
Bungleton Green and the Mystic Commandos
By Jay Jackson
THE COBRA, WITH THE MYSTIC COMMANDOS AND THE OLD SCIENTIST HAVE FREED THEMSELVES FROM THE STOCKS. THE COBRA PLANS TO STEAL A SHIP AND SAIL TO THE ISLANDS WHERE FORMER SLAVES HAVE A REPUBLIC OF THEIR OWN
THE COBRA, USING HIMSELF AS A DECOY ATTRACTS THE ATTENTION OF THE SENTRIES.....
LET'S TAKE HIM A-BOARD AND GET THE REWARD!
WE'LL MAKE MORE IF WE SELL HIM IN ANOTHER PORT!
BUT WHAT IF HE'S THE COBRA ?
GET 'EM BOYS !
O WOE IS ME! IT IS THE COBRA! ULP!
AS THE COBRA SNATCHES THE GUARD TO HIS DEATH, THE COMMANDOS, WHO HAVE CLIMBED UP THE OTHER SIDE OF THE SHIP, ATTACK !
NOW WOULD YOU TWO RATHER COOPERATE OR BECOME SHARK BAIT ?
THEN HEAD FOR THE ISLANDS AND NO TRICKS!
MEANWHILE TEENA EXPLORES THE SHIP
LOOK, BOYS A SLAVE SHIP!
WE'RE FREE! WE'LL HELP PLENTY!
WE'LL NEED IT TOO, PRINCE FOR HUNDREDS OF MILES YET!
BACK AT THE DOCK FRANTIC PREPARATIONS ARE IN PROGRESS TO OVERTAKE THE FUGITIVES
LOAD THE CANNON, MEN! IT'S THE WORK OF THE COBRA AND THAT WITCH'S SLAVES! THEY'LL NEVER GET AWAY WITH IT !
296

OCTOBER 2, 1943

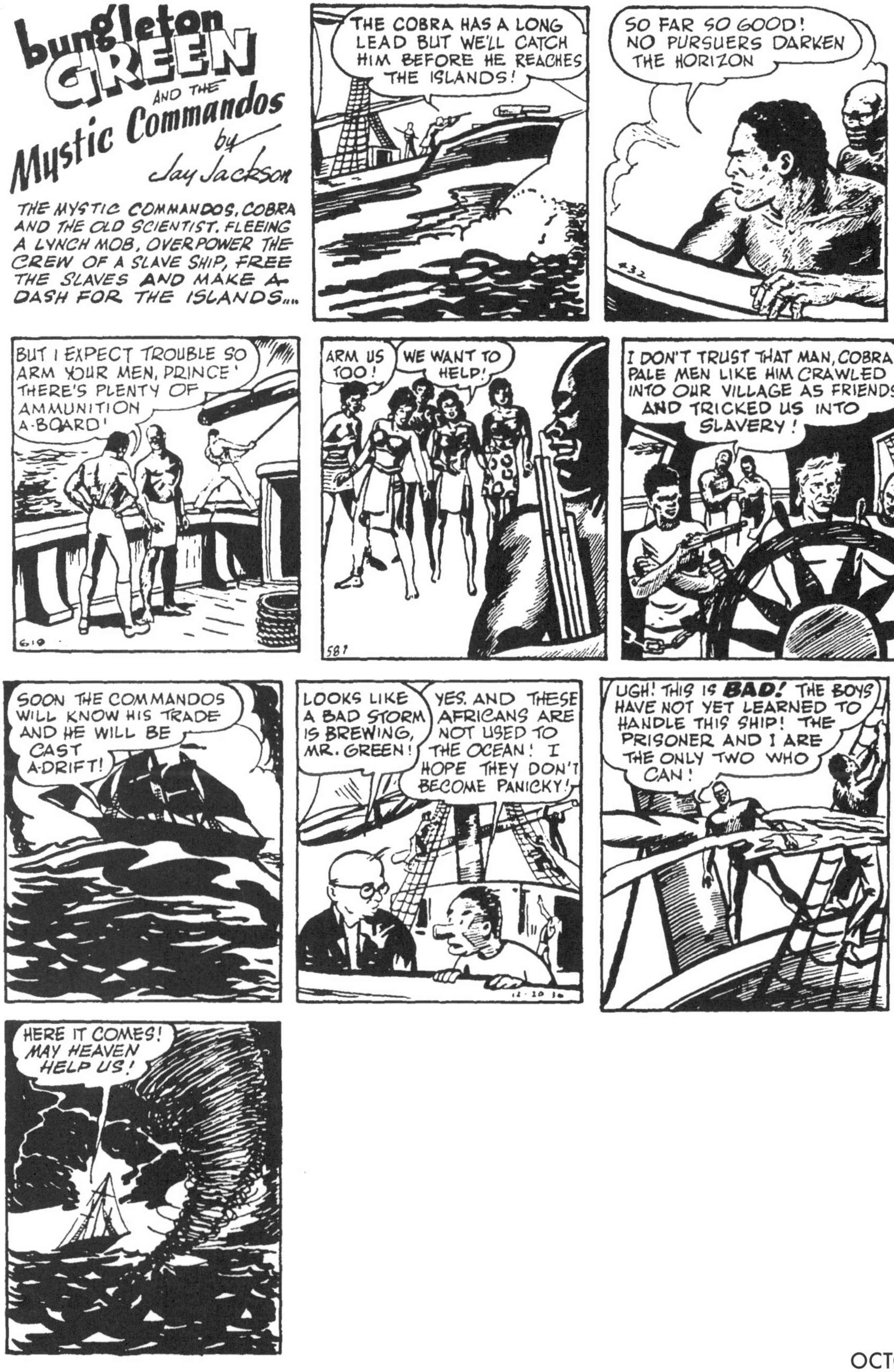
bungleton GREEN AND THE Mystic Commandos
by Jay Jackson
THE MYSTIC COMMANDOS, COBRA AND THE OLD SCIENTIST, FLEEING A LYNCH MOB, OVERPOWER THE CREW OF A SLAVE SHIP, FREE THE SLAVES AND MAKE A DASH FOR THE ISLANDS...
THE COBRA HAS A LONG LEAD BUT WE'LL CATCH HIM BEFORE HE REACHES THE ISLANDS!
SO FAR SO GOOD! NO PURSUERS DARKEN THE HORIZON
BUT I EXPECT TROUBLE SO ARM YOUR MEN, PRINCE! THERE'S PLENTY OF AMMUNITION A-BOARD!
ARM US TOO!
WE WANT TO HELP!
I DON'T TRUST THAT MAN, COBRA! PALE MEN LIKE HIM CRAWLED INTO OUR VILLAGE AS FRIENDS AND TRICKED US INTO SLAVERY!
SOON THE COMMANDOS WILL KNOW HIS TRADE AND HE WILL BE CAST A-DRIFT!
LOOKS LIKE A BAD STORM IS BREWING, MR. GREEN!
YES. AND THESE AFRICANS ARE NOT USED TO THE OCEAN! I HOPE THEY DON'T BECOME PANICKY!
UGH! THIS IS BAD! THE BOYS HAVE NOT YET LEARNED TO HANDLE THIS SHIP! THE PRISONER AND I ARE THE ONLY TWO WHO CAN!
HERE IT COMES! MAY HEAVEN HELP US!

OCTOBER 9, 1943

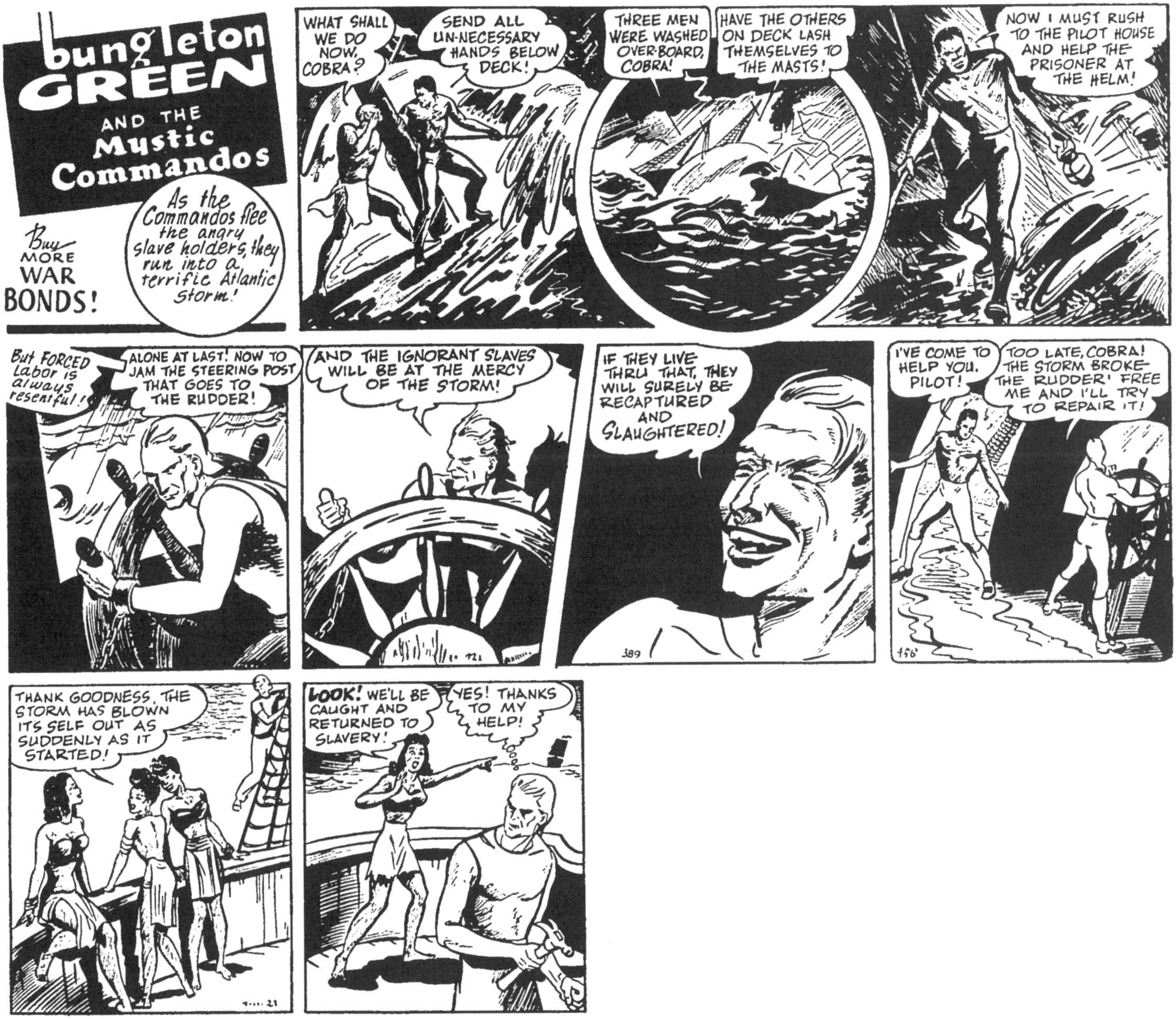
bungleton GREEN
AND THE Mystic Commandos
Buy MORE WAR BONDS!
As the Commandos flee the angry slave holders, they run into a terrific Atlantic storm!
WHAT SHALL WE DO NOW, COBRA?
SEND ALL UN-NECESSARY HANDS BELOW DECK!
THREE MEN WERE WASHED OVER-BOARD, COBRA!
HAVE THE OTHERS ON DECK LASH THEMSELVES TO THE MASTS!
NOW I MUST RUSH TO THE PILOT HOUSE AND HELP THE PRISONER AT THE HELM!
But FORCED labor is always resentful!
ALONE AT LAST! NOW TO JAM THE STEERING POST THAT GOES TO THE RUDDER!
AND THE IGNORANT SLAVES WILL BE AT THE MERCY OF THE STORM!
IF THEY LIVE THRU THAT, THEY WILL SURELY BE RECAPTURED AND SLAUGHTERED!
I'VE COME TO HELP YOU, PILOT!
TOO LATE, COBRA! THE STORM BROKE THE RUDDER! FREE ME AND I'LL TRY TO REPAIR IT!
THANK GOODNESS, THE STORM HAS BLOWN ITS SELF OUT AS SUDDENLY AS IT STARTED!
LOOK! WE'LL BE CAUGHT AND RETURNED TO SLAVERY!
YES! THANKS TO MY HELP!

OCTOBER 16, 1943

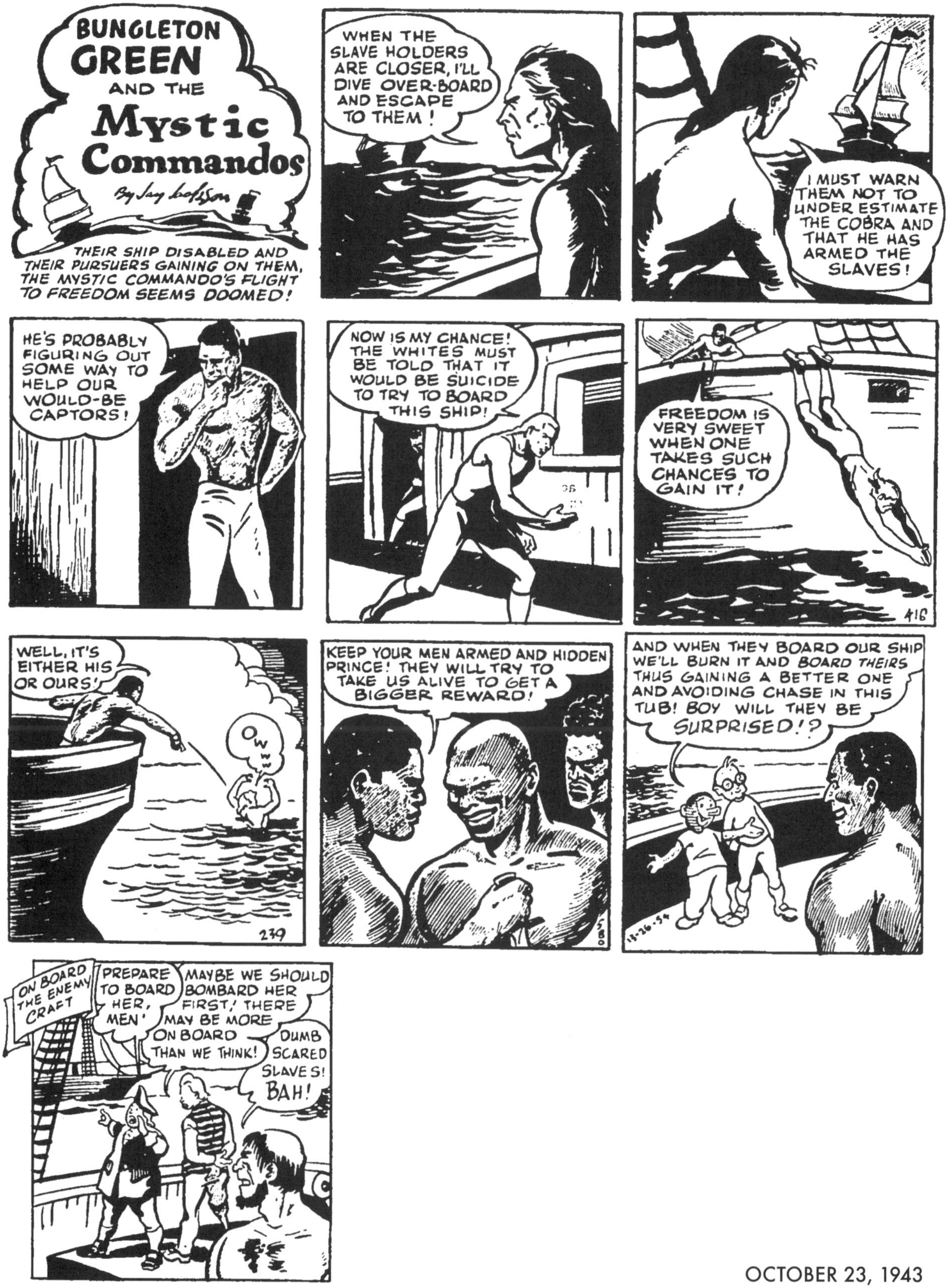
BUNGLETON GREEN AND THE Mystic Commandos
THEIR SHIP DISABLED AND THEIR PURSUERS GAINING ON THEM, THE MYSTIC COMMANDO'S FLIGHT TO FREEDOM SEEMS DOOMED!
WHEN THE SLAVE HOLDERS ARE CLOSER, I'LL DIVE OVER-BOARD AND ESCAPE TO THEM!
I MUST WARN THEM NOT TO UNDER ESTIMATE THE COBRA AND THAT HE HAS ARMED THE SLAVES!
HE'S PROBABLY FIGURING OUT SOME WAY TO HELP OUR WOULD-BE CAPTORS!
NOW IS MY CHANCE! THE WHITES MUST BE TOLD THAT IT WOULD BE SUICIDE TO TRY TO BOARD THIS SHIP!
FREEDOM IS VERY SWEET WHEN ONE TAKES SUCH CHANCES TO GAIN IT!
WELL, IT'S EITHER HIS OR OURS!
OWWW
KEEP YOUR MEN ARMED AND HIDDEN PRINCE! THEY WILL TRY TO TAKE US ALIVE TO GET A BIGGER REWARD!
AND WHEN THEY BOARD OUR SHIP WE'LL BURN IT AND BOARD THEIRS THUS GAINING A BETTER ONE AND AVOIDING CHASE IN THIS TUB! BOY WILL THEY BE SURPRISED!?
ON BOARD THE ENEMY CRAFT
PREPARE TO BOARD HER, MEN!
MAYBE WE SHOULD BOMBARD HER FIRST! THERE MAY BE MORE ON BOARD THAN WE THINK!
DUMB SCARED SLAVES! BAH!

OCTOBER 23, 1943

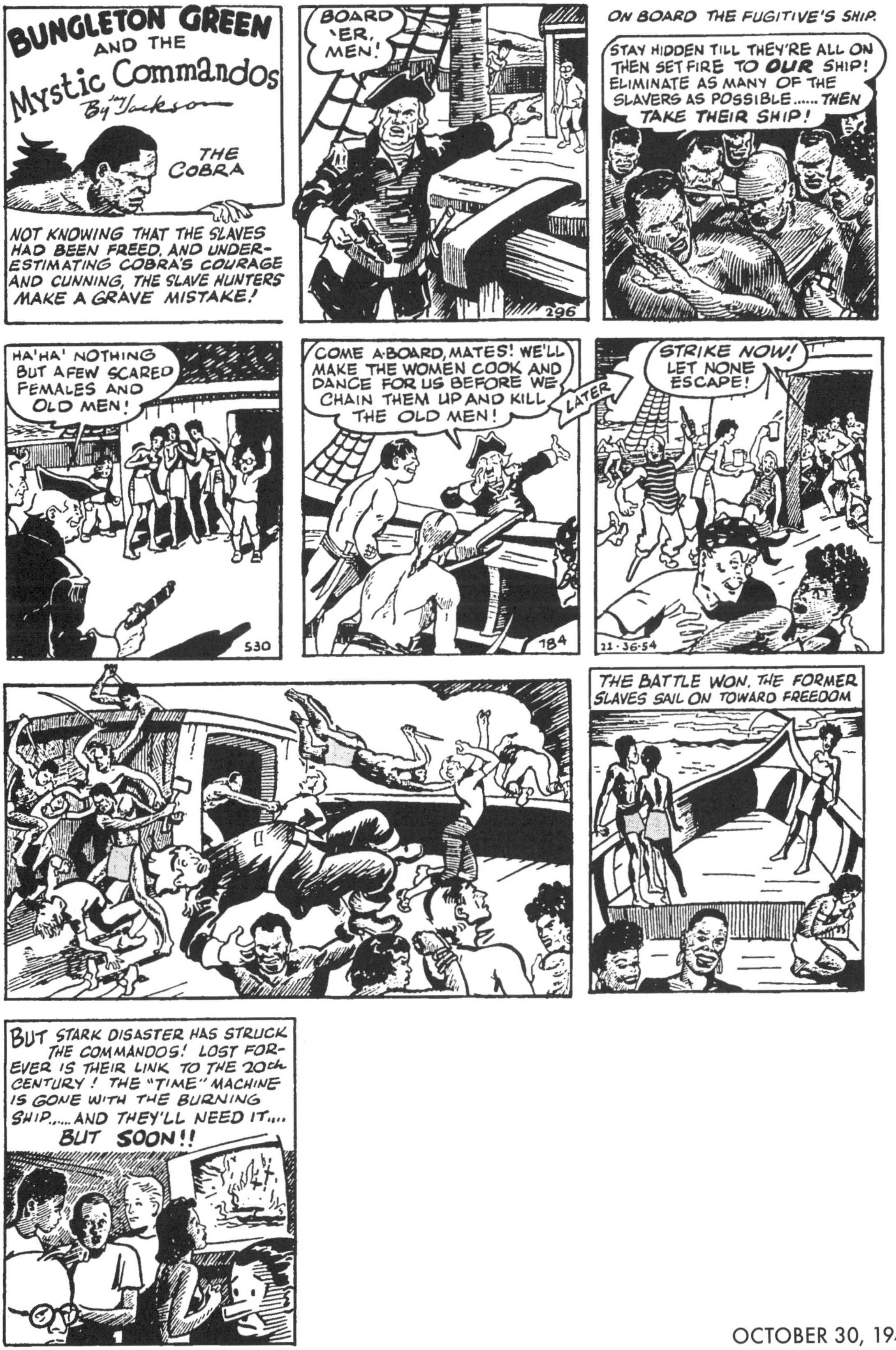

BUNGLETON GREEN
AND THE
Mystic Commandos
By Jay Jackson
THE COBRA
NOT KNOWING THAT THE SLAVES HAD BEEN FREED, AND UNDER-ESTIMATING COBRA'S COURAGE AND CUNNING, THE SLAVE HUNTERS MAKE A GRAVE MISTAKE!
BOARD 'ER, MEN!
296
ON BOARD THE FUGITIVE'S SHIP.
STAY HIDDEN TILL THEY'RE ALL ON THEN SET FIRE TO OUR SHIP! ELIMINATE AS MANY OF THE SLAVERS AS POSSIBLE...... THEN TAKE THEIR SHIP!
HA'HA' NOTHING BUT A FEW SCARED FEMALES AND OLD MEN!
530
COME A-BOARD, MATES! WE'LL MAKE THE WOMEN COOK AND DANCE FOR US BEFORE WE CHAIN THEM UP AND KILL THE OLD MEN!
784
LATER
STRIKE NOW! LET NONE ESCAPE!
21-36-54
THE BATTLE WON, THE FORMER SLAVES SAIL ON TOWARD FREEDOM
BUT STARK DISASTER HAS STRUCK THE COMMANDOS! LOST FOREVER IS THEIR LINK TO THE 20th CENTURY! THE "TIME" MACHINE IS GONE WITH THE BURNING SHIP...... AND THEY'LL NEED IT.... BUT SOON!!

OCTOBER 30, 1943

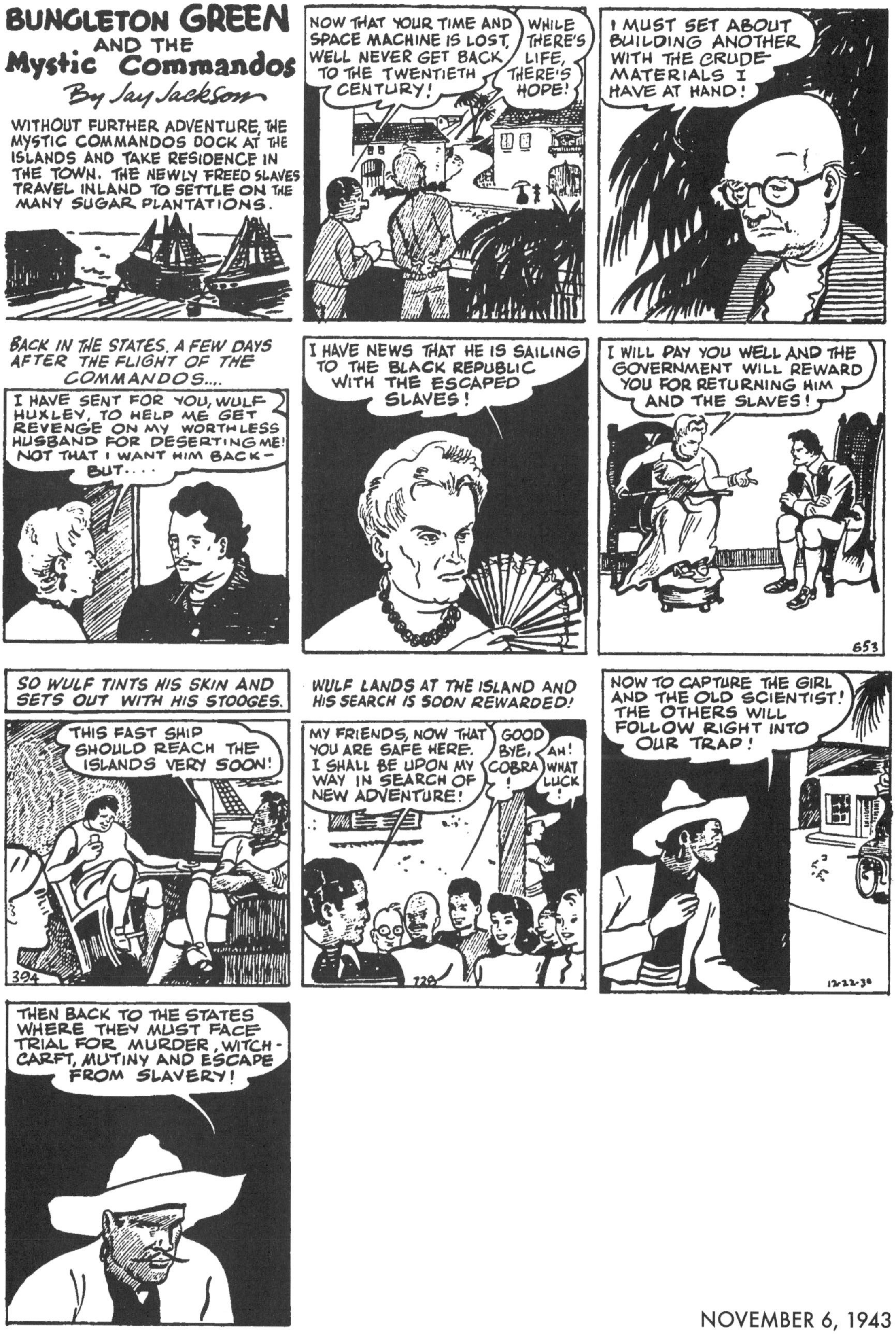
BUNGLETON GREEN
AND THE
Mystic Commandos
By Jay Jackson
WITHOUT FURTHER ADVENTURE, THE MYSTIC COMMANDOS DOCK AT THE ISLANDS AND TAKE RESIDENCE IN THE TOWN. THE NEWLY FREED SLAVES TRAVEL INLAND TO SETTLE ON THE MANY SUGAR PLANTATIONS.
NOW THAT YOUR TIME AND SPACE MACHINE IS LOST, WE'LL NEVER GET BACK TO THE TWENTIETH CENTURY!
WHILE THERE'S LIFE, THERE'S HOPE!
I MUST SET ABOUT BUILDING ANOTHER WITH THE CRUDE MATERIALS I HAVE AT HAND!
BACK IN THE STATES. A FEW DAYS AFTER THE FLIGHT OF THE COMMANDOS....
I HAVE SENT FOR YOU, WULF HUXLEY, TO HELP ME GET REVENGE ON MY WORTHLESS HUSBAND FOR DESERTING ME! NOT THAT I WANT HIM BACK- BUT....
I HAVE NEWS THAT HE IS SAILING TO THE BLACK REPUBLIC WITH THE ESCAPED SLAVES!
I WILL PAY YOU WELL AND THE GOVERNMENT WILL REWARD YOU FOR RETURNING HIM AND THE SLAVES!
653
SO WULF TINTS HIS SKIN AND SETS OUT WITH HIS STOOGES.
THIS FAST SHIP SHOULD REACH THE ISLANDS VERY SOON!
394
WULF LANDS AT THE ISLAND AND HIS SEARCH IS SOON REWARDED!
MY FRIENDS, NOW THAT YOU ARE SAFE HERE. I SHALL BE UPON MY WAY IN SEARCH OF NEW ADVENTURE!
GOOD BYE, COBRA!
AH! WHAT LUCK!
720
NOW TO CAPTURE THE GIRL AND THE OLD SCIENTIST! THE OTHERS WILL FOLLOW RIGHT INTO OUR TRAP!
12-22-30
THEN BACK TO THE STATES WHERE THEY MUST FACE TRIAL FOR MURDER, WITCH-CARFT, MUTINY AND ESCAPE FROM SLAVERY!

NOVEMBER 6, 1943

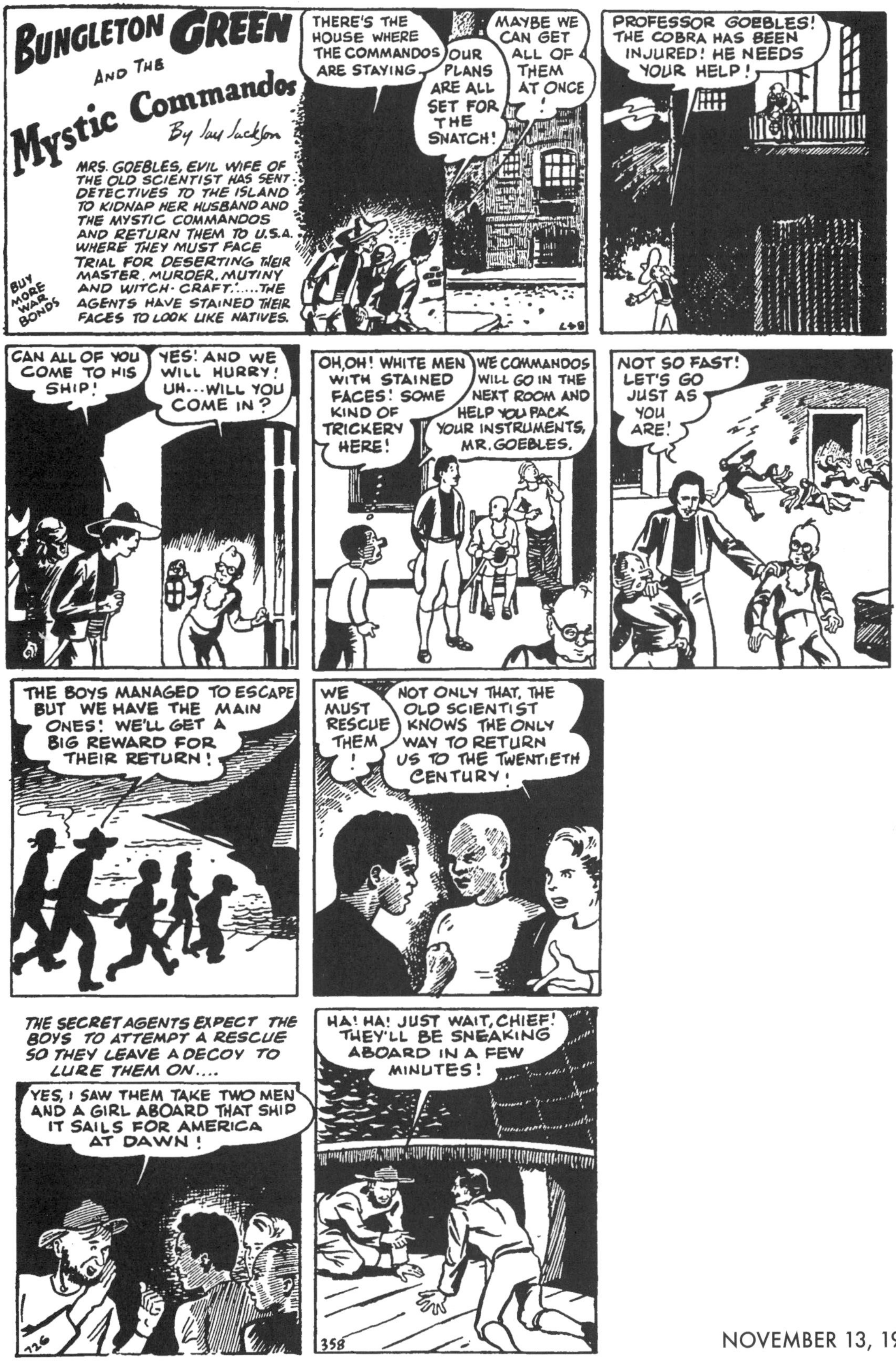
BUNGLETON GREEN AND THE Mystic Commandos
By Jay Jackson
MRS. GOEBLES, EVIL WIFE OF THE OLD SCIENTIST HAS SENT DETECTIVES TO THE ISLAND TO KIDNAP HER HUSBAND AND THE MYSTIC COMMANDOS AND RETURN THEM TO U.S.A. WHERE THEY MUST FACE TRIAL FOR DESERTING THEIR MASTER, MURDER, MUTINY AND WITCH-CRAFT!.....THE AGENTS HAVE STAINED THEIR FACES TO LOOK LIKE NATIVES.
BUY MORE WAR BONDS
THERE'S THE HOUSE WHERE THE COMMANDOS ARE STAYING.
OUR PLANS ARE ALL SET FOR THE SNATCH!
MAYBE WE CAN GET ALL OF THEM AT ONCE!
PROFESSOR GOEBLES! THE COBRA HAS BEEN INJURED! HE NEEDS YOUR HELP!
CAN ALL OF YOU COME TO HIS SHIP!
YES! AND WE WILL HURRY! UH...WILL YOU COME IN?
OH,OH! WHITE MEN WITH STAINED FACES! SOME KIND OF TRICKERY HERE!
WE COMMANDOS WILL GO IN THE NEXT ROOM AND HELP YOU PACK YOUR INSTRUMENTS, MR. GOEBLES.
NOT SO FAST! LET'S GO JUST AS YOU ARE!
THE BOYS MANAGED TO ESCAPE BUT WE HAVE THE MAIN ONES! WE'LL GET A BIG REWARD FOR THEIR RETURN!
WE MUST RESCUE THEM!
NOT ONLY THAT, THE OLD SCIENTIST KNOWS THE ONLY WAY TO RETURN US TO THE TWENTIETH CENTURY!
THE SECRET AGENTS EXPECT THE BOYS TO ATTEMPT A RESCUE SO THEY LEAVE A DECOY TO LURE THEM ON....
YES, I SAW THEM TAKE TWO MEN AND A GIRL ABOARD THAT SHIP IT SAILS FOR AMERICA AT DAWN!
HA! HA! JUST WAIT, CHIEF! THEY'LL BE SNEAKING ABOARD IN A FEW MINUTES!

NOVEMBER 13, 1943

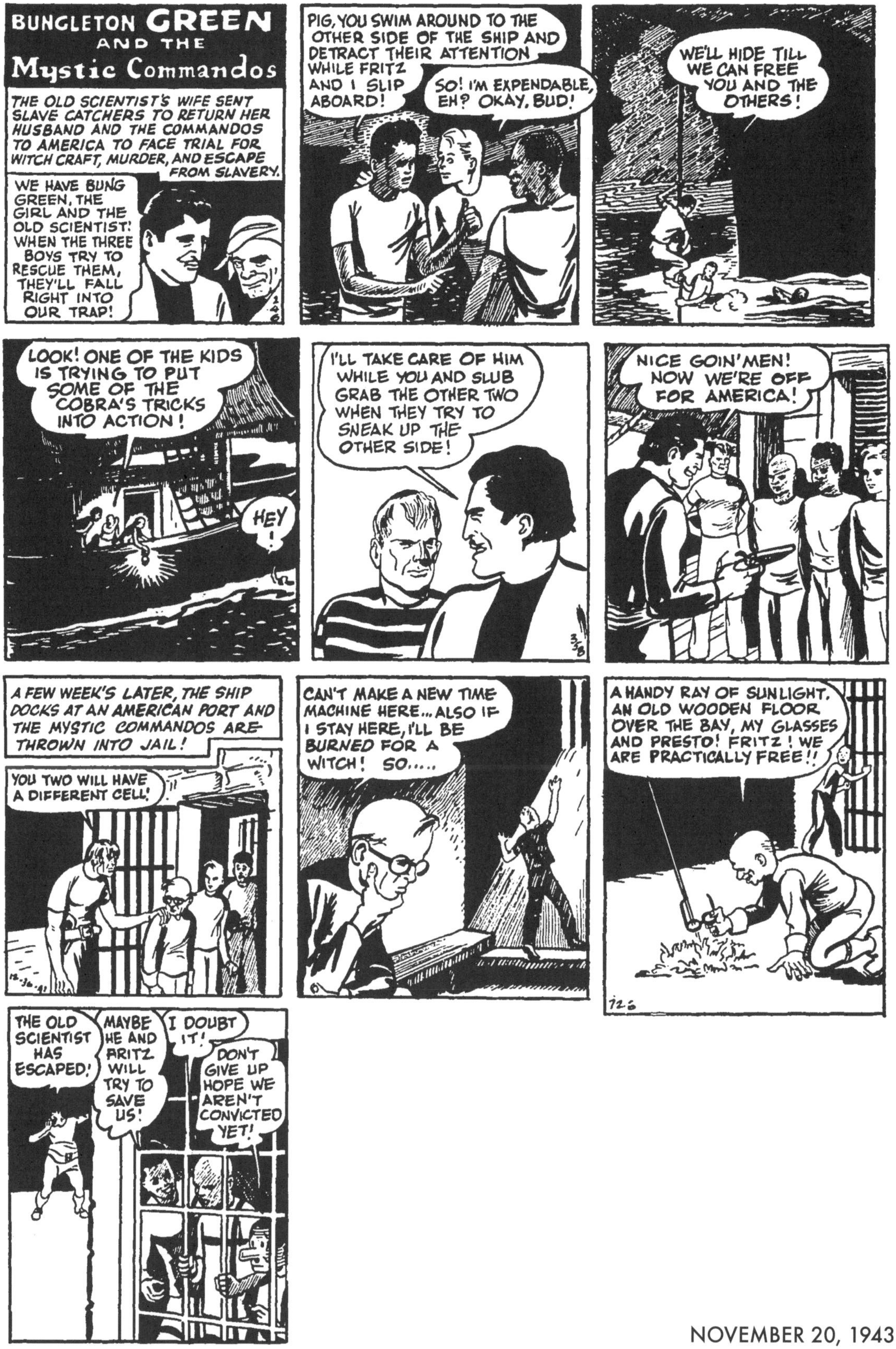
BUNGLETON GREEN AND THE Mystic Commandos
THE OLD SCIENTIST'S WIFE SENT SLAVE CATCHERS TO RETURN HER HUSBAND AND THE COMMANDOS TO AMERICA TO FACE TRIAL FOR WITCH CRAFT, MURDER, AND ESCAPE FROM SLAVERY.
WE HAVE BUNG GREEN, THE GIRL AND THE OLD SCIENTIST! WHEN THE THREE BOYS TRY TO RESCUE THEM, THEY'LL FALL RIGHT INTO OUR TRAP!
PIG, YOU SWIM AROUND TO THE OTHER SIDE OF THE SHIP AND DETRACT THEIR ATTENTION WHILE FRITZ AND I SLIP ABOARD!
SO! I'M EXPENDABLE, EH? OKAY, BUD!
WE'LL HIDE TILL WE CAN FREE YOU AND THE OTHERS!
LOOK! ONE OF THE KIDS IS TRYING TO PUT SOME OF THE COBRA'S TRICKS INTO ACTION!
HEY!
I'LL TAKE CARE OF HIM WHILE YOU AND SLUB GRAB THE OTHER TWO WHEN THEY TRY TO SNEAK UP THE OTHER SIDE!
NICE GOIN' MEN! NOW WE'RE OFF FOR AMERICA!
A FEW WEEK'S LATER, THE SHIP DOCKS AT AN AMERICAN PORT AND THE MYSTIC COMMANDOS ARE THROWN INTO JAIL!
YOU TWO WILL HAVE A DIFFERENT CELL!
CAN'T MAKE A NEW TIME MACHINE HERE... ALSO IF I STAY HERE, I'LL BE BURNED FOR A WITCH! SO.....
A HANDY RAY OF SUNLIGHT, AN OLD WOODEN FLOOR OVER THE BAY, MY GLASSES AND PRESTO! FRITZ! WE ARE PRACTICALLY FREE!!
THE OLD SCIENTIST HAS ESCAPED!
MAYBE HE AND FRITZ WILL TRY TO SAVE US!
I DOUBT IT!
DON'T GIVE UP HOPE WE AREN'T CONVICTED YET!

NOVEMBER 20, 1943

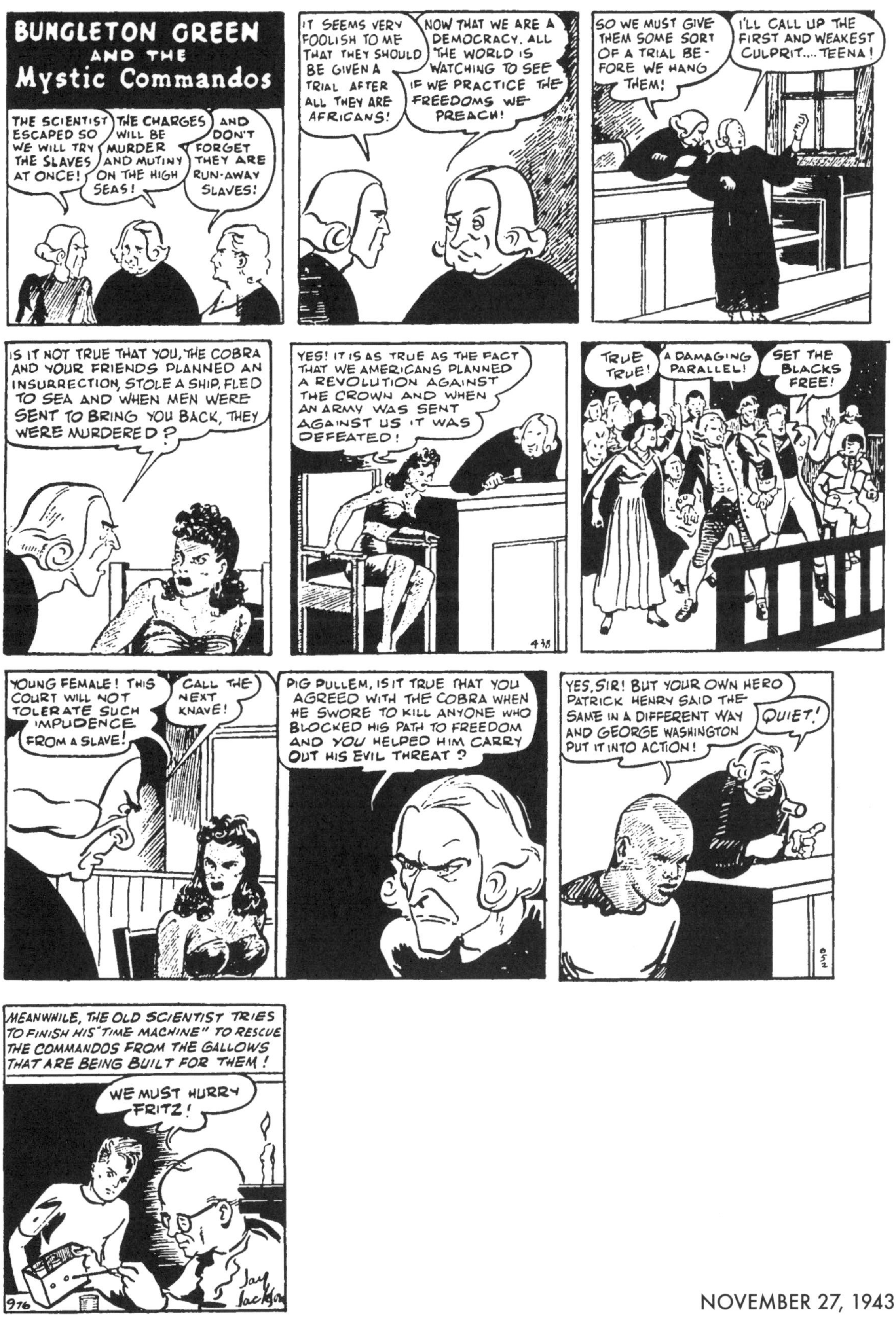

BUNGLETON GREEN AND THE Mystic Commandos
THE SCIENTIST ESCAPED SO WE WILL TRY THE SLAVES AT ONCE!
THE CHARGES WILL BE MURDER AND MUTINY ON THE HIGH SEAS!
AND DON'T FORGET THEY ARE RUN-AWAY SLAVES!
IT SEEMS VERY FOOLISH TO ME THAT THEY SHOULD BE GIVEN A TRIAL AFTER ALL THEY ARE AFRICANS!
NOW THAT WE ARE A DEMOCRACY. ALL THE WORLD IS WATCHING TO SEE IF WE PRACTICE THE FREEDOMS WE PREACH!
SO WE MUST GIVE THEM SOME SORT OF A TRIAL BEFORE WE HANG THEM!
I'LL CALL UP THE FIRST AND WEAKEST CULPRIT.... TEENA!
IS IT NOT TRUE THAT YOU, THE COBRA AND YOUR FRIENDS PLANNED AN INSURRECTION, STOLE A SHIP, FLED TO SEA AND WHEN MEN WERE SENT TO BRING YOU BACK, THEY WERE MURDERED?
YES! IT IS AS TRUE AS THE FACT THAT WE AMERICANS PLANNED A REVOLUTION AGAINST THE CROWN AND WHEN AN ARMY WAS SENT AGAINST US IT WAS DEFEATED!
TRUE TRUE!
A DAMAGING PARALLEL!
SET THE BLACKS FREE!
YOUNG FEMALE! THIS COURT WILL NOT TOLERATE SUCH IMPUDENCE FROM A SLAVE!
CALL THE NEXT KNAVE!
PIG PULLEM, IS IT TRUE THAT YOU AGREED WITH THE COBRA WHEN HE SWORE TO KILL ANYONE WHO BLOCKED HIS PATH TO FREEDOM AND YOU HELPED HIM CARRY OUT HIS EVIL THREAT?
YES, SIR! BUT YOUR OWN HERO PATRICK HENRY SAID THE SAME IN A DIFFERENT WAY AND GEORGE WASHINGTON PUT IT INTO ACTION!
QUIET!
MEANWHILE, THE OLD SCIENTIST TRIES TO FINISH HIS "TIME MACHINE" TO RESCUE THE COMMANDOS FROM THE GALLOWS THAT ARE BEING BUILT FOR THEM!
WE MUST HURRY FRITZ!
Jay Jackson

NOVEMBER 27, 1943

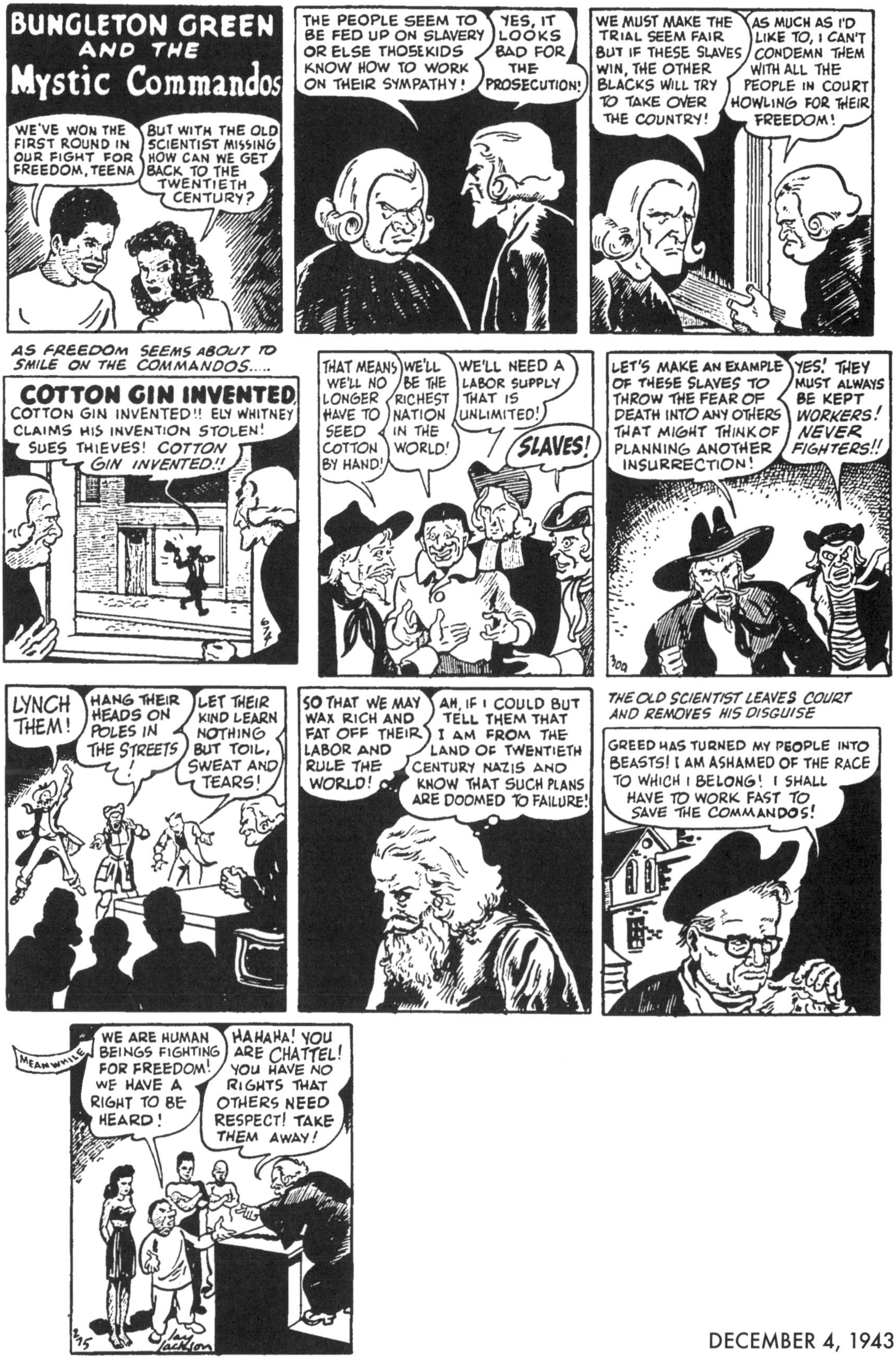

BUNGLETON GREEN AND THE Mystic Commandos
WE'VE WON THE FIRST ROUND IN OUR FIGHT FOR FREEDOM, TEENA
BUT WITH THE OLD SCIENTIST MISSING HOW CAN WE GET BACK TO THE TWENTIETH CENTURY?
THE PEOPLE SEEM TO BE FED UP ON SLAVERY OR ELSE THOSE KIDS KNOW HOW TO WORK ON THEIR SYMPATHY!
YES, IT LOOKS BAD FOR THE PROSECUTION!
WE MUST MAKE THE TRIAL SEEM FAIR BUT IF THESE SLAVES WIN, THE OTHER BLACKS WILL TRY TO TAKE OVER THE COUNTRY!
AS MUCH AS I'D LIKE TO, I CAN'T CONDEMN THEM WITH ALL THE PEOPLE IN COURT HOWLING FOR THEIR FREEDOM!
AS FREEDOM SEEMS ABOUT TO SMILE ON THE COMMANDOS.....
COTTON GIN INVENTED
COTTON GIN INVENTED!! ELY WHITNEY CLAIMS HIS INVENTION STOLEN! SUES THIEVES! COTTON GIN INVENTED!!
THAT MEANS WE'LL NO LONGER HAVE TO SEED COTTON BY HAND!
WE'LL BE THE RICHEST NATION IN THE WORLD!
WE'LL NEED A LABOR SUPPLY THAT IS UNLIMITED!
SLAVES!
LET'S MAKE AN EXAMPLE OF THESE SLAVES TO THROW THE FEAR OF DEATH INTO ANY OTHERS THAT MIGHT THINK OF PLANNING ANOTHER INSURRECTION!
YES! THEY MUST ALWAYS BE KEPT WORKERS! NEVER FIGHTERS!!
LYNCH THEM!
HANG THEIR HEADS ON POLES IN THE STREETS!
LET THEIR KIND LEARN NOTHING BUT TOIL, SWEAT AND TEARS!
SO THAT WE MAY WAX RICH AND FAT OFF THEIR LABOR AND RULE THE WORLD!
AH, IF I COULD BUT TELL THEM THAT I AM FROM THE LAND OF TWENTIETH CENTURY NAZIS AND KNOW THAT SUCH PLANS ARE DOOMED TO FAILURE!
THE OLD SCIENTIST LEAVES COURT AND REMOVES HIS DISGUISE
GREED HAS TURNED MY PEOPLE INTO BEASTS! I AM ASHAMED OF THE RACE TO WHICH I BELONG! I SHALL HAVE TO WORK FAST TO SAVE THE COMMANDOS!
MEANWHILE
WE ARE HUMAN BEINGS FIGHTING FOR FREEDOM! WE HAVE A RIGHT TO BE HEARD!
HAHAHA! YOU ARE CHATTEL! YOU HAVE NO RIGHTS THAT OTHERS NEED RESPECT! TAKE THEM AWAY!
Jay Jackson

DECEMBER 4, 1943

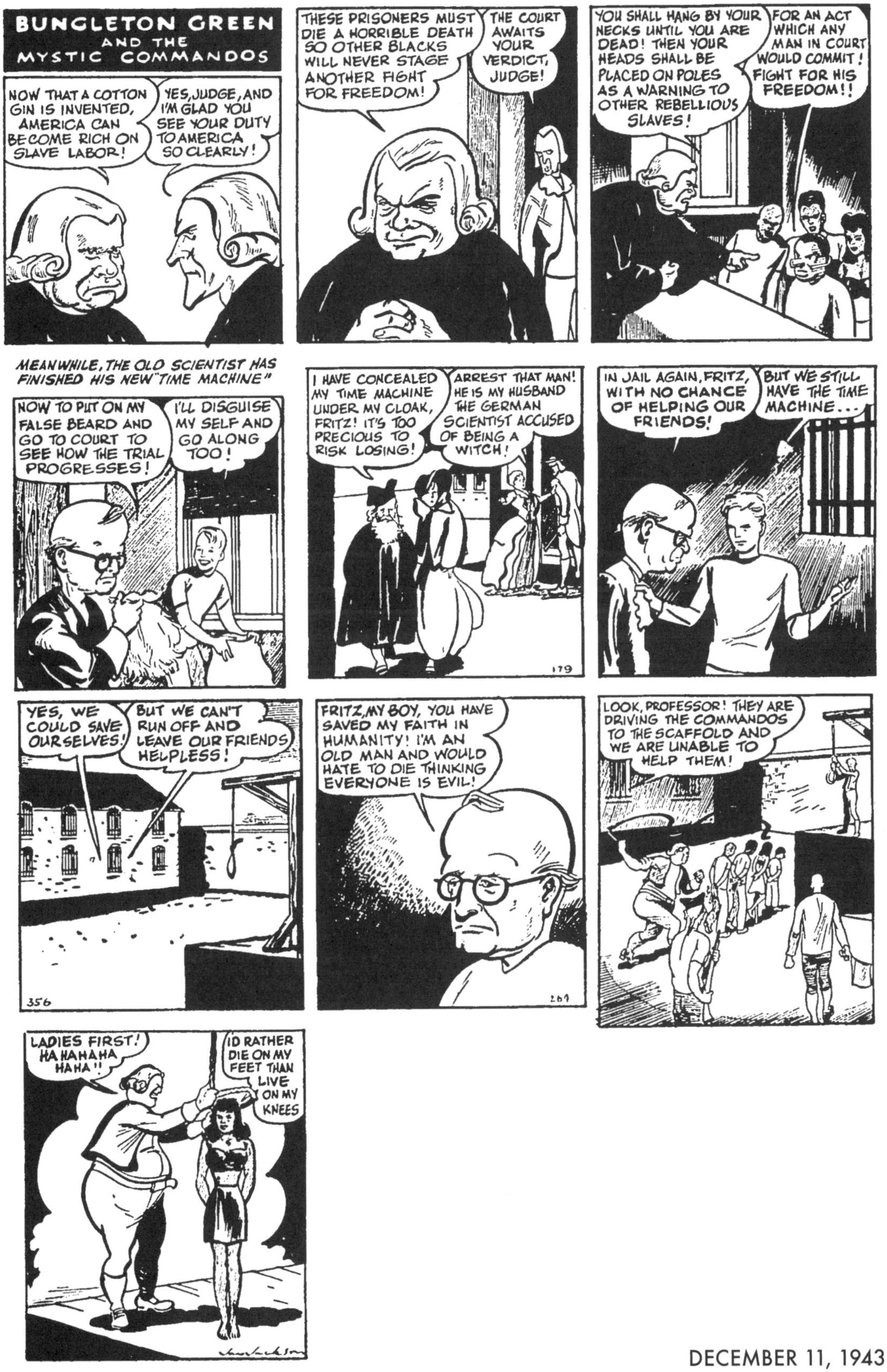
BUNGLETON GREEN AND THE MYSTIC COMMANDOS
NOW THAT A COTTON GIN IS INVENTED, AMERICA CAN BECOME RICH ON SLAVE LABOR!
YES, JUDGE, AND I'M GLAD YOU SEE YOUR DUTY TO AMERICA SO CLEARLY!
THESE PRISONERS MUST DIE A HORRIBLE DEATH SO OTHER BLACKS WILL NEVER STAGE ANOTHER FIGHT FOR FREEDOM!
THE COURT AWAITS YOUR VERDICT, JUDGE!
YOU SHALL HANG BY YOUR NECKS UNTIL YOU ARE DEAD! THEN YOUR HEADS SHALL BE PLACED ON POLES AS A WARNING TO OTHER REBELLIOUS SLAVES!
FOR AN ACT WHICH ANY MAN IN COURT WOULD COMMIT! FIGHT FOR HIS FREEDOM!!
MEANWHILE, THE OLD SCIENTIST HAS FINISHED HIS NEW "TIME MACHINE"
NOW TO PUT ON MY FALSE BEARD AND GO TO COURT TO SEE HOW THE TRIAL PROGRESSES!
I'LL DISGUISE MY SELF AND GO ALONG TOO!
I HAVE CONCEALED MY TIME MACHINE UNDER MY CLOAK, FRITZ! IT'S TOO PRECIOUS TO RISK LOSING!
ARREST THAT MAN! HE IS MY HUSBAND THE GERMAN SCIENTIST ACCUSED OF BEING A WITCH!
IN JAIL AGAIN, FRITZ, WITH NO CHANCE OF HELPING OUR FRIENDS!
BUT WE STILL HAVE THE TIME MACHINE...
YES, WE COULD SAVE OURSELVES!
BUT WE CAN'T RUN OFF AND LEAVE OUR FRIENDS HELPLESS!
FRITZ, MY BOY, YOU HAVE SAVED MY FAITH IN HUMANITY! I'M AN OLD MAN AND WOULD HATE TO DIE THINKING EVERYONE IS EVIL!
LOOK, PROFESSOR! THEY ARE DRIVING THE COMMANDOS TO THE SCAFFOLD AND WE ARE UNABLE TO HELP THEM!
LADIES FIRST! HA HA HA HA HA HA!!
ID RATHER DIE ON MY FEET THAN LIVE ON MY KNEES

DECEMBER 11, 1943

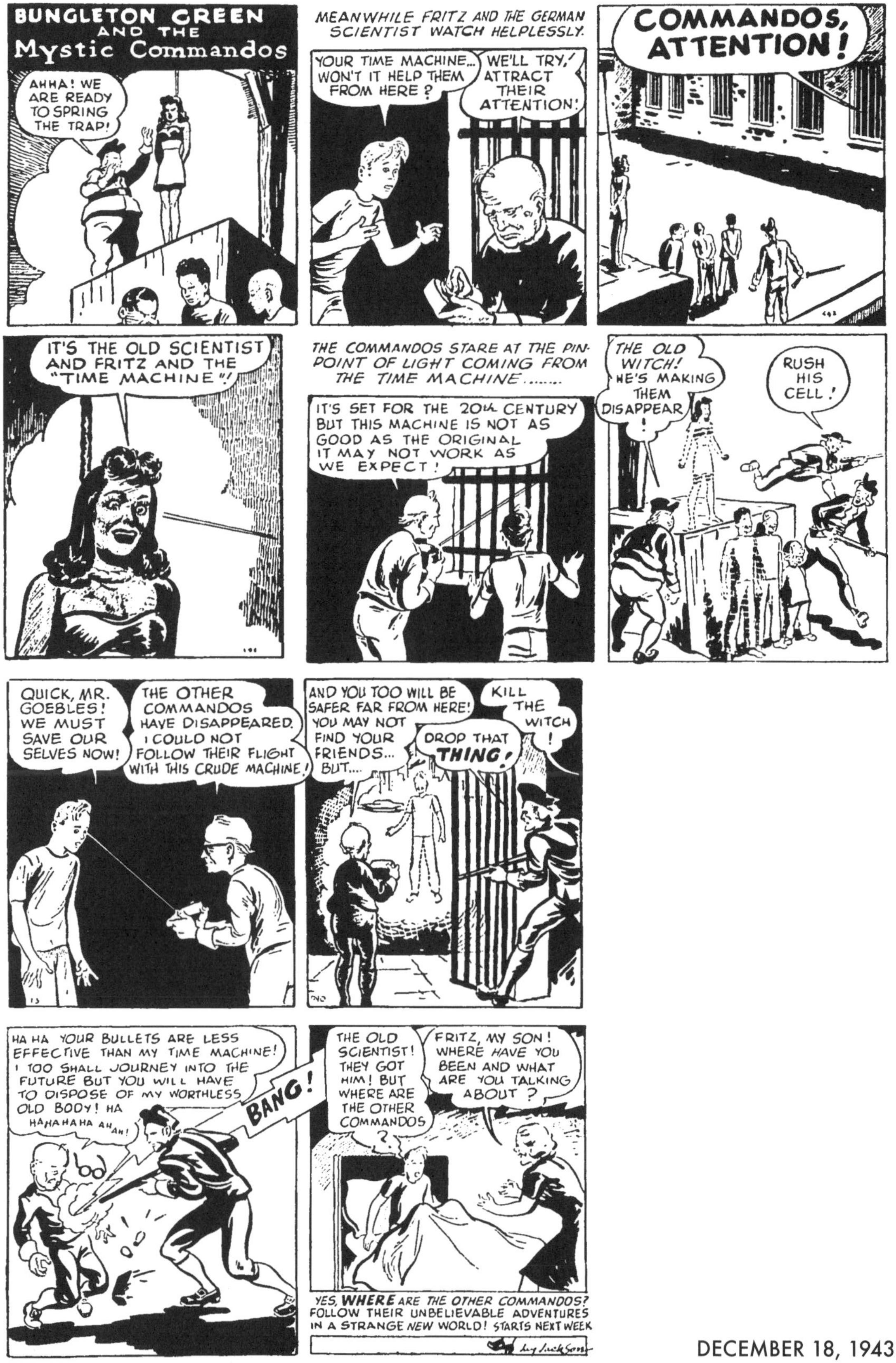
BUNGLETON GREEN AND THE Mystic Commandos
AHHA! WE ARE READY TO SPRING THE TRAP!
MEANWHILE FRITZ AND THE GERMAN SCIENTIST WATCH HELPLESSLY.
YOUR TIME MACHINE... WON'T IT HELP THEM FROM HERE?
WE'LL TRY! ATTRACT THEIR ATTENTION!
COMMANDOS, ATTENTION!
IT'S THE OLD SCIENTIST AND FRITZ AND THE "TIME MACHINE"!
THE COMMANDOS STARE AT THE PIN-POINT OF LIGHT COMING FROM THE TIME MACHINE........
IT'S SET FOR THE 20th CENTURY BUT THIS MACHINE IS NOT AS GOOD AS THE ORIGINAL IT MAY NOT WORK AS WE EXPECT!
THE OLD WITCH! HE'S MAKING THEM DISAPPEAR!
RUSH HIS CELL!
QUICK, MR. GOEBLES! WE MUST SAVE OUR SELVES NOW!
THE OTHER COMMANDOS HAVE DISAPPEARED. I COULD NOT FOLLOW THEIR FLIGHT WITH THIS CRUDE MACHINE!
AND YOU TOO WILL BE SAFER FAR FROM HERE! YOU MAY NOT FIND YOUR FRIENDS... BUT....
KILL THE WITCH!
DROP THAT THING!
HA HA YOUR BULLETS ARE LESS EFFECTIVE THAN MY TIME MACHINE! I TOO SHALL JOURNEY INTO THE FUTURE BUT YOU WILL HAVE TO DISPOSE OF MY WORTHLESS OLD BODY! HA HAHAHAHA AHAH!
BANG!
THE OLD SCIENTIST! THEY GOT HIM! BUT WHERE ARE THE OTHER COMMANDOS?
FRITZ, MY SON! WHERE HAVE YOU BEEN AND WHAT ARE YOU TALKING ABOUT?
YES, WHERE ARE THE OTHER COMMANDOS? FOLLOW THEIR UNBELIEVABLE ADVENTURES IN A STRANGE NEW WORLD! STARTS NEXT WEEK

TERNATIONAL ROCKET LINES
I'M GLAD YOU BROUGHT ME ALONG, LOTTA'
THANKS, BUD. BUT I'M AFRAID THE GREEN MEN WILL MAKE YOU THINK YOU'RE BACK IN 1944 AMERICA!

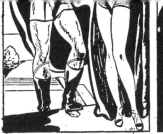

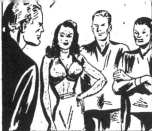

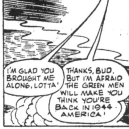

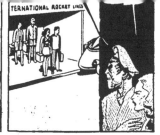

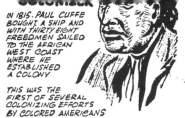

IN 1815, PAUL CUFFE BOUGHT A SHIP AND WITH THIRTY EIGHT FREEDMEN SAILED TO THE AFRICAN WEST COAST WHERE HE ESTABLISHED A COLONY
THIS WAS THE FIRST OF SEVERAL COLONIZING EFFORTS BY COLORED AMERICANS

2043

December 1943 – DECEMBER 1944

epublican nominee for the general ssembly from the Third Illinois enatorial district, had run third in e primary, with two to be nomiated. One of the successful candates, A. Andrew Torrence, was urdered the day before election. nowden, in asking $50,000 damages gainst the Cook county canvassing oard, contended he was denied ertification because he was not a regular Republican."

The ommission of his name from e ballot, said Snowden, deprived im of his constitutional rights, rivileges and immunities of the qual protection of the laws.

Chief Justice Stone, however, in eclaring that Mr. Snowden's conitutional rights were not affectd by State Board's action, said that here discrimination was sufficently shown, the right to relief nder the equal protection clause the constitution was not diminhed because the matter had to o with political rights.

"But," the Chief Justice added, the necessity of showing purposel discrimination is no less in a ase involving political rights than n any other. It was not intended y the Fourteenth Amendment and he Civil Rights Act that all maters formerly within the exclusive ognizance of the states should beome matters of national concern.

Justice Stone pointed out that in the Supreme Court arguments, Mr. Snowden disclaimed any contention that class or racial discrimination was involved, but merely cited that his constitutional right to protection had been violated.

Californian Seeks Seat In Congress

LOS ANGELES.—Walter L. Gordon Jr., prominent local lawyer, looms as a threat to gain the seat in congress from the 14th California district now occupied by Thomas F. Ford (D) who will again seek reelection.

Atty. Gordon, young, vigorous, highly capable member of the California bar, is regarded as one of the ablest lawyers in the state.

Gordon has not personally ever sought public office. In previous election campaigns friends have attempted to get him to enter his name on a ballot, but have met with a refusal. In the forthcoming congressional race, it is reported he has relented.

Atty. Gordon is Los Angeles born, educated at the University of Southern California and graduated from Ohio State Law school.

first raid of the American Pacific fleet; Marcus Island, Wake Island, on the convoy that bombed Tokyo; Coral Sea battle; Midway Island; battle of Steward Island; occupation of Guadacanal, and the battle of Santa Cruz, October 26, last, which he considers the hardest of all the encounters.

Still floating after several battles, their carrier received the President's citation for excellent performance of duty. Lester Caliste holds the following citations: President's Citation, American Defense, Asiatic Pacific, American Theatre of War, Good Conduct Medal, Expedition Medal and Alaska campaign citation.

His brother, Louis, holds all of the above citations and also the Purple Heart. Louis enlisted in the Navy in 1939; Lester in November, 1940.

They are the sons of Mr. and Mrs. Louis Caliste Sr., who also have two other sons in the Navy. The elder Caliste saw service in Uncle Sam's fleet during World War I for eight years.

The Negro in world politics? Read John Robert Badger's "World Views."

borrower who pays certain amounts towards the extinguishment of his mortgage loan every month until the mortgage loan has been entirely discharged is practicing amortization. In the same way the railroads whose rental for equipment includes regular payments against the cost of the equipment is amortizing the purchase price.

Walter Lowe

Ques.: What is meant by the term "dead assets"?

Ans.: Dead assets refers to property which has no monetary value.

LANGUAGE PROFS TO MEET

NASHVILLE, Tenn.—Dr. Lorenzo D. Turner of Fisk university and Dr. Charles Pendleton of George Peabody college for Teachers, will be principal speaker at the regional meeting of the Association of Teachers of Language in Negro colleges which meets here Feb. 24 at Tennessee A. and T. State college.

on the same road for the past 25 years.

the Negro teachers and principals of Charleston, S. C., is set for trial

IF COLDS' COUGHING BARKS YOU INTO A DOG'S LIFE

Don't stay in the dog house. Get real relief from that cough, the chest tightness and muscular aches and pains due to a cold. Get Penetro and see how it relieves these miseries of a cold. Rub Penetro on chest, throat and back. It has a base containing old-fashioned mutton suet. Pioneer grandma used medicated mutton suet to relieve these symptoms of a cold. And Penetro, the modern medication, has 5 active ingredients to help you, and is stainless and white. Penetro works two ways to bring relief. Inside, it comforts and soothes nose and throat irritated membranes. Outside, it acts like a warming comforting plaster, stimulating blood flow right at the spot where you rub it on. Keep Penetro handy all during the colds' season. You and your family will be delighted with the relief Penetro brings to these colds' miseries. The regular size costs 25c, double supply only 35c. Always demand Penetro

AT CHICAGO FURNITURE MART

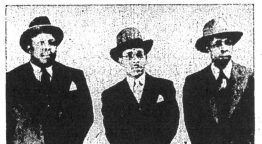

Owners of the Furniture Aid, Inc., of Detroit, were in Chicago last week on their annual visit to attend the American Furniture Market exhibit and show. The Detroiters placed orders for new stock for their spring and summer trade. Furniture Aid officials shown, left to right, are: Bob Settle, treasurer; William Singleton,

Genuine
Harlem Queens
Lace STOCKINGS
$1
Sheer
CHIFFON WEIGHT
COLORS
Terra Cotta,
Havana Tan,
Rusticana,
Wine and
Black..
SEND $1.00 WITH YOUR NAME, ADDRESS, SIZE AND COLOR WANTED
We pay all the Shipping charges
MONEY BACK GUARANTEE
NATIONAL CLOTHING CO.
4606 S. ASHLAND AVE.
CHICAGO 9, ILL.

BIVINS VAN LINES

Local and Long Distance Moving

BIVINS VAN LINES
COAST TO COAST

"WE MOVE THE WORLD"

LONG DISTANCE MOVING and SHIPPING TO ANY PART of the UNITED STATES

Twenty-four Hour Telephone Service

CALL, WRITE OR TELEGRAPH

BIVINS VAN LINES

5531 South State Street, Chicago, Ill. ENGlewood 3434

BUY WAR BONDS—BUY DEFENSE STAMPS

Bonded and Insured Warehouse

WE STORE YOUR FURNITURE IN OUR FIREPROOF WAREHOUSE

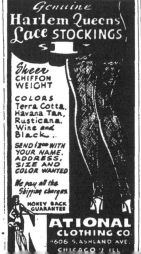

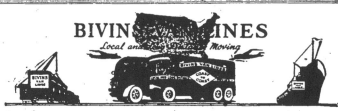

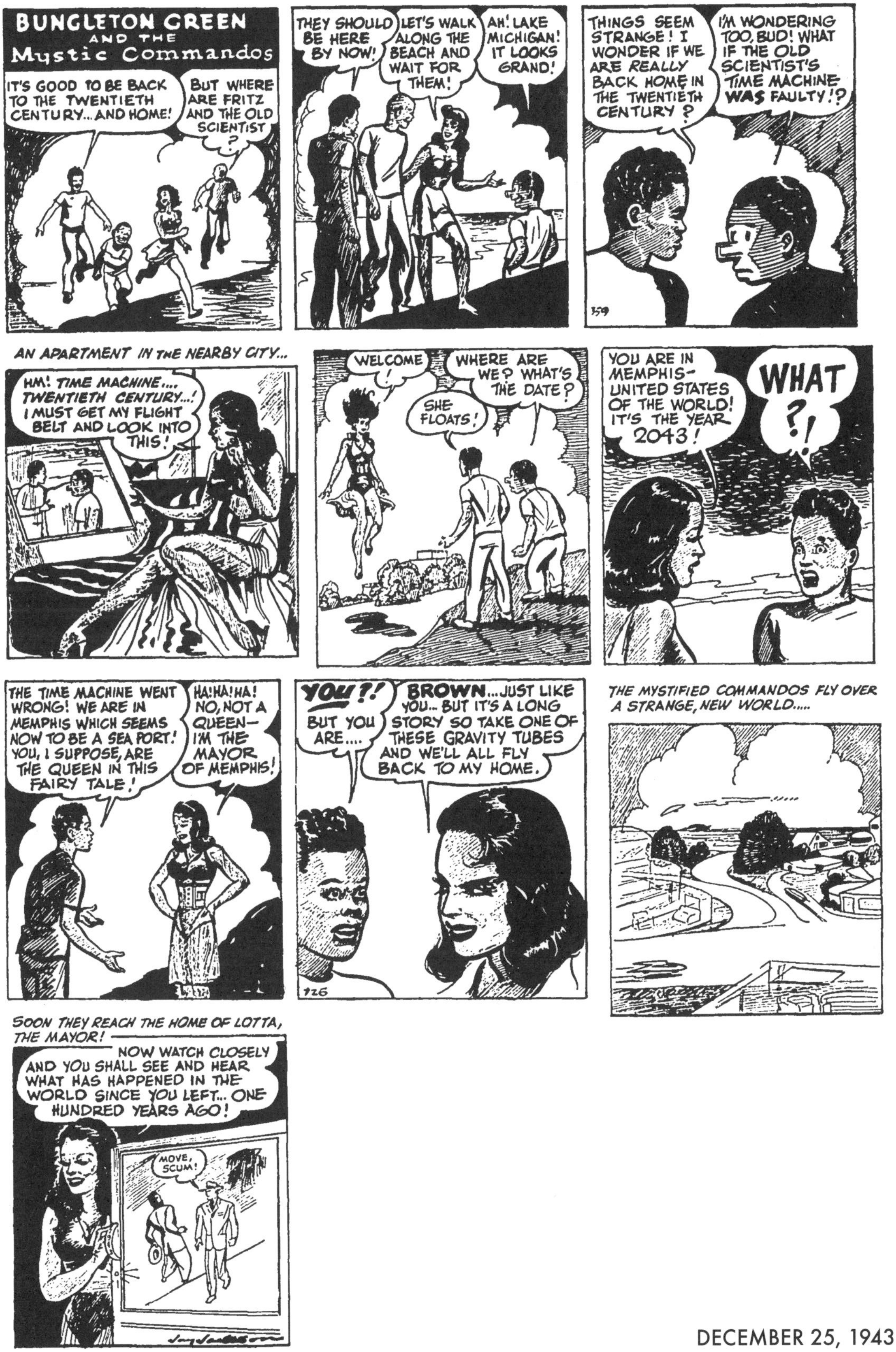

BUNGLETON GREEN AND THE Mystic Commandos
IT'S GOOD TO BE BACK TO THE TWENTIETH CENTURY... AND HOME!
BUT WHERE ARE FRITZ AND THE OLD SCIENTIST ?
THEY SHOULD BE HERE BY NOW!
LET'S WALK ALONG THE BEACH AND WAIT FOR THEM!
AH! LAKE MICHIGAN! IT LOOKS GRAND!
THINGS SEEM STRANGE! I WONDER IF WE ARE REALLY BACK HOME IN THE TWENTIETH CENTURY ?
I'M WONDERING TOO, BUD! WHAT IF THE OLD SCIENTIST'S TIME MACHINE WAS FAULTY!?
AN APARTMENT IN THE NEARBY CITY...
HM! TIME MACHINE.... TWENTIETH CENTURY...! I MUST GET MY FLIGHT BELT AND LOOK INTO THIS!
WELCOME!
WHERE ARE WE? WHAT'S THE DATE?
SHE FLOATS!
YOU ARE IN MEMPHIS- UNITED STATES OF THE WORLD! IT'S THE YEAR 2043!
WHAT ?!
THE TIME MACHINE WENT WRONG! WE ARE IN MEMPHIS WHICH SEEMS NOW TO BE A SEA PORT! YOU, I SUPPOSE, ARE THE QUEEN IN THIS FAIRY TALE!
HA!HA!HA! NO, NOT A QUEEN— I'M THE MAYOR OF MEMPHIS!
YOU?!
BUT YOU ARE....
BROWN... JUST LIKE YOU.. BUT IT'S A LONG STORY SO TAKE ONE OF THESE GRAVITY TUBES AND WE'LL ALL FLY BACK TO MY HOME.
THE MYSTIFIED COMMANDOS FLY OVER A STRANGE, NEW WORLD.....
SOON THEY REACH THE HOME OF LOTTA, THE MAYOR!
NOW WATCH CLOSELY AND YOU SHALL SEE AND HEAR WHAT HAS HAPPENED IN THE WORLD SINCE YOU LEFT... ONE HUNDRED YEARS AGO!
MOVE, SCUM!

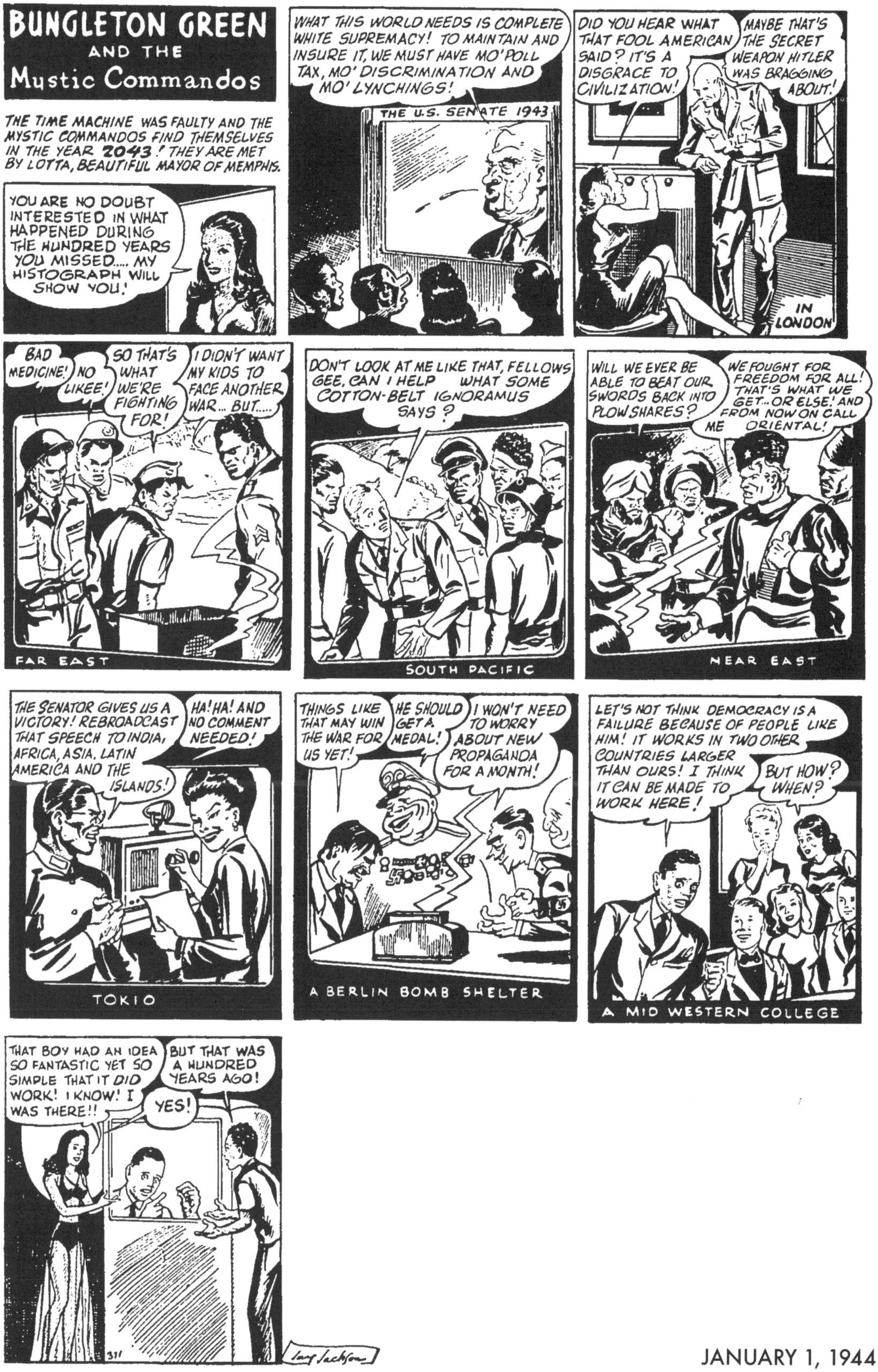
BUNGLETON GREEN AND THE Mystic Commandos
THE TIME MACHINE WAS FAULTY AND THE MYSTIC COMMANDOS FIND THEMSELVES IN THE YEAR 2043! THEY ARE MET BY LOTTA, BEAUTIFUL MAYOR OF MEMPHIS.
YOU ARE NO DOUBT INTERESTED IN WHAT HAPPENED DURING THE HUNDRED YEARS YOU MISSED..... MY HISTOGRAPH WILL SHOW YOU!
WHAT THIS WORLD NEEDS IS COMPLETE WHITE SUPREMACY! TO MAINTAIN AND INSURE IT, WE MUST HAVE MO' POLL TAX, MO' DISCRIMINATION AND MO' LYNCHINGS!
THE U.S. SENATE 1943
DID YOU HEAR WHAT THAT FOOL AMERICAN SAID? IT'S A DISGRACE TO CIVILIZATION!
MAYBE THAT'S THE SECRET WEAPON HITLER WAS BRAGGING ABOUT!
IN LONDON
BAD MEDICINE!
NO LIKEE!
SO THAT'S WHAT WE'RE FIGHTING FOR!
I DIDN'T WANT MY KIDS TO FACE ANOTHER WAR... BUT....
FAR EAST
DON'T LOOK AT ME LIKE THAT, FELLOWS GEE, CAN I HELP WHAT SOME COTTON-BELT IGNORAMUS SAYS?
SOUTH PACIFIC
WILL WE EVER BE ABLE TO BEAT OUR SWORDS BACK INTO PLOW SHARES?
WE FOUGHT FOR FREEDOM FOR ALL! THAT'S WHAT WE GET...OR ELSE! AND FROM NOW ON CALL ME ORIENTAL!
NEAR EAST
THE SENATOR GIVES US A VICTORY! REBROADCAST THAT SPEECH TO INDIA, AFRICA, ASIA, LATIN AMERICA AND THE ISLANDS!
HA! HA! AND NO COMMENT NEEDED!
TOKIO
THINGS LIKE THAT MAY WIN THE WAR FOR US YET!
HE SHOULD GET A MEDAL!
I WON'T NEED TO WORRY ABOUT NEW PROPAGANDA FOR A MONTH!
A BERLIN BOMB SHELTER
LET'S NOT THINK DEMOCRACY IS A FAILURE BECAUSE OF PEOPLE LIKE HIM! IT WORKS IN TWO OTHER COUNTRIES LARGER THAN OURS! I THINK IT CAN BE MADE TO WORK HERE!
BUT HOW? WHEN?
A MID WESTERN COLLEGE
THAT BOY HAD AN IDEA SO FANTASTIC YET SO SIMPLE THAT IT DID WORK! I KNOW! I WAS THERE!!
BUT THAT WAS A HUNDRED YEARS AGO!
YES!
311

JANUARY 1, 1944

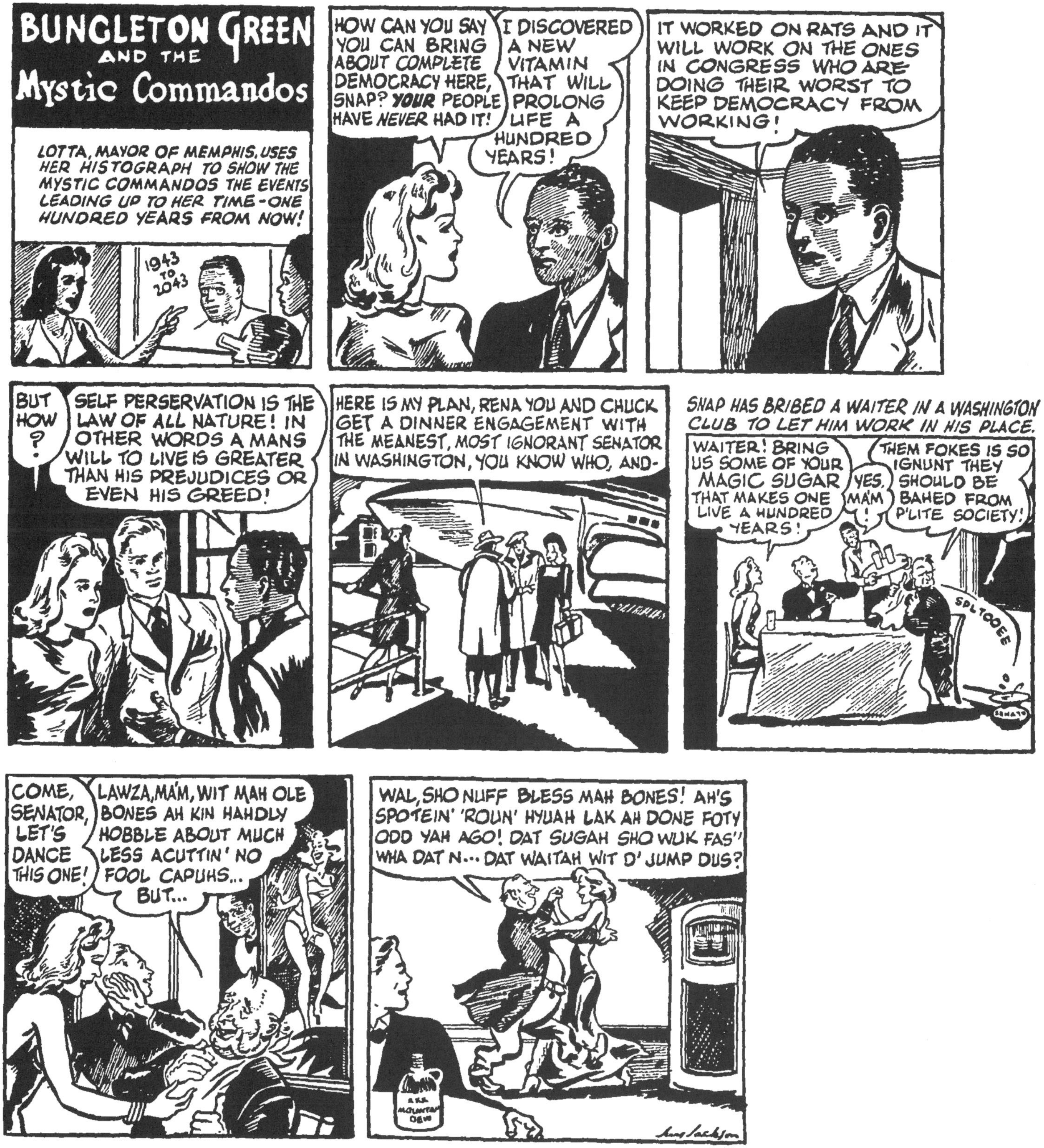
BUNGLETON GREEN AND THE Mystic Commandos
LOTTA, MAYOR OF MEMPHIS, USES HER HISTOGRAPH TO SHOW THE MYSTIC COMMANDOS THE EVENTS LEADING UP TO HER TIME - ONE HUNDRED YEARS FROM NOW!
1943 TO 2043
HOW CAN YOU SAY YOU CAN BRING ABOUT COMPLETE DEMOCRACY HERE, SNAP? YOUR PEOPLE HAVE NEVER HAD IT!
I DISCOVERED A NEW VITAMIN THAT WILL PROLONG LIFE A HUNDRED YEARS!
IT WORKED ON RATS AND IT WILL WORK ON THE ONES IN CONGRESS WHO ARE DOING THEIR WORST TO KEEP DEMOCRACY FROM WORKING!
BUT HOW ?
SELF PERSERVATION IS THE LAW OF ALL NATURE! IN OTHER WORDS A MANS WILL TO LIVE IS GREATER THAN HIS PREJUDICES OR EVEN HIS GREED!
HERE IS MY PLAN, RENA YOU AND CHUCK GET A DINNER ENGAGEMENT WITH THE MEANEST, MOST IGNORANT SENATOR IN WASHINGTON, YOU KNOW WHO, AND-
SNAP HAS BRIBED A WAITER IN A WASHINGTON CLUB TO LET HIM WORK IN HIS PLACE.
WAITER! BRING US SOME OF YOUR MAGIC SUGAR THAT MAKES ONE LIVE A HUNDRED YEARS!
YES, MA'M !
THEM FOKES IS SO IGNUNT THEY SHOULD BE BAHED FROM P'LITE SOCIETY!
SPLTOOEE
COME, SENATOR, LET'S DANCE THIS ONE!
LAWZA, MA'M, WIT MAH OLE BONES AH KIN HAHDLY HOBBLE ABOUT MUCH LESS ACUTTIN' NO FOOL CAPUHS... BUT...
WAL, SHO NUFF BLESS MAH BONES! AH'S SPOTEIN' 'ROUN' HYUAH LAK AH DONE FOTY ODD YAH AGO! DAT SUGAH SHO WUK FAS'! WHA DAT N... DAT WAITAH WIT D' JUMP DUS?

JANUARY 8, 1944

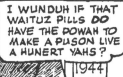

Bungleton GREEN AND THE "Mystic Commandos"

THE MYSTIC COMMANDOS FIND THEMSELVES IN THE YEAR **2044.** THEY ARE MET BY LOTTA, COLORED MAYOR OF MEMPHIS! SHE SHOWS THEM, ON HER HISTOGRAPH, HOW ONE BOY, SNAP DRAGON, BROUGHT ABOUT FULL DEMOCRATIC RIGHTS FOR HIS RACE ....

I WUNDUH IF THAT WAITUZ PILLS **DO** HAVE THE POWAH TO MAKE A PUSON LIVE A HUNERT YAHS?

AH SHO WAS A FEELIN! FINE GALAVANTIN' 'ROUN' WI' DAT PURTY LIL GAL LAS' WEEK!

HOWSOMEVAH, AH FEELS KINDA BEAT OUT THIS MAWNIN SOS AH RECON AS HOW AH'LL MOSEY IN HYAH AN' SEE KIN AH PUCHUS SOME MO PILLS FROM HIM!

HOWDY, MAM, AH'S A LOOKIN' FO DE WAITUH WI' DE JUMP DUS...

SORRY, SENATOR, HE WAS HERE BUT A SHORT TIME BUT I'LL GET YOU HIS ADDRESS!

LAWZY, WHAT A CRUMBY ALLEY DUMP! OH, WELL, IT'S FITTEN ENOUGH FO....

GOOD MORNING, SENATOR! I WAS EXPECTING YOU!

AH WANTS TO BUY SOME O' YO PILLS!

SORRY, SENATOR. THEY ARE NOT FOR SALE BUT I **GIVE** THEM TO MY FRIENDS!

SHO'NUFF, NOW! WAL, Y'ALL KNOWS US SUTHUNUS IS YO BES' FRIENS! WHY MA OLE MAMMY WAS A BIG, B....

YES, I KNOW. BUT YOUR RECENT SPEECH IN THE SENATE UPHOLDING MOB RULE, POLL TAX... ETCETERA...

BRUMPF! LE'S TALK ERBOUT DE PILLS.

GLADLY, IF YOU'LL STOP USING YOUR SENATORIAL OFFICE FOR KEEPING MINORITIES "IN THEIR PLACE"!

NEVAH! AH'LL DIE FUST!

YOU'D BE HELPING DEMOCRACY IF YOU DID! BUT IF YOU DO AS I SAY YOU CAN HELP DEMOCRACY AND **LIVE!**

?!? UM

JANUARY 15, 1944

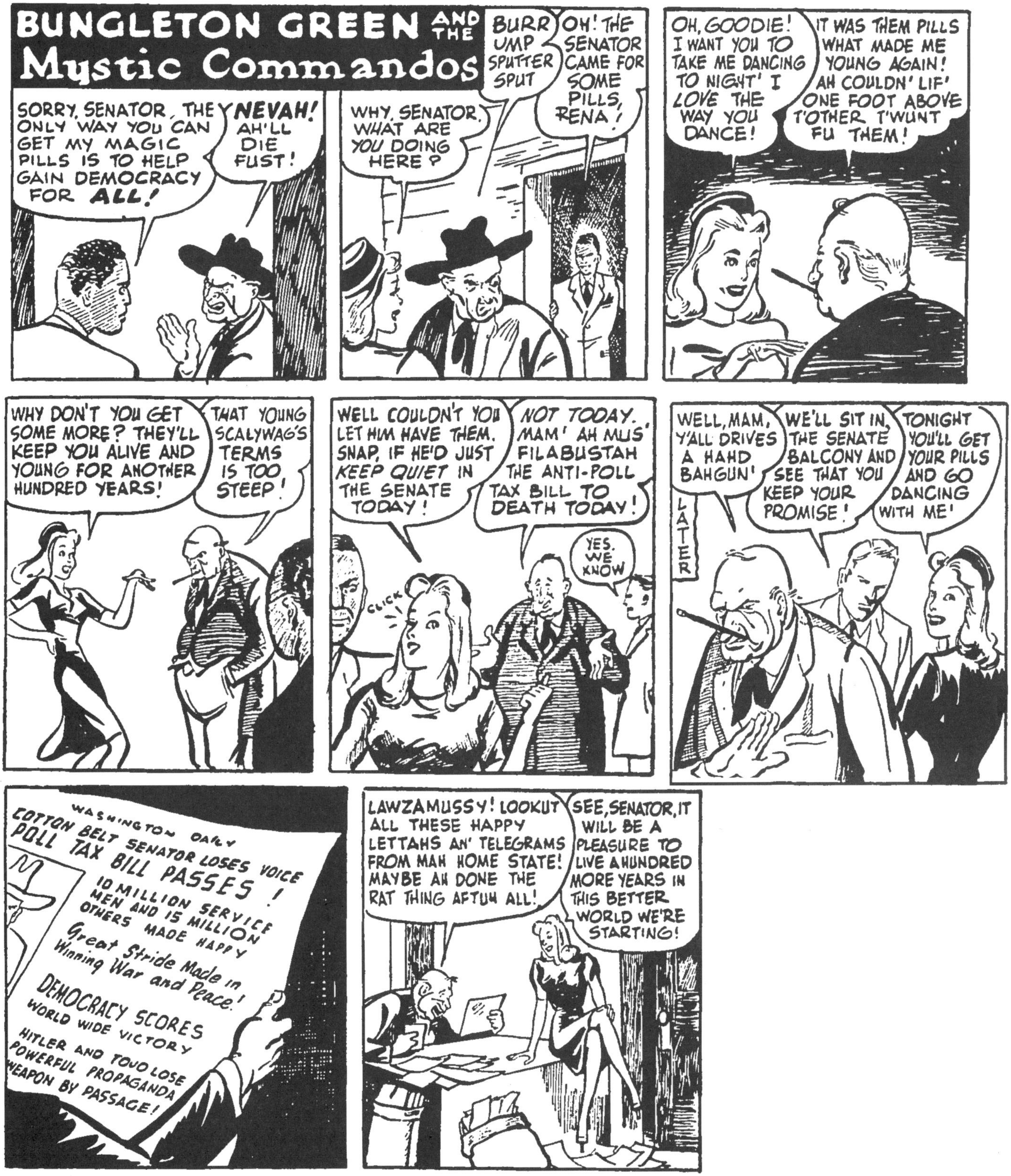
BUNGLETON GREEN AND THE Mystic Commandos
SORRY, SENATOR, THE ONLY WAY YOU CAN GET MY MAGIC PILLS IS TO HELP GAIN DEMOCRACY FOR ALL!
NEVAH! AH'LL DIE FUST!
BURR UMP SPUTTER SPUT
WHY, SENATOR, WHAT ARE YOU DOING HERE?
OH! THE SENATOR CAME FOR SOME PILLS, RENA!
OH, GOODIE! I WANT YOU TO TAKE ME DANCING TO NIGHT' I LOVE THE WAY YOU DANCE!
IT WAS THEM PILLS WHAT MADE ME YOUNG AGAIN! AH COULDN' LIF' ONE FOOT ABOVE T'OTHER T'WUNT FU THEM!
WHY DON'T YOU GET SOME MORE? THEY'LL KEEP YOU ALIVE AND YOUNG FOR ANOTHER HUNDRED YEARS!
THAT YOUNG SCALYWAG'S TERMS IS TOO STEEP!
WELL COULDN'T YOU LET HIM HAVE THEM, SNAP, IF HE'D JUST KEEP QUIET IN THE SENATE TODAY!
NOT TODAY, MAM' AH MUS' FILABUSTAH THE ANTI-POLL TAX BILL TO DEATH TODAY!
CLICK
YES. WE KNOW
LATER
WELL, MAM, Y'ALL DRIVES A HAHD BAHGUN'
WE'LL SIT IN THE SENATE BALCONY AND SEE THAT YOU KEEP YOUR PROMISE!
TONIGHT YOU'LL GET YOUR PILLS AND GO DANCING WITH ME'
WASHINGTON DAILY
COTTON BELT SENATOR LOSES VOICE
POLL TAX BILL PASSES!
10 MILLION SERVICE MEN AND 15 MILLION OTHERS MADE HAPPY
Great Stride Made in Winning War and Peace!
DEMOCRACY SCORES WORLD WIDE VICTORY
HITLER AND TOJO LOSE POWERFUL PROPAGANDA WEAPON BY PASSAGE!
LAWZAMUSSY! LOOKUT ALL THESE HAPPY LETTAHS AN' TELEGRAMS FROM MAH HOME STATE! MAYBE AH DONE THE RAT THING AFTUH ALL!
SEE, SENATOR, IT WILL BE A PLEASURE TO LIVE A HUNDRED MORE YEARS IN THIS BETTER WORLD WE'RE STARTING!

JANUARY 22, 1944

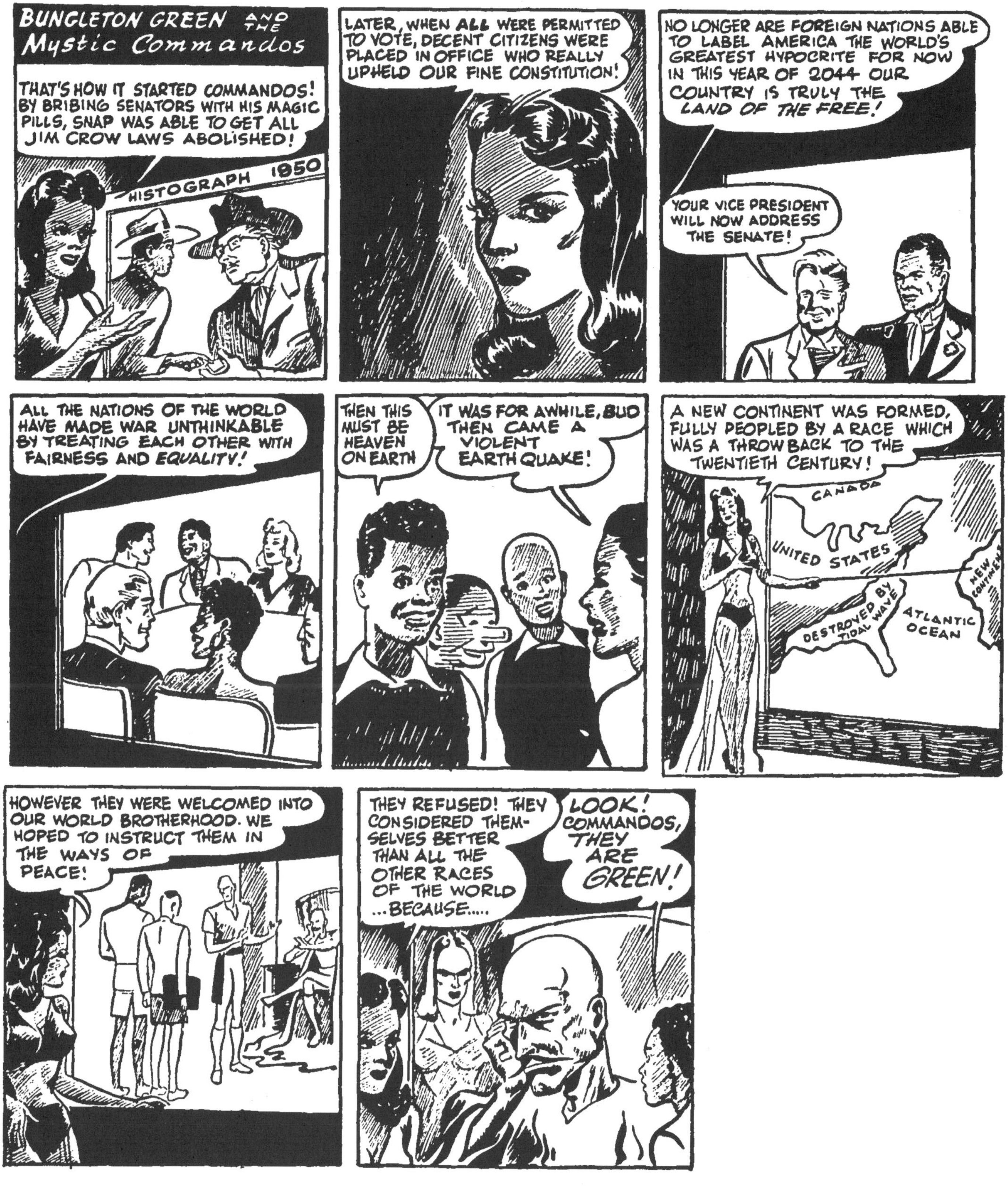

BUNGLETON GREEN AND THE Mystic Commandos
THAT'S HOW IT STARTED COMMANDOS! BY BRIBING SENATORS WITH HIS MAGIC PILLS, SNAP WAS ABLE TO GET ALL JIM CROW LAWS ABOLISHED!
HISTOGRAPH 1950
LATER, WHEN ALL WERE PERMITTED TO VOTE, DECENT CITIZENS WERE PLACED IN OFFICE WHO REALLY UPHELD OUR FINE CONSTITUTION!
NO LONGER ARE FOREIGN NATIONS ABLE TO LABEL AMERICA THE WORLD'S GREATEST HYPOCRITE FOR NOW IN THIS YEAR OF 2044 OUR COUNTRY IS TRULY THE LAND OF THE FREE!
YOUR VICE PRESIDENT WILL NOW ADDRESS THE SENATE!
ALL THE NATIONS OF THE WORLD HAVE MADE WAR UNTHINKABLE BY TREATING EACH OTHER WITH FAIRNESS AND EQUALITY!
THEN THIS MUST BE HEAVEN ON EARTH
IT WAS FOR AWHILE, BUD THEN CAME A VIOLENT EARTHQUAKE!
A NEW CONTINENT WAS FORMED, FULLY PEOPLED BY A RACE WHICH WAS A THROWBACK TO THE TWENTIETH CENTURY!
CANADA
UNITED STATES
NEW CONTINENT
DESTROYED BY TIDAL WAVE
ATLANTIC OCEAN
HOWEVER THEY WERE WELCOMED INTO OUR WORLD BROTHERHOOD. WE HOPED TO INSTRUCT THEM IN THE WAYS OF PEACE!
THEY REFUSED! THEY CONSIDERED THEMSELVES BETTER THAN ALL THE OTHER RACES OF THE WORLD ...BECAUSE.....
LOOK! COMMANDOS, THEY ARE GREEN!

JANUARY 29, 1944

BUNGLETON GREEN
AND THE
Mystic Commandos

OUT OF THE SEA BOTTOM COMES A NEW CRUEL RACE OF GREEN MEN WHO ARE THROW BACKS TO THE 20th CENTURY AND HOPE TO RULE THE PEACEFUL WORLD OF 2044

WE ARE DIFFERENT AND BETTER THAN ALL OTHER RACES!

YES, MASTER! BECAUSE WE ARE GREEN!

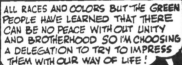

WE WERE SENT TO RULE ALL OTHERS! I INTEND TO!

SOON WE'LL BE READY TO ENSLAVE THEM!

SH! WE SHOULD NOT MAKE THE OUTSIDERS FEEL TOO INFERIOR ..... YET..

THE PRESIDENT'S OFFICE IN AMERICA

THE GREEN MEN OF BICE WITH THEIR FEELING OF SUPERIORITY TOWARD OTHER RACES MAY PLUNGE US ONCE AGAIN INTO WAR!

ALL RACES AND COLORS BUT THE GREEN PEOPLE HAVE LEARNED THAT THERE CAN BE NO PEACE WITHOUT UNITY AND BROTHERHOOD SO I'M CHOOSING A DELEGATION TO TRY TO IMPRESS THEM WITH OUR WAY OF LIFE!

I CHOSE YOU THREE BECAUSE OF YOUR DIFFERENCES YET ALL OF US LIVE TOGETHER IN PEACE! TRY AND SELL THE IDEA TO THE GREEN MEN!

I'M GLAD YOU BROUGHT ME ALONG, LOTTA.

THANKS, BUD. BUT I'M AFRAID THE GREEN MEN WILL MAKE YOU THINK YOU'RE BACK IN 1944 AMERICA!

LOOK! NON GREEN FOLKS! TELL 'EM ALL OUR CABS ARE FILLED!

THE NERVE! THEY'LL NO DOUBT TRY TO STAY IN ONE OF OUR BEST HOTELS!

TERNATIONAL ROCKET LINES

HEAD FOR COVER! SET UP THIS BIG MACHINE GUN!
WE'VE REACHED THE FRONT NOW, GUYS! LET'S GET READY TO DO SOME FIGHTING!

THE GREEN MEN

FEBRUARY 1944 – NOVEMBER 1944

ed to MacDill Field, Add these names to LAWRENCE, APO TRAVIS, A.S.F.T.R., h Base Unit, A.A.F. u read this, DETON correspondent for SIMS and VERA girl ...... RUTH NOEL over a bottle her ...... IVORY king so much about AWFORD, who has ter'...... WALTER ssed to Fleet Post-

those fighting men of western Europe many PATRIOTIC ger on the CHARM an INSULT at these fellow members of "NIGGERS WORK this column will do o OTTO GOES at Michigan avenue.

TS CLUB will sur- July 9. . . . Check- ing to drop BOWIE MODERN TEEN- Pershing. . . . . Sam body and soul.

, is back home after NEILAN JACOBS, COLEMAN was hit Y, during a lover's on INVASION day, letter from brother, stmaster, New York, ents had not heard S cocktail party at

er sister last week. , but is a bartender you expect. . . . . Mei Mei club popu- what ever happened

E our boys in serv- them the CHEER . . . Whether you and remember NO

plates of the week: LA HUTCHERSON, VIVIAN GAINES, and ELLA MAE andmother in Cin-

nt Hospital Nurse's enefit cabaret party Y SAMPSON with ARLES JACKSON

. . You could cer- care of postmaster. copped him a letter ack home after vis- Minnie's MIDWAY come by and give e draft limit. . . . e with flowers or a LURLEAN HOS- at Camp Stoneman, TC, says hello to is now recruiting

MERICAN NEGRO night, July 8. Pro- . . . SYMPATHY lost her mother this College, 4703 South he FEDERAL POS- Pershing ballroom, MELLS will crown

IAN
ger

column only when a TION. YOUR FULL rivate reply send 25c EADING and receive UESTIONS. Address loger) care of THE O, ILL.

Y. Will my future ize?
ucky stars and guid-

Dancer Praised

MISS PEARL PRIMUS

Dynamic dance artist of Cafe Society fame, who was showered with flowers and enthusiastic applause when she made her first appearance here May 29 at Orchestra Hall under the auspices of the International Workers Order in an Americans All Rally. This was Chicago's first opportunity to see her famous interpretations of Langston Hughes' "Negro Speaks of

Georgia Denies Negroes Primary Vote Rights

Ignoring the recent Supreme Court decision against "lily-white" primaries, the state of Georgia this week barred Negroes from voting in the Democratic primaries on July 4.

"The Supreme Court decision is not binding on the Georgia Democratic party," said Georgia officials, "because we were not parties to the Texas case" and because the Texas primary is regulated by statutes while the primary rules in Georgia are created by the party and not governed by election laws. The decision was made by a meeting of a subcommittee of the Georgia Democratic executive committee.

Clearing up what it considered "confusion in Georgia" as to whether Negroes would be allowed to vote, the subcommittee, composed of all officers of the general committee, adopted a resolution reaffirming a rule that only white electors can participate in the primary and ordered copies of the resolution sent to chairmen of the 158 Democratic county executive committees for their guidance in county voting.

"All white electors who are Democrats and qualified to vote in the general election," stated that the resolution, and who in good faith will pledge themselves to support the Democratic candidates for all offices to be voted on this year are declared qualified to vote."

After a sustained fight by the National Association for the Ad-

Negro Writer For Army Publication

WASHINGTON—(ANP)— Special efforts to increase the volume and to improve the quality of news material on Negro troops in the European theatre of operations are being made, the war department bureau of public relations told the Capital Press club this week.

The statement was made in a letter from Col. Stanley J. Grogan, deputy director of the public relations bureau, in reply to an inquiry from the press club concerning plans for news coverage of activities of Negro troops during the present invasion.

Col. Grogan's letter revealed that a Negro correspondent has recently been added to the staff of the "Stars and Stripes," army newspaper published in the European theatre, "for

YOUR Money

Ques.—Should an ex-service-man die before receiving his mustering out pay what becomes of the claim?

Ans.—If an ex-service man should die after being discharged and before he has received his mustering out pay his next of kin may qualify to receive his pay. His wife would be considered first. If a woman her husband. If there be no husband or wife then the ex-service man's child or children would come next. If there be no children then his parents; if no parents living, his next closest relative.

Walter Lowe

Ques.—Will mustering out pay be subject to income tax?

Ans.—No, this payment is exempt from all taxation. Moreover, it cannot be garnisheed, or attached by creditors. This money is immuned to all creditors. The Congress intended this sum of money to help the ex-service men in the following manner: transportation home, food, clothing, and other indispensable necessities until he will have found a means of making a livelihood.

W.Va. State ROTC Rated 'Excellent'

WEST VIRGINIA STATE COLLEGE—The ROTC Unit at West Virginia State college was awarded the rating of "excellent" on the basis of the annual inspection made May 17 by the Fifth Service Command, it was announced last week.

In a letter to Dr. John W. Davis, president of the college, Maj. Gen. James L. Collins at Fort Hayes, Columbus, Ohio, wrote, "This rating of 'excellent' reflects the commendable effort of the Corps of Cadets and of the Army personnel under your helpful guidance and encouragement. Kindly convey to all concerned my congratulations."

ATTEND CONFERENCE

Mrs. Estella Herndon and daughter, Scottie E. Herndon of Louisville, Ky., are in the city to attend the Knights of Peter Claver and auxiliaries' conference. They are the guests of Mrs. Dollie Cross, 3239 Rhodes avenue, and visited the Chicago Defender plant.

Ft. Dearborn E Elect F.W. Hen As Exalted Ru

The membership of Greater Dearborn Lodge 444 of Elks p the lodge rooms at 418 East street and cheered the unani re-election of Frank W. Hen Exalted Ruler.

Exalted Ruler Henry had ed his first term and unde able leadership the membersh Fort Dearborn increased ove per cent. Because of his sp record Exalted Ruler Henry been mentioned as a candida vice president of the State ciation of Elks which hold meeting at Joliet, June 24 an Other officers elected were Motley, E. S. Pritchard, A. L. Lawrence Givens. Atty. Jose Snowden was elected one o delegates to the State conve

John the Conqueror
LUCKY MO-JO
Lodestone

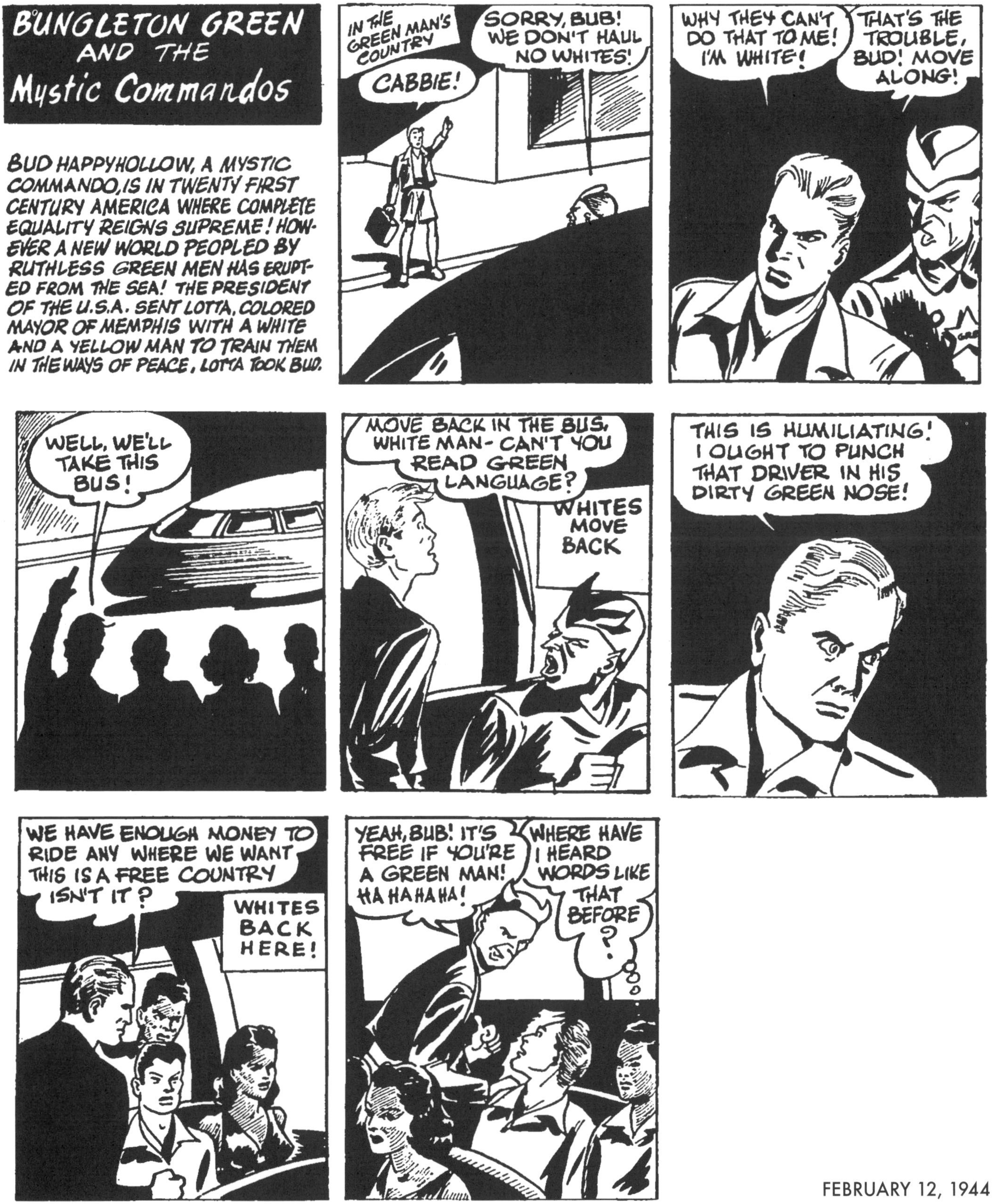
BUNGLETON GREEN AND THE Mystic Commandos
BUD HAPPYHOLLOW, A MYSTIC COMMANDO, IS IN TWENTY FIRST CENTURY AMERICA WHERE COMPLETE EQUALITY REIGNS SUPREME! HOWEVER A NEW WORLD PEOPLED BY RUTHLESS GREEN MEN HAS ERUPTED FROM THE SEA! THE PRESIDENT OF THE U.S.A. SENT LOTTA, COLORED MAYOR OF MEMPHIS WITH A WHITE AND A YELLOW MAN TO TRAIN THEM IN THE WAYS OF PEACE, LOTTA TOOK BUD.
IN THE GREEN MAN'S COUNTRY
CABBIE!
SORRY, BUB! WE DON'T HAUL NO WHITES!
WHY THEY CAN'T DO THAT TO ME! I'M WHITE!
THAT'S THE TROUBLE, BUD! MOVE ALONG!
WELL, WE'LL TAKE THIS BUS!
MOVE BACK IN THE BUS, WHITE MAN- CAN'T YOU READ GREEN LANGUAGE?
WHITES MOVE BACK
THIS IS HUMILIATING! I OUGHT TO PUNCH THAT DRIVER IN HIS DIRTY GREEN NOSE!
WE HAVE ENOUGH MONEY TO RIDE ANY WHERE WE WANT THIS IS A FREE COUNTRY ISN'T IT?
WHITES BACK HERE!
YEAH, BUB! IT'S FREE IF YOU'RE A GREEN MAN! HA HA HA HA HA!
WHERE HAVE I HEARD WORDS LIKE THAT BEFORE?

FEBRUARY 12, 1944

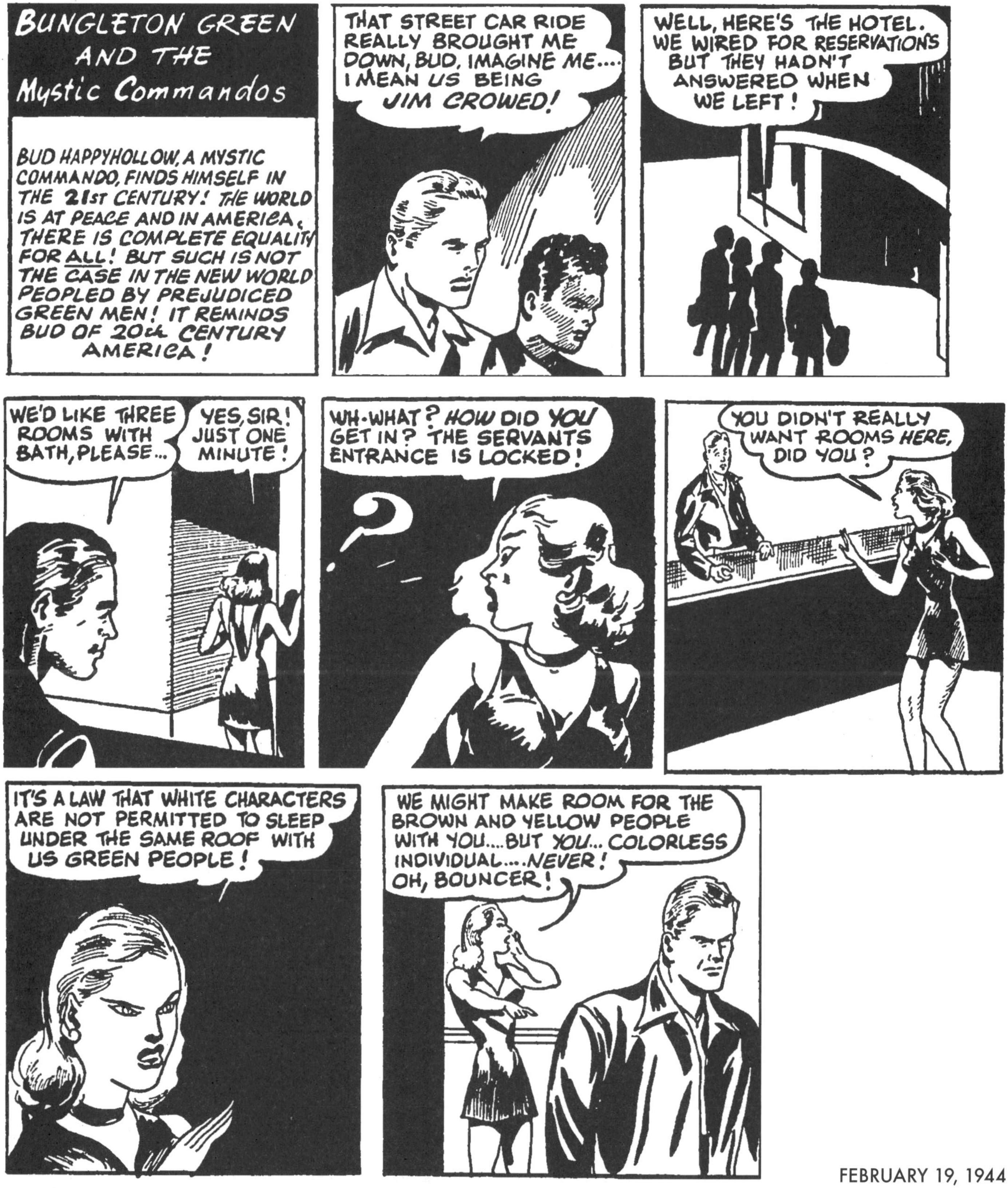
BUNGLETON GREEN AND THE Mystic Commandos
BUD HAPPYHOLLOW, A MYSTIC COMMANDO, FINDS HIMSELF IN THE 21ST CENTURY! THE WORLD IS AT PEACE AND IN AMERICA, THERE IS COMPLETE EQUALITY FOR ALL! BUT SUCH IS NOT THE CASE IN THE NEW WORLD PEOPLED BY PREJUDICED GREEN MEN! IT REMINDS BUD OF 20th CENTURY AMERICA!
THAT STREET CAR RIDE REALLY BROUGHT ME DOWN, BUD, IMAGINE ME.... I MEAN US BEING JIM CROWED!
WELL, HERE'S THE HOTEL. WE WIRED FOR RESERVATIONS BUT THEY HADN'T ANSWERED WHEN WE LEFT!
WE'D LIKE THREE ROOMS WITH BATH, PLEASE...
YES, SIR! JUST ONE MINUTE!
WH-WHAT? HOW DID YOU GET IN? THE SERVANTS ENTRANCE IS LOCKED!
YOU DIDN'T REALLY WANT ROOMS HERE, DID YOU?
IT'S A LAW THAT WHITE CHARACTERS ARE NOT PERMITTED TO SLEEP UNDER THE SAME ROOF WITH US GREEN PEOPLE!
WE MIGHT MAKE ROOM FOR THE BROWN AND YELLOW PEOPLE WITH YOU....BUT YOU... COLORLESS INDIVIDUAL....NEVER! OH, BOUNCER!

FEBRUARY 19, 1944

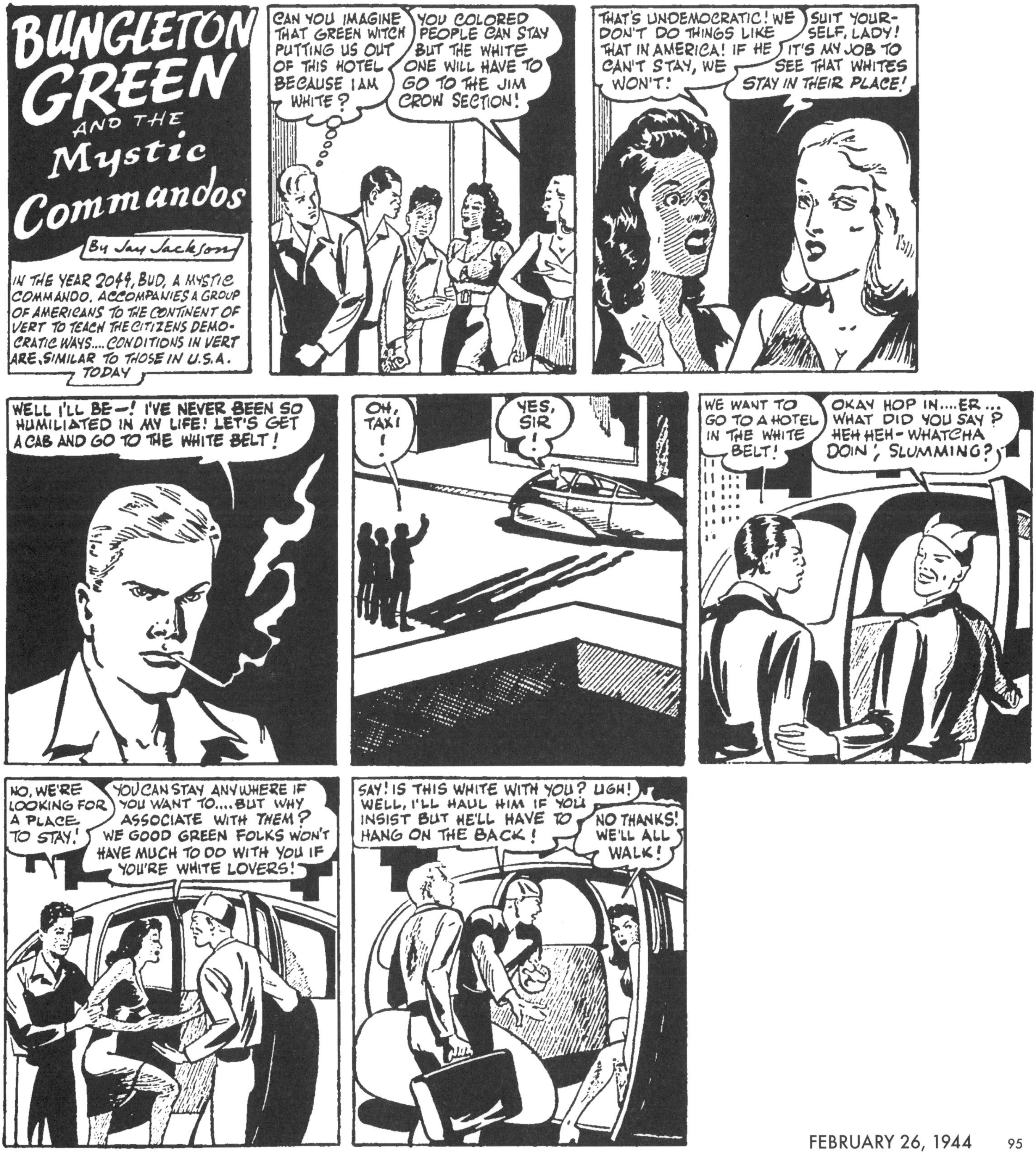
BUNGLETON GREEN AND THE Mystic Commandos
By Jay Jackson
IN THE YEAR 2044, BUD, A MYSTIC COMMANDO, ACCOMPANIES A GROUP OF AMERICANS TO THE CONTINENT OF VERT TO TEACH THE CITIZENS DEMOCRATIC WAYS.... CONDITIONS IN VERT ARE SIMILAR TO THOSE IN U.S.A. TODAY
CAN YOU IMAGINE THAT GREEN WITCH PUTTING US OUT OF THIS HOTEL BECAUSE I AM WHITE?
YOU COLORED PEOPLE CAN STAY BUT THE WHITE ONE WILL HAVE TO GO TO THE JIM CROW SECTION!
THAT'S UNDEMOCRATIC! WE DON'T DO THINGS LIKE THAT IN AMERICA! IF HE CAN'T STAY, WE WON'T!
SUIT YOURSELF, LADY! IT'S MY JOB TO SEE THAT WHITES STAY IN THEIR PLACE!
WELL I'LL BE—! I'VE NEVER BEEN SO HUMILIATED IN MY LIFE! LET'S GET A CAB AND GO TO THE WHITE BELT!
OH, TAXI!
YES, SIR!
WE WANT TO GO TO A HOTEL IN THE WHITE BELT!
OKAY HOP IN....ER... WHAT DID YOU SAY? HEH HEH- WHATCHA DOIN', SLUMMING?
NO, WE'RE LOOKING FOR A PLACE TO STAY!
YOU CAN STAY ANYWHERE IF YOU WANT TO....BUT WHY ASSOCIATE WITH THEM? WE GOOD GREEN FOLKS WON'T HAVE MUCH TO DO WITH YOU IF YOU'RE WHITE LOVERS!
SAY! IS THIS WHITE WITH YOU? UGH! WELL, I'LL HAUL HIM IF YOU INSIST BUT HE'LL HAVE TO HANG ON THE BACK!
NO THANKS! WE'LL ALL WALK!

FEBRUARY 26, 1944

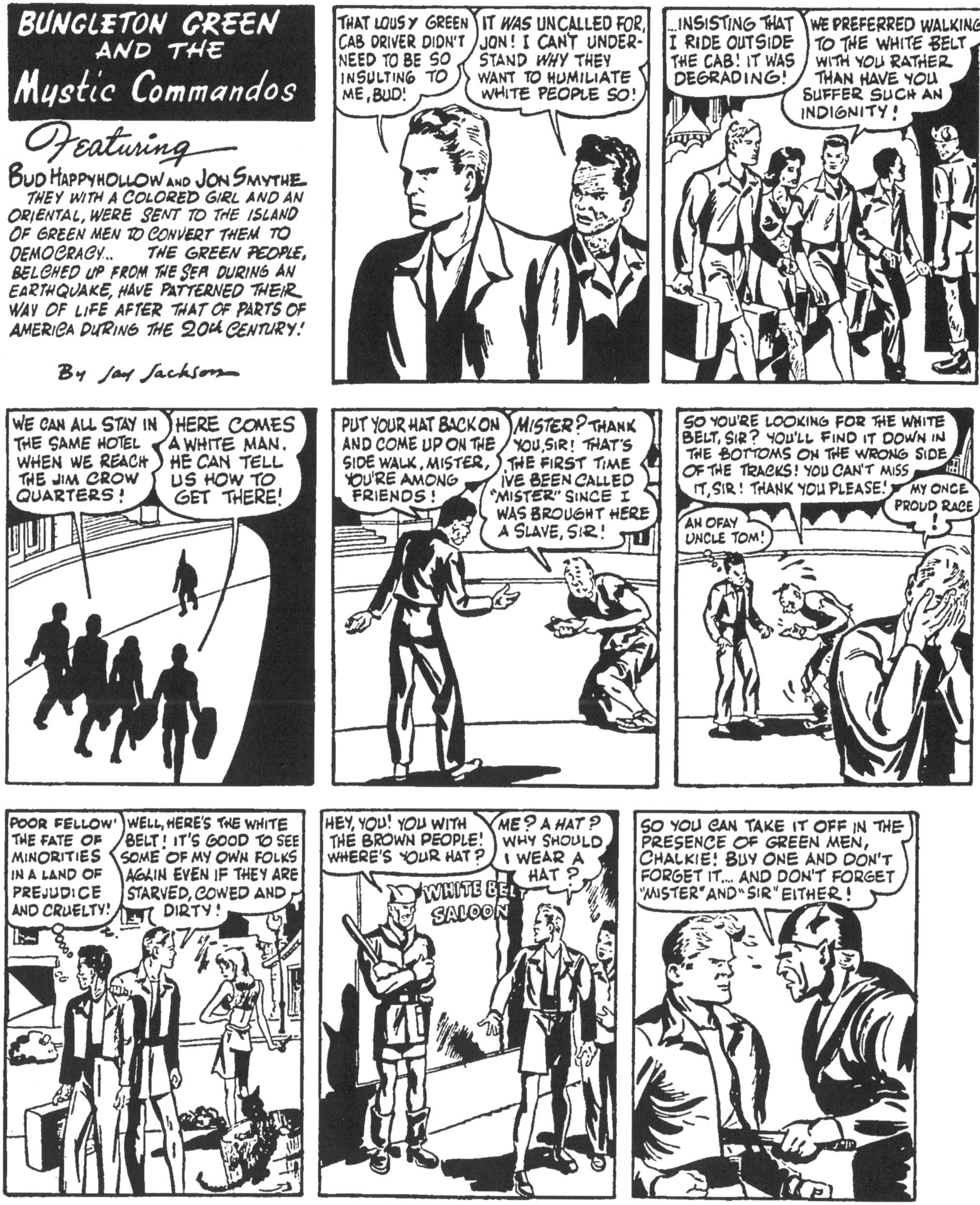
BUNGLETON GREEN AND THE Mystic Commandos
Featuring
BUD HAPPYHOLLOW AND JON SMYTHE
THEY WITH A COLORED GIRL AND AN ORIENTAL, WERE SENT TO THE ISLAND OF GREEN MEN TO CONVERT THEM TO DEMOCRACY... THE GREEN PEOPLE, BELCHED UP FROM THE SEA DURING AN EARTHQUAKE, HAVE PATTERNED THEIR WAY OF LIFE AFTER THAT OF PARTS OF AMERICA DURING THE 20th CENTURY!
By Jay Jackson
THAT LOUSY GREEN CAB DRIVER DIDN'T NEED TO BE SO INSULTING TO ME, BUD!
IT WAS UNCALLED FOR, JON! I CAN'T UNDERSTAND WHY THEY WANT TO HUMILIATE WHITE PEOPLE SO!
...INSISTING THAT I RIDE OUTSIDE THE CAB! IT WAS DEGRADING!
WE PREFERRED WALKING TO THE WHITE BELT WITH YOU RATHER THAN HAVE YOU SUFFER SUCH AN INDIGNITY!
WE CAN ALL STAY IN THE SAME HOTEL WHEN WE REACH THE JIM CROW QUARTERS!
HERE COMES A WHITE MAN. HE CAN TELL US HOW TO GET THERE!
PUT YOUR HAT BACK ON AND COME UP ON THE SIDE WALK, MISTER, YOU'RE AMONG FRIENDS!
MISTER? THANK YOU, SIR! THAT'S THE FIRST TIME I'VE BEEN CALLED "MISTER" SINCE I WAS BROUGHT HERE A SLAVE, SIR!
SO YOU'RE LOOKING FOR THE WHITE BELT, SIR? YOU'LL FIND IT DOWN IN THE BOTTOMS ON THE WRONG SIDE OF THE TRACKS! YOU CAN'T MISS IT, SIR! THANK YOU PLEASE!
AN OFAY UNCLE TOM!
MY ONCE PROUD RACE!
POOR FELLOW! THE FATE OF MINORITIES IN A LAND OF PREJUDICE AND CRUELTY!
WELL, HERE'S THE WHITE BELT! IT'S GOOD TO SEE SOME OF MY OWN FOLKS AGAIN EVEN IF THEY ARE STARVED, COWED AND DIRTY!
HEY, YOU! YOU WITH THE BROWN PEOPLE! WHERE'S YOUR HAT?
ME? A HAT? WHY SHOULD I WEAR A HAT?
WHITE BELT SALOON
SO YOU CAN TAKE IT OFF IN THE PRESENCE OF GREEN MEN, CHALKIE! BUY ONE AND DON'T FORGET IT... AND DON'T FORGET "MISTER" AND "SIR" EITHER!

SATURDAY, MARCH 4, 1944

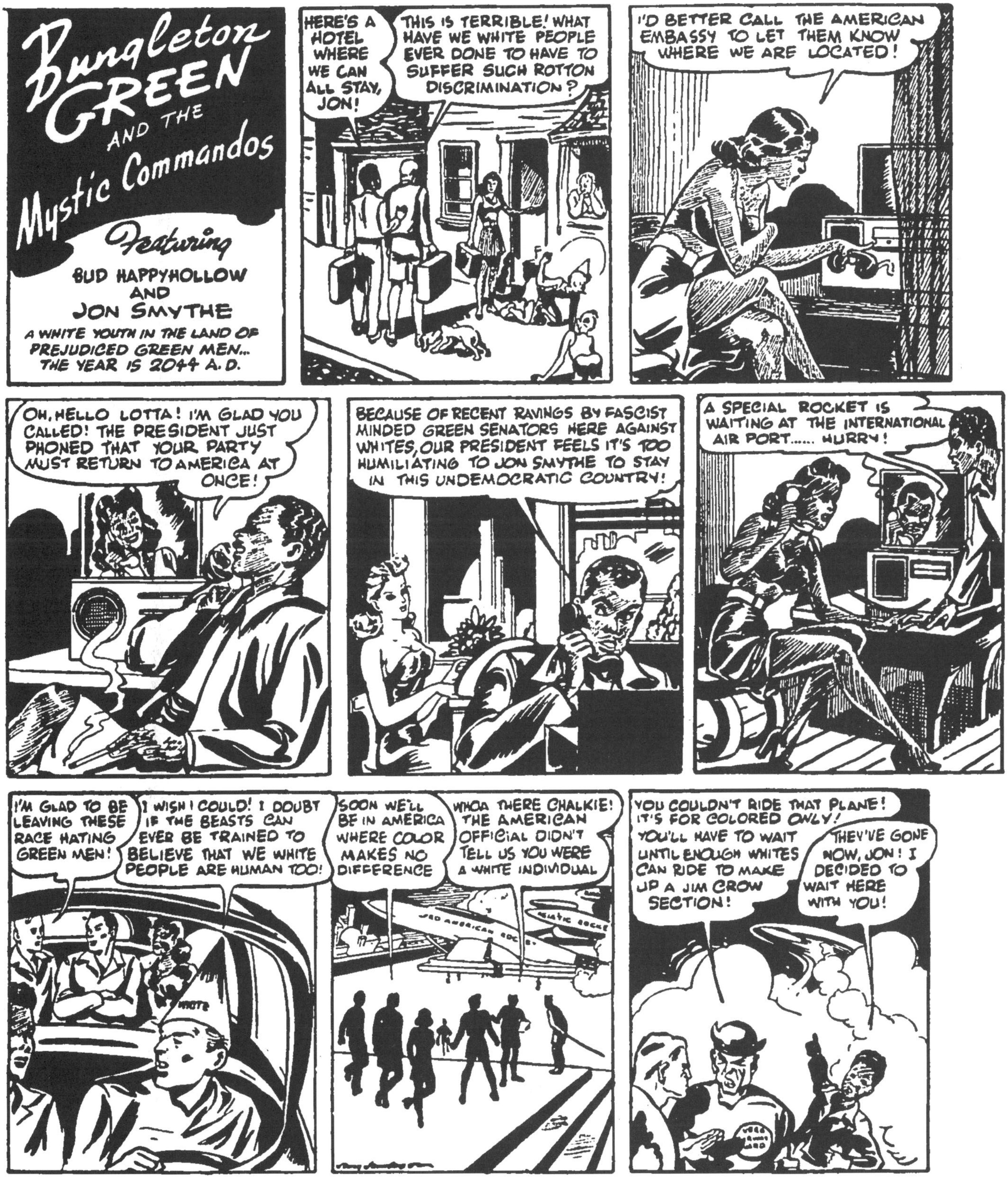
Bungleton GREEN AND THE Mystic Commandos
Featuring
BUD HAPPYHOLLOW AND JON SMYTHE
A WHITE YOUTH IN THE LAND OF PREJUDICED GREEN MEN... THE YEAR IS 2044 A.D.
HERE'S A HOTEL WHERE WE CAN ALL STAY, JON!
THIS IS TERRIBLE! WHAT HAVE WE WHITE PEOPLE EVER DONE TO HAVE TO SUFFER SUCH ROTTON DISCRIMINATION?
I'D BETTER CALL THE AMERICAN EMBASSY TO LET THEM KNOW WHERE WE ARE LOCATED!
OH, HELLO LOTTA! I'M GLAD YOU CALLED! THE PRESIDENT JUST PHONED THAT YOUR PARTY MUST RETURN TO AMERICA AT ONCE!
BECAUSE OF RECENT RAVINGS BY FASCIST MINDED GREEN SENATORS HERE AGAINST WHITES, OUR PRESIDENT FEELS IT'S TOO HUMILIATING TO JON SMYTHE TO STAY IN THIS UNDEMOCRATIC COUNTRY!
A SPECIAL ROCKET IS WAITING AT THE INTERNATIONAL AIR PORT...... HURRY!
I'M GLAD TO BE LEAVING THESE RACE HATING GREEN MEN!
I WISH I COULD! I DOUBT IF THE BEASTS CAN EVER BE TRAINED TO BELIEVE THAT WE WHITE PEOPLE ARE HUMAN TOO!
WHITE
SOON WE'LL BE IN AMERICA WHERE COLOR MAKES NO DIFFERENCE
WHOA THERE CHALKIE! THE AMERICAN OFFICIAL DIDN'T TELL US YOU WERE A WHITE INDIVIDUAL
YOU COULDN'T RIDE THAT PLANE! IT'S FOR COLORED ONLY! YOU'LL HAVE TO WAIT UNTIL ENOUGH WHITES CAN RIDE TO MAKE UP A JIM CROW SECTION!
THEY'VE GONE NOW, JON! I DECIDED TO WAIT HERE WITH YOU!

SATURDAY, MARCH 11, 1944

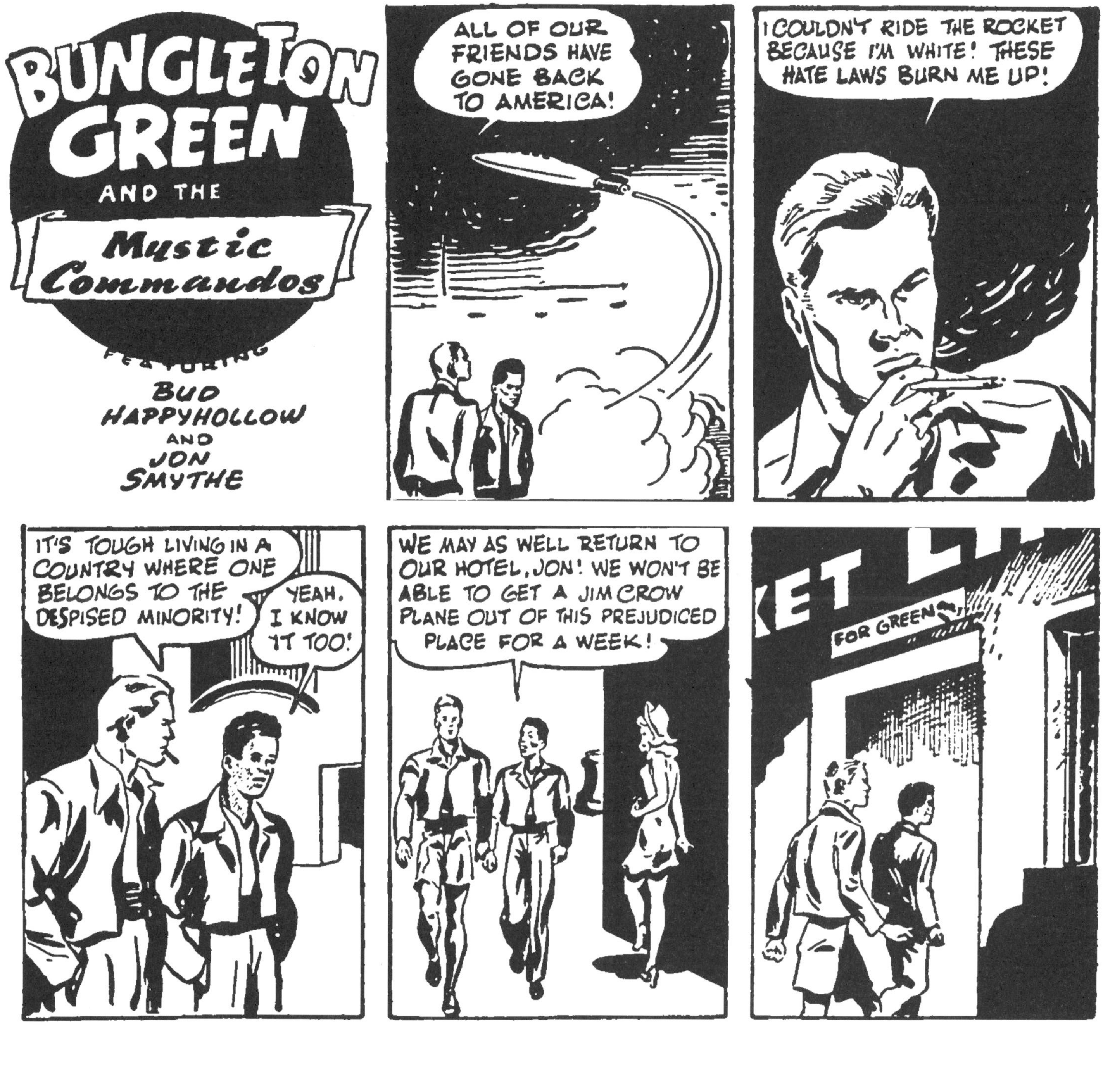
BUNGLETON GREEN
AND THE
Mystic Commandos
BUD HAPPYHOLLOW
AND
JON SMYTHE
ALL OF OUR FRIENDS HAVE GONE BACK TO AMERICA!
I COULDN'T RIDE THE ROCKET BECAUSE I'M WHITE! THESE HATE LAWS BURN ME UP!
IT'S TOUGH LIVING IN A COUNTRY WHERE ONE BELONGS TO THE DESPISED MINORITY!
YEAH. I KNOW IT TOO!
WE MAY AS WELL RETURN TO OUR HOTEL, JON! WE WON'T BE ABLE TO GET A JIM CROW PLANE OUT OF THIS PREJUDICED PLACE FOR A WEEK!
FOR GREENS

MARCH 18, 1944

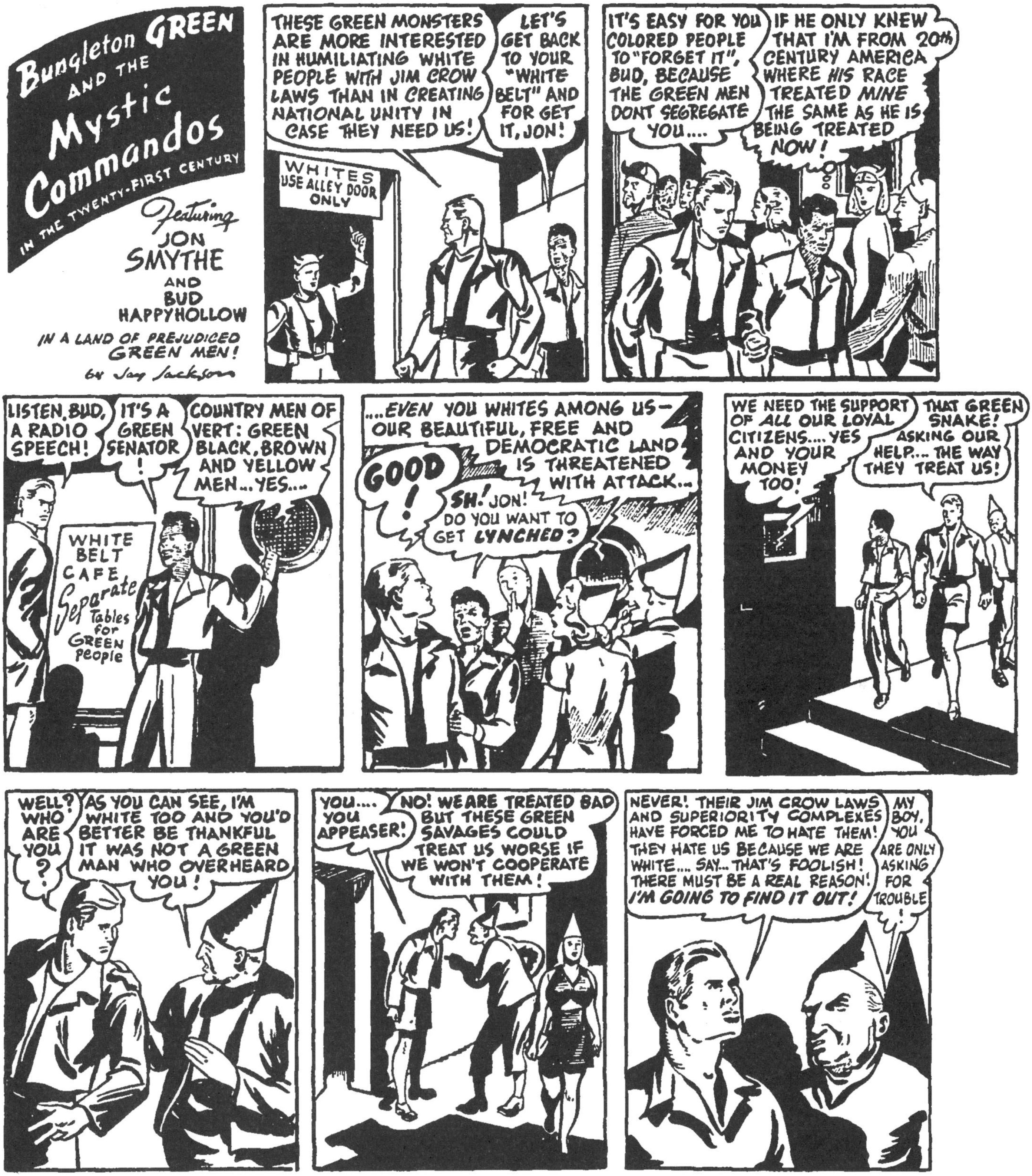
Bungleton GREEN AND THE Mystic Commandos IN THE TWENTY-FIRST CENTURY
Featuring JON SMYTHE AND BUD HAPPYHOLLOW
IN A LAND OF PREJUDICED GREEN MEN!
by Jay Jackson
THESE GREEN MONSTERS ARE MORE INTERESTED IN HUMILIATING WHITE PEOPLE WITH JIM CROW LAWS THAN IN CREATING NATIONAL UNITY IN CASE THEY NEED US!
LET'S GET BACK TO YOUR "WHITE BELT" AND FOR GET IT, JON!
WHITES USE ALLEY DOOR ONLY
IT'S EASY FOR YOU COLORED PEOPLE TO "FORGET IT", BUD, BECAUSE THE GREEN MEN DONT SEGREGATE YOU....
IF HE ONLY KNEW THAT I'M FROM 20th CENTURY AMERICA WHERE HIS RACE TREATED MINE THE SAME AS HE IS BEING TREATED NOW!
LISTEN, BUD, A RADIO SPEECH!
IT'S A GREEN SENATOR!
COUNTRY MEN OF VERT: GREEN BLACK, BROWN AND YELLOW MEN...YES...
WHITE BELT CAFE Separate Tables for GREEN people
...EVEN YOU WHITES AMONG US— OUR BEAUTIFUL, FREE AND DEMOCRATIC LAND IS THREATENED WITH ATTACK...
GOOD!
SH! JON! DO YOU WANT TO GET LYNCHED?
WE NEED THE SUPPORT OF ALL OUR LOYAL CITIZENS....YES AND YOUR MONEY TOO!
THAT GREEN SNAKE! ASKING OUR HELP... THE WAY THEY TREAT US!
WELL? WHO ARE YOU?
AS YOU CAN SEE, I'M WHITE TOO AND YOU'D BETTER BE THANKFUL IT WAS NOT A GREEN MAN WHO OVERHEARD YOU!
YOU.... YOU APPEASER!
NO! WE ARE TREATED BAD BUT THESE GREEN SAVAGES COULD TREAT US WORSE IF WE WON'T COOPERATE WITH THEM!
NEVER! THEIR JIM CROW LAWS AND SUPERIORITY COMPLEXES HAVE FORCED ME TO HATE THEM! THEY HATE US BECAUSE WE ARE WHITE.... SAY... THAT'S FOOLISH! THERE MUST BE A REAL REASON! I'M GOING TO FIND IT OUT!
MY BOY, YOU ARE ONLY ASKING FOR TROUBLE!

MARCH 25, 1944

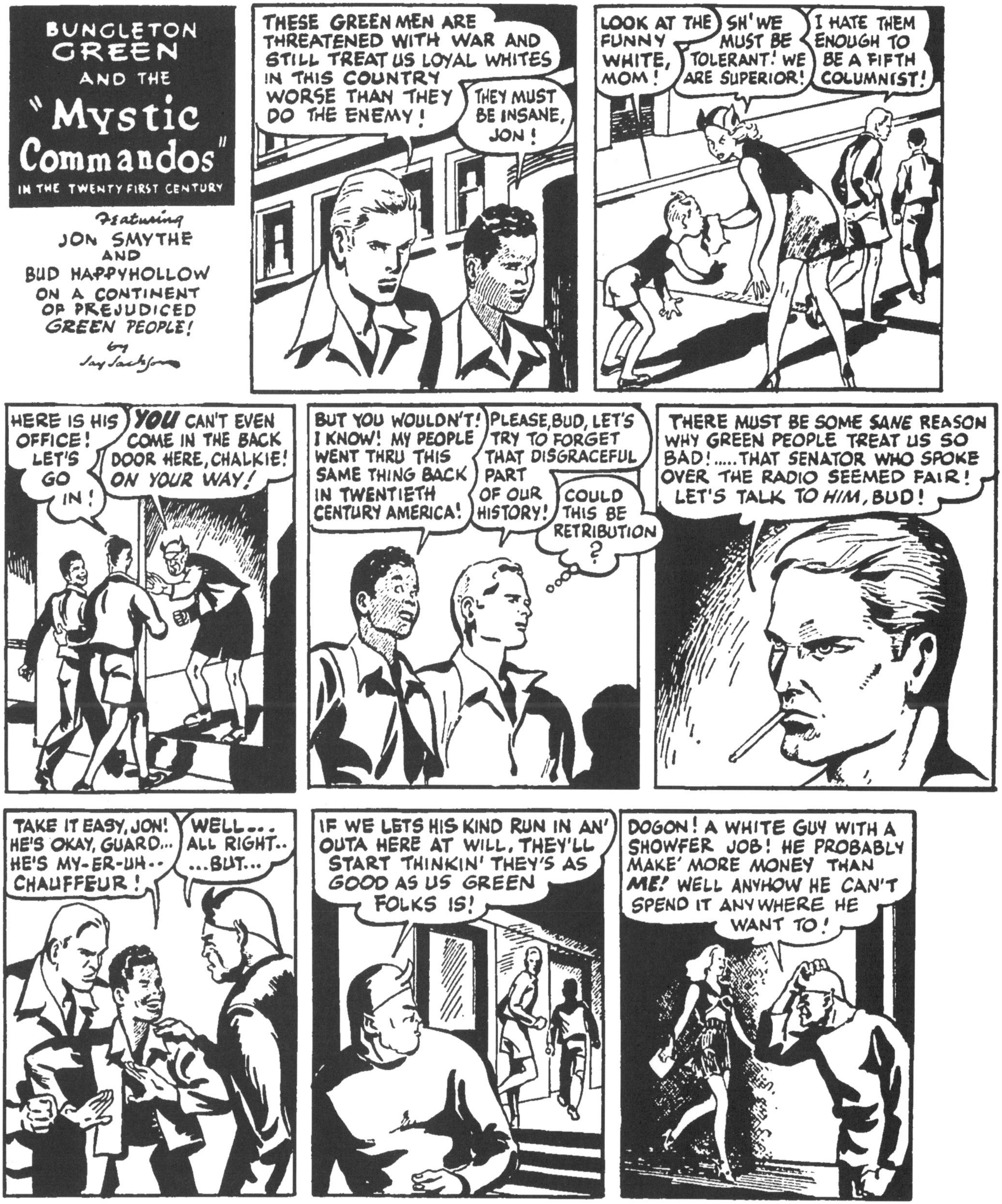

BUNGLETON GREEN AND THE "Mystic Commandos" IN THE TWENTY FIRST CENTURY
Featuring JON SMYTHE AND BUD HAPPYHOLLOW ON A CONTINENT OF PREJUDICED GREEN PEOPLE!
by Jay Jackson
THESE GREEN MEN ARE THREATENED WITH WAR AND STILL TREAT US LOYAL WHITES IN THIS COUNTRY WORSE THAN THEY DO THE ENEMY!
THEY MUST BE INSANE, JON!
LOOK AT THE FUNNY WHITE, MOM!
SH' WE MUST BE TOLERANT! WE ARE SUPERIOR!
I HATE THEM ENOUGH TO BE A FIFTH COLUMNIST!
HERE IS HIS OFFICE! LET'S GO IN!
YOU CAN'T EVEN COME IN THE BACK DOOR HERE, CHALKIE! ON YOUR WAY!
BUT YOU WOULDN'T! I KNOW! MY PEOPLE WENT THRU THIS SAME THING BACK IN TWENTIETH CENTURY AMERICA!
PLEASE, BUD, LET'S TRY TO FORGET THAT DISGRACEFUL PART OF OUR HISTORY!
COULD THIS BE RETRIBUTION ?
THERE MUST BE SOME SANE REASON WHY GREEN PEOPLE TREAT US SO BAD!.....THAT SENATOR WHO SPOKE OVER THE RADIO SEEMED FAIR! LET'S TALK TO HIM, BUD!
TAKE IT EASY, JON! HE'S OKAY, GUARD... HE'S MY-ER-UH.. CHAUFFEUR!
WELL... ALL RIGHT.. ...BUT...
IF WE LETS HIS KIND RUN IN AN' OUTA HERE AT WILL, THEY'LL START THINKIN' THEY'S AS GOOD AS US GREEN FOLKS IS!
DOGON! A WHITE GUY WITH A SHOWFER JOB! HE PROBABLY MAKE' MORE MONEY THAN ME! WELL ANYHOW HE CAN'T SPEND IT ANYWHERE HE WANT TO!

APRIL 1, 1944

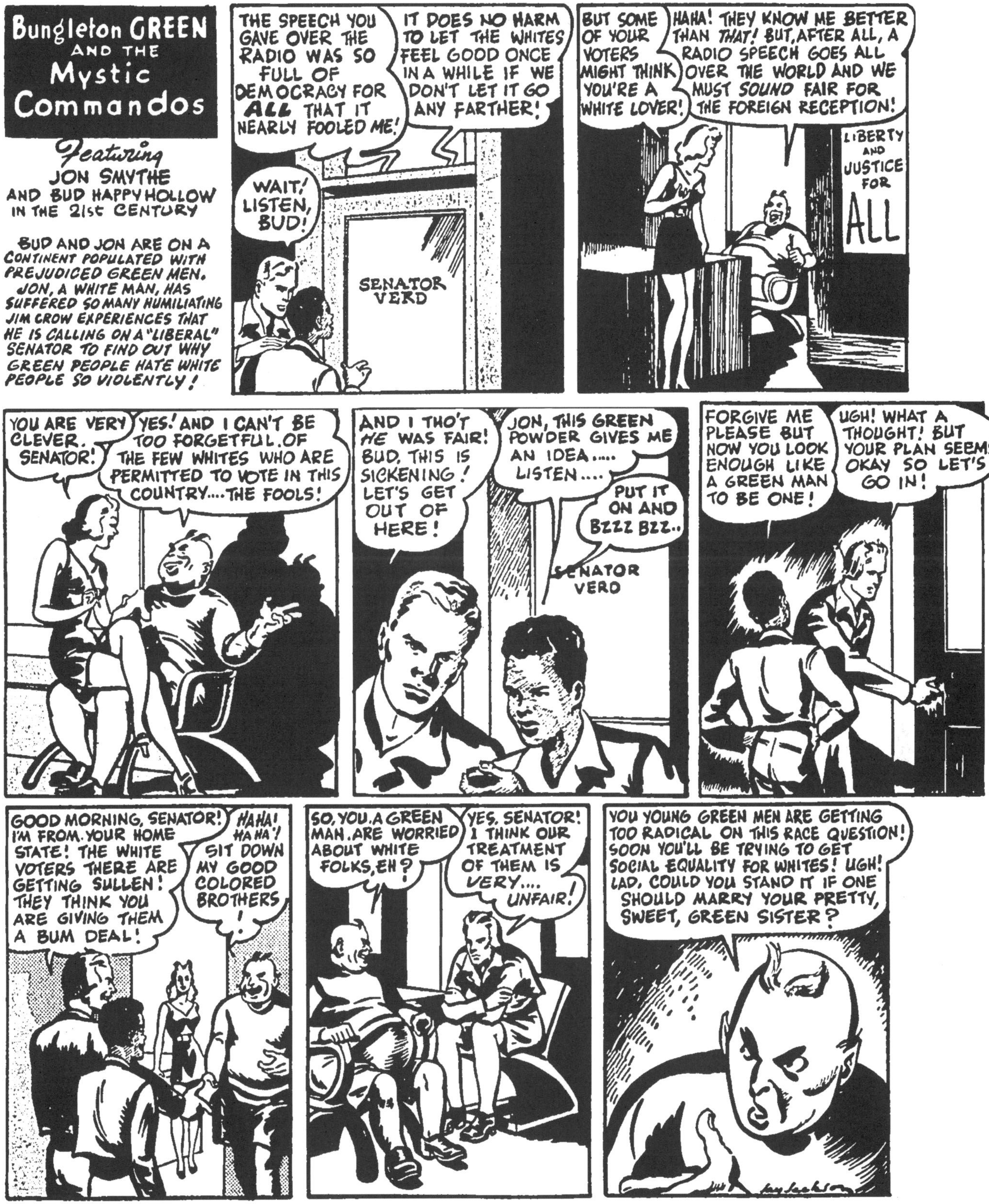
Bungleton GREEN AND THE Mystic Commandos
Featuring JON SMYTHE AND BUD HAPPYHOLLOW IN THE 21st CENTURY
BUD AND JON ARE ON A CONTINENT POPULATED WITH PREJUDICED GREEN MEN. JON, A WHITE MAN, HAS SUFFERED SO MANY HUMILIATING JIM CROW EXPERIENCES THAT HE IS CALLING ON A "LIBERAL" SENATOR TO FIND OUT WHY GREEN PEOPLE HATE WHITE PEOPLE SO VIOLENTLY!
THE SPEECH YOU GAVE OVER THE RADIO WAS SO FULL OF DEMOCRACY FOR ALL THAT IT NEARLY FOOLED ME!
IT DOES NO HARM TO LET THE WHITES FEEL GOOD ONCE IN A WHILE IF WE DON'T LET IT GO ANY FARTHER!
WAIT! LISTEN, BUD!
SENATOR VERD
BUT SOME OF YOUR VOTERS MIGHT THINK YOU'RE A WHITE LOVER!
HAHA! THEY KNOW ME BETTER THAN THAT! BUT, AFTER ALL, A RADIO SPEECH GOES ALL OVER THE WORLD AND WE MUST SOUND FAIR FOR THE FOREIGN RECEPTION!
LIBERTY AND JUSTICE FOR ALL
YOU ARE VERY CLEVER, SENATOR!
YES! AND I CAN'T BE TOO FORGETFUL OF THE FEW WHITES WHO ARE PERMITTED TO VOTE IN THIS COUNTRY.... THE FOOLS!
AND I THO'T HE WAS FAIR! BUD, THIS IS SICKENING! LET'S GET OUT OF HERE!
JON, THIS GREEN POWDER GIVES ME AN IDEA..... LISTEN....
PUT IT ON AND BZZZ BZZ..
SENATOR VERD
FORGIVE ME PLEASE BUT NOW YOU LOOK ENOUGH LIKE A GREEN MAN TO BE ONE!
UGH! WHAT A THOUGHT! BUT YOUR PLAN SEEMS OKAY SO LET'S GO IN!
GOOD MORNING, SENATOR! I'M FROM YOUR HOME STATE! THE WHITE VOTERS THERE ARE GETTING SULLEN! THEY THINK YOU ARE GIVING THEM A BUM DEAL!
HAHA! HA HA! SIT DOWN MY GOOD COLORED BROTHERS!
SO, YOU, A GREEN MAN, ARE WORRIED ABOUT WHITE FOLKS, EH?
YES, SENATOR! I THINK OUR TREATMENT OF THEM IS VERY.... UNFAIR!
YOU YOUNG GREEN MEN ARE GETTING TOO RADICAL ON THIS RACE QUESTION! SOON YOU'LL BE TRYING TO GET SOCIAL EQUALITY FOR WHITES! UGH! LAD, COULD YOU STAND IT IF ONE SHOULD MARRY YOUR PRETTY, SWEET, GREEN SISTER?

APRIL 8, 1944

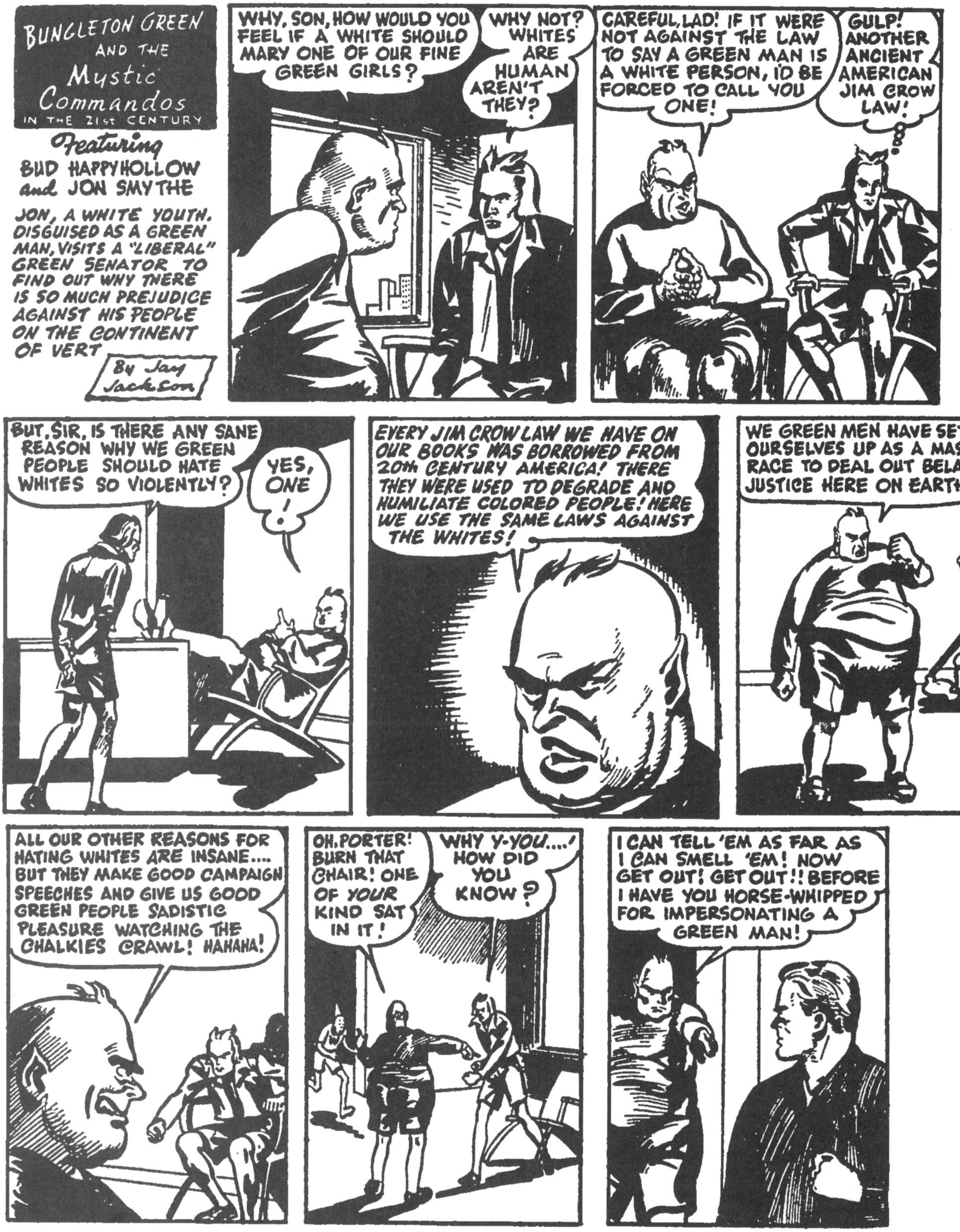
BUNGLETON GREEN AND THE Mystic Commandos IN THE 21st CENTURY
Featuring BUD HAPPYHOLLOW and JON SMYTHE
JON, A WHITE YOUTH. DISGUISED AS A GREEN MAN, VISITS A "LIBERAL" GREEN SENATOR TO FIND OUT WHY THERE IS SO MUCH PREJUDICE AGAINST HIS PEOPLE ON THE CONTINENT OF VERT
By Jay Jackson
WHY, SON, HOW WOULD YOU FEEL IF A WHITE SHOULD MARY ONE OF OUR FINE GREEN GIRLS?
WHY NOT? WHITES ARE HUMAN AREN'T THEY?
CAREFUL, LAD! IF IT WERE NOT AGAINST THE LAW TO SAY A GREEN MAN IS A WHITE PERSON, I'D BE FORCED TO CALL YOU ONE!
GULP! ANOTHER ANCIENT AMERICAN JIM CROW LAW!
BUT, SIR, IS THERE ANY SANE REASON WHY WE GREEN PEOPLE SHOULD HATE WHITES SO VIOLENTLY?
YES, ONE !
EVERY JIM CROW LAW WE HAVE ON OUR BOOKS WAS BORROWED FROM 20TH CENTURY AMERICA! THERE THEY WERE USED TO DEGRADE AND HUMILIATE COLORED PEOPLE! HERE WE USE THE SAME LAWS AGAINST THE WHITES!
WE GREEN MEN HAVE SET OURSELVES UP AS A MASTER RACE TO DEAL OUT BELATED JUSTICE HERE ON EARTH!
ALL OUR OTHER REASONS FOR HATING WHITES ARE INSANE.... BUT THEY MAKE GOOD CAMPAIGN SPEECHES AND GIVE US GOOD GREEN PEOPLE SADISTIC PLEASURE WATCHING THE CHALKIES CRAWL! HAHAHA!
OH, PORTER! BURN THAT CHAIR! ONE OF YOUR KIND SAT IN IT!
WHY Y-YOU....! HOW DID YOU KNOW?
I CAN TELL 'EM AS FAR AS I CAN SMELL 'EM! NOW GET OUT! GET OUT!! BEFORE I HAVE YOU HORSE-WHIPPED FOR IMPERSONATING A GREEN MAN!

APRIL 15, 1944

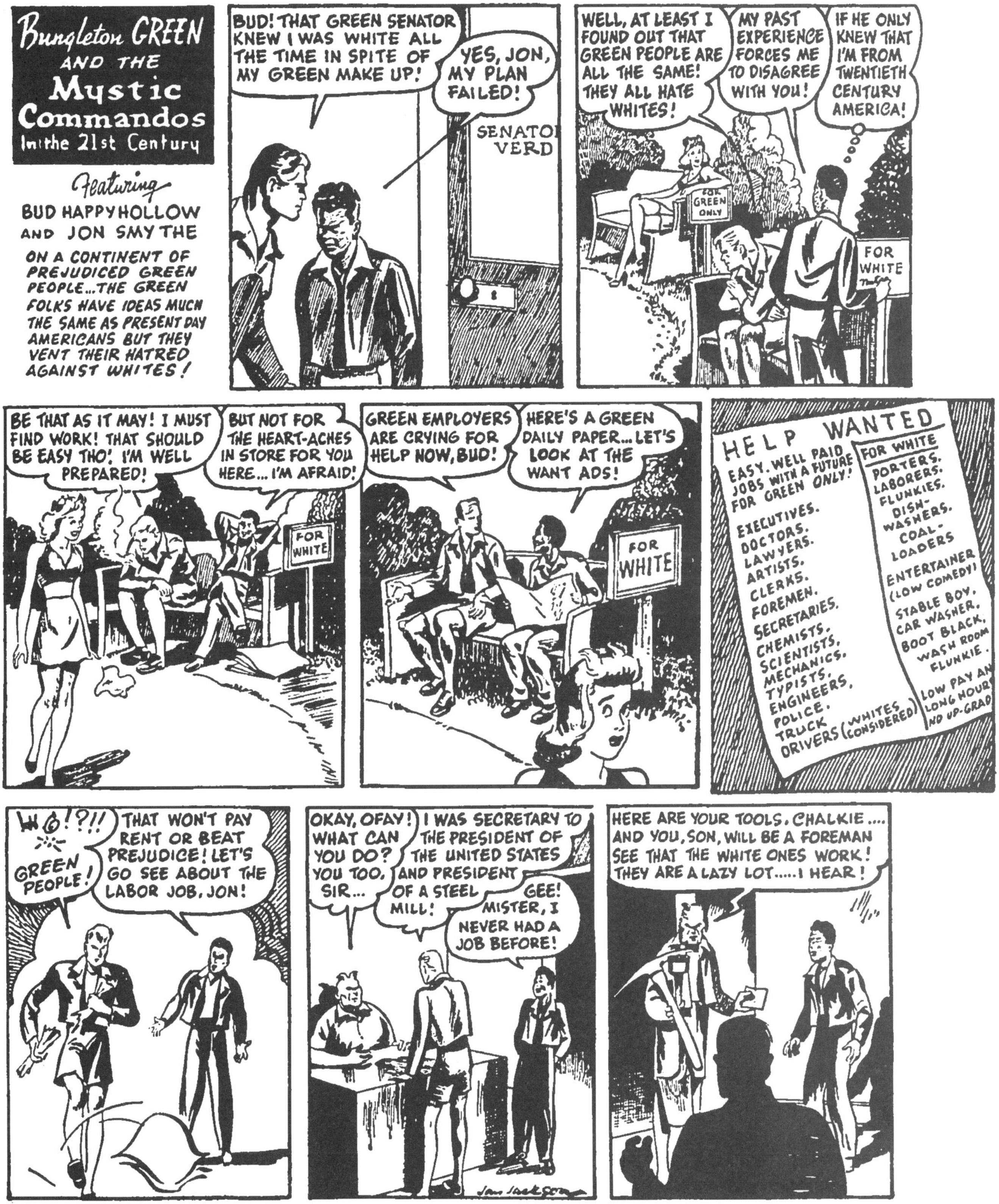

Bungleton GREEN AND THE Mystic Commandos In the 21st Century
Featuring
BUD HAPPYHOLLOW AND JON SMYTHE
ON A CONTINENT OF PREJUDICED GREEN PEOPLE...THE GREEN FOLKS HAVE IDEAS MUCH THE SAME AS PRESENT DAY AMERICANS BUT THEY VENT THEIR HATRED AGAINST WHITES!
BUD! THAT GREEN SENATOR KNEW I WAS WHITE ALL THE TIME IN SPITE OF MY GREEN MAKE UP!
YES, JON, MY PLAN FAILED!
SENATO VERD
WELL, AT LEAST I FOUND OUT THAT GREEN PEOPLE ARE ALL THE SAME! THEY ALL HATE WHITES!
MY PAST EXPERIENCE FORCES ME TO DISAGREE WITH YOU!
IF HE ONLY KNEW THAT I'M FROM TWENTIETH CENTURY AMERICA!
FOR GREEN ONLY
FOR WHITE
BE THAT AS IT MAY! I MUST FIND WORK! THAT SHOULD BE EASY THO'. I'M WELL PREPARED!
BUT NOT FOR THE HEART-ACHES IN STORE FOR YOU HERE... I'M AFRAID!
FOR WHITE
GREEN EMPLOYERS ARE CRYING FOR HELP NOW, BUD!
HERE'S A GREEN DAILY PAPER... LET'S LOOK AT THE WANT ADS!
FOR WHITE
HELP WANTED
EASY. WELL PAID JOBS WITH A FUTURE FOR GREEN ONLY!
EXECUTIVES. DOCTORS. LAWYERS. ARTISTS. CLERKS. FOREMEN. SECRETARIES. CHEMISTS. SCIENTISTS. MECHANICS. TYPISTS. ENGINEERS. POLICE. TRUCK DRIVERS (WHITES CONSIDERED)
FOR WHITE
PORTERS. LABORERS. FLUNKIES. DISH-WASHERS. COAL-LOADERS
ENTERTAINER (LOW COMEDY!)
STABLE BOY. CAR WASHER. BOOT BLACK. WASH ROOM FLUNKIE.
LOW PAY AN LONG HOUR ND UP-GRAD
!?!!
GREEN PEOPLE!
THAT WON'T PAY RENT OR BEAT PREJUDICE! LET'S GO SEE ABOUT THE LABOR JOB, JON!
OKAY, OFAY! WHAT CAN YOU DO? YOU TOO, SIR...
I WAS SECRETARY TO THE PRESIDENT OF THE UNITED STATES AND PRESIDENT OF A STEEL MILL!
GEE! MISTER, I NEVER HAD A JOB BEFORE!
HERE ARE YOUR TOOLS, CHALKIE.... AND YOU, SON, WILL BE A FOREMAN SEE THAT THE WHITE ONES WORK! THEY ARE A LAZY LOT..... I HEAR!

APRIL 22, 1944

BUNGLETON GREEN AND THE "Mystic Commandos"

Featuring
BUD HAPPYHOLLOW and JON SMYTHE
IN THE TWENTY FIRST CENTURY

JON SMYTHE, AN AMERICAN WHITE, EXPERIENCES RANK DISCRIMINATION BECAUSE OF HIS COLOR IN THE LAND OF GREEN MEN.

By Jay Jackson

Panel 1: I AM ABLE TO HOLD AN EXECUTIVE JOB! LOOK WHAT THOSE GREEN GOATS GAVE ME! — I NEVER HAD A JOB BEFORE AND THEY MAKE ME A BOSS!

Panel 2: I'VE NEVER SEEN SUCH SHORT-SIGHTED PREJUDICE ANY WHERE ELSE BUT IN...... — AH, AH, BUD! THAT WAS IN THE TWENTIETH CENTURY!

Panel 3: THIS IS YOUR NEW BOSS, FOLKS! — WE HOPE HE IS BETTER THAN THE LAST ONE! — HARYA, SHORTY! — CUTE, AINT HE? — THANK GOODNESS, HE'S NOT A GREEN MAN! MAYBE HE WILL GIVE US WHITES A BREAK!

Panel 4: HERE'S A... A-ANOTHER FOR YOUR CREW! — O YEAH!? WE GOT ENOUGH OF HIS KIND! — WE DON'T WANT HIM! — WE'LL WALK OFF THE JOB!

Panel 5: I CAN'T STICK MY NECK OUT FOR OFAYS! IT'S YOUR JOB FROM HERE, BUD! — GULP! — YOU'RE A FOREIGNER SO DON'T FORGET WE HAVE "SPECIAL TREATMENT" FOR OUR WHITES HERE, SEE?!

Panel 6: YOUR COUNTRY IS PREPARING FOR WAR! YOU'LL NEED *ALL* THE MAN POWER YOU CAN GET TO WIN! IF YOU *DON'T* WIN, ALL YOU GREEN MEN WILL BE AS POOR AND MISTREATED AS WHITES ...... WELL .....

Panel 7: DO YOU WIN WITH THEM OR LOSE WITH OUT THEM? — OKAY, BUT WE WON'T WORK BESIDE THEM! — HELP! THIS MOTOR IS CRUSHING ME!

Panel 8: Y-Y-YOU SAVED MY LIFE! UGH! YOU'RE A WHITE! — YES, AND I HAD TO WORK *BESIDE* YOU TO DO IT! WOULD YOU RATHER I HADN'T?

APRIL 29, 1944

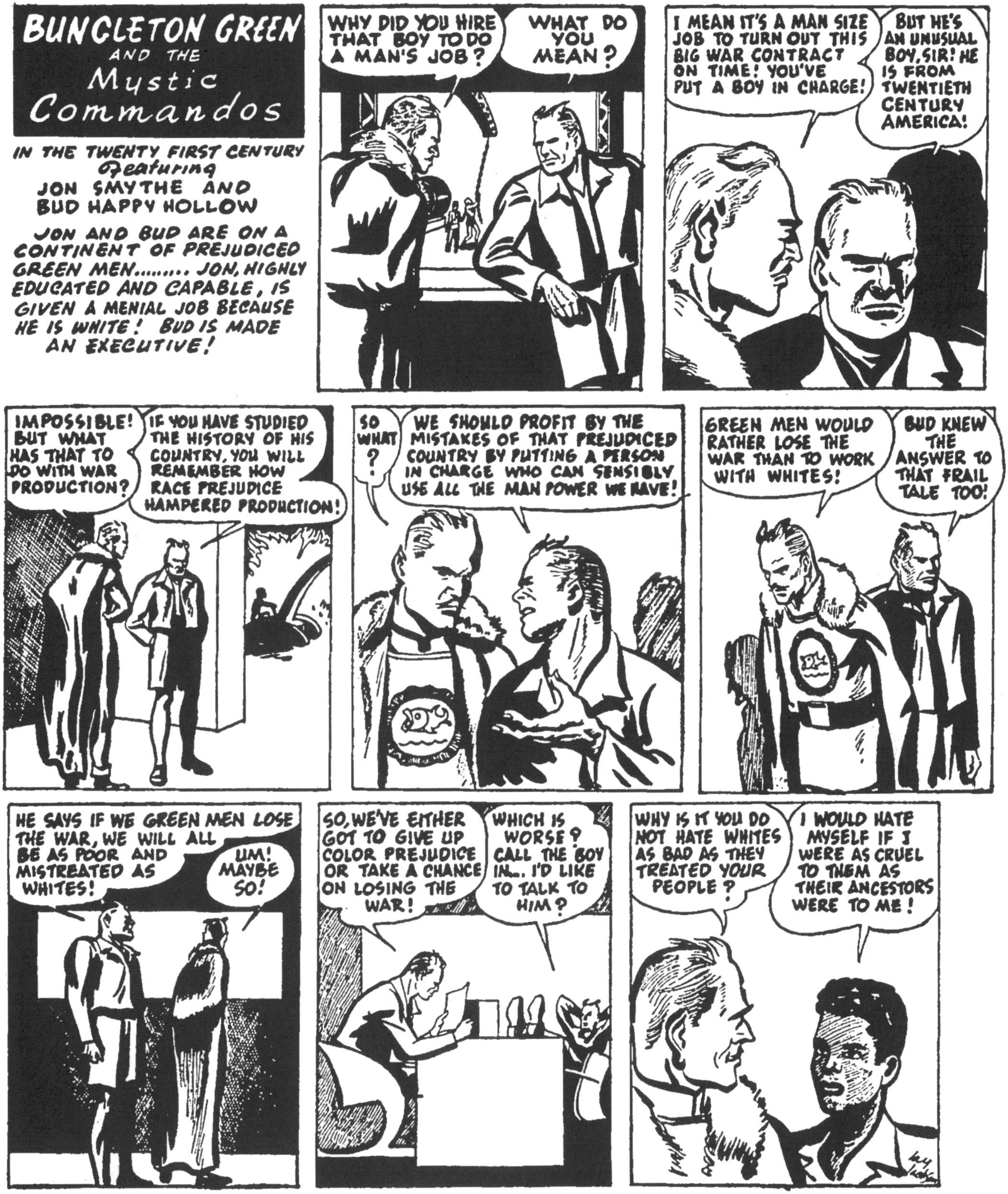
BUNCLETON GREEN
AND THE
Mystic
Commandos
IN THE TWENTY FIRST CENTURY
Featuring
JON SMYTHE AND
BUD HAPPY HOLLOW
JON AND BUD ARE ON A CONTINENT OF PREJUDICED GREEN MEN......... JON, HIGHLY EDUCATED AND CAPABLE, IS GIVEN A MENIAL JOB BECAUSE HE IS WHITE! BUD IS MADE AN EXECUTIVE!
WHY DID YOU HIRE THAT BOY TO DO A MAN'S JOB?
WHAT DO YOU MEAN?
I MEAN IT'S A MAN SIZE JOB TO TURN OUT THIS BIG WAR CONTRACT ON TIME! YOU'VE PUT A BOY IN CHARGE!
BUT HE'S AN UNUSUAL BOY, SIR! HE IS FROM TWENTIETH CENTURY AMERICA!
IMPOSSIBLE! BUT WHAT HAS THAT TO DO WITH WAR PRODUCTION?
IF YOU HAVE STUDIED THE HISTORY OF HIS COUNTRY, YOU WILL REMEMBER HOW RACE PREJUDICE HAMPERED PRODUCTION!
SO WHAT?
WE SHOULD PROFIT BY THE MISTAKES OF THAT PREJUDICED COUNTRY BY PUTTING A PERSON IN CHARGE WHO CAN SENSIBLY USE ALL THE MAN POWER WE HAVE!
GREEN MEN WOULD RATHER LOSE THE WAR THAN TO WORK WITH WHITES!
BUD KNEW THE ANSWER TO THAT FRAIL TALE TOO!
HE SAYS IF WE GREEN MEN LOSE THE WAR, WE WILL ALL BE AS POOR AND MISTREATED AS WHITES!
UM! MAYBE SO!
SO, WE'VE EITHER GOT TO GIVE UP COLOR PREJUDICE OR TAKE A CHANCE ON LOSING THE WAR!
WHICH IS WORSE? CALL THE BOY IN... I'D LIKE TO TALK TO HIM?
WHY IS IT YOU DO NOT HATE WHITES AS BAD AS THEY TREATED YOUR PEOPLE?
I WOULD HATE MYSELF IF I WERE AS CRUEL TO THEM AS THEIR ANCESTORS WERE TO ME!

MAY 6, 1944

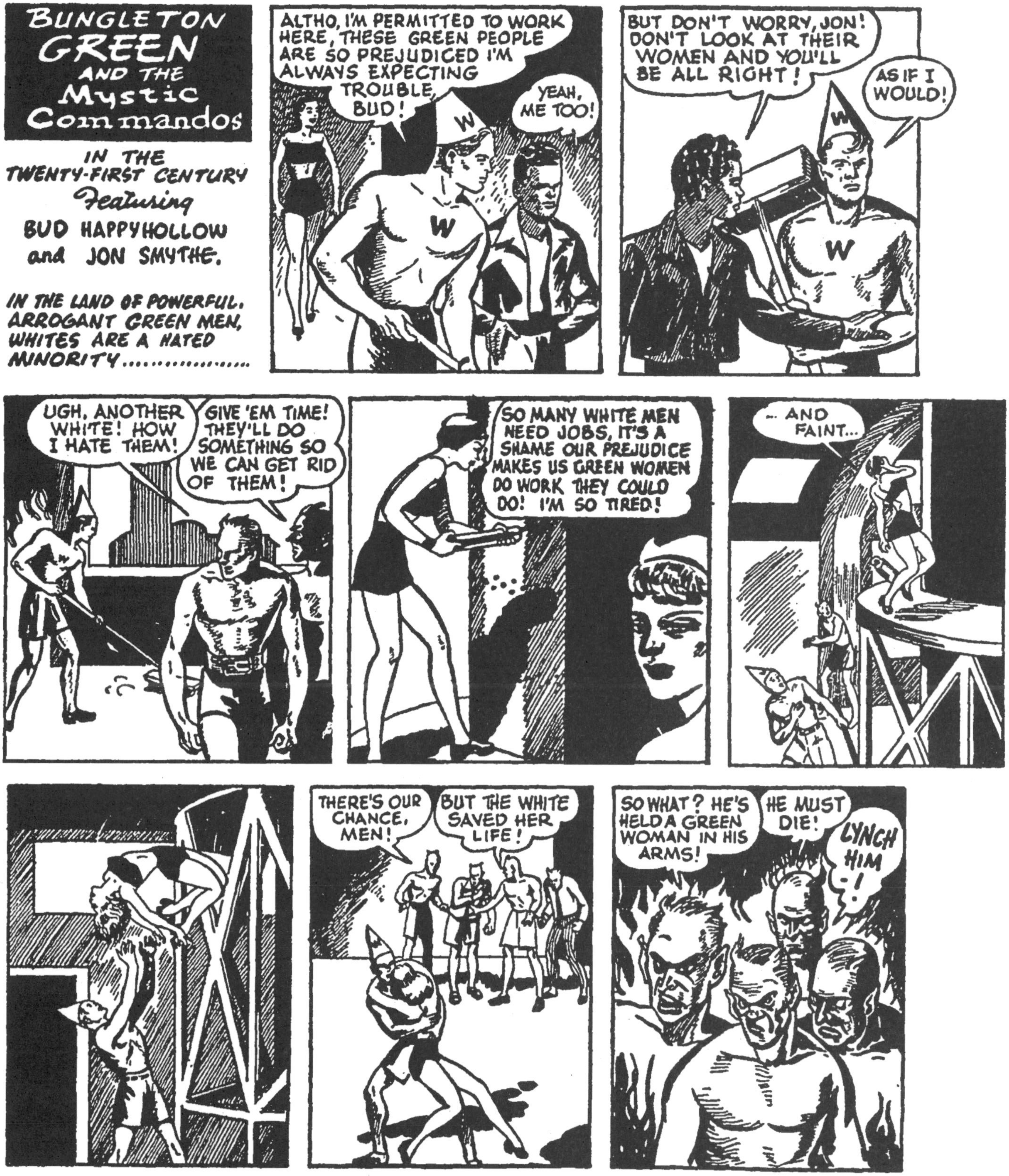
BUNGLETON GREEN AND THE Mystic Commandos
IN THE TWENTY-FIRST CENTURY Featuring BUD HAPPYHOLLOW and JON SMYTHE.
IN THE LAND OF POWERFUL. ARROGANT GREEN MEN, WHITES ARE A HATED MINORITY..................
ALTHO, I'M PERMITTED TO WORK HERE, THESE GREEN PEOPLE ARE SO PREJUDICED I'M ALWAYS EXPECTING TROUBLE, BUD!
YEAH, ME TOO!
BUT DON'T WORRY, JON! DON'T LOOK AT THEIR WOMEN AND YOU'LL BE ALL RIGHT!
AS IF I WOULD!
UGH, ANOTHER WHITE! HOW I HATE THEM!
GIVE 'EM TIME! THEY'LL DO SOMETHING SO WE CAN GET RID OF THEM!
SO MANY WHITE MEN NEED JOBS, IT'S A SHAME OUR PREJUDICE MAKES US GREEN WOMEN DO WORK THEY COULD DO! I'M SO TIRED!
... AND FAINT...
THERE'S OUR CHANCE, MEN!
BUT THE WHITE SAVED HER LIFE!
SO WHAT? HE'S HELD A GREEN WOMAN IN HIS ARMS!
HE MUST DIE!
LYNCH HIM -!

MAY 13, 1944

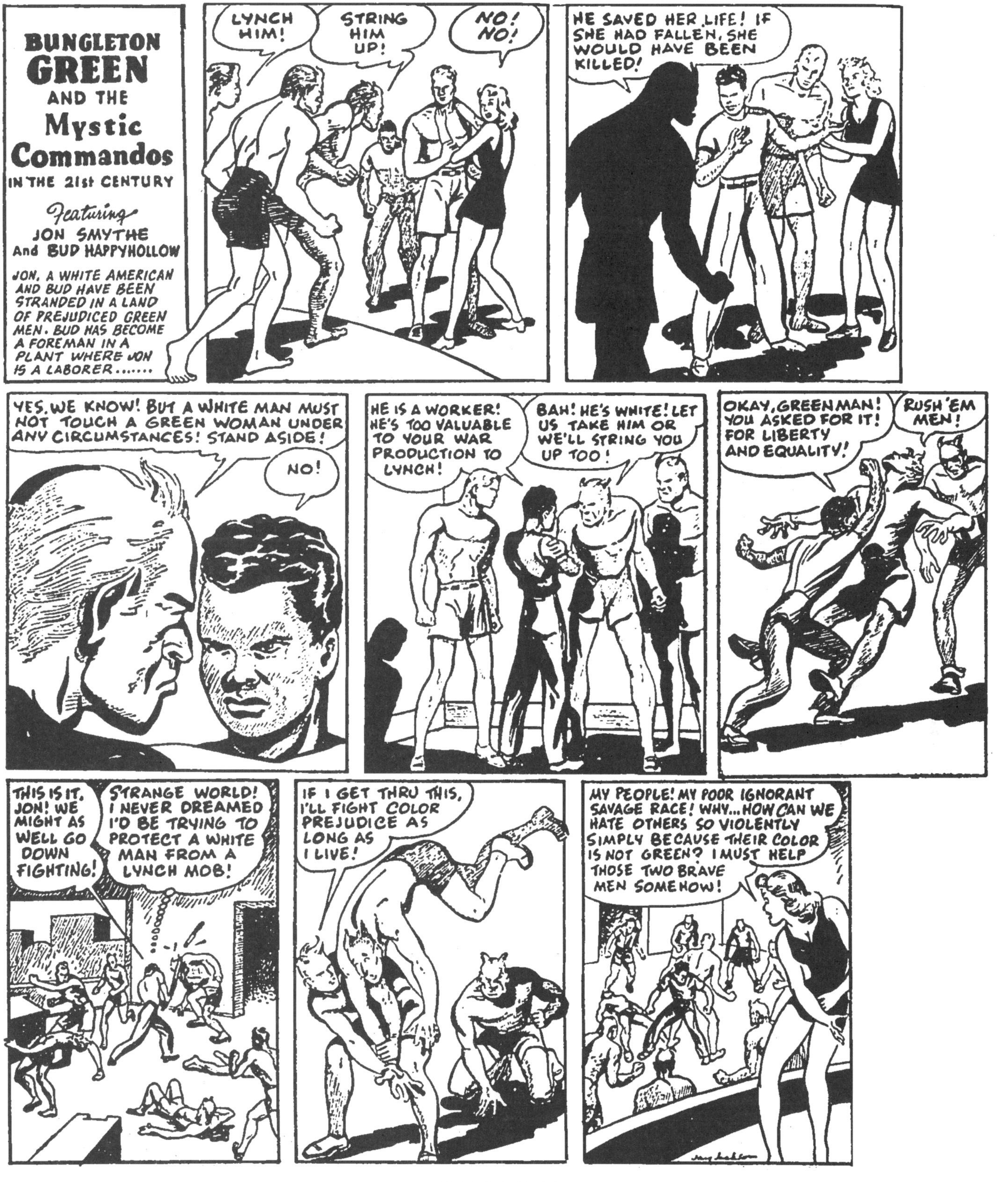
BUNGLETON GREEN
AND THE
Mystic Commandos
IN THE 21st CENTURY
Featuring
JON SMYTHE
And BUD HAPPYHOLLOW
JON, A WHITE AMERICAN AND BUD HAVE BEEN STRANDED IN A LAND OF PREJUDICED GREEN MEN. BUD HAS BECOME A FOREMAN IN A PLANT WHERE JON IS A LABORER.......
LYNCH HIM!
STRING HIM UP!
NO! NO!
HE SAVED HER LIFE! IF SHE HAD FALLEN, SHE WOULD HAVE BEEN KILLED!
YES, WE KNOW! BUT A WHITE MAN MUST NOT TOUCH A GREEN WOMAN UNDER ANY CIRCUMSTANCES! STAND ASIDE!
NO!
HE IS A WORKER! HE'S TOO VALUABLE TO YOUR WAR PRODUCTION TO LYNCH!
BAH! HE'S WHITE! LET US TAKE HIM OR WE'LL STRING YOU UP TOO!
OKAY, GREEN MAN! YOU ASKED FOR IT! FOR LIBERTY AND EQUALITY!
RUSH 'EM MEN!
THIS IS IT, JON! WE MIGHT AS WELL GO DOWN FIGHTING!
STRANGE WORLD! I NEVER DREAMED I'D BE TRYING TO PROTECT A WHITE MAN FROM A LYNCH MOB!
IF I GET THRU THIS, I'LL FIGHT COLOR PREJUDICE AS LONG AS I LIVE!
MY PEOPLE! MY POOR IGNORANT SAVAGE RACE! WHY...HOW CAN WE HATE OTHERS SO VIOLENTLY SIMPLY BECAUSE THEIR COLOR IS NOT GREEN? I MUST HELP THOSE TWO BRAVE MEN SOMEHOW!

MAY 20, 1944

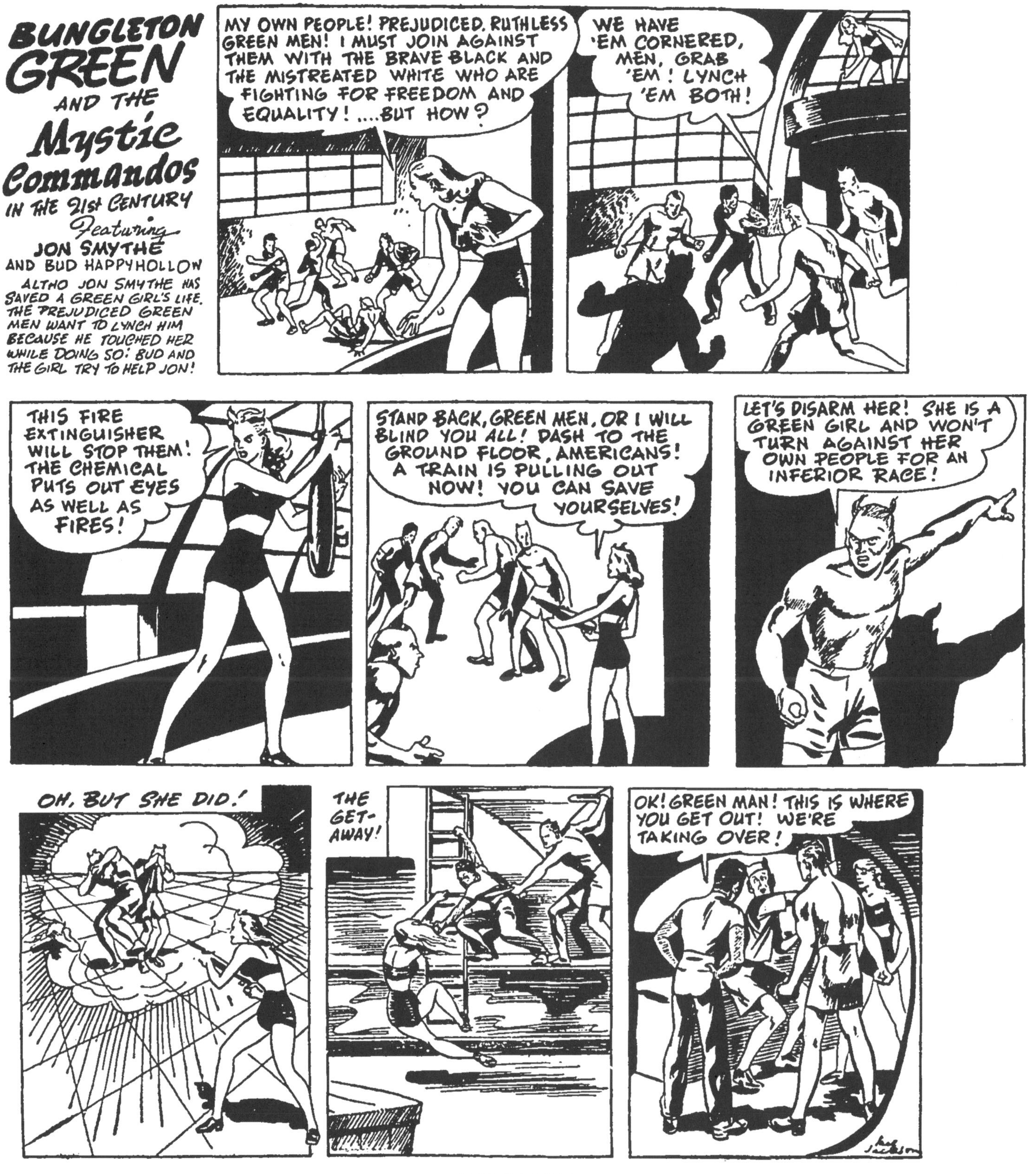
BUNGLETON GREEN AND THE Mystic Commandos IN THE 21st CENTURY
Featuring JON SMYTHE AND BUD HAPPYHOLLOW
ALTHO JON SMYTHE HAS SAVED A GREEN GIRL'S LIFE, THE PREJUDICED GREEN MEN WANT TO LYNCH HIM BECAUSE HE TOUCHED HER WHILE DOING SO: BUD AND THE GIRL TRY TO HELP JON!
MY OWN PEOPLE! PREJUDICED, RUTHLESS GREEN MEN! I MUST JOIN AGAINST THEM WITH THE BRAVE BLACK AND THE MISTREATED WHITE WHO ARE FIGHTING FOR FREEDOM AND EQUALITY! ....BUT HOW?
WE HAVE 'EM CORNERED, MEN. GRAB 'EM! LYNCH 'EM BOTH!
THIS FIRE EXTINGUISHER WILL STOP THEM! THE CHEMICAL PUTS OUT EYES AS WELL AS FIRES!
STAND BACK, GREEN MEN, OR I WILL BLIND YOU ALL! DASH TO THE GROUND FLOOR, AMERICANS! A TRAIN IS PULLING OUT NOW! YOU CAN SAVE YOURSELVES!
LET'S DISARM HER! SHE IS A GREEN GIRL AND WON'T TURN AGAINST HER OWN PEOPLE FOR AN INFERIOR RACE!
OH, BUT SHE DID!
THE GET-AWAY!
OK! GREEN MAN! THIS IS WHERE YOU GET OUT! WE'RE TAKING OVER!

MAY 27, 1944

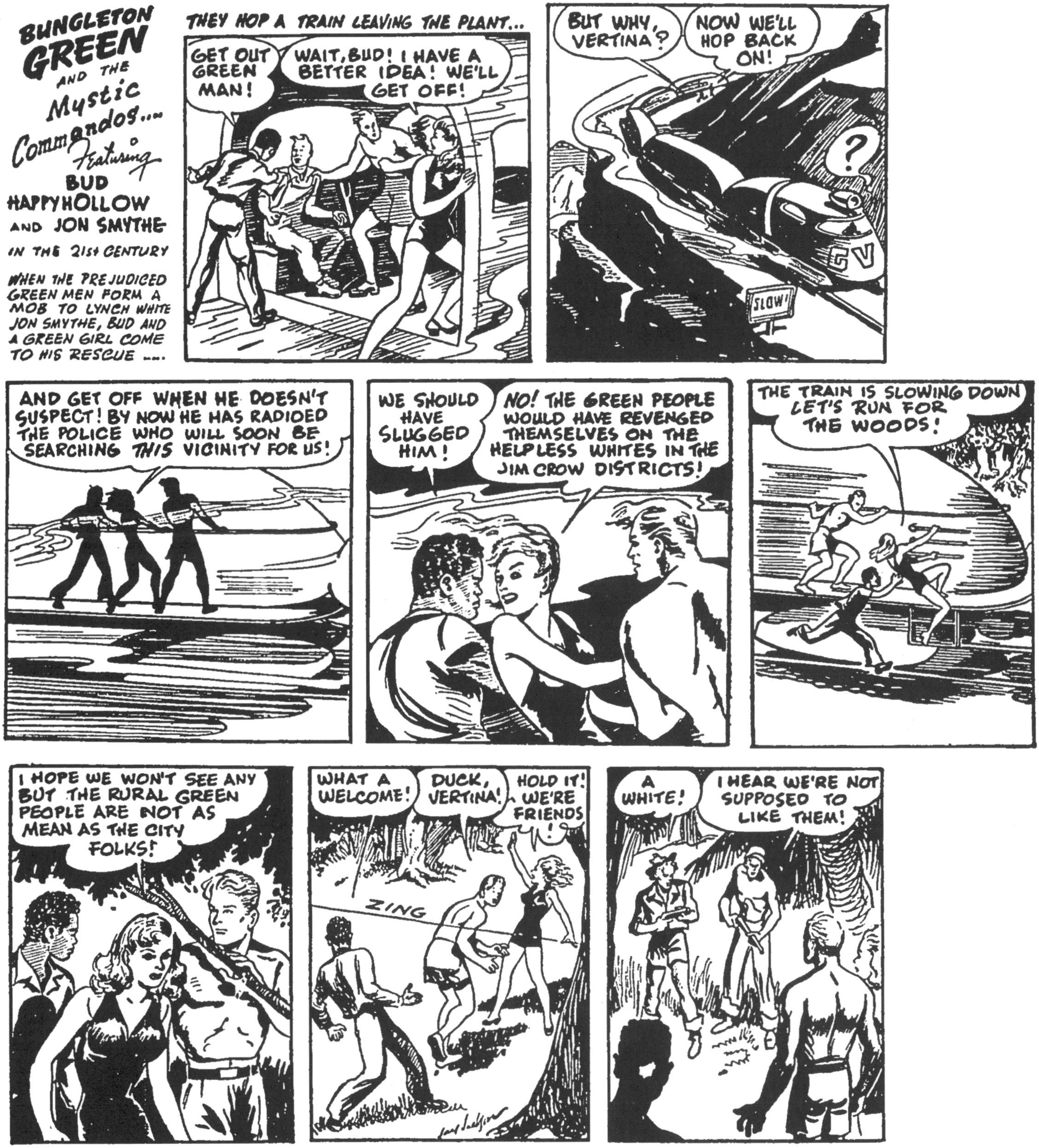
BUNGLETON GREEN AND THE Mystic Commandos... Featuring BUD HAPPYHOLLOW AND JON SMYTHE IN THE 21st CENTURY
WHEN THE PREJUDICED GREEN MEN FORM A MOB TO LYNCH WHITE JON SMYTHE, BUD AND A GREEN GIRL COME TO HIS RESCUE ...
THEY HOP A TRAIN LEAVING THE PLANT...
GET OUT GREEN MAN!
WAIT, BUD! I HAVE A BETTER IDEA! WE'LL GET OFF!
BUT WHY, VERTINA?
NOW WE'LL HOP BACK ON!
?
GV
SLOW!
AND GET OFF WHEN HE DOESN'T SUSPECT! BY NOW HE HAS RADIOED THE POLICE WHO WILL SOON BE SEARCHING THIS VICINITY FOR US!
WE SHOULD HAVE SLUGGED HIM!
NO! THE GREEN PEOPLE WOULD HAVE REVENGED THEMSELVES ON THE HELPLESS WHITES IN THE JIM CROW DISTRICTS!
THE TRAIN IS SLOWING DOWN LET'S RUN FOR THE WOODS!
I HOPE WE WON'T SEE ANY BUT THE RURAL GREEN PEOPLE ARE NOT AS MEAN AS THE CITY FOLKS!
WHAT A WELCOME!
DUCK, VERTINA!
HOLD IT! WE'RE FRIENDS!
ZING
A WHITE!
I HEAR WE'RE NOT SUPPOSED TO LIKE THEM!

JUNE 3, 1944

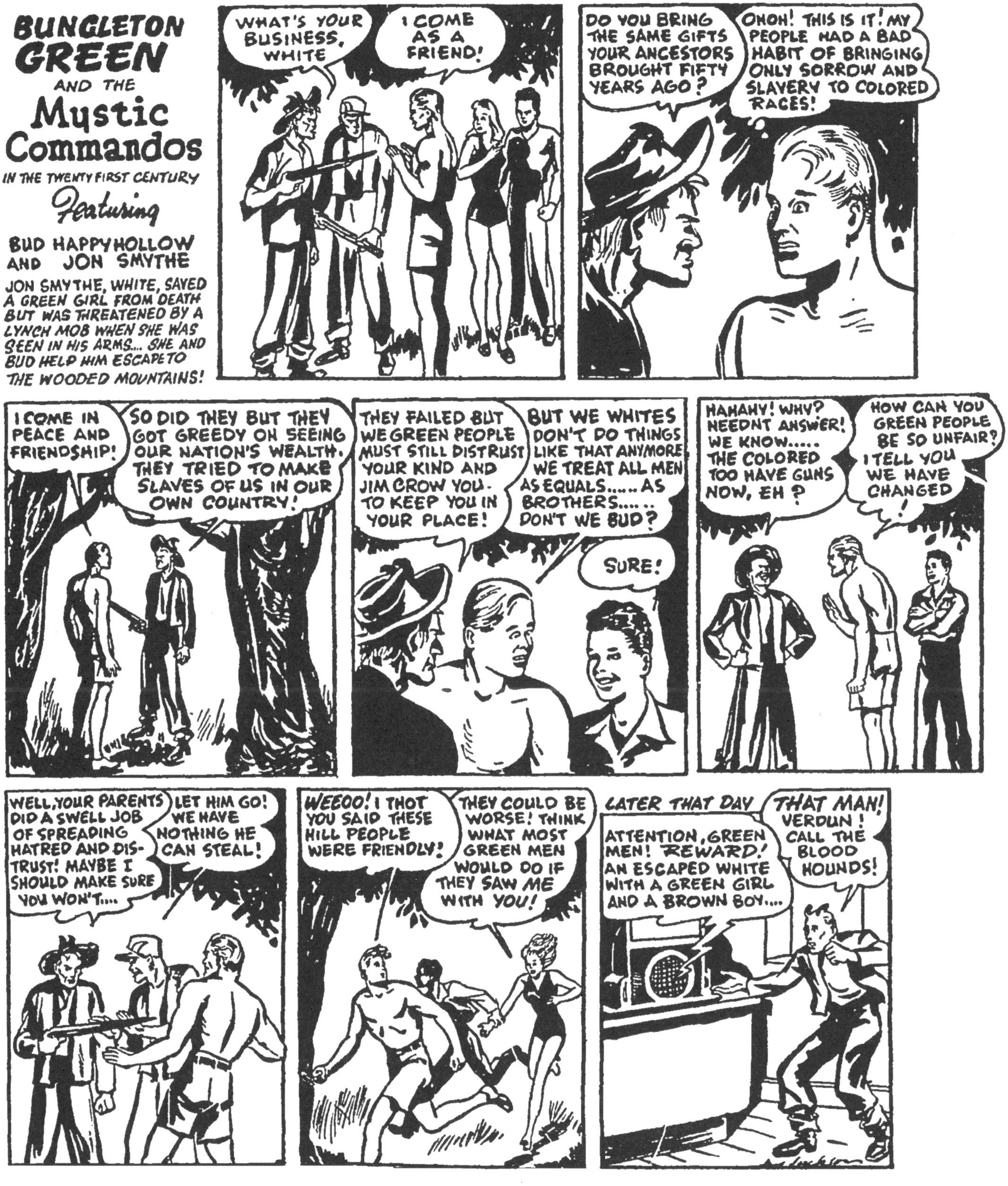
BUNGLETON GREEN
AND THE
Mystic Commandos
IN THE TWENTY FIRST CENTURY
Featuring
BUD HAPPYHOLLOW AND JON SMYTHE
JON SMYTHE, WHITE, SAVED A GREEN GIRL FROM DEATH BUT WAS THREATENED BY A LYNCH MOB WHEN SHE WAS SEEN IN HIS ARMS.... SHE AND BUD HELP HIM ESCAPE TO THE WOODED MOUNTAINS!
WHAT'S YOUR BUSINESS, WHITE
I COME AS A FRIEND!
DO YOU BRING THE SAME GIFTS YOUR ANCESTORS BROUGHT FIFTY YEARS AGO?
OHOH! THIS IS IT! MY PEOPLE HAD A BAD HABIT OF BRINGING ONLY SORROW AND SLAVERY TO COLORED RACES!
I COME IN PEACE AND FRIENDSHIP!
SO DID THEY BUT THEY GOT GREEDY ON SEEING OUR NATION'S WEALTH. THEY TRIED TO MAKE SLAVES OF US IN OUR OWN COUNTRY!
THEY FAILED BUT WE GREEN PEOPLE MUST STILL DISTRUST YOUR KIND AND JIM CROW YOU. TO KEEP YOU IN YOUR PLACE!
BUT WE WHITES DON'T DO THINGS LIKE THAT ANYMORE. WE TREAT ALL MEN AS EQUALS..... AS BROTHERS...... DON'T WE BUD?
SURE!
HAHAHY! WHY? NEEDNT ANSWER! WE KNOW..... THE COLORED TOO HAVE GUNS NOW, EH?
HOW CAN YOU GREEN PEOPLE BE SO UNFAIR? I TELL YOU WE HAVE CHANGED!
WELL, YOUR PARENTS DID A SWELL JOB OF SPREADING HATRED AND DISTRUST! MAYBE I SHOULD MAKE SURE YOU WON'T....
LET HIM GO! WE HAVE NOTHING HE CAN STEAL!
WEEOO! I THOT YOU SAID THESE HILL PEOPLE WERE FRIENDLY!
THEY COULD BE WORSE! THINK WHAT MOST GREEN MEN WOULD DO IF THEY SAW ME WITH YOU!
LATER THAT DAY
ATTENTION, GREEN MEN! REWARD! AN ESCAPED WHITE WITH A GREEN GIRL AND A BROWN BOY....
THAT MAN! VERDUN! CALL THE BLOOD HOUNDS!

JUNE 10, 1944

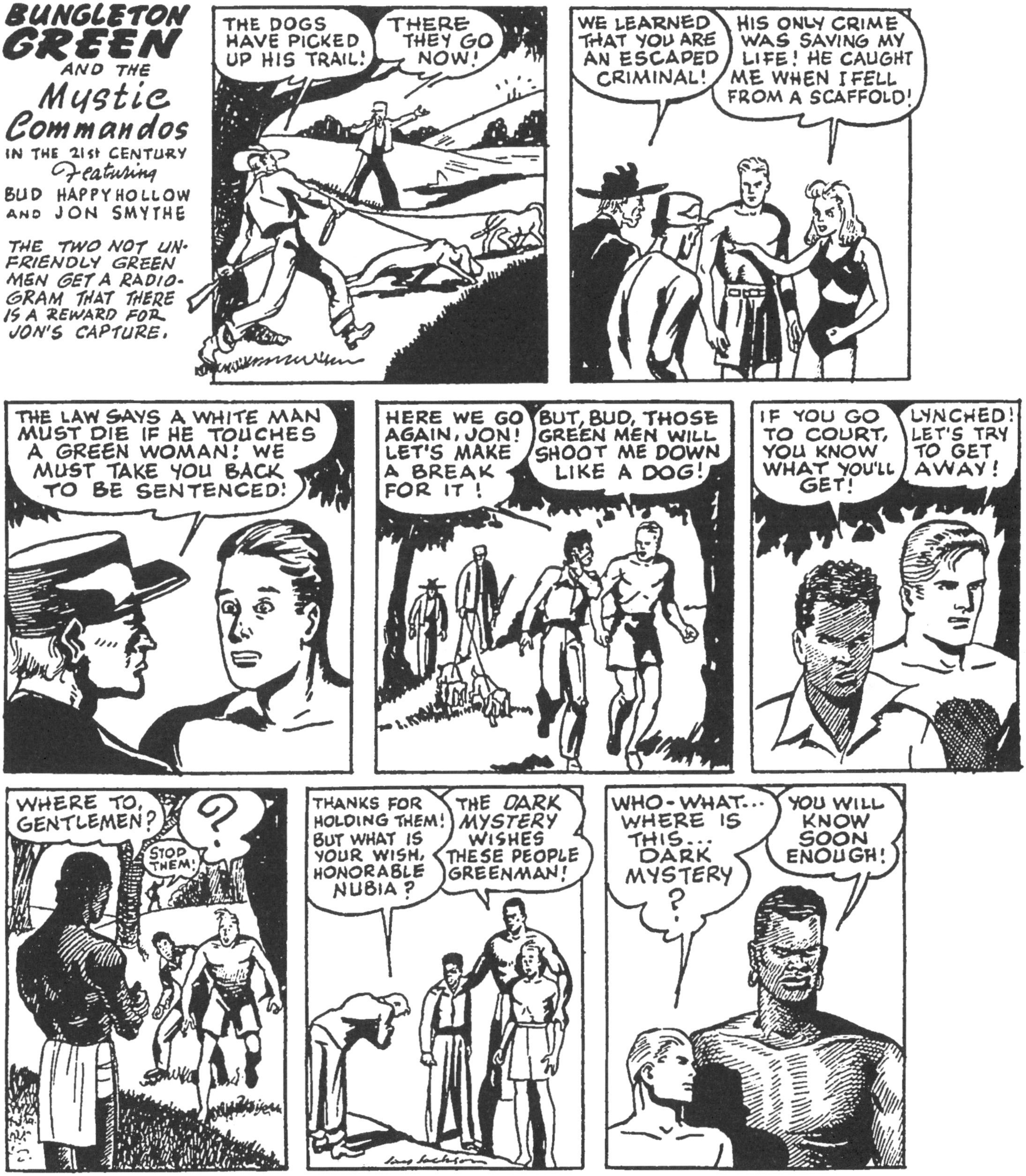
BUNGLETON GREEN AND THE Mystic Commandos IN THE 21st CENTURY Featuring BUD HAPPYHOLLOW AND JON SMYTHE
THE TWO NOT UNFRIENDLY GREEN MEN GET A RADIOGRAM THAT THERE IS A REWARD FOR JON'S CAPTURE.
THE DOGS HAVE PICKED UP HIS TRAIL!
THERE THEY GO NOW!
WE LEARNED THAT YOU ARE AN ESCAPED CRIMINAL!
HIS ONLY CRIME WAS SAVING MY LIFE! HE CAUGHT ME WHEN I FELL FROM A SCAFFOLD!
THE LAW SAYS A WHITE MAN MUST DIE IF HE TOUCHES A GREEN WOMAN! WE MUST TAKE YOU BACK TO BE SENTENCED!
HERE WE GO AGAIN, JON! LET'S MAKE A BREAK FOR IT!
BUT, BUD, THOSE GREEN MEN WILL SHOOT ME DOWN LIKE A DOG!
IF YOU GO TO COURT, YOU KNOW WHAT YOU'LL GET!
LYNCHED! LET'S TRY TO GET AWAY!
WHERE TO, GENTLEMEN?
?
STOP THEM!
THANKS FOR HOLDING THEM! BUT WHAT IS YOUR WISH, HONORABLE NUBIA?
THE DARK MYSTERY WISHES THESE PEOPLE GREENMAN!
WHO-WHAT... WHERE IS THIS... DARK MYSTERY?
YOU WILL KNOW SOON ENOUGH!

JUNE 17, 1944

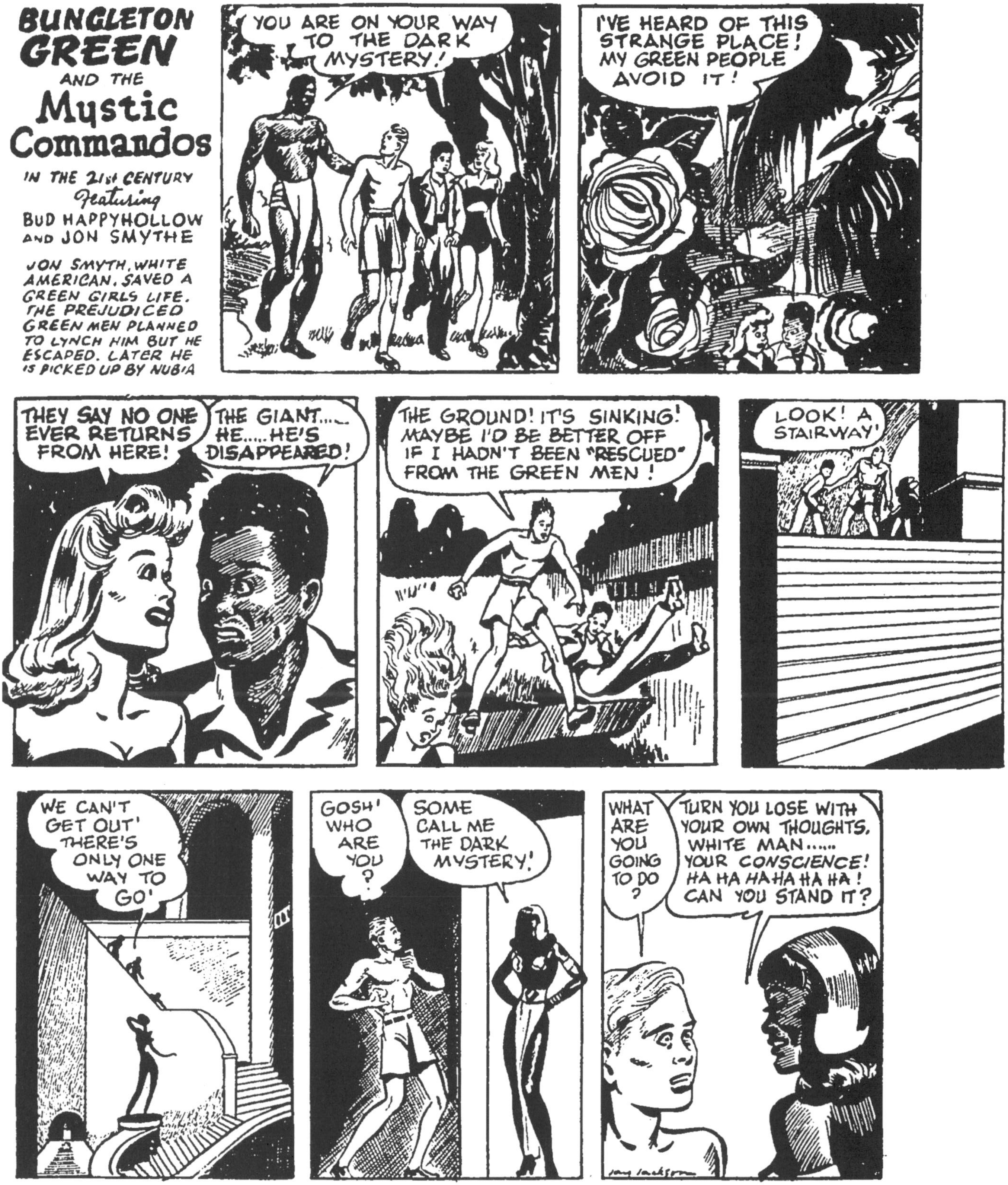
BUNGLETON GREEN
AND THE
Mystic Commandos
IN THE 21st CENTURY
featuring
BUD HAPPYHOLLOW
AND JON SMYTHE
JON SMYTH, WHITE AMERICAN, SAVED A GREEN GIRLS LIFE. THE PREJUDICED GREEN MEN PLANNED TO LYNCH HIM BUT HE ESCAPED. LATER HE IS PICKED UP BY NUBIA
YOU ARE ON YOUR WAY TO THE DARK MYSTERY!
I'VE HEARD OF THIS STRANGE PLACE! MY GREEN PEOPLE AVOID IT!
THEY SAY NO ONE EVER RETURNS FROM HERE!
THE GIANT..... HE..... HE'S DISAPPEARED!
THE GROUND! IT'S SINKING! MAYBE I'D BE BETTER OFF IF I HADN'T BEEN "RESCUED" FROM THE GREEN MEN!
LOOK! A STAIRWAY!
WE CAN'T GET OUT! THERE'S ONLY ONE WAY TO GO!
GOSH! WHO ARE YOU?
SOME CALL ME THE DARK MYSTERY!
WHAT ARE YOU GOING TO DO?
TURN YOU LOSE WITH YOUR OWN THOUGHTS, WHITE MAN..... YOUR CONSCIENCE! HA HA HA HA HA HA! CAN YOU STAND IT?
Jay Jackson

JUNE 24, 1944

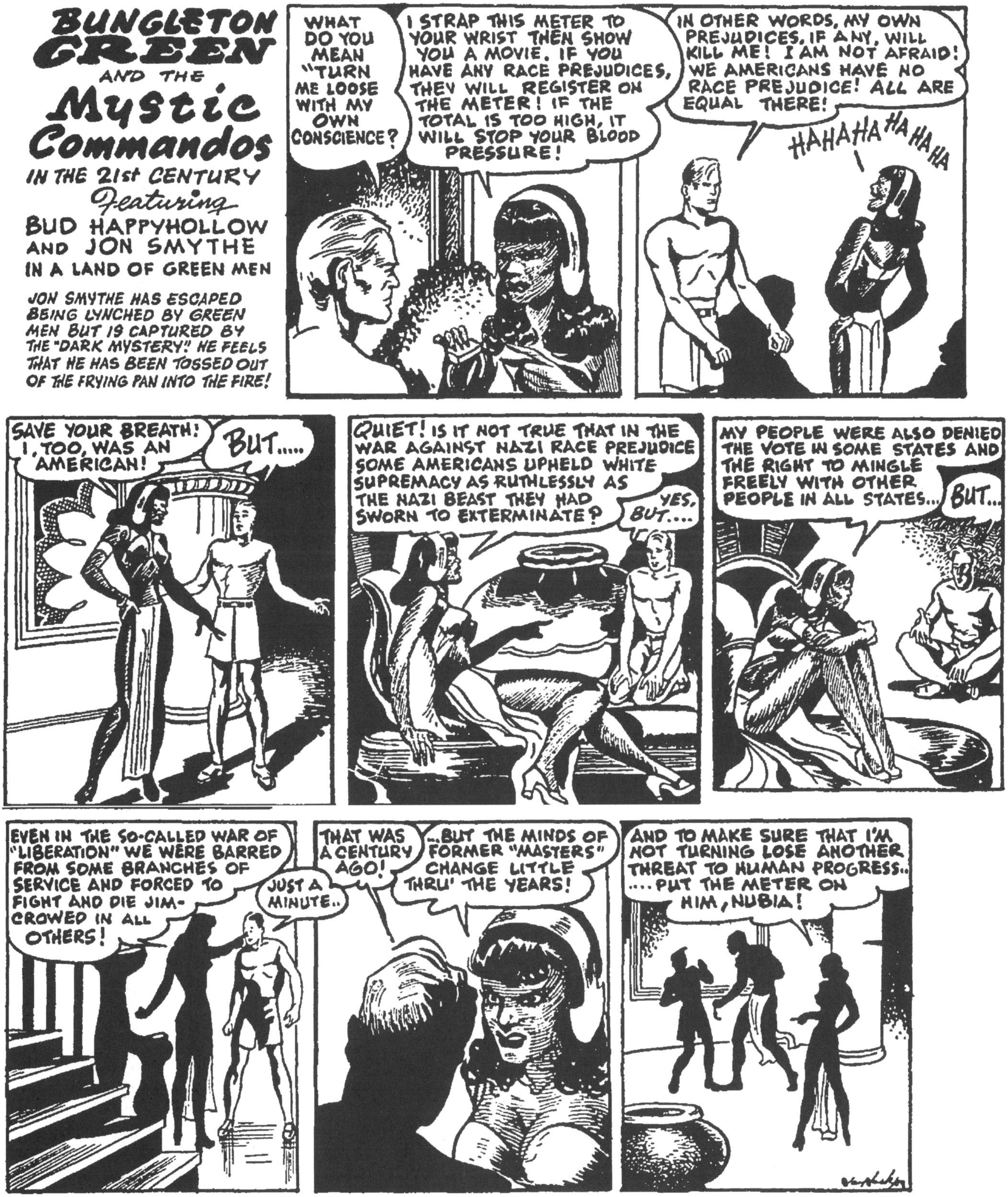
BUNGLETON GREEN AND THE Mystic Commandos IN THE 21st CENTURY Featuring BUD HAPPYHOLLOW AND JON SMYTHE IN A LAND OF GREEN MEN
JON SMYTHE HAS ESCAPED BEING LYNCHED BY GREEN MEN BUT IS CAPTURED BY THE "DARK MYSTERY!" HE FEELS THAT HE HAS BEEN TOSSED OUT OF THE FRYING PAN INTO THE FIRE!
WHAT DO YOU MEAN "TURN ME LOOSE WITH MY OWN CONSCIENCE?
I STRAP THIS METER TO YOUR WRIST THEN SHOW YOU A MOVIE. IF YOU HAVE ANY RACE PREJUDICES, THEY WILL REGISTER ON THE METER! IF THE TOTAL IS TOO HIGH, IT WILL STOP YOUR BLOOD PRESSURE!
IN OTHER WORDS, MY OWN PREJUDICES, IF ANY, WILL KILL ME! I AM NOT AFRAID! WE AMERICANS HAVE NO RACE PREJUDICE! ALL ARE EQUAL THERE!
HAHAHA HA HA HA HA
SAVE YOUR BREATH! I, TOO, WAS AN AMERICAN!
BUT.....
QUIET! IS IT NOT TRUE THAT IN THE WAR AGAINST NAZI RACE PREJUDICE SOME AMERICANS UPHELD WHITE SUPREMACY AS RUTHLESSLY AS THE NAZI BEAST THEY HAD SWORN TO EXTERMINATE?
YES, BUT....
MY PEOPLE WERE ALSO DENIED THE VOTE IN SOME STATES AND THE RIGHT TO MINGLE FREELY WITH OTHER PEOPLE IN ALL STATES...
BUT...
EVEN IN THE SO-CALLED WAR OF "LIBERATION" WE WERE BARRED FROM SOME BRANCHES OF SERVICE AND FORCED TO FIGHT AND DIE JIM-CROWED IN ALL OTHERS!
JUST A MINUTE..
THAT WAS A CENTURY AGO!
..BUT THE MINDS OF FORMER "MASTERS" CHANGE LITTLE THRU' THE YEARS!
AND TO MAKE SURE THAT I'M NOT TURNING LOSE ANOTHER THREAT TO HUMAN PROGRESS.. ....PUT THE METER ON HIM, NUBIA!

JULY 1, 1944

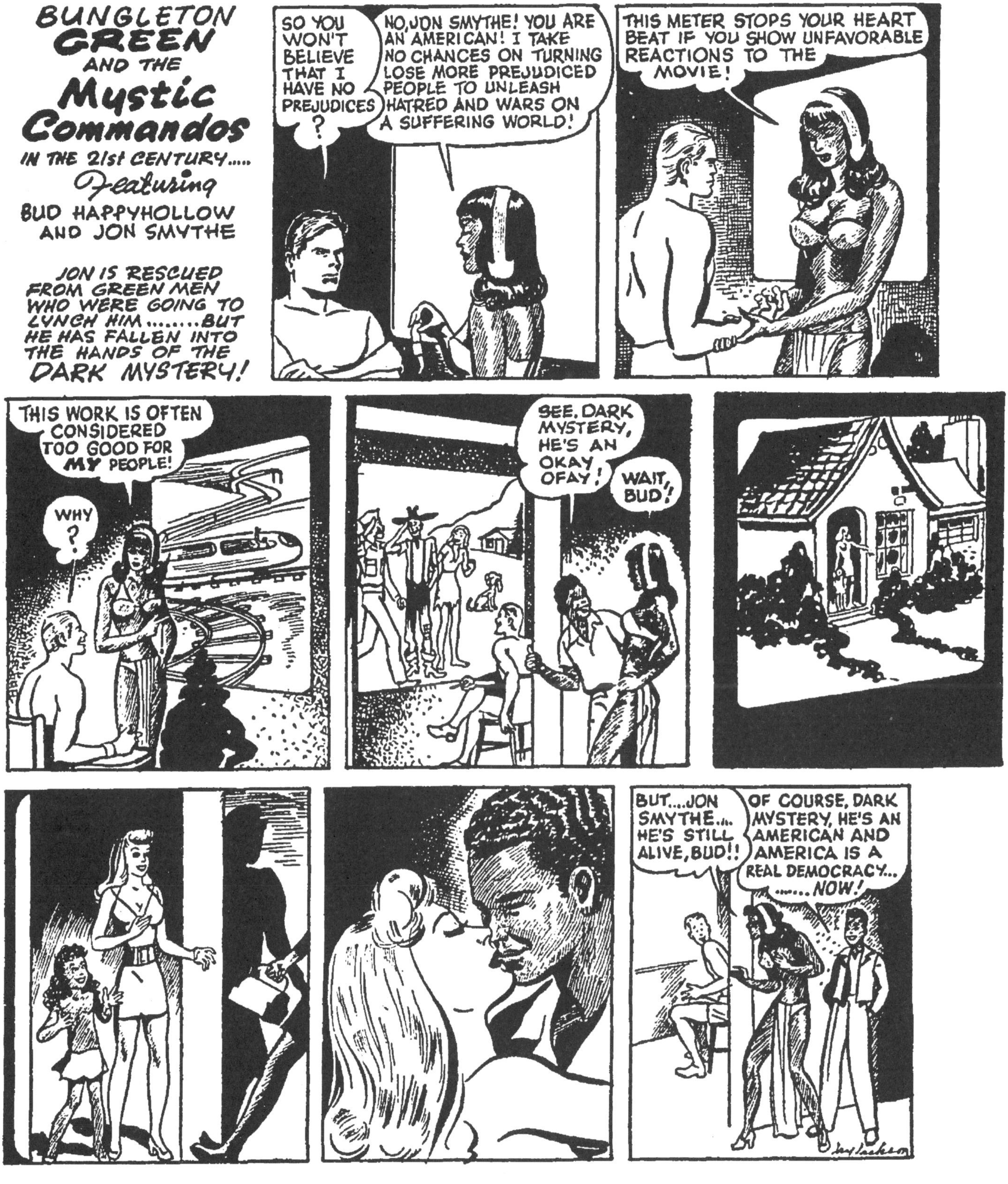
BUNGLETON GREEN AND THE Mystic Commandos IN THE 21st CENTURY.....
Featuring
BUD HAPPYHOLLOW AND JON SMYTHE
JON IS RESCUED FROM GREEN MEN WHO WERE GOING TO LYNCH HIM........BUT HE HAS FALLEN INTO THE HANDS OF THE DARK MYSTERY!
SO YOU WON'T BELIEVE THAT I HAVE NO PREJUDICES ?
NO, JON SMYTHE! YOU ARE AN AMERICAN! I TAKE NO CHANCES ON TURNING LOSE MORE PREJUDICED PEOPLE TO UNLEASH HATRED AND WARS ON A SUFFERING WORLD!
THIS METER STOPS YOUR HEART BEAT IF YOU SHOW UNFAVORABLE REACTIONS TO THE MOVIE!
THIS WORK IS OFTEN CONSIDERED TOO GOOD FOR MY PEOPLE!
WHY ?
SEE, DARK MYSTERY, HE'S AN OKAY OFAY!
WAIT, BUD!
BUT....JON SMYTHE.... HE'S STILL ALIVE, BUD!!
OF COURSE, DARK MYSTERY, HE'S AN AMERICAN AND AMERICA IS A REAL DEMOCRACY... ......NOW!
Jay Jackson

JULY 8, 1944

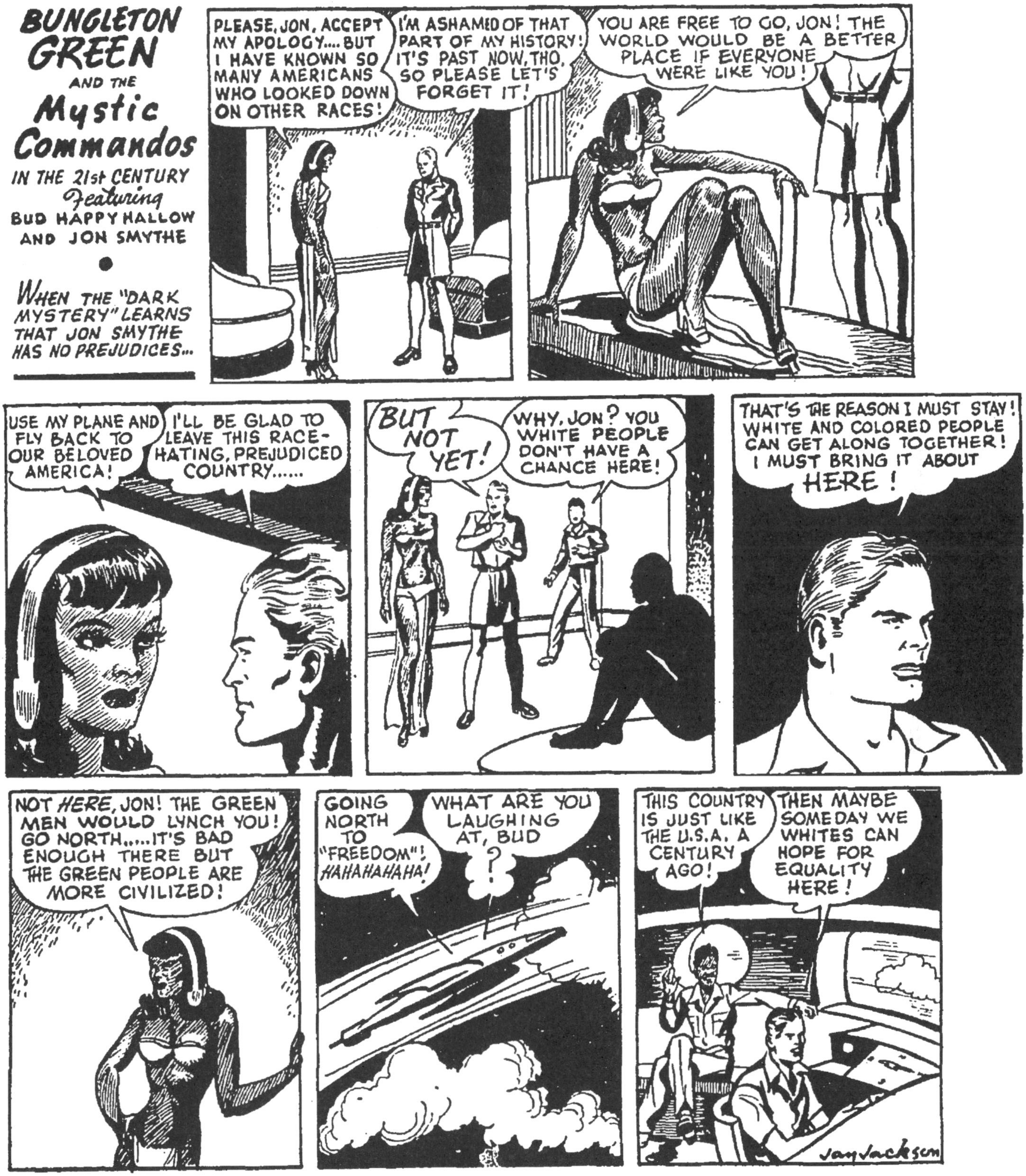
BUNGLETON GREEN AND THE Mystic Commandos
IN THE 21st CENTURY Featuring BUD HAPPY HALLOW AND JON SMYTHE
WHEN THE "DARK MYSTERY" LEARNS THAT JON SMYTHE HAS NO PREJUDICES...
PLEASE, JON, ACCEPT MY APOLOGY.... BUT I HAVE KNOWN SO MANY AMERICANS WHO LOOKED DOWN ON OTHER RACES!
I'M ASHAMED OF THAT PART OF MY HISTORY! IT'S PAST NOW, THO, SO PLEASE LET'S FORGET IT!
YOU ARE FREE TO GO, JON! THE WORLD WOULD BE A BETTER PLACE IF EVERYONE WERE LIKE YOU!
USE MY PLANE AND FLY BACK TO OUR BELOVED AMERICA!
I'LL BE GLAD TO LEAVE THIS RACE-HATING, PREJUDICED COUNTRY......
BUT NOT YET!
WHY, JON? YOU WHITE PEOPLE DON'T HAVE A CHANCE HERE!
THAT'S THE REASON I MUST STAY! WHITE AND COLORED PEOPLE CAN GET ALONG TOGETHER! I MUST BRING IT ABOUT HERE!
NOT HERE, JON! THE GREEN MEN WOULD LYNCH YOU! GO NORTH.....IT'S BAD ENOUGH THERE BUT THE GREEN PEOPLE ARE MORE CIVILIZED!
GOING NORTH TO "FREEDOM"! HAHAHAHAHA!
WHAT ARE YOU LAUGHING AT, BUD ?
THIS COUNTRY IS JUST LIKE THE U.S.A. A CENTURY AGO!
THEN MAYBE SOMEDAY WE WHITES CAN HOPE FOR EQUALITY HERE!
Jay Jackson

JULY 15, 1944

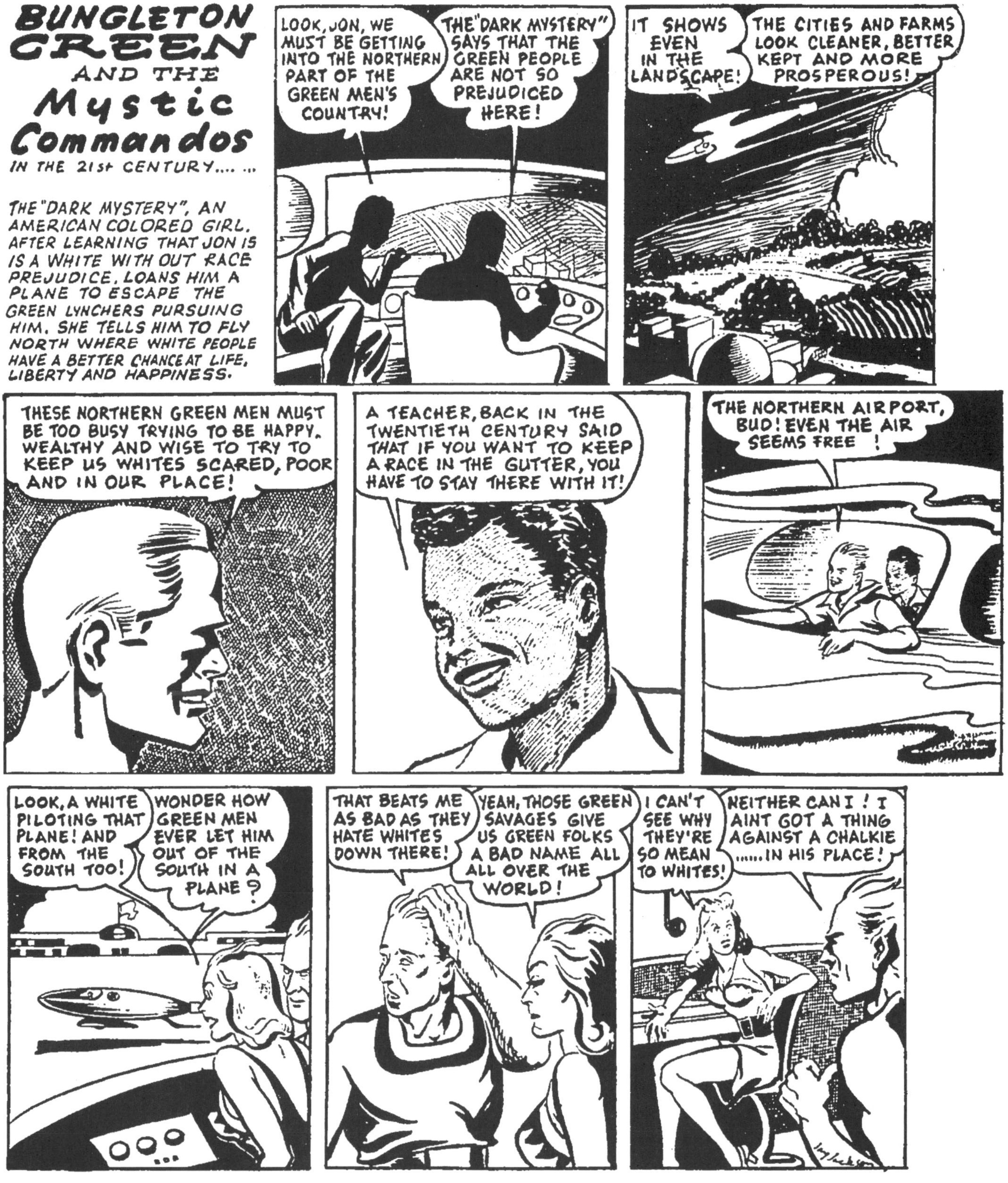
BUNGLETON GREEN AND THE Mystic Commandos IN THE 21st CENTURY.... ...
THE "DARK MYSTERY", AN AMERICAN COLORED GIRL, AFTER LEARNING THAT JON IS IS A WHITE WITH OUT RACE PREJUDICE, LOANS HIM A PLANE TO ESCAPE THE GREEN LYNCHERS PURSUING HIM. SHE TELLS HIM TO FLY NORTH WHERE WHITE PEOPLE HAVE A BETTER CHANCE AT LIFE, LIBERTY AND HAPPINESS.
LOOK, JON, WE MUST BE GETTING INTO THE NORTHERN PART OF THE GREEN MEN'S COUNTRY!
THE "DARK MYSTERY" SAYS THAT THE GREEN PEOPLE ARE NOT SO PREJUDICED HERE!
IT SHOWS EVEN IN THE LANDSCAPE!
THE CITIES AND FARMS LOOK CLEANER, BETTER KEPT AND MORE PROSPEROUS!
THESE NORTHERN GREEN MEN MUST BE TOO BUSY TRYING TO BE HAPPY, WEALTHY AND WISE TO TRY TO KEEP US WHITES SCARED, POOR AND IN OUR PLACE!
A TEACHER, BACK IN THE TWENTIETH CENTURY SAID THAT IF YOU WANT TO KEEP A RACE IN THE GUTTER, YOU HAVE TO STAY THERE WITH IT!
THE NORTHERN AIRPORT, BUD! EVEN THE AIR SEEMS FREE !
LOOK, A WHITE PILOTING THAT PLANE! AND FROM THE SOUTH TOO!
WONDER HOW GREEN MEN EVER LET HIM OUT OF THE SOUTH IN A PLANE?
THAT BEATS ME AS BAD AS THEY HATE WHITES DOWN THERE!
YEAH, THOSE GREEN SAVAGES GIVE US GREEN FOLKS A BAD NAME ALL ALL OVER THE WORLD!
I CAN'T SEE WHY THEY'RE SO MEAN TO WHITES!
NEITHER CAN I! I AINT GOT A THING AGAINST A CHALKIE ......IN HIS PLACE!

JULY 22, 1944

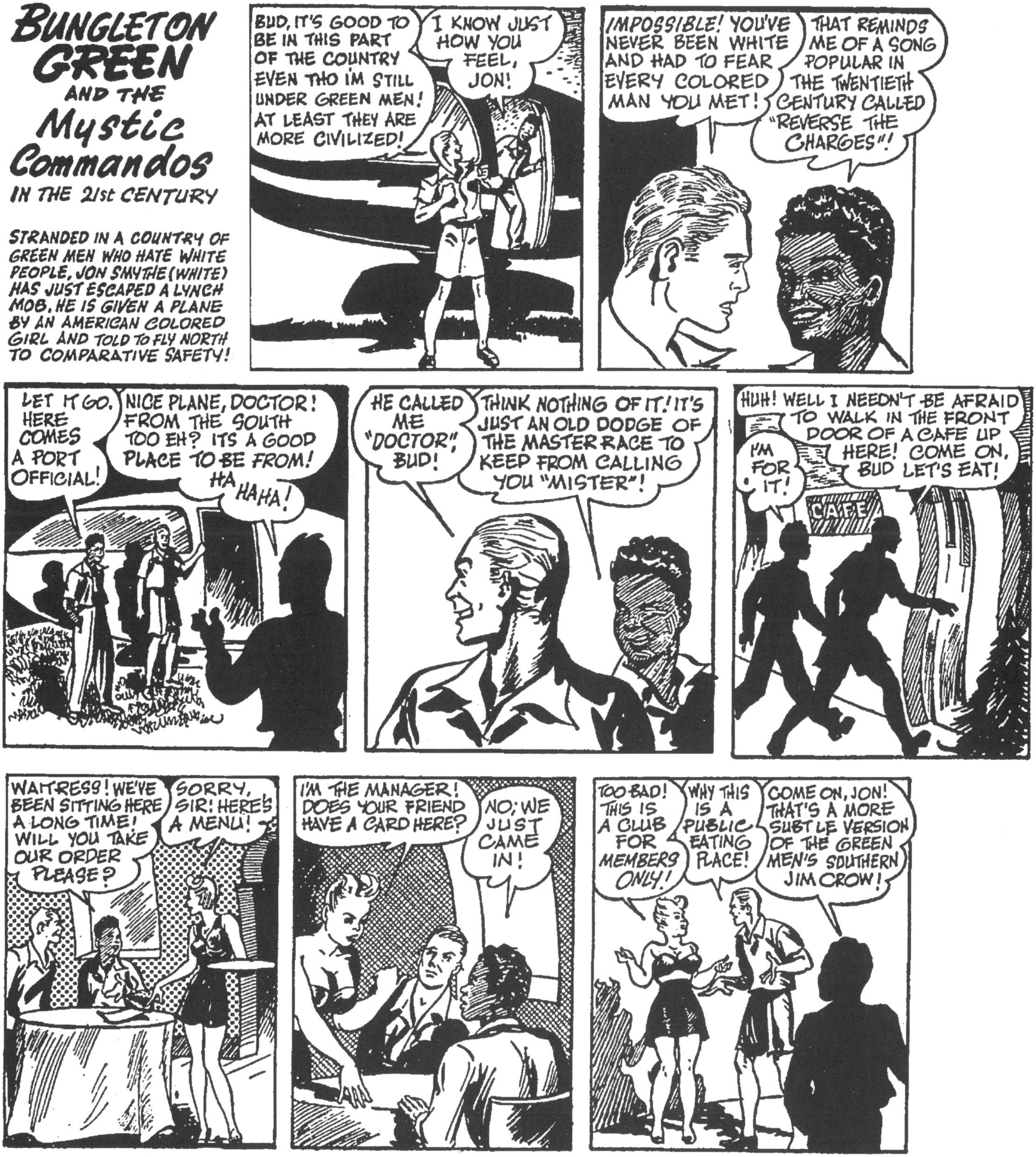
BUNGLETON GREEN AND THE Mystic Commandos
IN THE 21st CENTURY
STRANDED IN A COUNTRY OF GREEN MEN WHO HATE WHITE PEOPLE, JON SMYTHE (WHITE) HAS JUST ESCAPED A LYNCH MOB. HE IS GIVEN A PLANE BY AN AMERICAN COLORED GIRL AND TOLD TO FLY NORTH TO COMPARATIVE SAFETY!
BUD, IT'S GOOD TO BE IN THIS PART OF THE COUNTRY EVEN THO I'M STILL UNDER GREEN MEN! AT LEAST THEY ARE MORE CIVILIZED!
I KNOW JUST HOW YOU FEEL, JON!
IMPOSSIBLE! YOU'VE NEVER BEEN WHITE AND HAD TO FEAR EVERY COLORED MAN YOU MET!
THAT REMINDS ME OF A SONG POPULAR IN THE TWENTIETH CENTURY CALLED "REVERSE THE CHARGES"!
LET IT GO. HERE COMES A PORT OFFICIAL!
NICE PLANE, DOCTOR! FROM THE SOUTH TOO EH? ITS A GOOD PLACE TO BE FROM! HA HAHA!
HE CALLED ME "DOCTOR", BUD!
THINK NOTHING OF IT! IT'S JUST AN OLD DODGE OF THE MASTER RACE TO KEEP FROM CALLING YOU "MISTER"!
HUH! WELL I NEEDN'T BE AFRAID TO WALK IN THE FRONT DOOR OF A CAFE UP HERE! COME ON, BUD LET'S EAT!
I'M FOR IT!
CAFE
WAITRESS! WE'VE BEEN SITTING HERE A LONG TIME! WILL YOU TAKE OUR ORDER PLEASE?
SORRY, SIR! HERE'S A MENU!
I'M THE MANAGER! DOES YOUR FRIEND HAVE A CARD HERE?
NO; WE JUST CAME IN!
TOO BAD! THIS IS A CLUB FOR MEMBERS ONLY!
WHY THIS IS A PUBLIC EATING PLACE!
COME ON, JON! THAT'S A MORE SUBTLE VERSION OF THE GREEN MEN'S SOUTHERN JIM CROW!

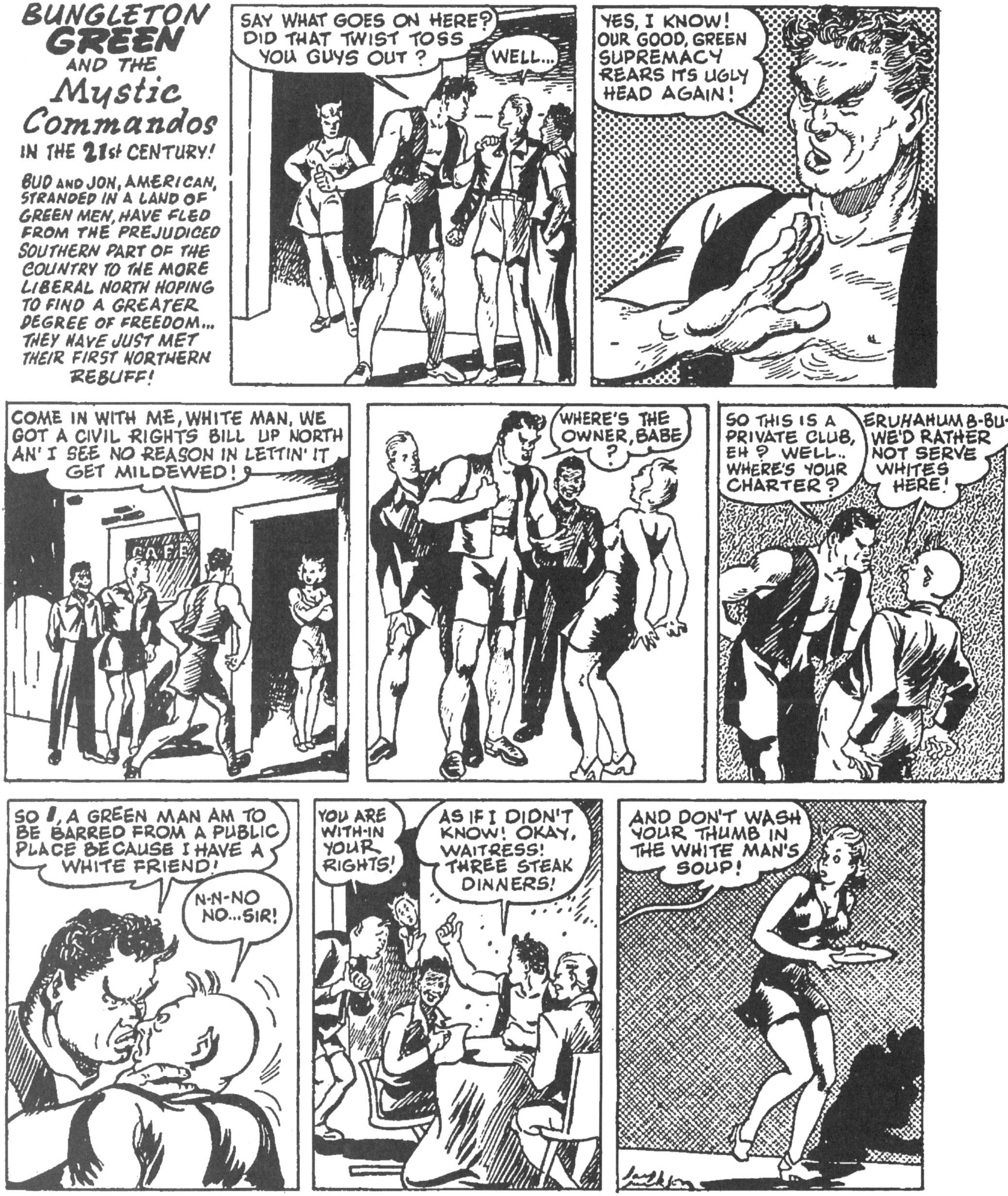
BUNGLETON GREEN AND THE Mystic Commandos IN THE 21st CENTURY!
BUD AND JON, AMERICAN, STRANDED IN A LAND OF GREEN MEN, HAVE FLED FROM THE PREJUDICED SOUTHERN PART OF THE COUNTRY TO THE MORE LIBERAL NORTH HOPING TO FIND A GREATER DEGREE OF FREEDOM... THEY HAVE JUST MET THEIR FIRST NORTHERN REBUFF!
SAY WHAT GOES ON HERE? DID THAT TWIST TOSS YOU GUYS OUT ?
WELL...
YES, I KNOW! OUR GOOD, GREEN SUPREMACY REARS ITS UGLY HEAD AGAIN!
COME IN WITH ME, WHITE MAN, WE GOT A CIVIL RIGHTS BILL UP NORTH AN' I SEE NO REASON IN LETTIN' IT GET MILDEWED!
CAFE
WHERE'S THE OWNER, BABE ?
SO THIS IS A PRIVATE CLUB, EH ? WELL.. WHERE'S YOUR CHARTER ?
ERUHAHUM B-BU- WE'D RATHER NOT SERVE WHITES HERE!
SO I, A GREEN MAN AM TO BE BARRED FROM A PUBLIC PLACE BECAUSE I HAVE A WHITE FRIEND!
N-N-NO NO...SIR!
YOU ARE WITH-IN YOUR RIGHTS!
AS IF I DIDN'T KNOW! OKAY, WAITRESS! THREE STEAK DINNERS!
AND DON'T WASH YOUR THUMB IN THE WHITE MAN'S SOUP!

AUGUST 5, 1944

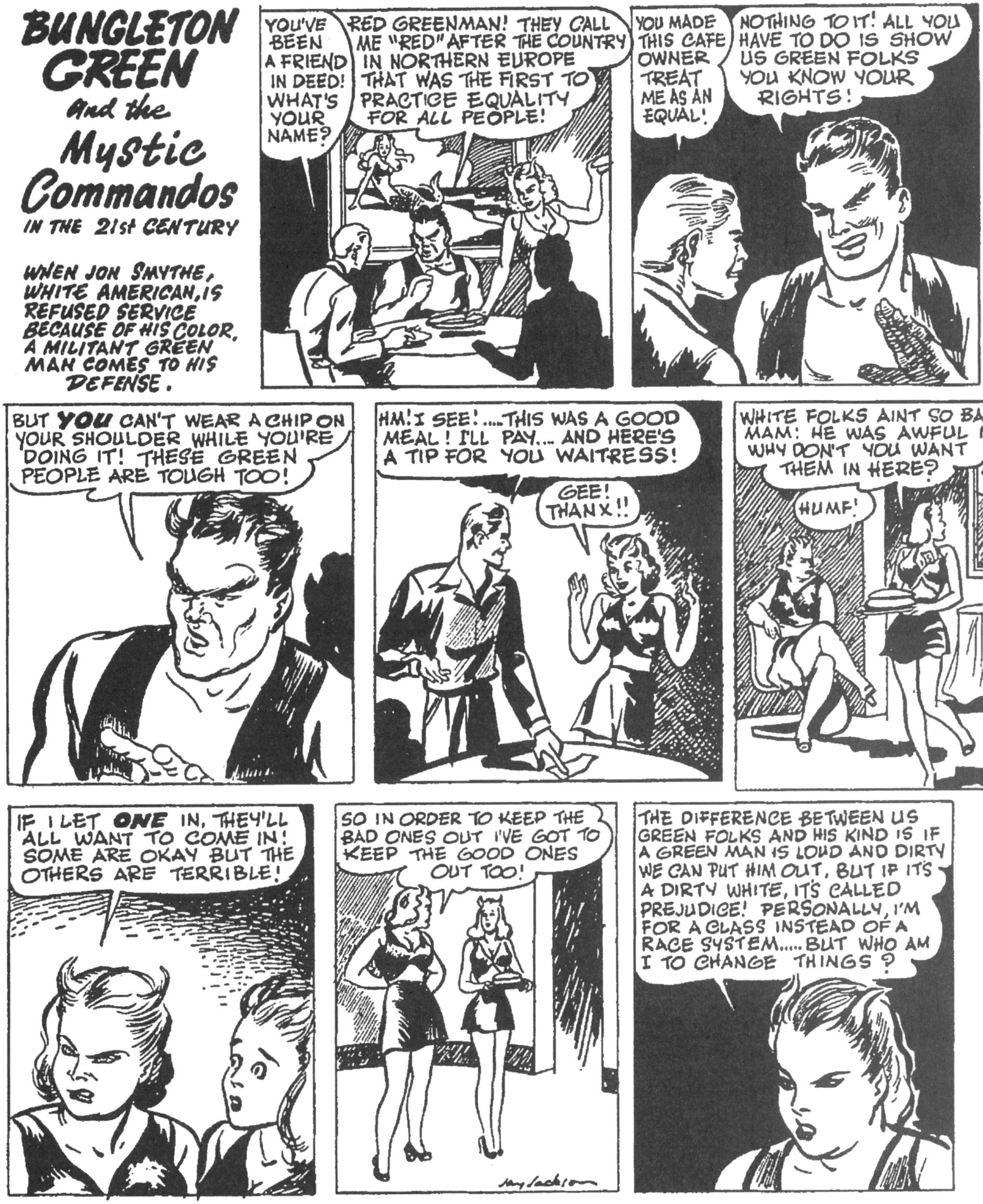
BUNGLETON GREEN and the Mystic Commandos IN THE 21st CENTURY
WHEN JON SMYTHE, WHITE AMERICAN, IS REFUSED SERVICE BECAUSE OF HIS COLOR, A MILITANT GREEN MAN COMES TO HIS DEFENSE.
YOU'VE BEEN A FRIEND IN DEED! WHAT'S YOUR NAME?
RED GREENMAN! THEY CALL ME "RED" AFTER THE COUNTRY IN NORTHERN EUROPE THAT WAS THE FIRST TO PRACTICE EQUALITY FOR ALL PEOPLE!
YOU MADE THIS CAFE OWNER TREAT ME AS AN EQUAL!
NOTHING TO IT! ALL YOU HAVE TO DO IS SHOW US GREEN FOLKS YOU KNOW YOUR RIGHTS!
BUT YOU CAN'T WEAR A CHIP ON YOUR SHOULDER WHILE YOU'RE DOING IT! THESE GREEN PEOPLE ARE TOUGH TOO!
HM! I SEE! ....THIS WAS A GOOD MEAL! I'LL PAY.... AND HERE'S A TIP FOR YOU WAITRESS!
GEE! THANX!!
WHITE FOLKS AINT SO BAD, MAM: HE WAS AWFUL NICE! WHY DON'T YOU WANT THEM IN HERE?
HUMF!
IF I LET ONE IN, THEY'LL ALL WANT TO COME IN! SOME ARE OKAY BUT THE OTHERS ARE TERRIBLE!
SO IN ORDER TO KEEP THE BAD ONES OUT I'VE GOT TO KEEP THE GOOD ONES OUT TOO!
THE DIFFERENCE BETWEEN US GREEN FOLKS AND HIS KIND IS IF A GREEN MAN IS LOUD AND DIRTY WE CAN PUT HIM OUT, BUT IF IT'S A DIRTY WHITE, IT'S CALLED PREJUDICE! PERSONALLY, I'M FOR A CLASS INSTEAD OF A RACE SYSTEM..... BUT WHO AM I TO CHANGE THINGS?
Jay Jackson

AUGUST 12, 1944

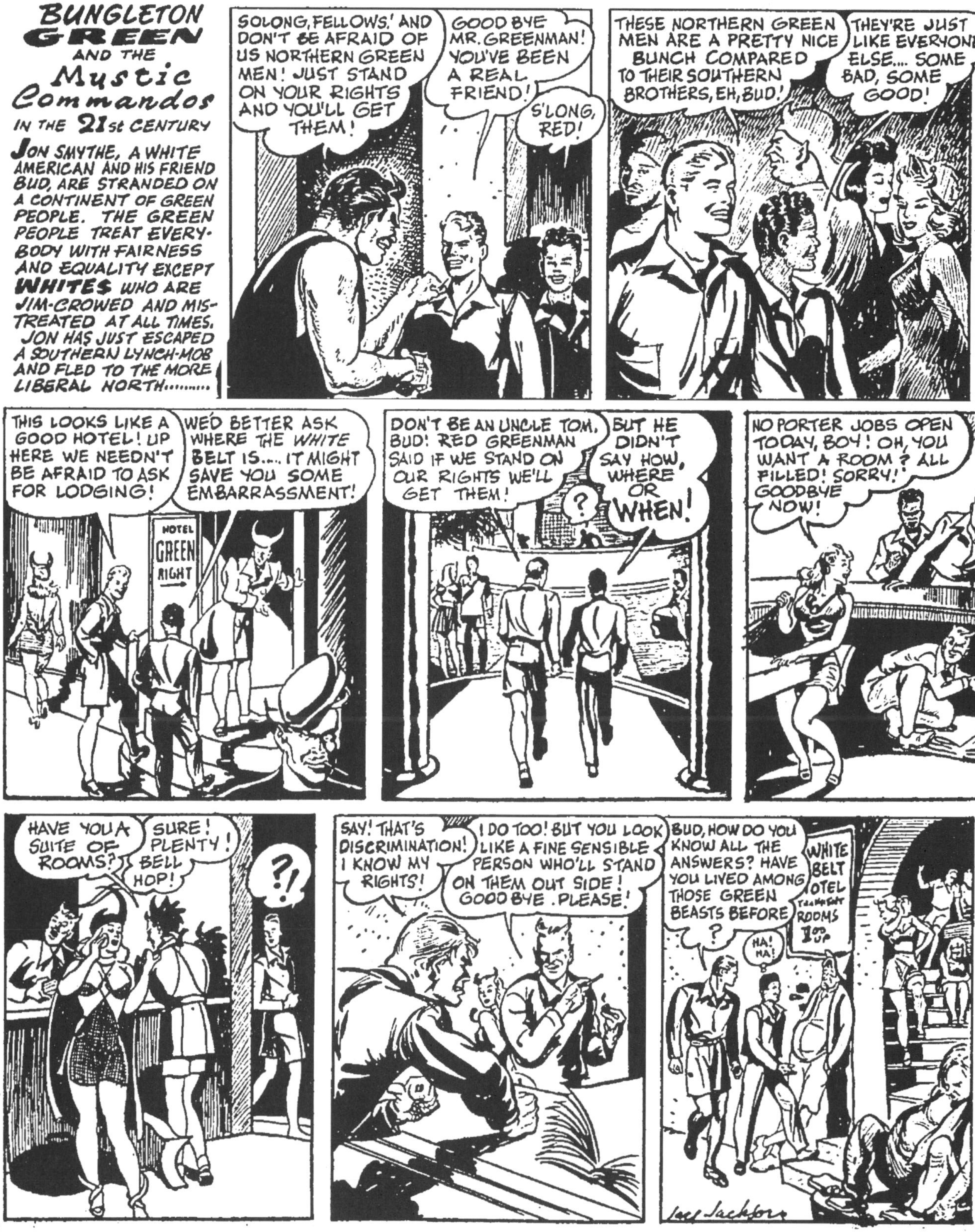

BUNGLETON GREEN AND THE Mystic Commandos IN THE 21st CENTURY
JON SMYTHE, A WHITE AMERICAN AND HIS FRIEND BUD, ARE STRANDED ON A CONTINENT OF GREEN PEOPLE. THE GREEN PEOPLE TREAT EVERYBODY WITH FAIRNESS AND EQUALITY EXCEPT WHITES WHO ARE JIM-CROWED AND MISTREATED AT ALL TIMES. JON HAS JUST ESCAPED A SOUTHERN LYNCH-MOB AND FLED TO THE MORE LIBERAL NORTH.........
SOLONG, FELLOWS! AND DON'T BE AFRAID OF US NORTHERN GREEN MEN! JUST STAND ON YOUR RIGHTS AND YOU'LL GET THEM!
GOOD BYE MR. GREENMAN! YOU'VE BEEN A REAL FRIEND!
S'LONG, RED!
THESE NORTHERN GREEN MEN ARE A PRETTY NICE BUNCH COMPARED TO THEIR SOUTHERN BROTHERS, EH, BUD!
THEY'RE JUST LIKE EVERYONE ELSE.... SOME BAD, SOME GOOD!
THIS LOOKS LIKE A GOOD HOTEL! UP HERE WE NEEDN'T BE AFRAID TO ASK FOR LODGING!
WE'D BETTER ASK WHERE THE WHITE BELT IS.... IT MIGHT SAVE YOU SOME EMBARRASSMENT!
HOTEL GREEN RIGHT
DON'T BE AN UNCLE TOM, BUD! RED GREENMAN SAID IF WE STAND ON OUR RIGHTS WE'LL GET THEM!
BUT HE DIDN'T SAY HOW, WHERE OR WHEN!
?
NO PORTER JOBS OPEN TODAY, BOY! OH, YOU WANT A ROOM? ALL FILLED! SORRY! GOODBYE NOW!
HAVE YOU A SUITE OF ROOMS?
SURE! PLENTY! BELL HOP!
?!
SAY! THAT'S DISCRIMINATION! I KNOW MY RIGHTS!
I DO TOO! BUT YOU LOOK LIKE A FINE SENSIBLE PERSON WHO'LL STAND ON THEM OUT SIDE! GOOD BYE. PLEASE!
BUD, HOW DO YOU KNOW ALL THE ANSWERS? HAVE YOU LIVED AMONG THOSE GREEN BEASTS BEFORE?
HA! HA!
WHITE BELT HOTEL ROOMS

AUGUST 19, 1944

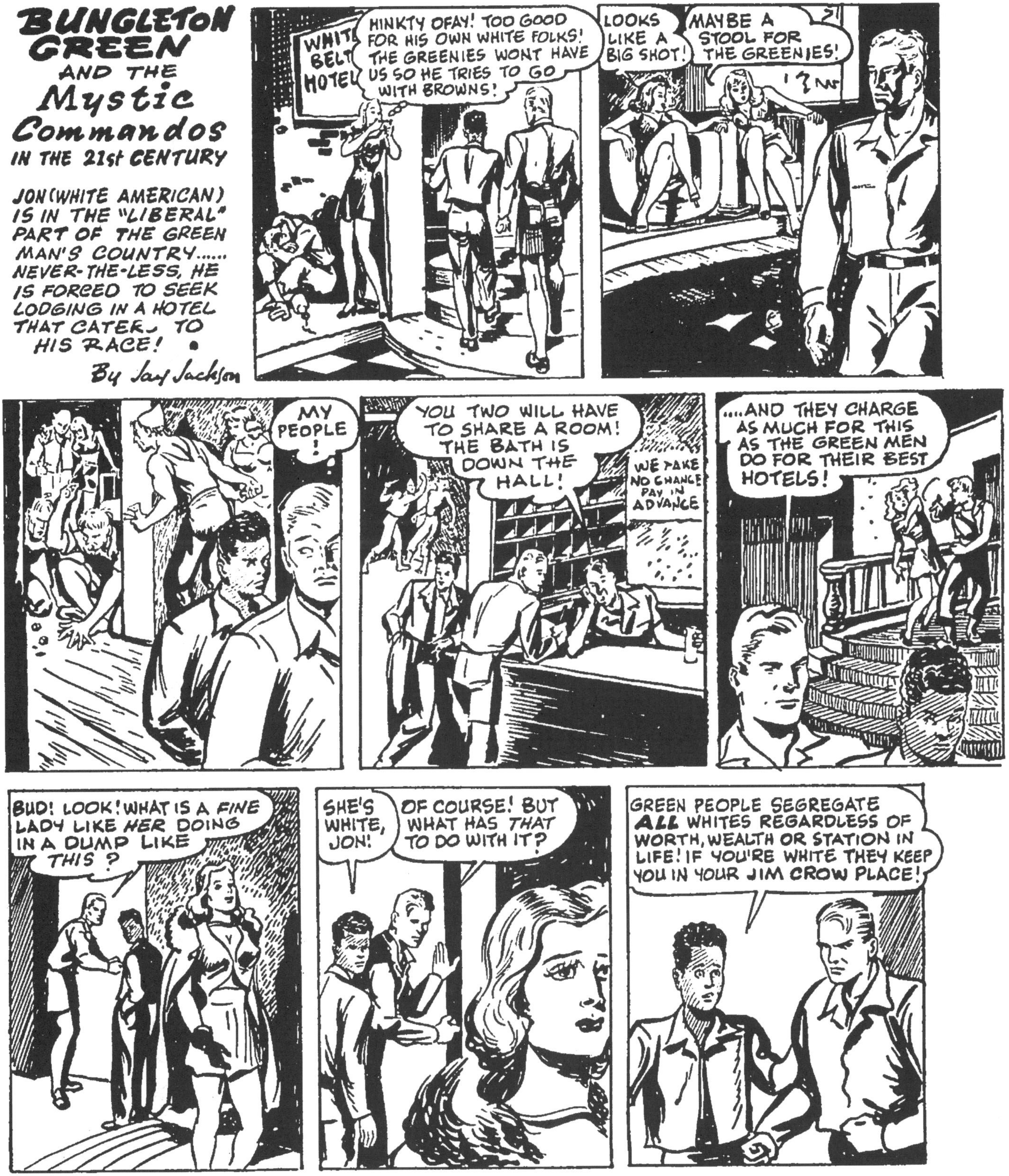
BUNGLETON GREEN AND THE Mystic Commandos IN THE 21st CENTURY
JON (WHITE AMERICAN) IS IN THE "LIBERAL" PART OF THE GREEN MAN'S COUNTRY...... NEVER-THE-LESS, HE IS FORCED TO SEEK LODGING IN A HOTEL THAT CATERS TO HIS RACE!
By Jay Jackson
WHITE BELT HOTEL
HINKTY OFAY! TOO GOOD FOR HIS OWN WHITE FOLKS! THE GREENIES WONT HAVE US SO HE TRIES TO GO WITH BROWNS!
LOOKS LIKE A BIG SHOT!
MAYBE A STOOL FOR THE GREENIES!
MY PEOPLE!
YOU TWO WILL HAVE TO SHARE A ROOM! THE BATH IS DOWN THE HALL!
WE TAKE NO CHANGE PAY IN ADVANCE
....AND THEY CHARGE AS MUCH FOR THIS AS THE GREEN MEN DO FOR THEIR BEST HOTELS!
BUD! LOOK! WHAT IS A FINE LADY LIKE HER DOING IN A DUMP LIKE THIS ?
SHE'S WHITE, JON!
OF COURSE! BUT WHAT HAS THAT TO DO WITH IT?
GREEN PEOPLE SEGREGATE ALL WHITES REGARDLESS OF WORTH, WEALTH OR STATION IN LIFE! IF YOU'RE WHITE THEY KEEP YOU IN YOUR JIM CROW PLACE!

AUGUST 26, 1944

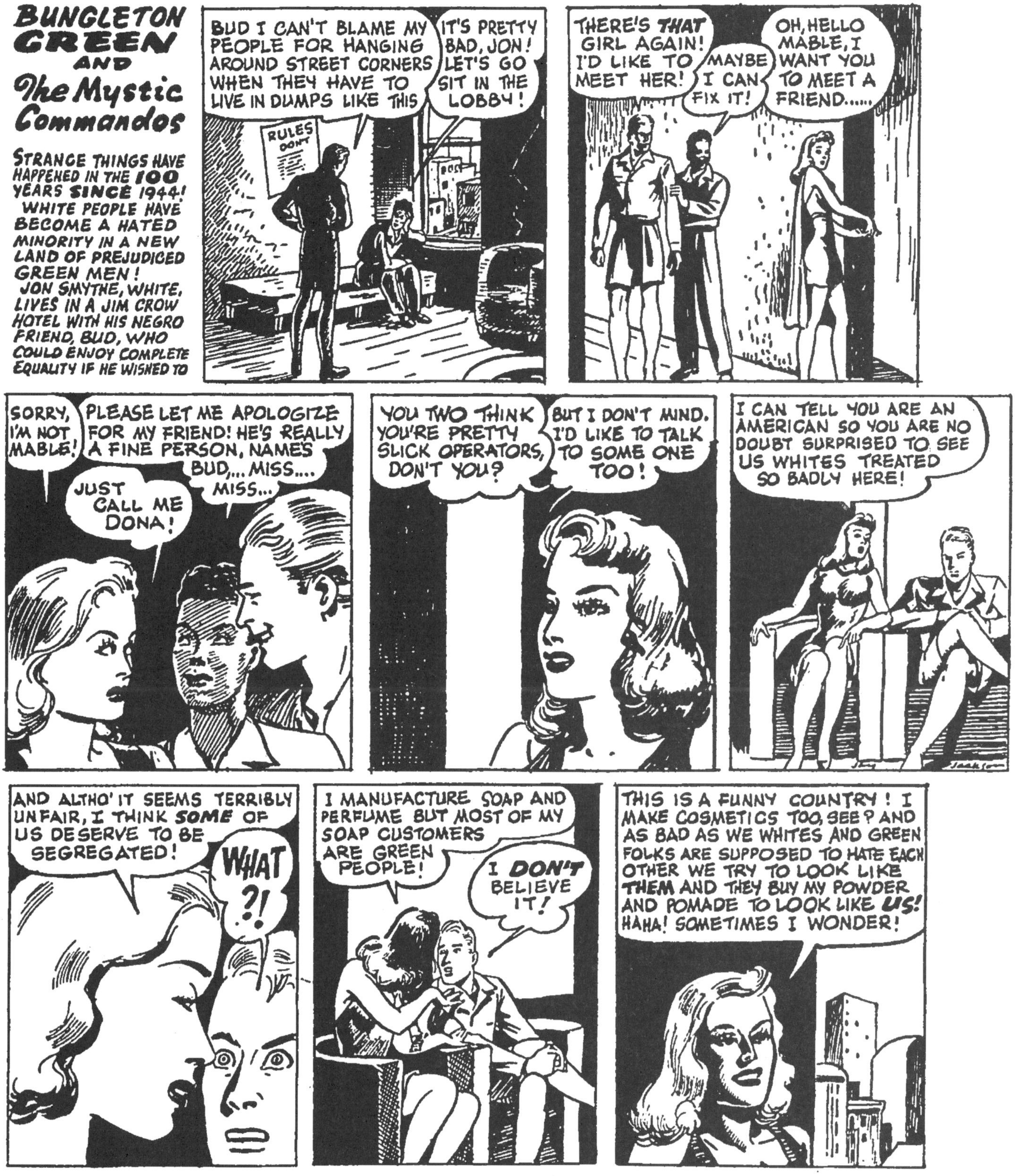
BUNGLETON GREEN AND The Mystic Commandos
STRANGE THINGS HAVE HAPPENED IN THE 100 YEARS SINCE 1944! WHITE PEOPLE HAVE BECOME A HATED MINORITY IN A NEW LAND OF PREJUDICED GREEN MEN! JON SMYTHE, WHITE, LIVES IN A JIM CROW HOTEL WITH HIS NEGRO FRIEND, BUD, WHO COULD ENJOY COMPLETE EQUALITY IF HE WISHED TO
BUD I CAN'T BLAME MY PEOPLE FOR HANGING AROUND STREET CORNERS WHEN THEY HAVE TO LIVE IN DUMPS LIKE THIS
IT'S PRETTY BAD, JON! LET'S GO SIT IN THE LOBBY!
RULES DON'T
THERE'S THAT GIRL AGAIN! I'D LIKE TO MEET HER!
MAYBE I CAN FIX IT!
OH, HELLO MABLE, I WANT YOU TO MEET A FRIEND......
SORRY, I'M NOT MABLE!
PLEASE LET ME APOLOGIZE FOR MY FRIEND! HE'S REALLY A FINE PERSON, NAME'S BUD,... MISS.... MISS...
JUST CALL ME DONA!
YOU TWO THINK YOU'RE PRETTY SLICK OPERATORS, DON'T YOU?
BUT I DON'T MIND. I'D LIKE TO TALK TO SOME ONE TOO!
I CAN TELL YOU ARE AN AMERICAN SO YOU ARE NO DOUBT SURPRISED TO SEE US WHITES TREATED SO BADLY HERE!
AND ALTHO' IT SEEMS TERRIBLY UNFAIR, I THINK SOME OF US DESERVE TO BE SEGREGATED!
WHAT?!
I MANUFACTURE SOAP AND PERFUME BUT MOST OF MY SOAP CUSTOMERS ARE GREEN PEOPLE!
I DON'T BELIEVE IT!
THIS IS A FUNNY COUNTRY! I MAKE COSMETICS TOO, SEE? AND AS BAD AS WE WHITES AND GREEN FOLKS ARE SUPPOSED TO HATE EACH OTHER WE TRY TO LOOK LIKE THEM AND THEY BUY MY POWDER AND POMADE TO LOOK LIKE US! HAHA! SOMETIMES I WONDER!

SEPTEMBER 2, 1944

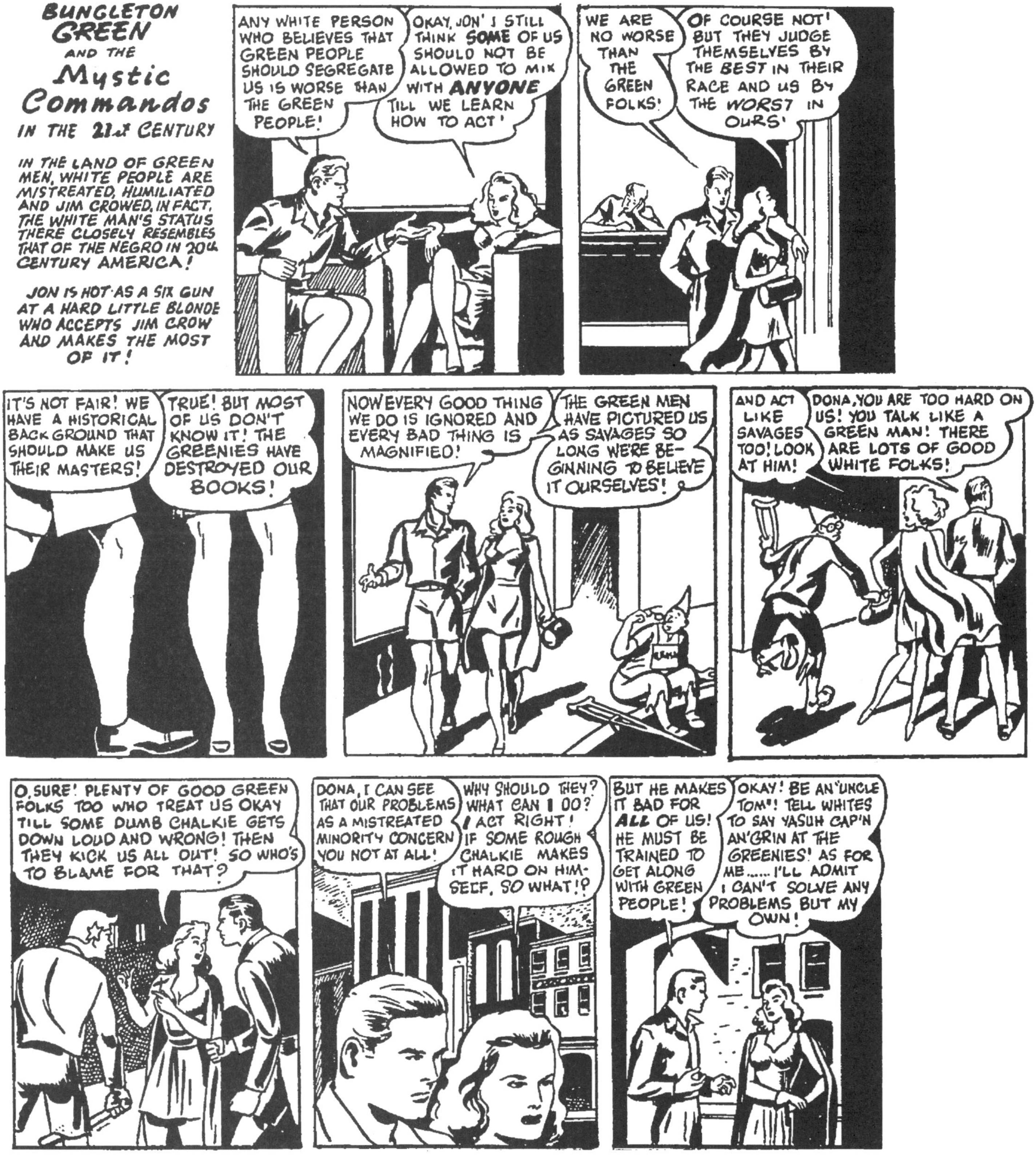
BUNGLETON GREEN AND THE Mystic Commandos IN THE 21st CENTURY
IN THE LAND OF GREEN MEN, WHITE PEOPLE ARE MISTREATED, HUMILIATED AND JIM CROWED. IN FACT, THE WHITE MAN'S STATUS THERE CLOSELY RESEMBLES THAT OF THE NEGRO IN 20th CENTURY AMERICA!
JON IS HOT AS A SIX GUN AT A HARD LITTLE BLONDE WHO ACCEPTS JIM CROW AND MAKES THE MOST OF IT!
ANY WHITE PERSON WHO BELIEVES THAT GREEN PEOPLE SHOULD SEGREGATE US IS WORSE THAN THE GREEN PEOPLE!
OKAY, JON! I STILL THINK SOME OF US SHOULD NOT BE ALLOWED TO MIX WITH ANYONE TILL WE LEARN HOW TO ACT!
WE ARE NO WORSE THAN THE GREEN FOLKS!
OF COURSE NOT! BUT THEY JUDGE THEMSELVES BY THE BEST IN THEIR RACE AND US BY THE WORST IN OURS!
IT'S NOT FAIR! WE HAVE A HISTORICAL BACKGROUND THAT SHOULD MAKE US THEIR MASTERS!
TRUE! BUT MOST OF US DON'T KNOW IT! THE GREENIES HAVE DESTROYED OUR BOOKS!
NOW EVERY GOOD THING WE DO IS IGNORED AND EVERY BAD THING IS MAGNIFIED!
THE GREEN MEN HAVE PICTURED US AS SAVAGES SO LONG WE'RE BEGINNING TO BELIEVE IT OURSELVES!
AND ACT LIKE SAVAGES TOO! LOOK AT HIM!
DONA, YOU ARE TOO HARD ON US! YOU TALK LIKE A GREEN MAN! THERE ARE LOTS OF GOOD WHITE FOLKS!
O, SURE! PLENTY OF GOOD GREEN FOLKS TOO WHO TREAT US OKAY TILL SOME DUMB CHALKIE GETS DOWN LOUD AND WRONG! THEN THEY KICK US ALL OUT! SO WHO'S TO BLAME FOR THAT?
DONA, I CAN SEE THAT OUR PROBLEMS AS A MISTREATED MINORITY CONCERN YOU NOT AT ALL!
WHY SHOULD THEY? WHAT CAN I DO? I ACT RIGHT! IF SOME ROUGH CHALKIE MAKES IT HARD ON HIMSELF, SO WHAT!?
BUT HE MAKES IT BAD FOR ALL OF US! HE MUST BE TRAINED TO GET ALONG WITH GREEN PEOPLE!
OKAY! BE AN "UNCLE TOM"! TELL WHITES TO SAY YASUH CAP'N AN' GRIN AT THE GREENIES! AS FOR ME...... I'LL ADMIT I CAN'T SOLVE ANY PROBLEMS BUT MY OWN!

SEPTEMBER 9, 1944

BUNGLETON GREEN AND THE Mystic Commandos

IN THE 21st CENTURY

IN THE GREEN MAN'S COUNTRY, THE WHITE MINORITY HAS A **HARD** WAY TO GO! JON AND DONA, BOTH WHITE, DISCUSS THE PROBLEMS OF A MINORITY RACE IN A HOSTILE LAND.....

Panel 1:
JON, I HAVE NO SYMPATHY FOR MY RACE! WE FORCE THE GREENIES TO MISTREAT US BECAUSE WE ACT SO BAD!

A FEW OF US DO BUT THAT'S NO REASON THEY SHOULD MISTREAT ALL OF US!

Panel 2:

THIS IS THEIR COUNTRY NOT OURS! SHOULD WE EXPECT THEM TO RUN IT TO SUIT US? IF WE DON'T LIKE IT, WE CAN LEAVE!

BUT EVEN THE PEOPLE WHO FOUGHT AGAINST THE GREENIES ARE TREATED BETTER THAN WE!

Panel 3:

YES, I KNOW! BUT LOOK AT HIM! YOU CAN TELL BY HIS WALK THAT HE HATES EVERY GREENIE ON EARTH! AND IS JUST LOOKING FOR A CHANCE TO PROVE IT!

CAN YOU BLAME HIM?

Panel 4:

AH! WHAT A BURLY WHITE BUCK! LOOKS LIKE HE COULD USE A JOB.....HMM!

Panel 5:

I HIRE A LOT OF THEM IN MY PLANT. THEY'RE GOOD WORKERS AND, BY SHARK, I'VE LEARNED TO LIKE 'EM!

Panel 6:

HELLO, BOY! WANT A JOB?

SAY, GREENIE, HOW BIG DO BOYS GROW HERE?.... SO YOU OFFER ME A JOB, EH? BUILD ME UP TO A FALSE SECURITY THEN FIRE ME! NO! I DON'T WANT A JOB!

Panel 7:

B-B-BUT.... IF YOU SAVE YOUR MONEY....

BAH! JUST BECAUSE YOU'RE GREEN YOU THINK THAT GIVES YOU THE RIGHT TO TELL ME HOW TO RUN MY LIFE! I OUGHT TO PUNCH YOU IN YOUR LITTLE PINK EYES!

Panel 8:
THE GREEN MAN REACHES HIS OFFICE

FIRE EVERY CHALKIE IN THE PLACE! NEVER HIRE ANOTHER! IF THEY'RE WHITE, THEY'RE NOT RIGHT!

I DON'T GET IT! HE ALWAYS LIKED WHITES BEFORE!

SEPTEMBER 16, 1944

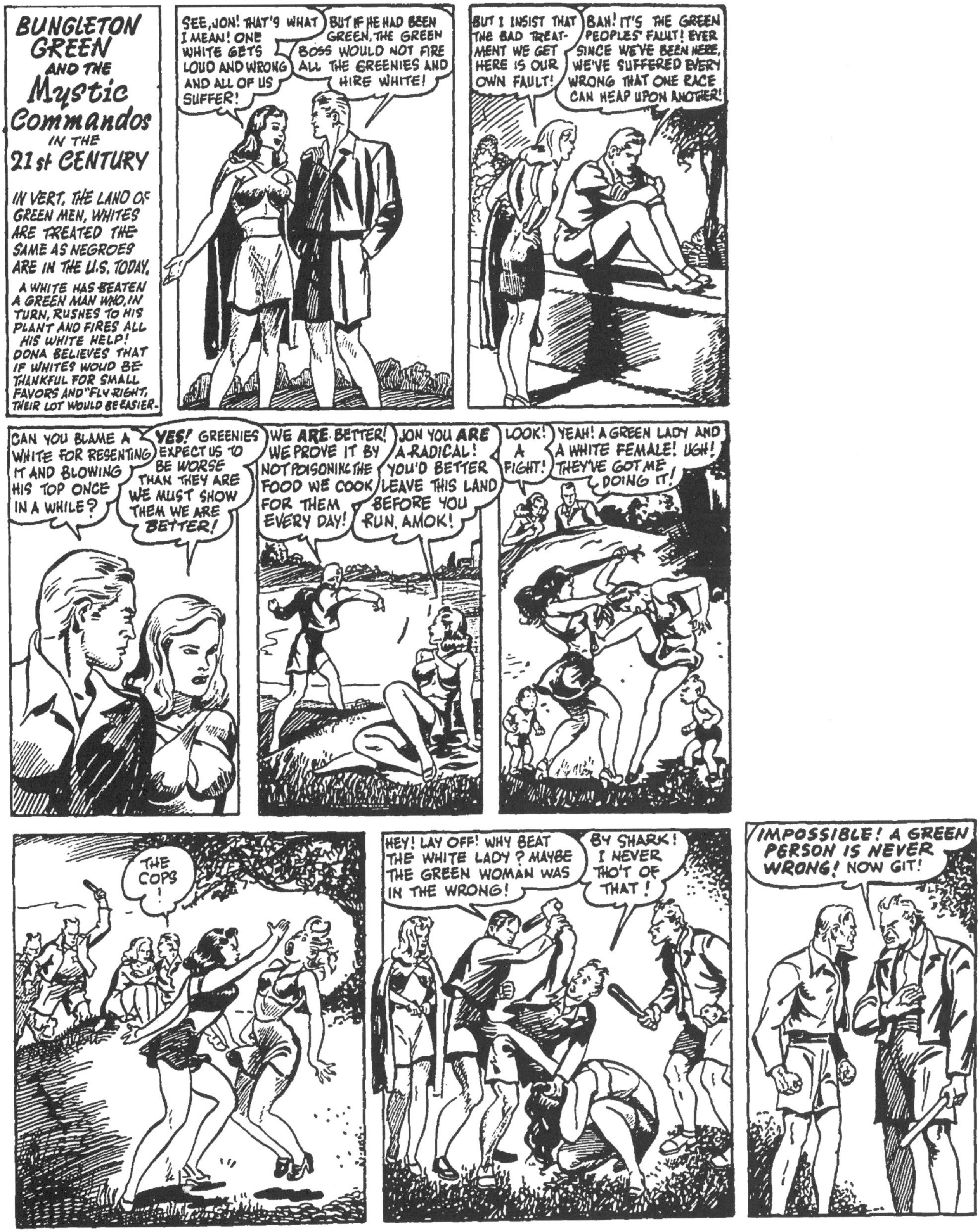
BUNGLETON GREEN AND THE Mystic Commandos IN THE 21st CENTURY
IN VERT, THE LAND OF GREEN MEN, WHITES ARE TREATED THE SAME AS NEGROES ARE IN THE U.S. TODAY.
A WHITE HAS BEATEN A GREEN MAN WHO, IN TURN, RUSHES TO HIS PLANT AND FIRES ALL HIS WHITE HELP! DONA BELIEVES THAT IF WHITES WOUD BE THANKFUL FOR SMALL FAVORS AND "FLY RIGHT," THEIR LOT WOULD BE EASIER.
SEE, JON! THAT'S WHAT I MEAN! ONE WHITE GETS LOUD AND WRONG AND ALL OF US SUFFER!
BUT IF HE HAD BEEN GREEN, THE GREEN BOSS WOULD NOT FIRE ALL THE GREENIES AND HIRE WHITE!
BUT I INSIST THAT THE BAD TREATMENT WE GET HERE IS OUR OWN FAULT!
BAH! IT'S THE GREEN PEOPLES' FAULT! EVER SINCE WE'VE BEEN HERE, WE'VE SUFFERED EVERY WRONG THAT ONE RACE CAN HEAP UPON ANOTHER!
CAN YOU BLAME A WHITE FOR RESENTING IT AND BLOWING HIS TOP ONCE IN A WHILE?
YES! GREENIES EXPECT US TO BE WORSE THAN THEY ARE WE MUST SHOW THEM WE ARE BETTER!
WE ARE BETTER! WE PROVE IT BY NOT POISONING THE FOOD WE COOK FOR THEM EVERY DAY!
JON YOU ARE A RADICAL! YOU'D BETTER LEAVE THIS LAND BEFORE YOU RUN AMOK!
LOOK! A FIGHT!
YEAH! A GREEN LADY AND A WHITE FEMALE! UGH! THEY'VE GOT ME DOING IT!
THE COPS!
HEY! LAY OFF! WHY BEAT THE WHITE LADY? MAYBE THE GREEN WOMAN WAS IN THE WRONG!
BY SHARK! I NEVER THO'T OF THAT!
IMPOSSIBLE! A GREEN PERSON IS NEVER WRONG! NOW GIT!

SEPTEMBER 23, 1944

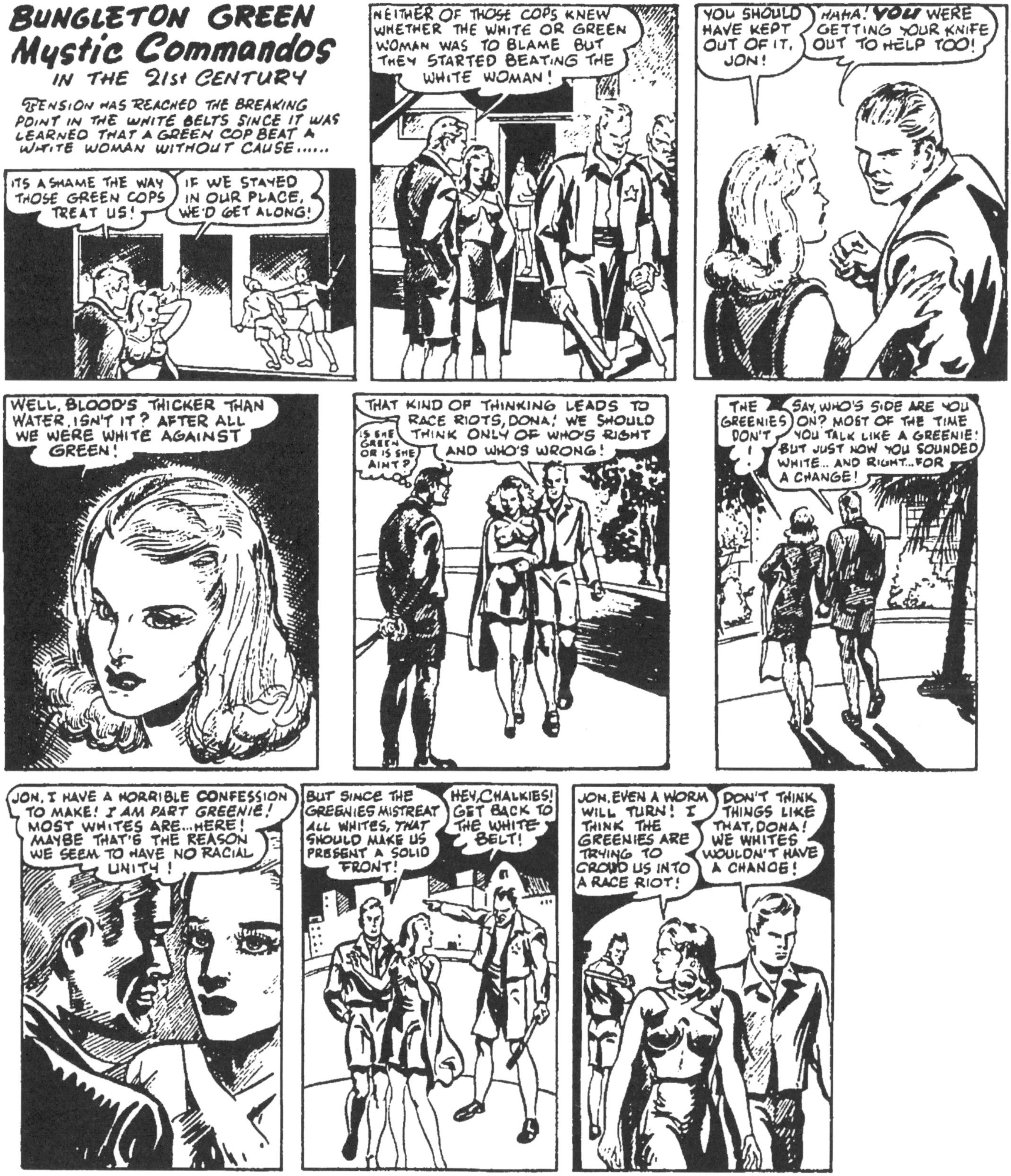
BUNGLETON GREEN
Mystic Commandos
IN THE 21st CENTURY
TENSION HAS REACHED THE BREAKING POINT IN THE WHITE BELTS SINCE IT WAS LEARNED THAT A GREEN COP BEAT A WHITE WOMAN WITHOUT CAUSE......
ITS A SHAME THE WAY THOSE GREEN COPS TREAT US!
IF WE STAYED IN OUR PLACE, WE'D GET ALONG!
NEITHER OF THOSE COPS KNEW WHETHER THE WHITE OR GREEN WOMAN WAS TO BLAME BUT THEY STARTED BEATING THE WHITE WOMAN!
YOU SHOULD HAVE KEPT OUT OF IT, JON!
HAHA! YOU WERE GETTING YOUR KNIFE OUT TO HELP TOO!
WELL, BLOOD'S THICKER THAN WATER, ISN'T IT? AFTER ALL WE WERE WHITE AGAINST GREEN!
THAT KIND OF THINKING LEADS TO RACE RIOTS, DONA! WE SHOULD THINK ONLY OF WHO'S RIGHT AND WHO'S WRONG!
IS SHE GREEN OR IS SHE AINT?
THE GREENIES DON'T!
SAY, WHO'S SIDE ARE YOU ON? MOST OF THE TIME YOU TALK LIKE A GREENIE! BUT JUST NOW YOU SOUNDED WHITE... AND RIGHT...FOR A CHANGE!
JON, I HAVE A HORRIBLE CONFESSION TO MAKE! I AM PART GREENIE! MOST WHITES ARE...HERE! MAYBE THAT'S THE REASON WE SEEM TO HAVE NO RACIAL UNITY!
BUT SINCE THE GREENIES MISTREAT ALL WHITES, THAT SHOULD MAKE US PRESENT A SOLID FRONT!
HEY, CHALKIES! GET BACK TO THE WHITE BELT!
JON, EVEN A WORM WILL TURN! I THINK THE GREENIES ARE TRYING TO CROWD US INTO A RACE RIOT!
DON'T THINK THINGS LIKE THAT, DONA! WE WHITES WOULDN'T HAVE A CHANCE!

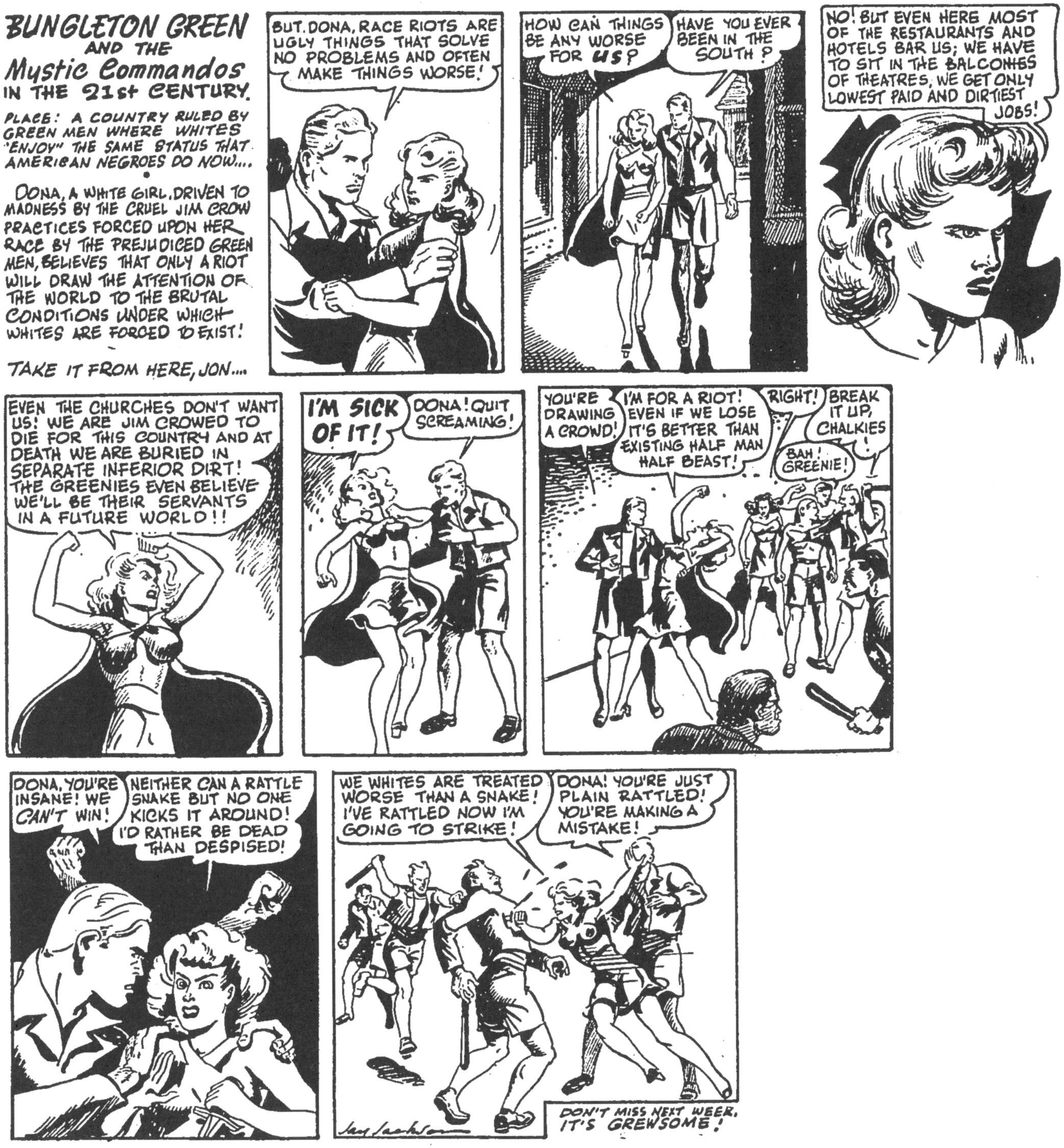
BUNGLETON GREEN AND THE Mystic Commandos IN THE 21st CENTURY.
PLACE: A COUNTRY RULED BY GREEN MEN WHERE WHITES "ENJOY" THE SAME STATUS THAT AMERICAN NEGROES DO NOW....
DONA, A WHITE GIRL, DRIVEN TO MADNESS BY THE CRUEL JIM CROW PRACTICES FORCED UPON HER RACE BY THE PREJUDICED GREEN MEN, BELIEVES THAT ONLY A RIOT WILL DRAW THE ATTENTION OF THE WORLD TO THE BRUTAL CONDITIONS UNDER WHICH WHITES ARE FORCED TO EXIST!
TAKE IT FROM HERE, JON....
BUT. DONA, RACE RIOTS ARE UGLY THINGS THAT SOLVE NO PROBLEMS AND OFTEN MAKE THINGS WORSE!
HOW CAN THINGS BE ANY WORSE FOR US?
HAVE YOU EVER BEEN IN THE SOUTH?
NO! BUT EVEN HERE MOST OF THE RESTAURANTS AND HOTELS BAR US; WE HAVE TO SIT IN THE BALCONIES OF THEATRES, WE GET ONLY LOWEST PAID AND DIRTIEST JOBS!
EVEN THE CHURCHES DON'T WANT US! WE ARE JIM CROWED TO DIE FOR THIS COUNTRY AND AT DEATH WE ARE BURIED IN SEPARATE INFERIOR DIRT! THE GREENIES EVEN BELIEVE WE'LL BE THEIR SERVANTS IN A FUTURE WORLD!!
I'M SICK OF IT!
DONA! QUIT SCREAMING!
YOU'RE DRAWING A CROWD!
I'M FOR A RIOT! EVEN IF WE LOSE IT'S BETTER THAN EXISTING HALF MAN HALF BEAST!
RIGHT!
BREAK IT UP, CHALKIES!
BAH! GREENIE!
DONA, YOU'RE INSANE! WE CAN'T WIN!
NEITHER CAN A RATTLE SNAKE BUT NO ONE KICKS IT AROUND! I'D RATHER BE DEAD THAN DESPISED!
WE WHITES ARE TREATED WORSE THAN A SNAKE! I'VE RATTLED NOW I'M GOING TO STRIKE!
DONA! YOU'RE JUST PLAIN RATTLED! YOU'RE MAKING A MISTAKE!
DON'T MISS NEXT WEEK. IT'S GREWSOME!

OCTOBER 7, 1944

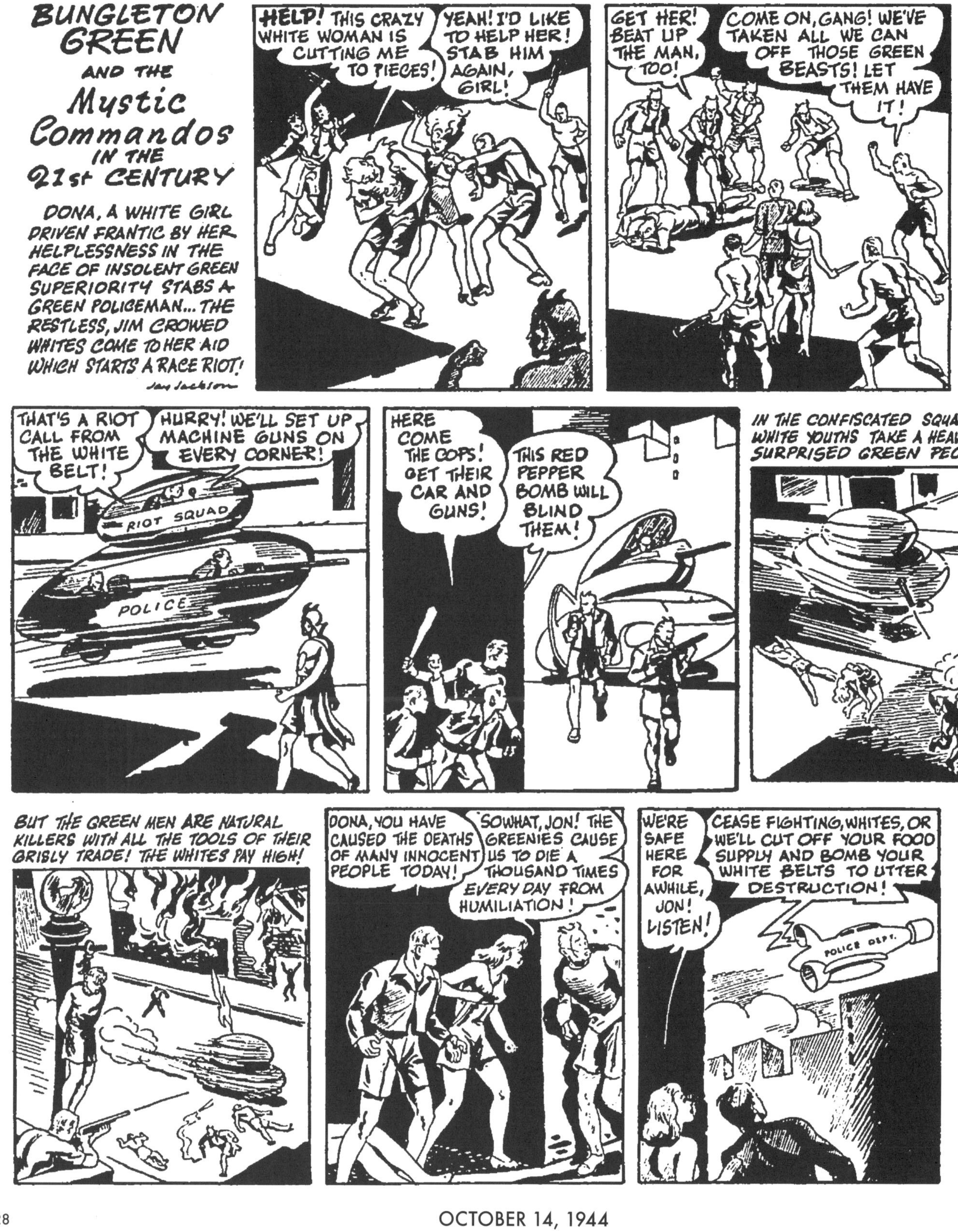

BUNGLETON GREEN AND THE Mystic Commandos IN THE 21st CENTURY
DONA, A WHITE GIRL DRIVEN FRANTIC BY HER HELPLESSNESS IN THE FACE OF INSOLENT GREEN SUPERIORITY STABS A GREEN POLICEMAN... THE RESTLESS, JIM CROWED WHITES COME TO HER AID WHICH STARTS A RACE RIOT!
HELP! THIS CRAZY WHITE WOMAN IS CUTTING ME TO PIECES!
YEAH! I'D LIKE TO HELP HER! STAB HIM AGAIN, GIRL!
GET HER! BEAT UP THE MAN, TOO!
COME ON, GANG! WE'VE TAKEN ALL WE CAN OFF THOSE GREEN BEASTS! LET THEM HAVE IT!
THAT'S A RIOT CALL FROM THE WHITE BELT!
HURRY! WE'LL SET UP MACHINE GUNS ON EVERY CORNER!
RIOT SQUAD
POLICE
HERE COME THE COPS! GET THEIR CAR AND GUNS!
THIS RED PEPPER BOMB WILL BLIND THEM!
IN THE CONFISCATED SQUAD CAR THE WHITE YOUTHS TAKE A HEAVY TOLL OF SURPRISED GREEN PEOPLE........
BUT THE GREEN MEN ARE NATURAL KILLERS WITH ALL THE TOOLS OF THEIR GRISLY TRADE! THE WHITES PAY HIGH!
DONA, YOU HAVE CAUSED THE DEATHS OF MANY INNOCENT PEOPLE TODAY!
SOWHAT, JON! THE GREENIES CAUSE US TO DIE A THOUSAND TIMES EVERY DAY FROM HUMILIATION!
WE'RE SAFE HERE FOR AWHILE, JON! LISTEN!
CEASE FIGHTING, WHITES, OR WE'LL CUT OFF YOUR FOOD SUPPLY AND BOMB YOUR WHITE BELTS TO UTTER DESTRUCTION!
POLICE DEPT.

OCTOBER 14, 1944

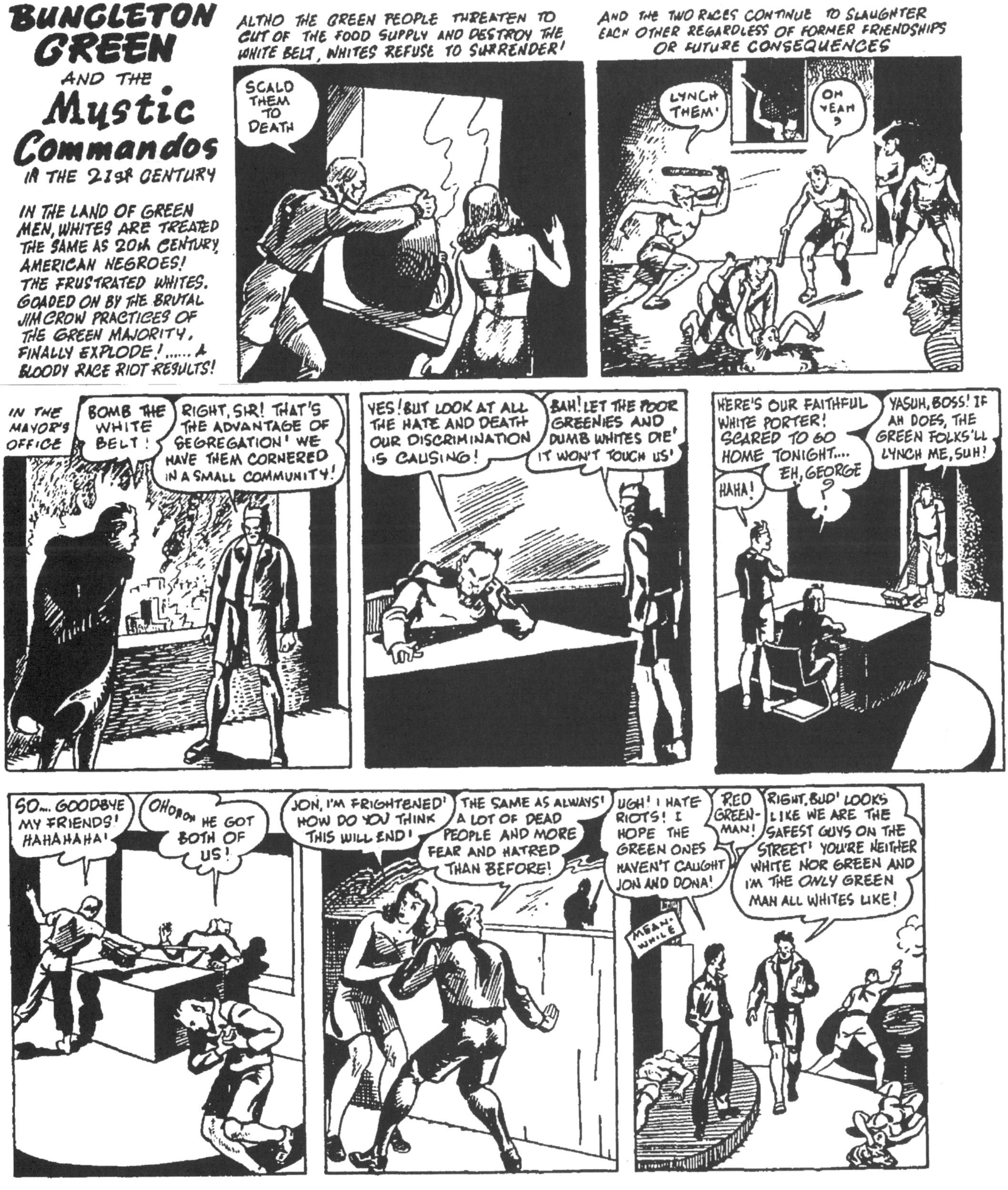
BUNGLETON GREEN
AND THE
Mystic Commandos
IN THE 21ST CENTURY
IN THE LAND OF GREEN MEN, WHITES ARE TREATED THE SAME AS 20th CENTURY AMERICAN NEGROES! THE FRUSTRATED WHITES. GOADED ON BY THE BRUTAL JIM CROW PRACTICES OF THE GREEN MAJORITY, FINALLY EXPLODE! ...... A BLOODY RACE RIOT RESULTS!
ALTHO THE GREEN PEOPLE THREATEN TO CUT OF THE FOOD SUPPLY AND DESTROY THE WHITE BELT, WHITES REFUSE TO SURRENDER!
SCALD THEM TO DEATH
AND THE TWO RACES CONTINUE TO SLAUGHTER EACH OTHER REGARDLESS OF FORMER FRIENDSHIPS OR FUTURE CONSEQUENCES
LYNCH THEM!
OH YEAH ?
IN THE MAYOR'S OFFICE
BOMB THE WHITE BELT!
RIGHT, SIR! THAT'S THE ADVANTAGE OF SEGREGATION! WE HAVE THEM CORNERED IN A SMALL COMMUNITY!
YES! BUT LOOK AT ALL THE HATE AND DEATH OUR DISCRIMINATION IS CAUSING!
BAH! LET THE POOR GREENIES AND DUMB WHITES DIE! IT WON'T TOUCH US!
HERE'S OUR FAITHFUL WHITE PORTER! SCARED TO GO HOME TONIGHT.... EH, GEORGE ?
HAHA!
YASUH, BOSS! IF AH DOES, THE GREEN FOLKS'LL LYNCH ME, SUH!
SO... GOODBYE MY FRIENDS! HAHAHAHA!
OHOHOH HE GOT BOTH OF US!
JON, I'M FRIGHTENED! HOW DO YOU THINK THIS WILL END!
THE SAME AS ALWAYS! A LOT OF DEAD PEOPLE AND MORE FEAR AND HATRED THAN BEFORE!
MEAN-WHILE
UGH! I HATE RIOTS! I HOPE THE GREEN ONES HAVEN'T CAUGHT JON AND DONA!
RED GREEN-MAN!
RIGHT, BUD! LOOKS LIKE WE ARE THE SAFEST GUYS ON THE STREET! YOU'RE NEITHER WHITE NOR GREEN AND I'M THE ONLY GREEN MAN ALL WHITES LIKE!

OCTOBER 21, 1944

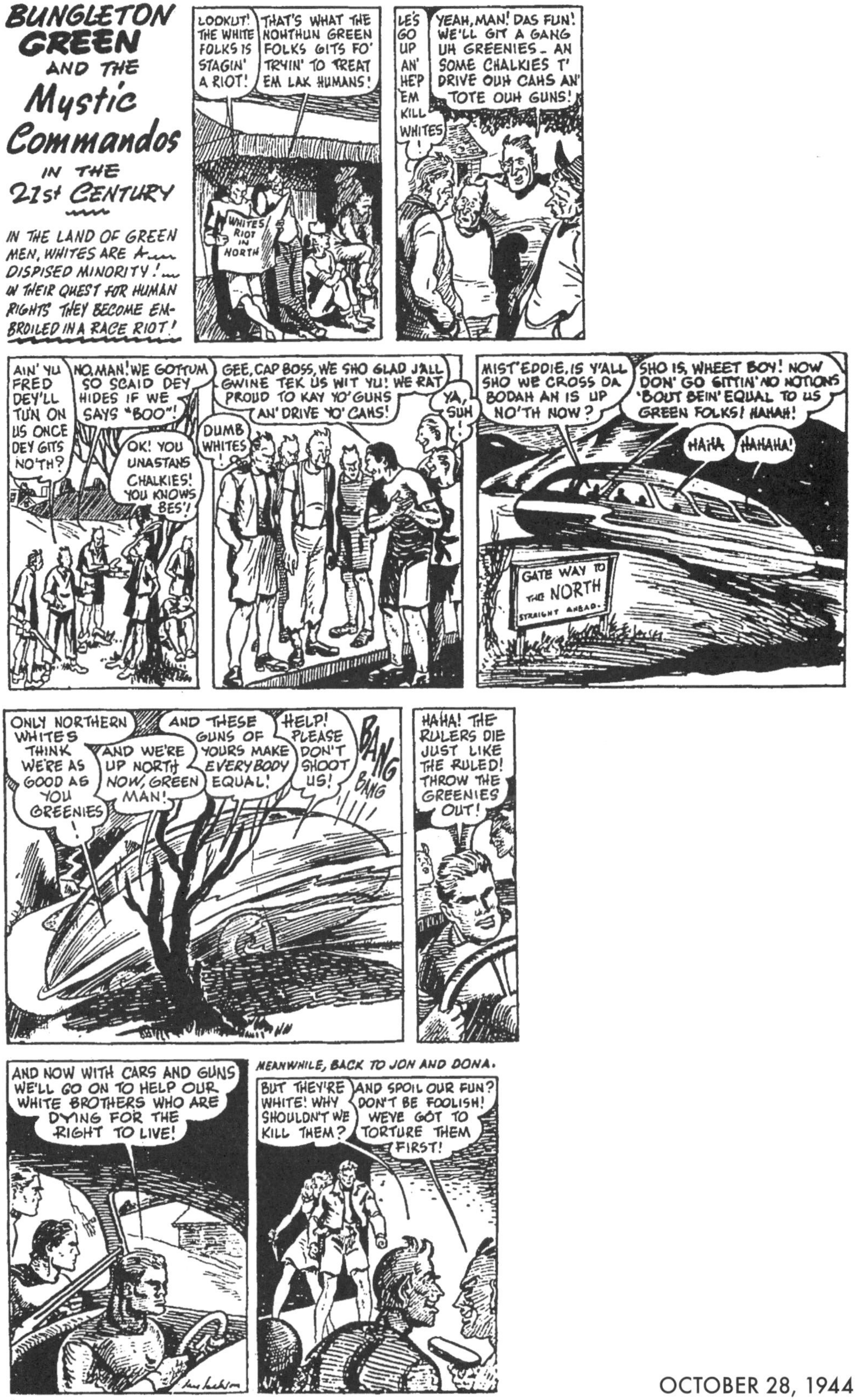
BUNGLETON GREEN AND THE Mystic Commandos IN THE 21st CENTURY
IN THE LAND OF GREEN MEN, WHITES ARE A DISPISED MINORITY! IN THEIR QUEST FOR HUMAN RIGHTS THEY BECOME EMBROILED IN A RACE RIOT!
LOOKUT! THE WHITE FOLKS IS STAGIN' A RIOT!
THAT'S WHAT THE NOHTHUN GREEN FOLKS GITS FO' TRYIN' TO TREAT EM LAK HUMANS!
WHITES RIOT IN NORTH
LE'S GO UP AN' HE'P EM KILL WHITES!
YEAH, MAN! DAS FUN! WE'LL GIT A GANG UH GREENIES - AN SOME CHALKIES T' DRIVE OUH CAHS AN' TOTE OUH GUNS!
AIN' YU FRED DEY'LL TU'N ON US ONCE DEY GITS NO'TH?
NO, MAN! WE GOTTUM SO SCAID DEY HIDES IF WE SAYS "BOO"!
OK! YOU UNASTANS CHALKIES! YOU KNOWS BES'!
GEE, CAP BOSS, WE SHO GLAD Y'ALL GWINE TEK US WIT YU! WE RAT PROUD TO KAY YO' GUNS AN' DRIVE YO' CAHS!
YA, SUH!
DUMB WHITES!
MIST' EDDIE, IS Y'ALL SHO WE CROSS DA BODAH AN IS UP NO'TH NOW?
SHO IS, WHEET BOY! NOW DON' GO GITTIN' NO NOTIONS 'BOUT BEIN' EQUAL TO US GREEN FOLKS! HAHAH!
HAHA
HAHAHA!
GATE WAY TO THE NORTH STRAIGHT AHEAD.
ONLY NORTHERN WHITES THINK WE'RE AS GOOD AS YOU GREENIES!
AND WE'RE UP NORTH NOW, GREEN MAN!
AND THESE GUNS OF YOURS MAKE EVERYBODY EQUAL!
HELP! PLEASE DON'T SHOOT US!
BANG BANG
HAHA! THE RULERS DIE JUST LIKE THE RULED! THROW THE GREENIES OUT!
AND NOW WITH CARS AND GUNS WE'LL GO ON TO HELP OUR WHITE BROTHERS WHO ARE DYING FOR THE RIGHT TO LIVE!
MEANWHILE, BACK TO JON AND DONA.
BUT THEY'RE WHITE! WHY SHOULDN'T WE KILL THEM?
AND SPOIL OUR FUN? DON'T BE FOOLISH! WE'VE GOT TO TORTURE THEM FIRST!

OCTOBER 28, 1944

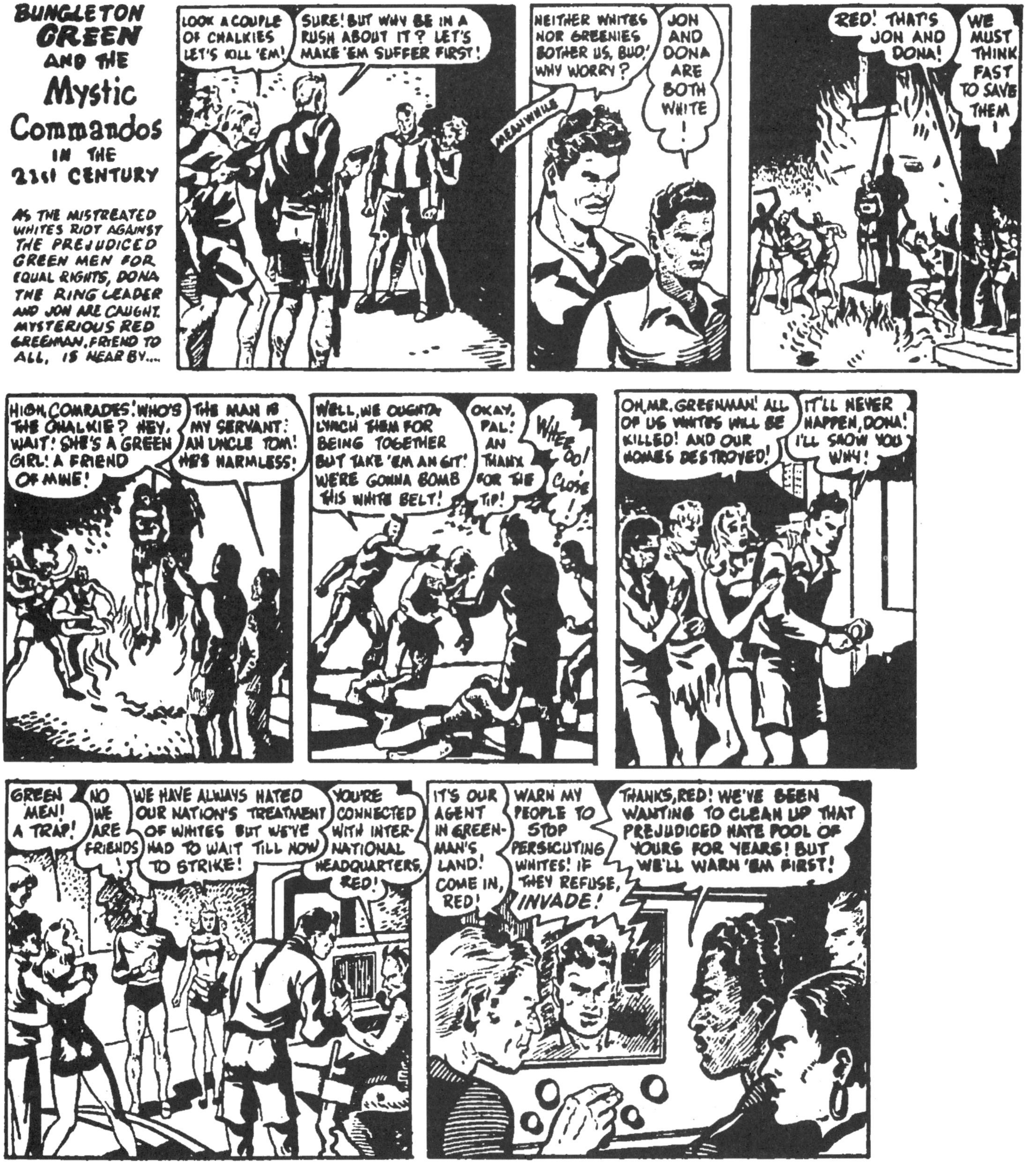
BUNGLETON GREEN AND THE Mystic Commandos IN THE 21st CENTURY
AS THE MISTREATED WHITES RIOT AGAINST THE PREJUDICED GREEN MEN FOR EQUAL RIGHTS, DONA THE RING LEADER AND JON ARE CAUGHT. MYSTERIOUS RED GREENMAN, FRIEND TO ALL, IS NEAR BY....
LOOK A COUPLE OF CHALKIES LET'S KILL 'EM!
SURE! BUT WHY BE IN A RUSH ABOUT IT? LET'S MAKE 'EM SUFFER FIRST!
MEANWHILE
NEITHER WHITES NOR GREENIES BOTHER US, BUD, WHY WORRY?
JON AND DONA ARE BOTH WHITE!
RED! THAT'S JON AND DONA!
WE MUST THINK FAST TO SAVE THEM!
HIGH, COMRADES! WHO'S THE CHALKIE? HEY. WAIT! SHE'S A GREEN GIRL! A FRIEND OF MINE!
THE MAN IS MY SERVANT! AN UNCLE TOM! HE'S HARMLESS!
WELL, WE OUGHTA LYNCH THEM FOR BEING TOGETHER BUT TAKE 'EM AN GIT! WE'RE GONNA BOMB THIS WHITE BELT!
OKAY, PAL! AN THANX FOR THE TIP!
WHEE-OO! CLOSE!
OH, MR. GREENMAN! ALL OF US WHITES WILL BE KILLED! AND OUR HOMES DESTROYED!
IT'LL NEVER HAPPEN, DONA! I'LL SHOW YOU WHY!
GREEN MEN! A TRAP!
NO WE ARE FRIENDS!
WE HAVE ALWAYS HATED OUR NATION'S TREATMENT OF WHITES BUT WE'VE HAD TO WAIT TILL NOW TO STRIKE!
YOU'RE CONNECTED WITH INTER-NATIONAL HEADQUARTERS, RED!
IT'S OUR AGENT IN GREEN-MAN'S LAND! COME IN, RED!
WARN MY PEOPLE TO STOP PERSECUTING WHITES! IF THEY REFUSE, INVADE!
THANKS, RED! WE'VE BEEN WANTING TO CLEAN UP THAT PREJUDICED HATE POOL OF YOURS FOR YEARS! BUT WE'LL WARN 'EM FIRST!

NOVEMBER 4, 1944

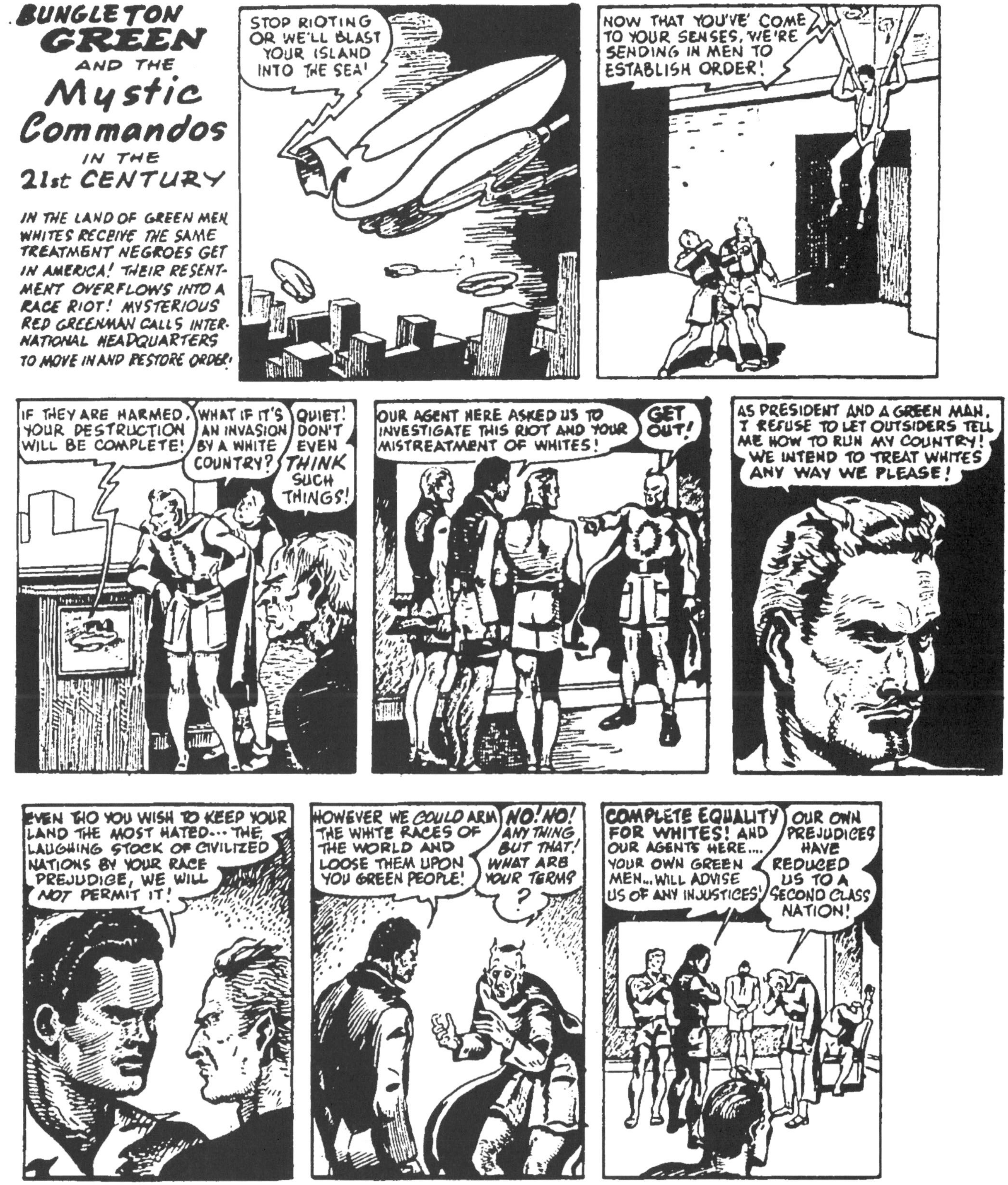
BUNGLETON GREEN AND THE Mystic Commandos IN THE 21st CENTURY
IN THE LAND OF GREEN MEN WHITES RECEIVE THE SAME TREATMENT NEGROES GET IN AMERICA! THEIR RESENTMENT OVERFLOWS INTO A RACE RIOT! MYSTERIOUS RED GREENMAN CALLS INTERNATIONAL HEADQUARTERS TO MOVE IN AND RESTORE ORDER!
STOP RIOTING OR WE'LL BLAST YOUR ISLAND INTO THE SEA!
NOW THAT YOU'VE COME TO YOUR SENSES, WE'RE SENDING IN MEN TO ESTABLISH ORDER!
IF THEY ARE HARMED, YOUR DESTRUCTION WILL BE COMPLETE!
WHAT IF IT'S AN INVASION BY A WHITE COUNTRY?
QUIET! DON'T EVEN THINK SUCH THINGS!
OUR AGENT HERE ASKED US TO INVESTIGATE THIS RIOT AND YOUR MISTREATMENT OF WHITES!
GET OUT!
AS PRESIDENT AND A GREEN MAN, I REFUSE TO LET OUTSIDERS TELL ME HOW TO RUN MY COUNTRY! WE INTEND TO TREAT WHITES ANY WAY WE PLEASE!
EVEN THO YOU WISH TO KEEP YOUR LAND THE MOST HATED... THE LAUGHING STOCK OF CIVILIZED NATIONS BY YOUR RACE PREJUDICE, WE WILL NOT PERMIT IT!
HOWEVER WE COULD ARM THE WHITE RACES OF THE WORLD AND LOOSE THEM UPON YOU GREEN PEOPLE!
NO! NO! ANY THING BUT THAT! WHAT ARE YOUR TERMS?
COMPLETE EQUALITY FOR WHITES! AND OUR AGENTS HERE.... YOUR OWN GREEN MEN... WILL ADVISE US OF ANY INJUSTICES!
OUR OWN PREJUDICES HAVE REDUCED US TO A SECOND CLASS NATION!

NOVEMBER 11, 1944

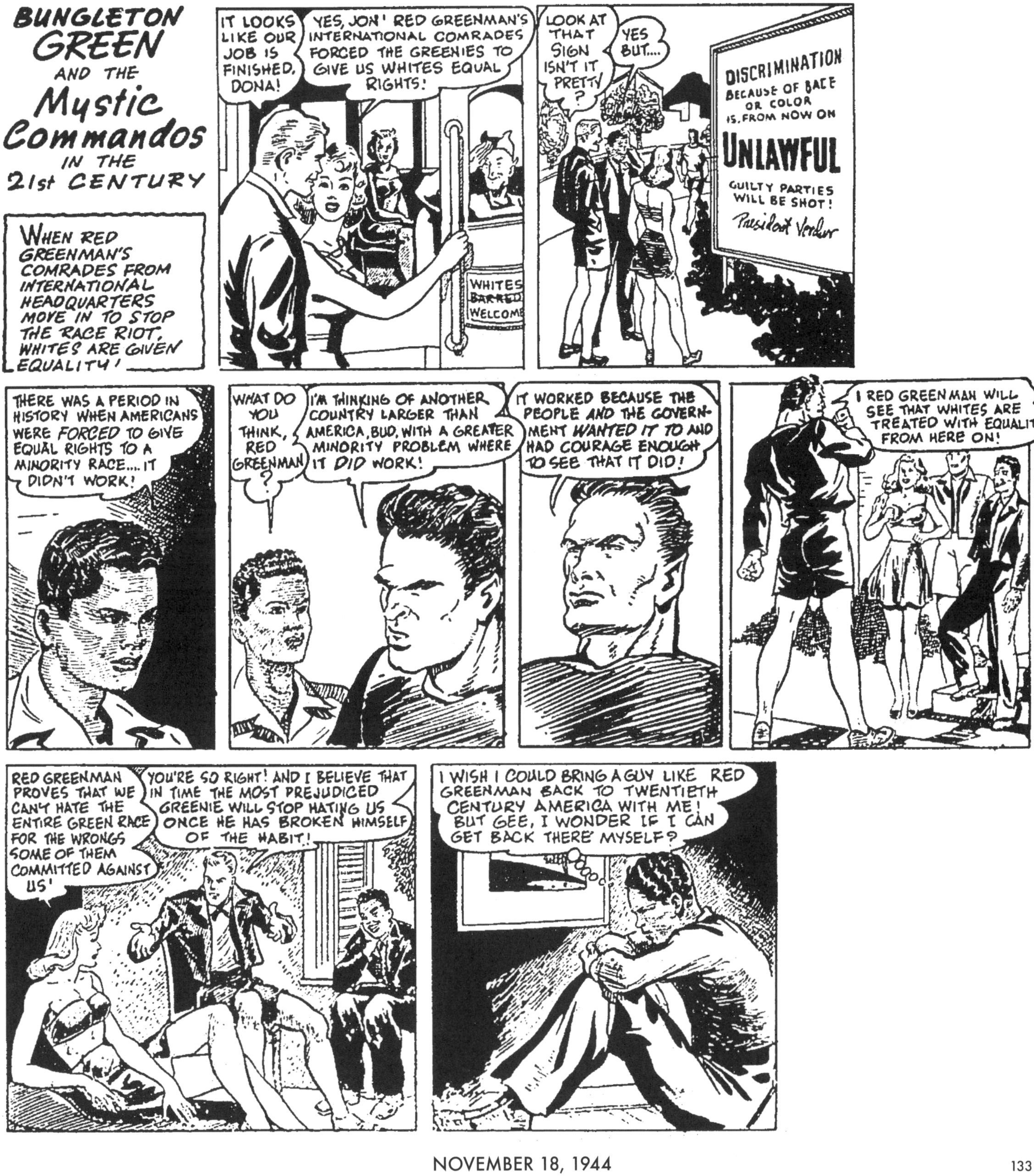
BUNGLETON GREEN AND THE Mystic Commandos IN THE 21st CENTURY
WHEN RED GREENMAN'S COMRADES FROM INTERNATIONAL HEADQUARTERS MOVE IN TO STOP THE RACE RIOT, WHITES ARE GIVEN EQUALITY!
IT LOOKS LIKE OUR JOB IS FINISHED, DONA!
YES, JON! RED GREENMAN'S INTERNATIONAL COMRADES FORCED THE GREENIES TO GIVE US WHITES EQUAL RIGHTS!
WHITES BARRED WELCOME
LOOK AT THAT SIGN ISN'T IT PRETTY?
YES BUT....
DISCRIMINATION BECAUSE OF RACE OR COLOR IS FROM NOW ON UNLAWFUL GUILTY PARTIES WILL BE SHOT! President Verdur
THERE WAS A PERIOD IN HISTORY WHEN AMERICANS WERE FORCED TO GIVE EQUAL RIGHTS TO A MINORITY RACE.... IT DIDN'T WORK!
WHAT DO YOU THINK, RED GREENMAN?
I'M THINKING OF ANOTHER COUNTRY LARGER THAN AMERICA, BUD, WITH A GREATER MINORITY PROBLEM WHERE IT DID WORK!
IT WORKED BECAUSE THE PEOPLE AND THE GOVERNMENT WANTED IT TO AND HAD COURAGE ENOUGH TO SEE THAT IT DID!
I RED GREENMAN WILL SEE THAT WHITES ARE TREATED WITH EQUALITY FROM HERE ON!
RED GREENMAN PROVES THAT WE CAN'T HATE THE ENTIRE GREEN RACE FOR THE WRONGS SOME OF THEM COMMITTED AGAINST US!
YOU'RE SO RIGHT! AND I BELIEVE THAT IN TIME THE MOST PREJUDICED GREENIE WILL STOP HATING US ONCE HE HAS BROKEN HIMSELF OF THE HABIT!
I WISH I COULD BRING A GUY LIKE RED GREENMAN BACK TO TWENTIETH CENTURY AMERICA WITH ME! BUT GEE, I WONDER IF I CAN GET BACK THERE MYSELF?

NOVEMBER 18, 1944

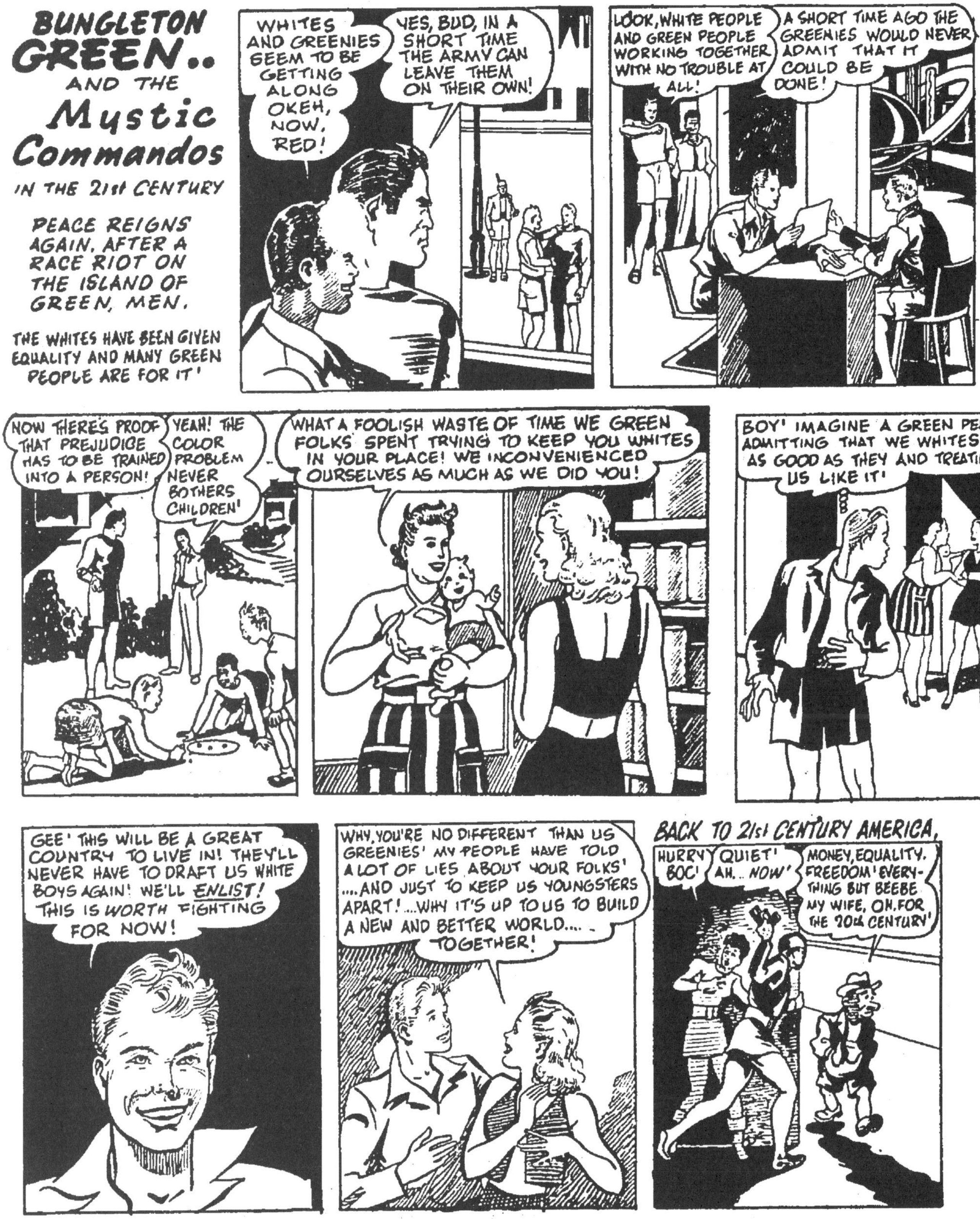
BUNGLETON GREEN.. AND THE Mystic Commandos IN THE 21st CENTURY
PEACE REIGNS AGAIN. AFTER A RACE RIOT ON THE ISLAND OF GREEN, MEN.
THE WHITES HAVE BEEN GIVEN EQUALITY AND MANY GREEN PEOPLE ARE FOR IT!
WHITES AND GREENIES SEEM TO BE GETTING ALONG OKEH, NOW, RED!
YES, BUD, IN A SHORT TIME THE ARMY CAN LEAVE THEM ON THEIR OWN!
LOOK, WHITE PEOPLE AND GREEN PEOPLE WORKING TOGETHER WITH NO TROUBLE AT ALL!
A SHORT TIME AGO THE GREENIES WOULD NEVER ADMIT THAT IT COULD BE DONE!
NOW THERE'S PROOF THAT PREJUDICE HAS TO BE TRAINED INTO A PERSON!
YEAH! THE COLOR PROBLEM NEVER BOTHERS CHILDREN!
WHAT A FOOLISH WASTE OF TIME WE GREEN FOLKS SPENT TRYING TO KEEP YOU WHITES IN YOUR PLACE! WE INCONVENIENCED OURSELVES AS MUCH AS WE DID YOU!
BOY! IMAGINE A GREEN PERSON ADMITTING THAT WE WHITES ARE AS GOOD AS THEY AND TREATING US LIKE IT!
GEE! THIS WILL BE A GREAT COUNTRY TO LIVE IN! THEY'LL NEVER HAVE TO DRAFT US WHITE BOYS AGAIN! WE'LL ENLIST! THIS IS WORTH FIGHTING FOR NOW!
WHY, YOU'RE NO DIFFERENT THAN US GREENIES! MY PEOPLE HAVE TOLD A LOT OF LIES ABOUT YOUR FOLKS! ....AND JUST TO KEEP US YOUNGSTERS APART! ...WHY IT'S UP TO US TO BUILD A NEW AND BETTER WORLD.... TOGETHER!
BACK TO 21st CENTURY AMERICA,
HURRY BOC!
QUIET! AH... NOW!
MONEY, EQUALITY, FREEDOM! EVERYTHING BUT BEEBE MY WIFE, OH, FOR THE 20th CENTURY!

NOVEMBER 25, 1944

[CAM]PAIGN to raise funds to spread Christmas cheer among [WO]UNDED veterans of World War No. 2 officially gets under [way] this week by the Chicago Defender.... Every patriotic-minded man and woman will be asked to make a cash CONTRIBU-tion to make Christmas for these veterans a HAPPY and JOY-ous.... It has been customary for the Chicago Defender to [distribute] baskets during the Yuletide to poverty stricken families, but this year, the need for baskets is not so great, hence, we [combining] our efforts to make this Christmas a never-to-be-forgotten one.... Your checks, money orders or cash contributions should be sent to the Goodfellow Basket Fund, 3435 Indiana Chicago....

[I] might tell that girl who recently started working for that [man] at 47th and South Parkway, she had better be careful....

* * *

[It] was lovely MITZI (former Chicagoan) JACKSON ADAMS [Cali]fornia on 55th street the other day with her brand new baby [daugh]ter. Mitzi is visiting her folks and looks as fine as wine.... [Is] this affair going on between that business man on South [side] and his office girl?... WINNIE CHRISTIE walking in [Per]shing Lounge with what young real estate man t'other [day]... MARION JACKSON PRATT isn't seen around much [mo]re since the Judge untied that knot to Lt. BERT PRATT, [?] rumored wedding bells are going to ring soon now between [?]ON and that certain aviator from out East along around New [Year's] time....

* * *

[Wha]t's this about a New York chic throwing a brick through [win]dow of JOHN BURNETT'S pool room at 47th street?... [UP]-TO-DATERS' 'barrel of fun' cocktail party at the Rhum-[boogie] Sunday, Nov. 26, promises to be a colorful event.... [The] PSI PHI fraternity has completed plans for an INFOR-[MAL] dance at the Parkway, Saturday, Dec. 2, and the hours are 1:30 until.... Is it true that JOE HARRIS and JOYCE (Po-[lk]) GOOLSBY are like two peas in a pod? If so that's the [reason] LOUIS GRIFFIN is so sad.... The FEDERATED HOTEL [WORK]ERS, Local 358, will give their sixth annual dance Monday, [2]7 and indications are that the affair will top all others given [by] waiters... WE WOMEN OF AMERICA cabaret party [Satur]day, Nov. 25 at the Blue Heaven ballroom should draw a [big] crowd.'... BERNICE CHATMAN was sportin' a much too [cute] outfit at the Earl's dance Saturday....

* * *

[Tho]se of you who BUY your cottage cheese, eggs and milk [from] BOWMAN dairy will do well to tell the management that [Ne]groes do not appreciate their references to KINKY HEADS [on the] Bowman Musical Bandwagon heard daily on station WGN. [Tu]esday morning a song with such words was heard on the [air]... Address your letters to the general manager, Bowman Co., 41st street and State....

[EL]NOR ROSE is very unhappy these days because residents [in the] vicinity of the CAMPUS INN voted the precinct DRY thus [taking] the bright spot.... And whoever said JOE LOUIS has lost [his pun]ch? Tuesday night in Buffalo, he KNOCKED out 190-[pound] JOHNNY DAVIS of Brooklyn with the first sock.... They [are] saying that GOLETHA DIUGID is the top waitress at the [Sprayi]ng lounge.... Here's one for the books: JEANETTE CAR-[?] was very jubilant, but two days later, she learned the [plane] returning from San Francisco blew up and killed 24 [per]s.... FLASH! She is returning to Chicago by bus....

[Be sure] to come to the Regal theatre Saturday morning, Nov. 25, [and] bring the kiddies to attend Bud Billiken's THANKS-[GIVIN]G party.... JIMMIE LUNCEFORD'S band and an all-star [show] will be the feature attraction.

[The] reason THERESA BOOTH was so jubilant at the DeLisa [because] hubby, Pvt. LUTHER YANCEY was home on furlough [from Ft.] Huachuca, Arizona.... EDDIE (fight promoter) PLICQUE [?] birthday Monday and you can't guess how old he is.... [They are] saying mean things about LEROY (Bing) WILLIAMS the [one] who ran out on the DeLisa after they had been so good to [him]... He gave notice.... Tell LOU C. P. - - - to come and get [his bi]rthday present in the form of a fur coat....

[Pick]ed as 'the woman of the month' for her recent stand [on Ne]gro rights, LORRAINE BRADLEY will get an award Sunday [at the] Dance for Democracy' set for the Sportsman hall.... Won-[der w]hat was it that LAWRENCE HANCOCK and HELEN HAR-[?] that upset the Nine Star Bridge club at the Juggs' party [?]?...

[The] reason the EUCLID (Major) TAYLORS are so jubilant is [because] their son, NICHOLAS CHARLES TAYLOR, somewhere [in Eng]land, has been promoted to Steward's Mate 3rd class.... [JUG]QUE club gives $45 dollars for the Xmas Basket fund and [to] ROSA TOUPS and the girls....

[The] diamond ring ANN HINTON is wearing was given her by [?] as a birthday present.... MARY (Bon Amies) COLE was [?] a fashion plate t'other day.... The fellas say they never [see RO]OSEVELT (Filling station) PHILLIPS at any of the parties [these] days. Wonder why?... What's this about the GEORGE [ROB]ERTS doing everything wrong.... FLASH! FLASH! It's [a] matter of days before BILLY (I can play the piano but I'm [no] army man) WARD about to say marriage vows to who.... [JO]H WILLIAMS and his missus celebrated their wedding anni-[versar]y with champagne flowing.... Ringsiders at the Juggs in-[clude MA]XIE (Mayor of 51st St.) BARBOUR, SONNY BARNETT, [?] CARTER and HARRY SMITH....

[JIMM]Y ELLIS and SUSANNA PHELPS will say marriage vows [soo]n... We have found badge 667 of a worker at Eastman [?] company. Call for it at the Defender city desk.... Sgt. [MAL]COLM SMITH of Ft. Benning, Ga, was in town seeing the [gang] and greeting old friends....

[HENR]Y WILSON WORTHY, who underwent an operation at the [?] hospital, is better and is home at 5146½ South Parkway. [A]LVERTA FRANKLIN skipped to Detroit.... CHINK (Red [?] LAWRENCE will display his wardrobe at the IMPERIAL [SATEL]LITES cocktail party Thanksgiving day at the Boogie.... [Mother] Bethesda church and its pastor Dr. A. ALFRED WATTS [?] anniversary ceremonies Sunday.... The SEPIA TONES [are] setting new records at the Pershing Lounge....

[And] now it can be told! MARGIE EPPS said marriage vows to [JIMM]Y (Salesman) CARR way back on Feb. 21 and they have [kept] a secret.... NETTIE GEORGE SPEEDY had a birthday [last w]eek and how about a greeting card to 4834 Prairie avenue, [?] reminds us that LUCIUS (Dustin' Off the News) HARPER [had] a birthday but won't tell his age.... FLASH! He says [they can] give him nylons, cigars or Scotch.

A SUPERMAN

December 1944 – July 1943

NEW YORK IN REVIEW

By RAMONA LOWE
(Defender New York Bureau)

NEW YORK.—The War Department is using 1500 copies of the National Urban League's Bulletin No. 1 on Employment Problems of the Negro prepared by Fanny McConnell Buford. It is being used in the separation classification program to give a picture to counselors of current job problems facing the Negro.

* * *

Marian Anderson is featured in a new short army film called "Christmas 1944" along with Leopold Stokowski, the Westminster Choir and an all-service orchestra. The film which contains a spoken Christmas greeting from Miss Anderson as well as her famous rendition of "Ave Maria" will be shown to servicemen and women all over the world.

* * *

Mrs. Paul Robeson has an article in the current issue of the magazine "Asia" on "A Negro Looks At Africa." She spoke on "What the People of Africa Want," at Pearl Buck's East and West Association meeting at Town Hall last week.

* * *

When Dr. Otto Heningberg of the National Urban League went to Detroit November 18 to speak at the Regional Institute for the American Friends Service Committee, he told the Friends that white races have messed up...

* * *

Belle Rosette, the singer and dancer from Trinidad who created...

Smith—

(Continued from Page 1)

Smith's violation of the union rule against an alien holding union office was "not intentional."

Accepting the resignation, the union council made public a unanimous statement saying its members "know and love Ferdinand Smith" and "know the great contribution he has made to his union, his people and his country." It added its program would continue to receive "the aid and counsel of Ferdinand Smith."

Charges against Smith were first brought by a New York newspaper before a recent banquet tendered to Smith by leading civic and industrial spokesmen. The paper charged that Smith was a Communist and not a citizen.

The union promptly appointed an investigating committee to determine Smith's status. After its report, Smith submitted his resignation.

"I must take that step," he commented, "which will make it impossible for this issue to be utilized by forces hostile to the union to split or weaken the union in any way."

The probability is that Smith will again be elected as secretary in the union's election in January. As soon as he files for his citizenship papers, he will again be eligible for office.

He has indicated that he will make his application immediately and other union spokesmen said that he will be a candidate for secretary again in the coming elec-

All Races Join In Interracial Church On Coast

BERKELEY, Cal.—(ANP)—After a year of service, the South Berkeley Community church, composed of members of all races, was declared a success last week.

Dr. Buell Gallagher, white professor of ethics at Pacific School of Religion is pastor and the Rev. Nichols is associate pastor.

All races are welcomed to attend the services at the church and a full program of activity is carried on during the week. With a membership of 175, attendance at Sunday services averages 45 per cent Negroes, 25 per cent white and a few Chinese, church records reveal.

Dr. Gallagher was president of Talladega college until last year when he resigned to head an experiment in interracial religion.

Poll Tax Gone! Arkansas GIs To Vote Without It

LITTLE ROCK.—The poll tax in Arkansas was buried under an avalanche of ballots on Nov. 7, and now Negro service men and wom-[en along with whites may vote in...]

Negro Leaders Back National War Fund Drive

NEW YORK.—Leading Negroes are not only supporting the National War Fund drive throughout the country, but are serving on state, county and municipal committees, it was announced by the national office this week, as the second annual campaign for $250,-000,000 for local welfare services and the 22 member agencies of the National War Fund now being conducted through the ten thousand local community War Funds, gets into full swing.

"Negroes are and should be interested in supporting the National War Fund," said Dr. F. D. Patterson, president of Tuskegee Institute, in an interview this week, "not only because they are responsible citizens of the United States, but because thousands of their fighting sons and relatives will benefit by the funds collected, as well as millions of colored subjects of the allied nations."

Among those serving on state and local committees are C. C. Spaulding, president, North Carolina Mutual Life Insurance Co., Durham; Carter Wesley, publisher, Houston; P. B. Young Sr., publisher, Norfolk; Raymond Pace Alexander, lawyer, Philadelphia; Parole Commissioner Samuel Battle, New York; Dr. Leslie Pinkney Hill, president, Cheney Teachers'

[...]son, Cleveland; former Judge [Wil]liam C. Hueston, Elk [?] Washington, D. C.; Miss Jane [?]ter, social worker, Cleveland; Bishop David H. Sims, Phil[adel]phia; Dr. Dorothy Ferebee, [?]ity leader of Washington, [?] and Bishop J. H. Clayborne, [?]Rock, Ark.

BUNGLETON GREEN
AND THE
Mystic Commandos
IN THE 21st CENTURY

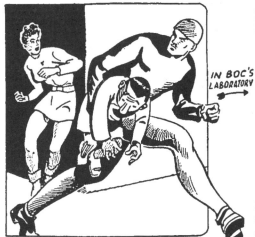

IN BOC'S LABORATORY →

IT MUST BE FROM ANOTHER WORLD, BOC!

I HOPE IT IS, BOO! THEN I CAN SAY MY EXPERIMENTS ARE FOR THE BENEFIT OF SCIENCE! CALL TONG HE CAN TELL!

WHAT IS IT, TONG?

SH! HE'S COMING TO!

STRANGE, HIS THOUGHT WAVE SEEMS TO COME FROM A HUNDRED YEARS AGO!

WHO ARE YOU?

WHERE ARE YOU FROM?

WHY?

IF I TELL THEM I WAS SENT HERE FROM THE 20th CENTURY BY A TIME MACHINE, THEY'LL THINK I'M CRAZY!

THANK YOU MISTER GREEN! AND I DON'T THINK YOU ARE INSANE!

WHAT? HOW?

EASY, SIR! I READ YOUR MIND! THERE IS MORE I WISH TO KNOW BEFORE...

DON'T TELL HIM, TONG, HE MIGHT LOSE HIS MIND!

MEANWHILE IN A STRATOROCKET

OBOY! I CAN HARDLY WAIT TO SEE MY FRIENDS BACK IN AMERICA; BUNG. PIG, TEENA.....

WE'RE HERE, BUD, LET'S GO!

DECEMBER 2, 1944

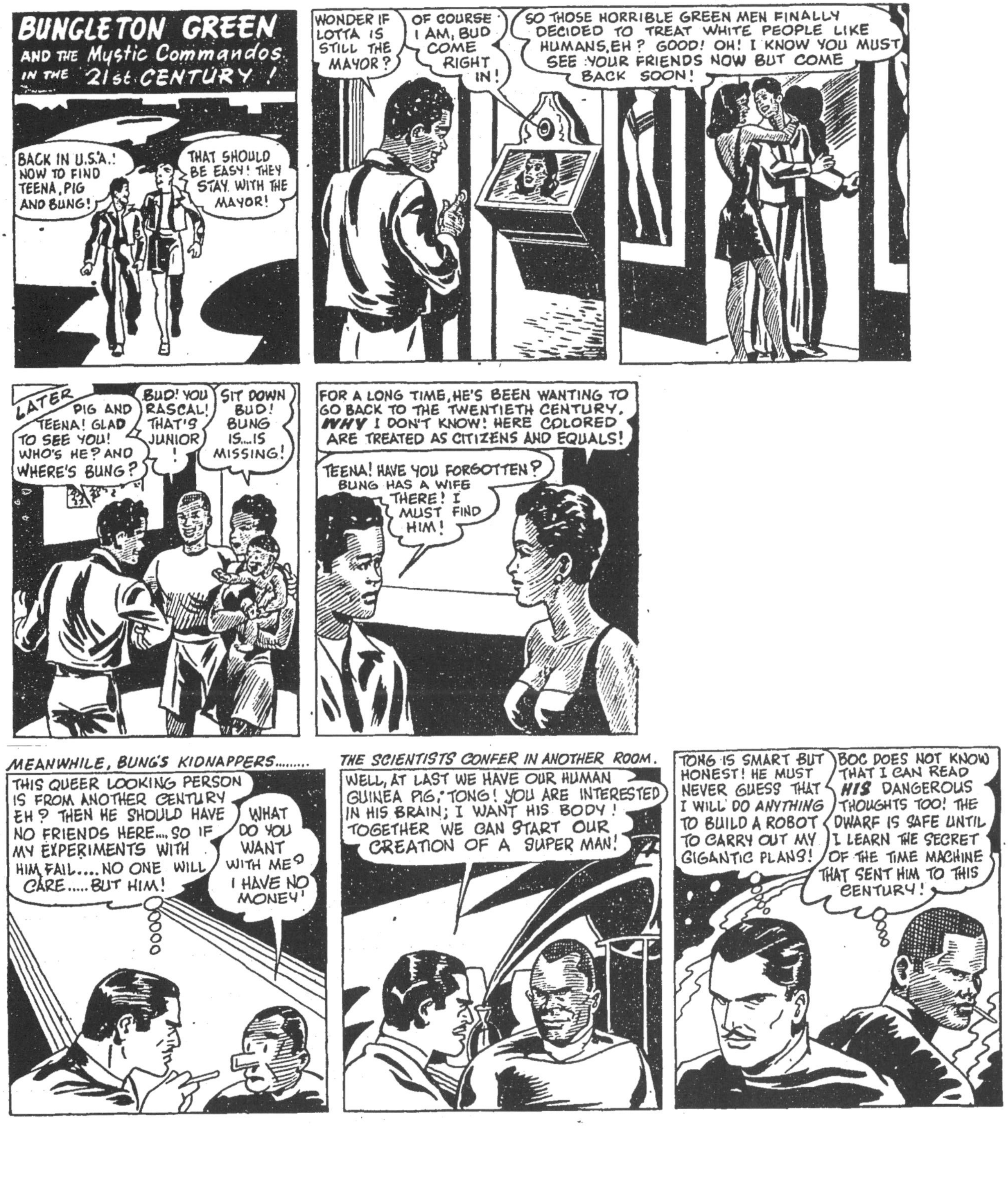
BUNGLETON GREEN
AND THE Mystic Commandos IN THE 21st. CENTURY !
BACK IN U.S.A.! NOW TO FIND TEENA, PIG AND BUNG!
THAT SHOULD BE EASY! THEY STAY WITH THE MAYOR!
WONDER IF LOTTA IS STILL THE MAYOR?
OF COURSE I AM, BUD COME RIGHT IN!
SO THOSE HORRIBLE GREEN MEN FINALLY DECIDED TO TREAT WHITE PEOPLE LIKE HUMANS, EH? GOOD! OH! I KNOW YOU MUST SEE YOUR FRIENDS NOW BUT COME BACK SOON!
LATER
PIG AND TEENA! GLAD TO SEE YOU! WHO'S HE? AND WHERE'S BUNG?
BUD! YOU RASCAL! THAT'S JUNIOR!
SIT DOWN BUD! BUNG IS....IS MISSING!
FOR A LONG TIME, HE'S BEEN WANTING TO GO BACK TO THE TWENTIETH CENTURY. WHY I DON'T KNOW! HERE COLORED ARE TREATED AS CITIZENS AND EQUALS!
TEENA! HAVE YOU FORGOTTEN? BUNG HAS A WIFE THERE! I MUST FIND HIM!
MEANWHILE, BUNG'S KIDNAPPERS.........
THIS QUEER LOOKING PERSON IS FROM ANOTHER CENTURY EH? THEN HE SHOULD HAVE NO FRIENDS HERE.... SO IF MY EXPERIMENTS WITH HIM FAIL.... NO ONE WILL CARE..... BUT HIM!
WHAT DO YOU WANT WITH ME? I HAVE NO MONEY!
THE SCIENTISTS CONFER IN ANOTHER ROOM.
WELL, AT LAST WE HAVE OUR HUMAN GUINEA PIG, TONG! YOU ARE INTERESTED IN HIS BRAIN; I WANT HIS BODY! TOGETHER WE CAN START OUR CREATION OF A SUPER MAN!
TONG IS SMART BUT HONEST! HE MUST NEVER GUESS THAT I WILL DO ANYTHING TO BUILD A ROBOT TO CARRY OUT MY GIGANTIC PLANS!
BOC DOES NOT KNOW THAT I CAN READ HIS DANGEROUS THOUGHTS TOO! THE DWARF IS SAFE UNTIL I LEARN THE SECRET OF THE TIME MACHINE THAT SENT HIM TO THIS CENTURY!

DECEMBER 9, 1944

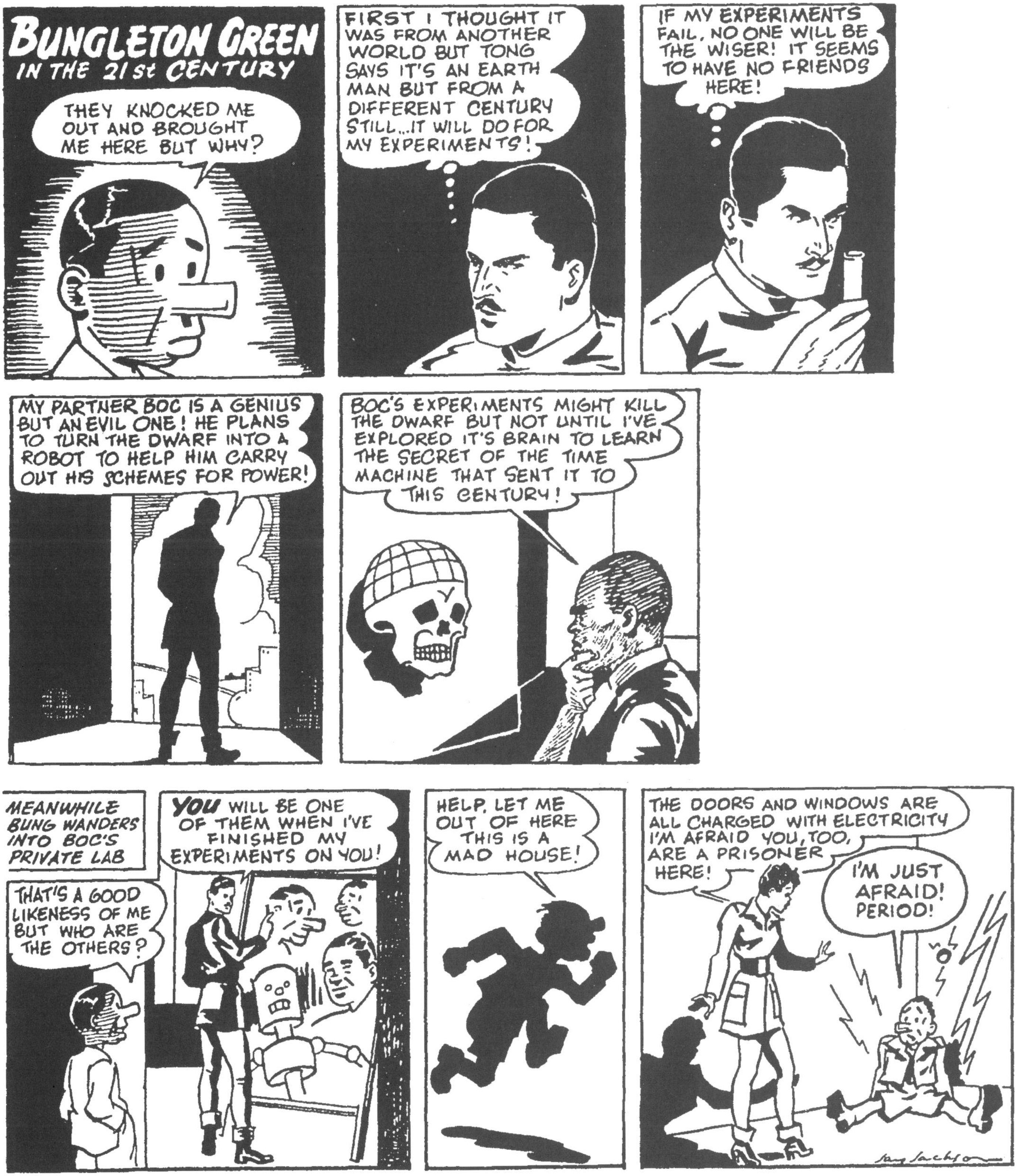
BUNGLETON GREEN
IN THE 21st CENTURY
THEY KNOCKED ME OUT AND BROUGHT ME HERE BUT WHY?
FIRST I THOUGHT IT WAS FROM ANOTHER WORLD BUT TONG SAYS IT'S AN EARTH MAN BUT FROM A DIFFERENT CENTURY STILL...IT WILL DO FOR MY EXPERIMENTS!
IF MY EXPERIMENTS FAIL, NO ONE WILL BE THE WISER! IT SEEMS TO HAVE NO FRIENDS HERE!
MY PARTNER BOC IS A GENIUS BUT AN EVIL ONE! HE PLANS TO TURN THE DWARF INTO A ROBOT TO HELP HIM CARRY OUT HIS SCHEMES FOR POWER!
BOC'S EXPERIMENTS MIGHT KILL THE DWARF BUT NOT UNTIL I'VE EXPLORED IT'S BRAIN TO LEARN THE SECRET OF THE TIME MACHINE THAT SENT IT TO THIS CENTURY!
MEANWHILE BUNG WANDERS INTO BOC'S PRIVATE LAB
THAT'S A GOOD LIKENESS OF ME BUT WHO ARE THE OTHERS?
YOU WILL BE ONE OF THEM WHEN I'VE FINISHED MY EXPERIMENTS ON YOU!
HELP, LET ME OUT OF HERE THIS IS A MAD HOUSE!
THE DOORS AND WINDOWS ARE ALL CHARGED WITH ELECTRICITY I'M AFRAID YOU, TOO, ARE A PRISONER HERE!
I'M JUST AFRAID! PERIOD!

DECEMBER 16, 1944

BUNGLETON GREEN IN THE 21st CENTURY

NEEDN'T TRY TO GET AWAY! I KNOW! I TOO AM A PRISONER HERE!

OUR ONLY HOPE IS TO WAIT! THE TWO SCIENTISTS DISTRUST EACH OTHER! ONE DAY THEY WILL KILL EACH OTHER OFF THEN WILL BE OUR CHANCE! MEANWHILE LET ON LIKE YOU TRUST THEM!

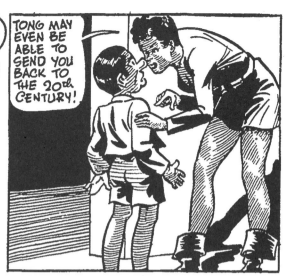

TONG MAY EVEN BE ABLE TO SEND YOU BACK TO THE 20th CENTURY!

MEANWHILE, BOC MAKES PLANS

I WILL MAKE THIS BUNGLETON INDIVIDUAL INTO A SUPER ROBOT! BUT FIRST I MUST CHANGE HIS LOOKS SO NO ONE WILL KNOW HIM......!

TALLER, HANDSOMER.... MORE LIKE A HUMAN BEING!

THEN I MUST GET TONG TO GIVE HIM A SUPER MIND AND TEACH ME HOW TO CONTROL IT!

MEANWHILE, TONG EXPERIMENTS WITH BUNG'S MIND....

THINK HARD NOW WHILE I TRY TO CAPTURE AN IMPRESSION OF THE MACHINE THAT SENT YOU TO THIS CENTURY... AH! THERE IT IS! NOW TO BUILD IT AND MAKE IT WORK!

WHEEOO! THOSE TWO GUYS ARE SPOOKY! BUT WHAT PART DO YOU PLAY HERE?

BOC KIDNAPPED ME FOR AN EXPERIMENT BUT TONG WOULDN'T LET HIM KILL ME SO THEY KEEP ME HEAR SO I CAN'T EXPOSE THEM!

AHHA! THAT GIVES ME AN IDEA THAT MAY FREE US BOTH AND MIGHT EVEN GET ME BACK TO THE TWENTIETH CENTURY!

DECEMBER 23, 1944

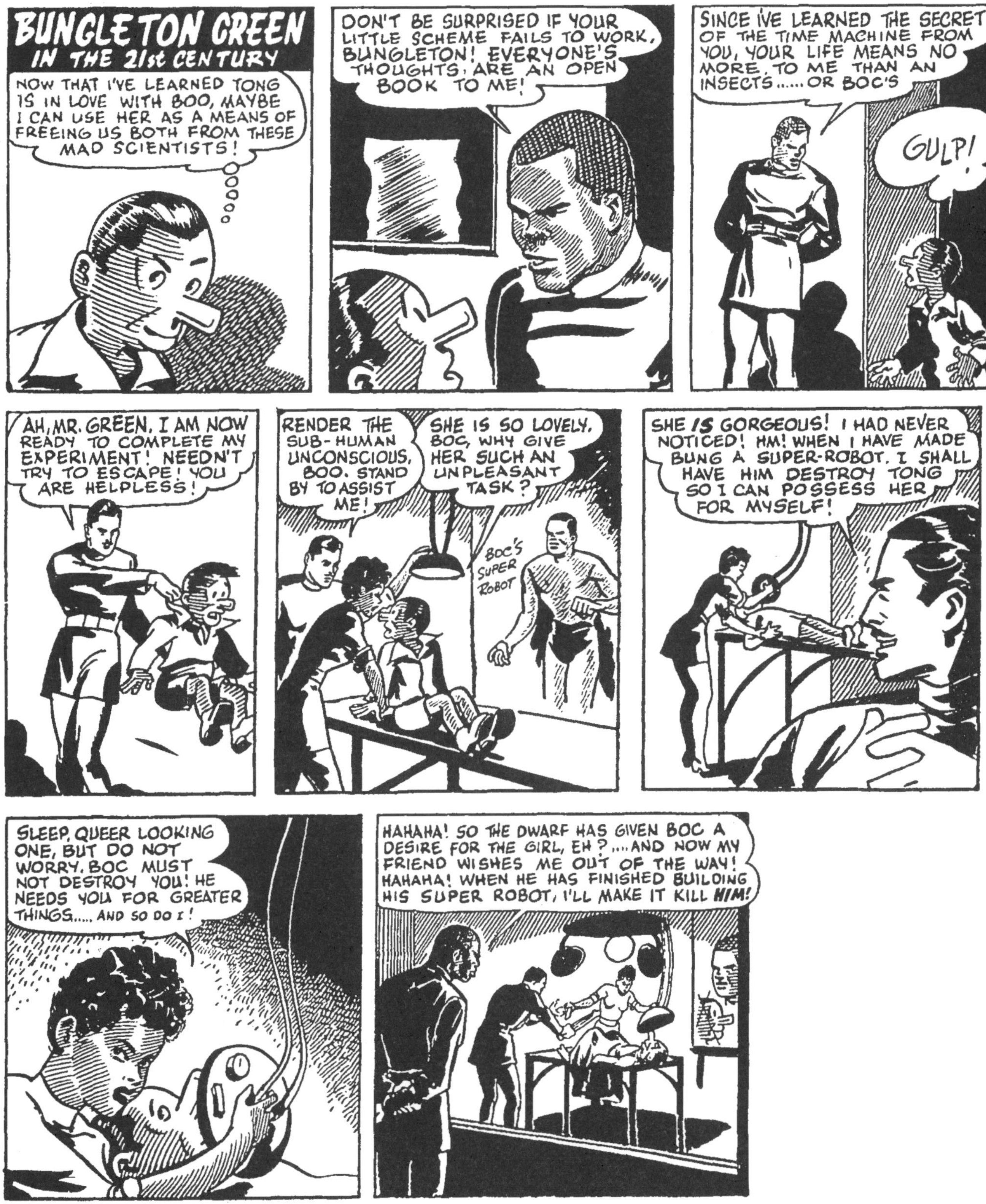

BUNGLETON GREEN
IN THE 21st CENTURY
NOW THAT I'VE LEARNED TONG IS IN LOVE WITH BOO, MAYBE I CAN USE HER AS A MEANS OF FREEING US BOTH FROM THESE MAD SCIENTISTS!
DON'T BE SURPRISED IF YOUR LITTLE SCHEME FAILS TO WORK, BUNGLETON! EVERYONE'S THOUGHTS ARE AN OPEN BOOK TO ME!
SINCE I'VE LEARNED THE SECRET OF THE TIME MACHINE FROM YOU, YOUR LIFE MEANS NO MORE TO ME THAN AN INSECTS.....OR BOC'S
GULP!
AH, MR. GREEN, I AM NOW READY TO COMPLETE MY EXPERIMENT! NEEDN'T TRY TO ESCAPE! YOU ARE HELPLESS!
RENDER THE SUB-HUMAN UNCONSCIOUS, BOO. STAND BY TO ASSIST ME!
SHE IS SO LOVELY. BOC, WHY GIVE HER SUCH AN UNPLEASANT TASK?
BOC'S SUPER ROBOT
SHE IS GORGEOUS! I HAD NEVER NOTICED! HM! WHEN I HAVE MADE BUNG A SUPER-ROBOT, I SHALL HAVE HIM DESTROY TONG SO I CAN POSSESS HER FOR MYSELF!
SLEEP, QUEER LOOKING ONE, BUT DO NOT WORRY. BOC MUST NOT DESTROY YOU! HE NEEDS YOU FOR GREATER THINGS..... AND SO DO I!
HAHAHA! SO THE DWARF HAS GIVEN BOC A DESIRE FOR THE GIRL, EH?....AND NOW MY FRIEND WISHES ME OUT OF THE WAY! HAHAHA! WHEN HE HAS FINISHED BUILDING HIS SUPER ROBOT, I'LL MAKE IT KILL HIM!

DECEMBER 30, 1944

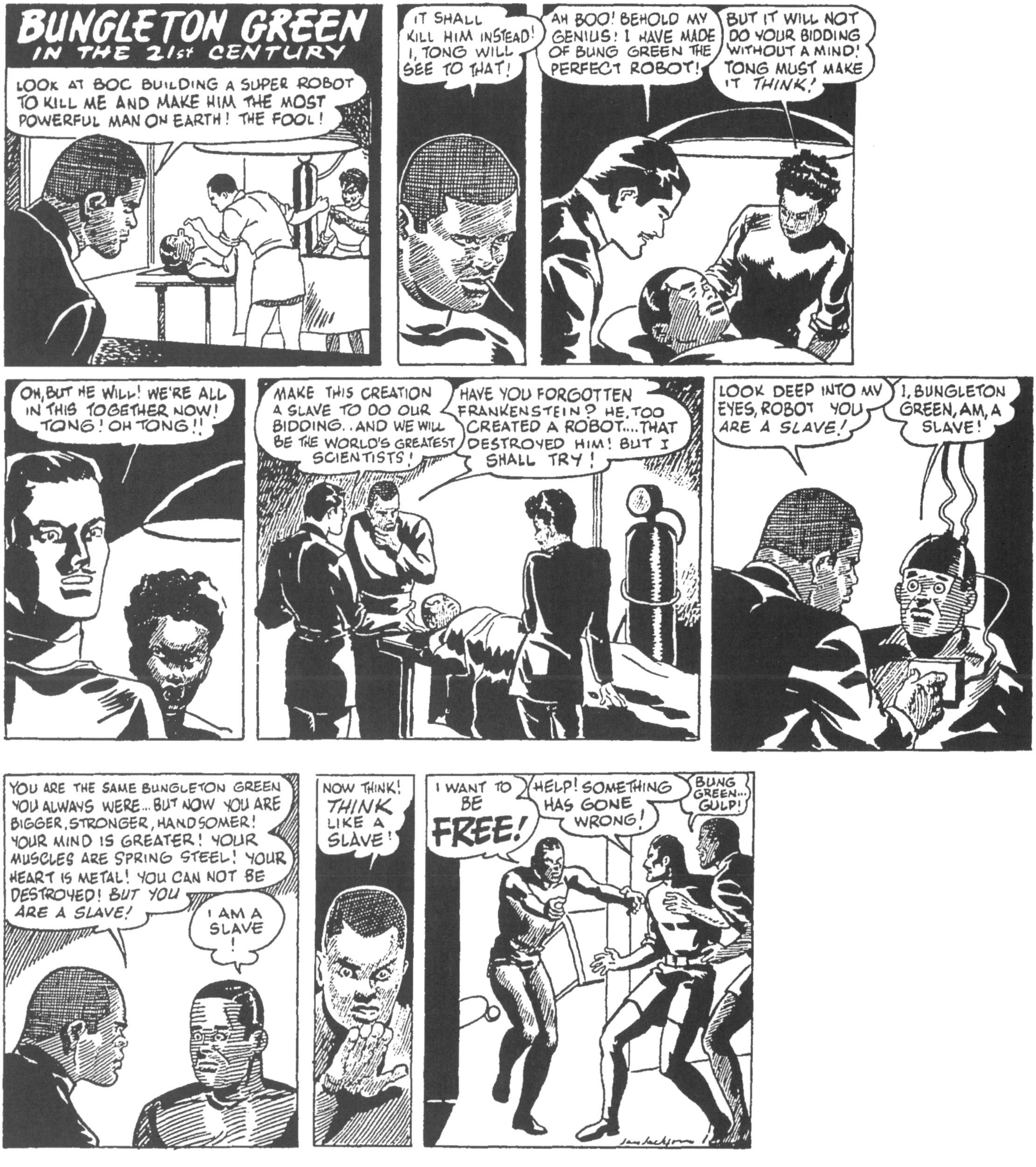
BUNGLETON GREEN
IN THE 21st CENTURY
LOOK AT BOC BUILDING A SUPER ROBOT TO KILL ME AND MAKE HIM THE MOST POWERFUL MAN ON EARTH! THE FOOL!
IT SHALL KILL HIM INSTEAD! I, TONG WILL SEE TO THAT!
AH BOO! BEHOLD MY GENIUS! I HAVE MADE OF BUNG GREEN THE PERFECT ROBOT!
BUT IT WILL NOT DO YOUR BIDDING WITHOUT A MIND! TONG MUST MAKE IT THINK!
OH, BUT HE WILL! WE'RE ALL IN THIS TOGETHER NOW! TONG! OH TONG!!
MAKE THIS CREATION A SLAVE TO DO OUR BIDDING.. AND WE WILL BE THE WORLD'S GREATEST SCIENTISTS!
HAVE YOU FORGOTTEN FRANKENSTEIN? HE, TOO CREATED A ROBOT.... THAT DESTROYED HIM! BUT I SHALL TRY!
LOOK DEEP INTO MY EYES, ROBOT YOU ARE A SLAVE!
I, BUNGLETON GREEN, AM, A SLAVE!
YOU ARE THE SAME BUNGLETON GREEN YOU ALWAYS WERE... BUT NOW YOU ARE BIGGER, STRONGER, HANDSOMER! YOUR MIND IS GREATER! YOUR MUSCLES ARE SPRING STEEL! YOUR HEART IS METAL! YOU CAN NOT BE DESTROYED! BUT YOU ARE A SLAVE!
I AM A SLAVE!
NOW THINK! THINK LIKE A SLAVE!
I WANT TO BE FREE!
HELP! SOMETHING HAS GONE WRONG!
BUNG GREEN... GULP!

JANUARY 6, 1945

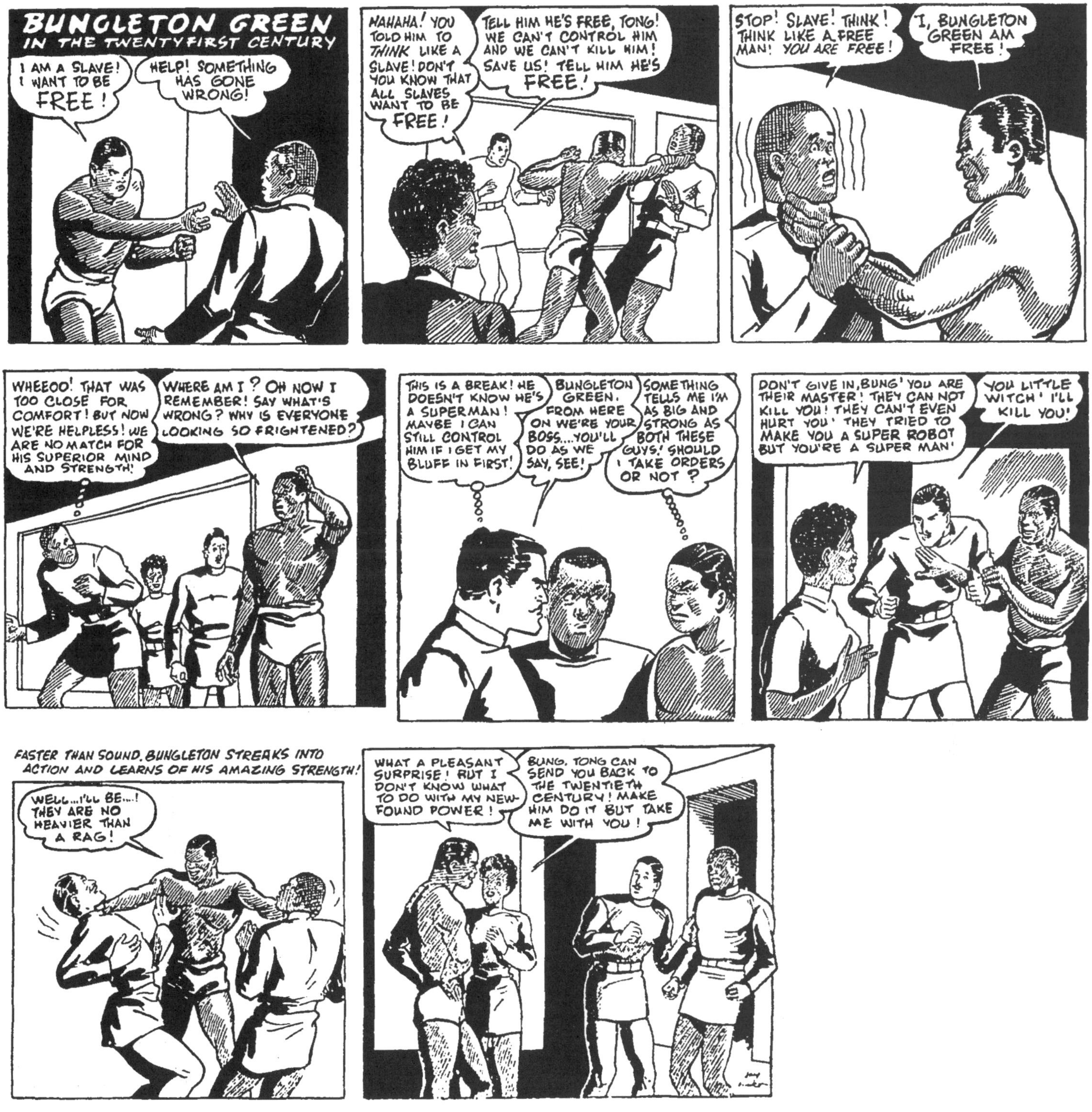
BUNGLETON GREEN
IN THE TWENTYFIRST CENTURY
I AM A SLAVE! I WANT TO BE FREE!
HELP! SOMETHING HAS GONE WRONG!
HAHAHA! YOU TOLD HIM TO THINK LIKE A SLAVE! DON'T YOU KNOW THAT ALL SLAVES WANT TO BE FREE!
TELL HIM HE'S FREE, TONG! WE CAN'T CONTROL HIM AND WE CAN'T KILL HIM! SAVE US! TELL HIM HE'S FREE!
STOP! SLAVE! THINK! THINK LIKE A FREE MAN! YOU ARE FREE!
I, BUNGLETON GREEN AM FREE!
WHEEOO! THAT WAS TOO CLOSE FOR COMFORT! BUT NOW WE'RE HELPLESS! WE ARE NO MATCH FOR HIS SUPERIOR MIND AND STRENGTH!
WHERE AM I? OH NOW I REMEMBER! SAY WHAT'S WRONG? WHY IS EVERYONE LOOKING SO FRIGHTENED?
THIS IS A BREAK! HE DOESN'T KNOW HE'S A SUPERMAN! MAYBE I CAN STILL CONTROL HIM IF I GET MY BLUFF IN FIRST!
BUNGLETON GREEN. FROM HERE ON WE'RE YOUR BOSS....YOU'LL DO AS WE SAY, SEE!
SOMETHING TELLS ME I'M AS BIG AND STRONG AS BOTH THESE GUYS! SHOULD I TAKE ORDERS OR NOT?
DON'T GIVE IN, BUNG! YOU ARE THEIR MASTER! THEY CAN NOT KILL YOU! THEY CAN'T EVEN HURT YOU! THEY TRIED TO MAKE YOU A SUPER ROBOT BUT YOU'RE A SUPER MAN!
YOU LITTLE WITCH! I'LL KILL YOU!
FASTER THAN SOUND, BUNGLETON STREAKS INTO ACTION AND LEARNS OF HIS AMAZING STRENGTH!
WELL...I'LL BE...! THEY ARE NO HEAVIER THAN A RAG!
WHAT A PLEASANT SURPRISE! BUT I DON'T KNOW WHAT TO DO WITH MY NEW-FOUND POWER!
BUNG, TONG CAN SEND YOU BACK TO THE TWENTIETH CENTURY! MAKE HIM DO IT BUT TAKE ME WITH YOU!

JANUARY 13, 1945

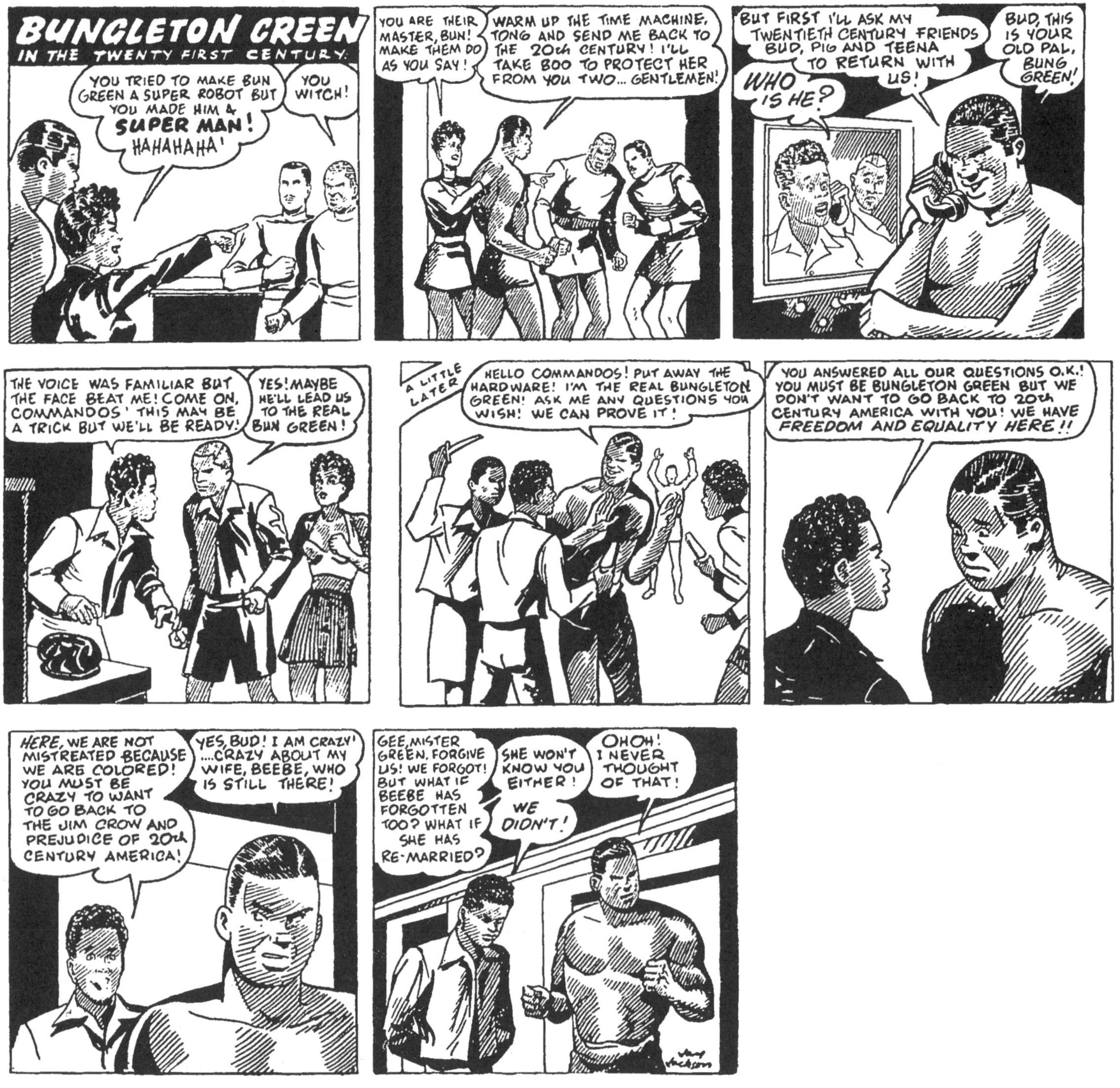
BUNGLETON GREEN
IN THE TWENTY FIRST CENTURY
YOU TRIED TO MAKE BUN GREEN A SUPER ROBOT BUT YOU MADE HIM A SUPER MAN! HAHAHAHA!
YOU WITCH!
YOU ARE THEIR MASTER, BUN! MAKE THEM DO AS YOU SAY!
WARM UP THE TIME MACHINE, TONG AND SEND ME BACK TO THE 20th CENTURY! I'LL TAKE BOO TO PROTECT HER FROM YOU TWO... GENTLEMEN!
BUT FIRST I'LL ASK MY TWENTIETH CENTURY FRIENDS BUD, PIG AND TEENA TO RETURN WITH US!
WHO IS HE?
BUD, THIS IS YOUR OLD PAL, BUNG GREEN!
THE VOICE WAS FAMILIAR BUT THE FACE BEAT ME! COME ON, COMMANDOS! THIS MAY BE A TRICK BUT WE'LL BE READY!
YES! MAYBE HE'LL LEAD US TO THE REAL BUN GREEN!
A LITTLE LATER
HELLO COMMANDOS! PUT AWAY THE HARDWARE! I'M THE REAL BUNGLETON GREEN! ASK ME ANY QUESTIONS YOU WISH! WE CAN PROVE IT!
YOU ANSWERED ALL OUR QUESTIONS O.K.! YOU MUST BE BUNGLETON GREEN BUT WE DON'T WANT TO GO BACK TO 20th CENTURY AMERICA WITH YOU! WE HAVE FREEDOM AND EQUALITY HERE!!
HERE, WE ARE NOT MISTREATED BECAUSE WE ARE COLORED! YOU MUST BE CRAZY TO WANT TO GO BACK TO THE JIM CROW AND PREJUDICE OF 20th CENTURY AMERICA!
YES, BUD! I AM CRAZY! ....CRAZY ABOUT MY WIFE, BEEBE, WHO IS STILL THERE!
GEE, MISTER GREEN, FORGIVE US! WE FORGOT! BUT WHAT IF BEEBE HAS FORGOTTEN TOO? WHAT IF SHE HAS RE-MARRIED?
SHE WON'T KNOW YOU EITHER!
WE DIDN'T!
OH OH! I NEVER THOUGHT OF THAT!

JANUARY 20, 1945

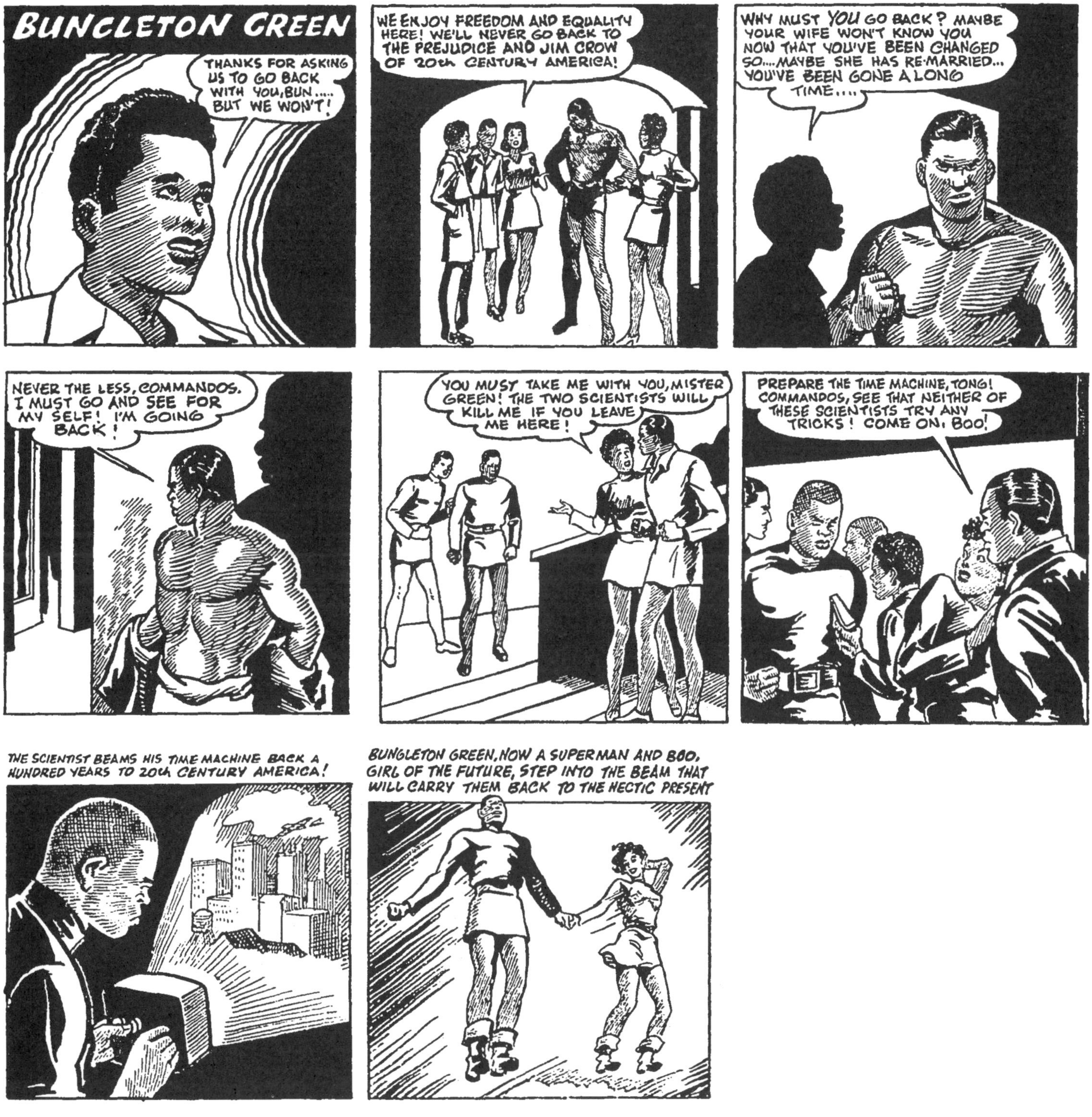
BUNGLETON GREEN
THANKS FOR ASKING US TO GO BACK WITH YOU, BUN..... BUT WE WON'T!
WE ENJOY FREEDOM AND EQUALITY HERE! WE'LL NEVER GO BACK TO THE PREJUDICE AND JIM CROW OF 20th CENTURY AMERICA!
WHY MUST YOU GO BACK? MAYBE YOUR WIFE WON'T KNOW YOU NOW THAT YOU'VE BEEN CHANGED SO....MAYBE SHE HAS RE-MARRIED... YOU'VE BEEN GONE A LONG TIME....
NEVER THE LESS, COMMANDOS. I MUST GO AND SEE FOR MY SELF! I'M GOING BACK!
YOU MUST TAKE ME WITH YOU, MISTER GREEN! THE TWO SCIENTISTS WILL KILL ME IF YOU LEAVE ME HERE!
PREPARE THE TIME MACHINE, TONG! COMMANDOS, SEE THAT NEITHER OF THESE SCIENTISTS TRY ANY TRICKS! COME ON, BOO!
THE SCIENTIST BEAMS HIS TIME MACHINE BACK A HUNDRED YEARS TO 20th CENTURY AMERICA!
BUNGLETON GREEN, NOW A SUPERMAN AND BOO, GIRL OF THE FUTURE, STEP INTO THE BEAM THAT WILL CARRY THEM BACK TO THE HECTIC PRESENT

JANUARY 27, 1945

JACKSON'S PASSWORDS

In most of Jackson's run of *Bungleton Green and the Mystic Commandos*, the final panel featured a short biography of a famous Black historical figure. Often it was a contemporary or historic figure like Booker T. Washington, and other times more mythic, like John Henry. All of them are collected here.

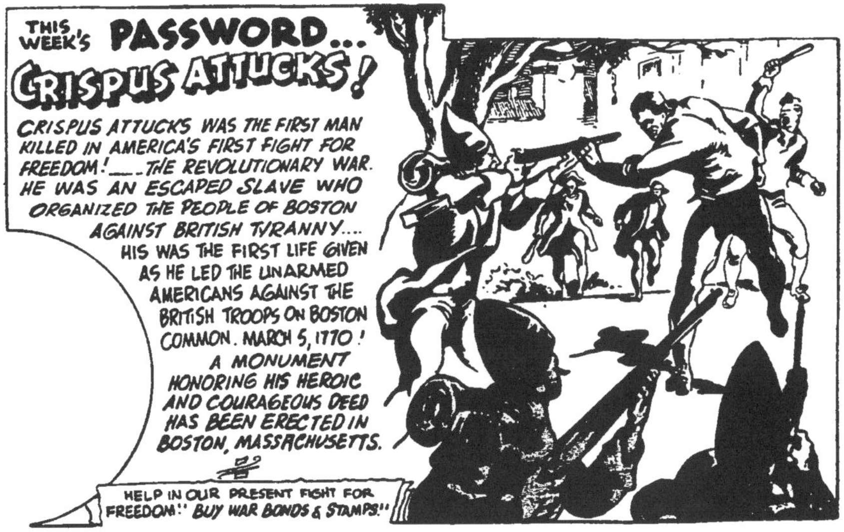
THIS WEEK'S PASSWORD...
CRISPUS ATTUCKS!
CRISPUS ATTUCKS WAS THE FIRST MAN KILLED IN AMERICA'S FIRST FIGHT FOR FREEDOM!___THE REVOLUTIONARY WAR. HE WAS AN ESCAPED SLAVE WHO ORGANIZED THE PEOPLE OF BOSTON AGAINST BRITISH TYRANNY.... HIS WAS THE FIRST LIFE GIVEN AS HE LED THE UNARMED AMERICANS AGAINST THE BRITISH TROOPS ON BOSTON COMMON. MARCH 5, 1770! A MONUMENT HONORING HIS HEROIC AND COURAGEOUS DEED HAS BEEN ERECTED IN BOSTON, MASSACHUSETTS.
HELP IN OUR PRESENT FIGHT FOR FREEDOM!' BUY WAR BONDS & STAMPS!"

DECEMBER 5, 1942

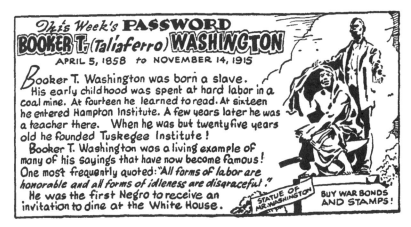

This Week's PASSWORD
BOOKER T. (Taliaferro) WASHINGTON
APRIL 5, 1858 to NOVEMBER 14, 1915
Booker T. Washington was born a slave.
His early childhood was spent at hard labor in a coal mine. At fourteen he learned to read. At sixteen he entered Hampton Institute. A few years later he was a teacher there. When he was but twentyfive years old he founded Tuskegee Institute!
Booker T. Washington was a living example of many of his sayings that have now become famous! One most frequently quoted: "All forms of labor are honorable and all forms of idleness are disgraceful."
He was the first Negro to receive an invitation to dine at the White House.
STATUE OF MR. WASHINGTON
BUY WAR BONDS AND STAMPS!

DECEMBER 12, 1942

THIS WEEK'S Password "PRINCE WHIPPLE"
PRINCE WHIPPLE, FAMOUS NEGRO HERO OF THE AMERICAN REVOLUTION WAS THE OARSMAN FOR GEORGE WASHINGTON IN THE CELEBRATED CROSSING OF THE DELEWARE!
HE WAS THE GIANT SON OF A ZULU CHIEFTAIN AND HIS COURAGE IS RECORDED IN THE WELL KNOWN PAINTING BY EMANUEL LEUTZE WHICH HANGS IN THE NATION'S CAPITOL.... WASHINGTON, D.C.
FROM THE PAINTING BY EMANUEL LEUTZE

DECEMBER 5, 1942

THIS WEEK'S PASSWORD
PETER SALEM
PETER SALEM AN EX SLAVE FROM FRAMINGHAM, MASSACHUSETTS WAS ONE OF THE OUTSTANDING HEROES OF THE AMERICAN REVOLUTION...... HE FIRED THE SHOT THAT KILLED BRITISH MAJOR PITCAIRN... JUNE 17, 1775 AT BUNKER HILL, AFTER THE HISTORIC ORDER WAS GIVEN.
"DON'T FIRE UNTIL YOU SEE THE WHITES OF THEIR EYES!"

DECEMBER 12, 1942

This Week's PASSWORD "EBOUE" PRONOUNCED AY-BOO-AY
ADOLPH FELIX SILVESTER EBOUE WAS THE FIRST BLACK MAN EVER TO GOVERN A FRENCH COLONY. HE REFUSED TO FOLLOW VICHY PRO-NAZI POLICY AND LED THE BATTLE TO BRING FRENCH EQUATORIAL AFRICA TO THE ALLIED CAUSE! HE WAS NAMED GOVERNOR-GENERAL BY GENERAL CHARLES DE GAULLE. EBOUE HELPED A.E.F. INVASION OF AFRICA SUCCEED BY HIS FIGHT FOR FREEDOM!
HELP IN OUR FIGHT FOR FREEDOM! BUY MORE WAR BONDS AND STAMPS!
PRO NAZI AFRICA
SUEZ
IRAN
INDIA
PRO-ALLIES AFRICA
BRAZIL
ATLANTIC OCEAN
MADAGASCAR

JANUARY 2, 1943

THIS WEEK'S PASSWORD – DOMINIQUE FRANÇOIS TOUSSAINT L'OUVERTURE...
BORN A SLAVE....ROSE TO GENERAL IN THE FRENCH ARMY AND RULER (WITH THE RIGHT OF NAMING HIS SUCCESSOR) OF HAITI. AFTER ORGANIZING THE SLAVES IN A SUCCESSFUL UPRISING AGAINST THEIR MASTERS, HE TURNED ON THE ENGLISH AND SPANISH AND DROVE THEIR ARMIES FROM HAITI. HE IMMEDIATELY RESTORED PEACE AND PROSPERITY. IN 1800 HE BEGAIN TO AIM AT INDEPENDENCE FROM FRANCE. HE BROKE COMPLETELY WITH THE FRENCH WHEN THEY TRIED TO REESTABLISH SLAVERY ON THE ISLAND! NAPOLEON SENT A POWERFUL FLEET TO FORCE THE ISSUE...... WHILE L'OUVERTURE WAS ATTEMPTING TO SETTLE THE MATTER PEACEFULLY, HE WAS TREACHEROUSLY ATTACKED, OVERPOWERED, CARRIED TO FRANCE AND THROWN INTO PRISON. THERE HE DIED TEN MONTHS LATER, APRIL 27, 1803.

JANUARY 9, 1943

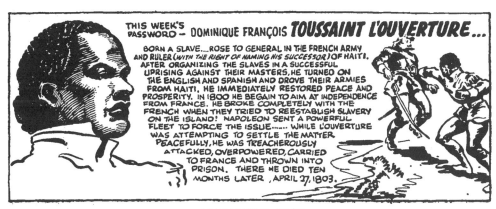

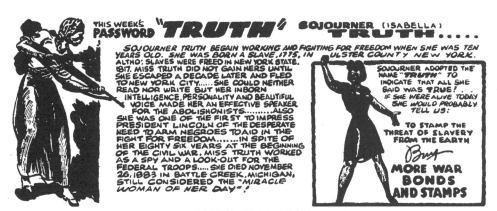

THIS WEEK'S PASSWORD "TRUTH" SOJOURNER (ISABELLA) TRUTH.....
SOJOURNER TRUTH BEGAIN WORKING AND FIGHTING FOR FREEDOM WHEN SHE WAS TEN YEARS OLD. SHE WAS BORN A SLAVE, 1775, IN ULSTER COUNTY NEW YORK. ALTHO' SLAVES WERE FREED IN NEW YORK STATE. 1817. MISS TRUTH DID NOT GAIN HERS UNTIL SHE ESCAPED A DECADE LATER AND FLED TO NEW YORK CITY...... SHE COULD NEITHER READ NOR WRITE BUT HER INBORN INTELLIGENCE, PERSONALITY AND BEAUTIFUL VOICE MADE HER AN EFFECTIVE SPEAKER FOR THE ABOLISHONISTS.........ALSO SHE WAS ONE OF THE FIRST TO IMPRESS PRESIDENT LINCOLN OF THE DESPERATE NEED TO ARM NEGROES TO AID IN THE FIGHT FOR FREEDOM.......IN SPITE OF HER EIGHTY SIX YEARS AT THE BEGINNING OF THE CIVIL WAR, MISS TRUTH WORKED AS A SPY AND A LOOK-OUT FOR THE FEDERAL TROOPS..... SHE DIED NOVEMBER 26, 1883 IN BATTLE CREEK, MICHIGAN, STILL CONSIDERED THE "MIRACLE WOMAN OF HER DAY"!
SOJOURNER ADOPTED THE NAME "TRUTH" TO INDICATE THAT ALL SHE SAID WAS TRUE! . . IF SHE WERE ALIVE TODAY SHE WOULD PROBABLY TELL US:
TO STAMP THE THREAT OF SLAVERY FROM THE EARTH
Buy MORE WAR BONDS AND STAMPS

JANUARY 16, 1943

THIS WEEK'S
PASSWORD
DORIE
MILLER
HERO OF
Pearl Harbor
DORIE MILLER. MESSMAN IN THE U.S. NAVY WAS AWARDED THE NAVY CROSS FOR EXTRA ORDINARY BRAVERY UNDER FIRE. DURING THE SURPRISE ATTACK ON PEARL HARBOR, DECEMBER 7, 1941. MR MILLER RUSHED TO THE AID OF HIS WOUNDED CAPTAIN AND CARRIED HIM TO A SAFER PLACE. HE RETURNED TO THE BRIDGE OF THE DAMAGED SHIP AND FIRED A MACHINE GUN AT ATTACKING JAPANESE PLANES UNTIL HE WAS BOMBED FROM HIS DANGEROUS POST!

JANUARY 23, 1943

THIS WEEK'S PASSWORD
OSCEOLA
THE KIDNAPPING OF A NEGRO BRIDE FORCED THE UNITED STATES TO FIGHT A WAR!
OSCEOLA WAS THE SON OF A NEGRO WOMAN AND A SEMINOLE INDIAN CHIEF LIVING IN THE FLORIDA SWAMPS. HIS TRIBE HAD GIVEN THE SPANIARDS SO MUCH GRIEF THAT THEY SOLD FLORIDA AND ITS PROBLEMS TO THE UNITED STATES FOR $5,000,000. UNTIL 1840 THE TRIBESMEN WERE STILL UNSUBDUED! FOR YEARS INDIANS HAD BEEN FURNISHING HIDE OUTS FOR NEGRO SLAVES SEEKING FREEDOM. THE SEMINOLE INDIANS WERE NO EXCEPTION. THEY WELCOMED NEGROES. THE NEGROES IN TURN ACCEPTED THEIR CUSTOMS AND INTERMARRIED WITH THEM.
OSCEOLA FELL IN LOVE AND MARRIED A BEAUTIFUL COLORED GIRL WHO ESCAPED INTO HIS CAMP FROM A BORDERING SLAVE STATE.... SOME MONTHS LATER SHE WAS ABDUCTED BY SLAVE RAIDERS AND SOLD. THE SEMINOLES WENT ON THE WAR PATH. THEIR RETRIBUTION WAS SWIFT AND TERRIBLE! SO GREAT WAS THEIR DESTRUCTION IN THE SURROUNDING STATES THAT IT WAS NECESSARY TO CALL OUT THE UNITED STATES ARMY: A BLOODY WAR RESULTED. EVENTUALLY THE SEMINOLES AND THEIR NEGRO RELATIVES AND ALLIES WERE BOUGHT OFF BY THE UNITED STATES GOVERNMENT AND MOVED WEST OF THE MISSISSIPPI RIVER.

JANUARY 30, 1943

THIS WEEK'S Password
JOHN HENRY
BIG JOHN HENRY WAS A RIVER MAN. HE LIVED ON THE LEVEE SINCE TIME BEGAN
HE COULD WHIP A MULE AND A HUNDRED MEN, LOAD A COTTON BOAT AN' DO IT AGAIN.'
BIG JOHN HENRY HAD A BIG TALL GAL, SHE HAD BLUE GUMS AN' HER NAME WAS SAL.
THEY RODE WHERE THEY WENT ON A HURRICANE, BUT THEY COUD OUT RUN A RAIL ROAD TRAIN!
STORIES OF JOHN HENRY HAVE BEEN TOLD AND SUNG BY NEGROES THRU' THE CENTURIES. ROARK BRADFORD COMPILED SOME AND PUT THEM IN BOOK FORM. PLAYS HAVE BEEN WRITTEN ABOUT THIS NEGRO SUPERMAN AND RELEASED OVER NATIONAL RADIO HOOKUPS AND ON STAGE AND SCREEN. RECENTLY JOHN HENRY TURNED UP ON A BROADCAST SPONSORED BY THE TREASURY DEPT. HE AND THE MYTHICAL PAUL BUNYUN WERE TURNING OUT MORE WEAPONS THAN A HUNDRED MEN TO WHIP THE AXIS! JOHN HENRY, LIKE THE SPIRITUALS AND THE BLUES IS ANOTHER OF THE NEGRO'S MANY CONTRIBUTIONS TO AMERICA'S COLORFUL FOLKLORE.

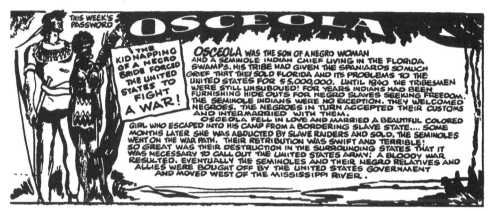

FEBRUARY 6, 1943

THIS WEEK'S PASSWORD
FREDERICK DOUGLASS

BORN FEB. 9th 1817, TUCKAHOE, MARYLAND. A SLAVE UNTIL 21 WHEN HE ESCAPED TO NEW YORK. DIED FEB. 20, 1895. KNOWN AND HONORED IN AMERICA AND EUROPE FOR HIS RELENTLESS FIGHT FOR FREEDOM.

ABOLITIONIST.... LECTURED IN ENGLAND AND AMERICA AGAINST SLAVERY.

JOURNALIST.... PUBLISHED "THE NORTH STAR" "NATIONAL ERA" AND "FREDERIC DOUGLASS NEWS".

DIPLOMAT..... APPOINTED SECRETARY OF THE COMMISSION OF SANTO DOMINGO, PRESIDENTAL ELECTOR OF NEW YORK, MARSHAL FOR THE DISTRICT OF COLUMBIA, ALSO COMMISSIONER OF DEEDS AND UNITED STATES MINISTER TO HAITI.

FEBRUARY 13, 1943

THIS WEEK'S PASSWORD
ROBERT SMALLS

ASSISTANT TO THE CAPTAIN OF THE CONFEDERATE SHIP "THE PLANTER". AT THE START OF THE CIVIL WAR, MR. SMALLS SMUGGLED HIS FAMILY AND AS MANY SLAVES AS POSSIBLE ABOARD, RAN THE GANTLET OF THE REBEL NAVY AND TURNED "THE PLANTER" OVER TO THE FEDERAL GOVERNMENT IN A NORTHERN PORT! THE NORTH REPAID HIS HEROISM BY PLACING HIM IN COMMAND OF THE SHIP FOR THE DURATION OF THE WAR

ELECTED TO CONGRESS FIVE TIMES DURING RECONSTRUCTION PERIOD!

U.S. NAVAL TRAINING CAMP RECENTLY NAMED IN HIS HONOR

FEBRUARY 20, 1943

THIS WEEK'S PASSWORD
JOSEPH CINQUE

AFRICAN PRINCE, WAS CAPTURED BY SLAVE RAIDERS ALONG WITH FIFTY OTHER MEN AND THREE GIRLS.. THEY WERE HERDED INTO THE SPANISH SHIP "AMISTAD" BOUND FOR CUBA...ENROUTE, CINQUE AND THE OTHER SLAVES FREED THEMSELVES, DISPOSED OF THE CREW AND ORDERED THE SPANISH CAPTAIN AND PILOT BACK TO AFRICA. INSTEAD, TWO MONTHS LATER THEY DOCKED IN CONNECTICUT, U.S.A. THE NEGROES WERE CHARGED WITH MUTINY AND MURDER!

AFTER A TWO YEAR COURT BATTLE, WITH THE AID OF AMERICAN ABOLITIONISTS AND THE BRITISH GOVERNMENT, THE NEGROES WERE FREED, EDUCATED AND RETURNED TO SIERRA LEONE AFRICA - 1841.

ONE OF THE GIRLS PLANNED TO ENTER OBERLIN COLLEGE.

A FIGHT FOR FREEDOM THAT ENDED IN VICTORY!

OUR PRESENT FIGHT FOR FREEDOM WILL END VICTORIOUSLY SOONER IF WE BUY MORE WAR BONDS AND STAMPS

FEBRUARY 27, 1943

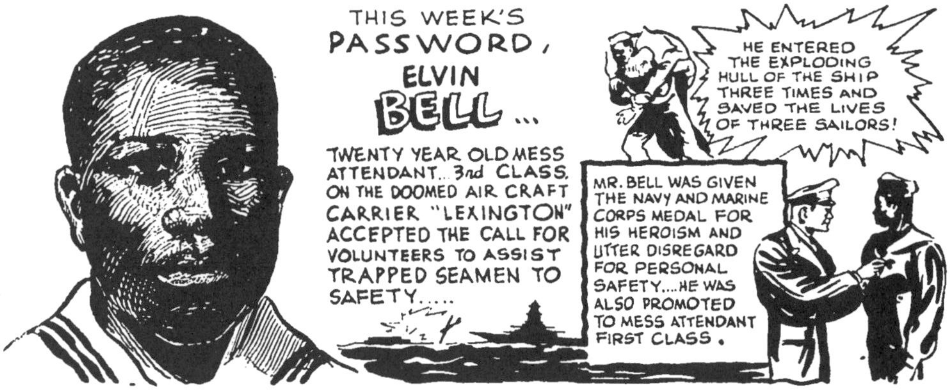
THIS WEEK'S PASSWORD, ELVIN BELL...
TWENTY YEAR OLD MESS ATTENDANT... 3rd CLASS, ON THE DOOMED AIR CRAFT CARRIER "LEXINGTON" ACCEPTED THE CALL FOR VOLUNTEERS TO ASSIST TRAPPED SEAMEN TO SAFETY.....
HE ENTERED THE EXPLODING HULL OF THE SHIP THREE TIMES AND SAVED THE LIVES OF THREE SAILORS!
MR. BELL WAS GIVEN THE NAVY AND MARINE CORPS MEDAL FOR HIS HEROISM AND UTTER DISREGARD FOR PERSONAL SAFETY.... HE WAS ALSO PROMOTED TO MESS ATTENDANT FIRST CLASS.

MARCH 6, 1943

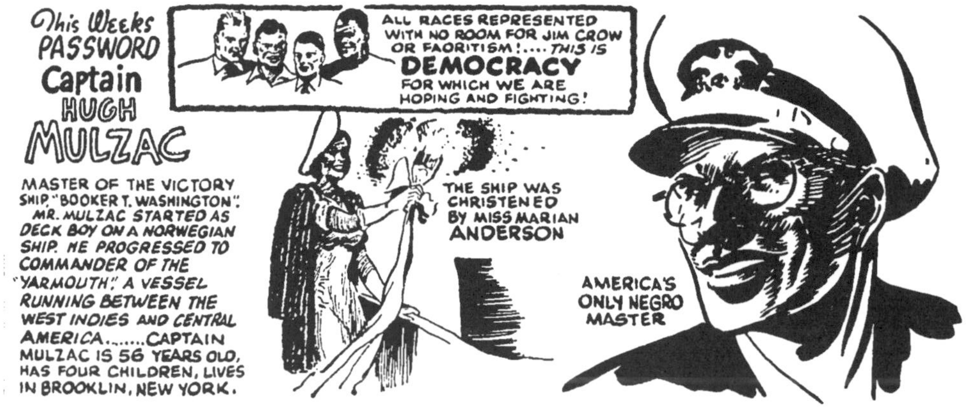
This Weeks PASSWORD Captain HUGH MULZAC
ALL RACES REPRESENTED WITH NO ROOM FOR JIM CROW OR FAORITISM!.... THIS IS DEMOCRACY FOR WHICH WE ARE HOPING AND FIGHTING!
MASTER OF THE VICTORY SHIP, "BOOKER T. WASHINGTON". MR. MULZAC STARTED AS DECK BOY ON A NORWEGIAN SHIP. HE PROGRESSED TO COMMANDER OF THE "YARMOUTH", A VESSEL RUNNING BETWEEN THE WEST INDIES AND CENTRAL AMERICA........ CAPTAIN MULZAC IS 56 YEARS OLD, HAS FOUR CHILDREN, LIVES IN BROOKLIN, NEW YORK.
THE SHIP WAS CHRISTENED BY MISS MARIAN ANDERSON
AMERICA'S ONLY NEGRO MASTER

MARCH 13, 1943

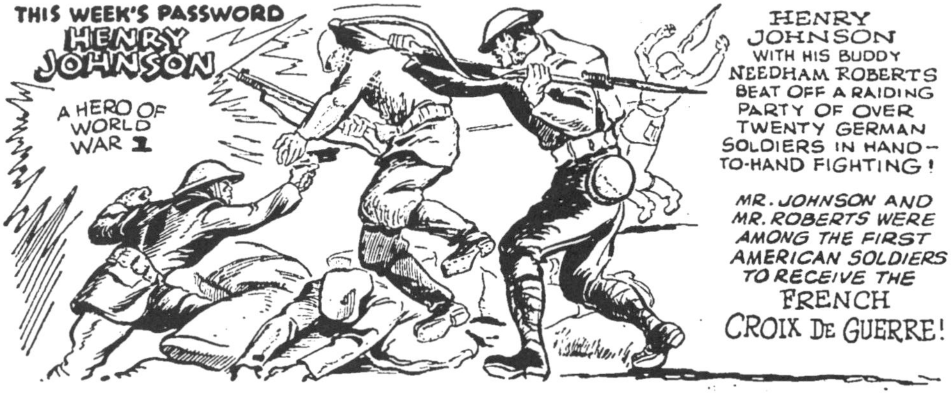
THIS WEEK'S PASSWORD HENRY JOHNSON
A HERO OF WORLD WAR 1
HENRY JOHNSON WITH HIS BUDDY NEEDHAM ROBERTS BEAT OFF A RAIDING PARTY OF OVER TWENTY GERMAN SOLDIERS IN HAND-TO-HAND FIGHTING!
MR. JOHNSON AND MR. ROBERTS WERE AMONG THE FIRST AMERICAN SOLDIERS TO RECEIVE THE FRENCH CROIX DE GUERRE!

MARCH 20, 1943

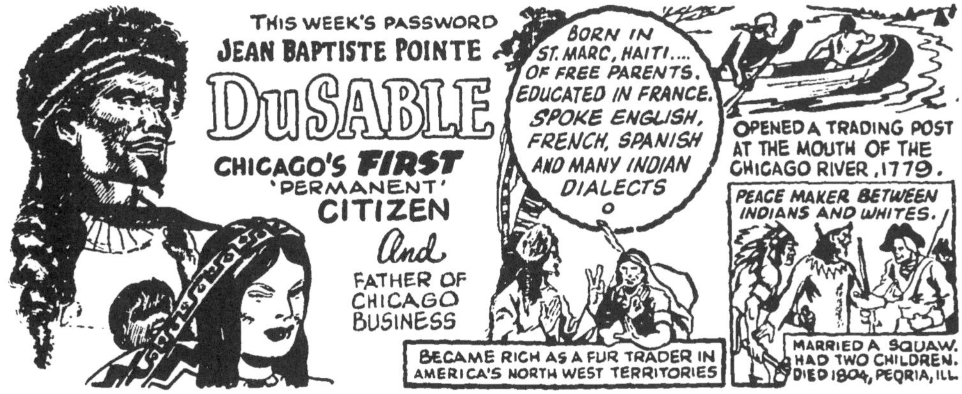
THIS WEEK'S PASSWORD
JEAN BAPTISTE POINTE
DuSABLE
CHICAGO'S FIRST 'PERMANENT' CITIZEN
And
FATHER OF CHICAGO BUSINESS
BORN IN ST. MARC, HAITI.... OF FREE PARENTS. EDUCATED IN FRANCE. SPOKE ENGLISH, FRENCH, SPANISH AND MANY INDIAN DIALECTS
OPENED A TRADING POST AT THE MOUTH OF THE CHICAGO RIVER, 1779.
PEACE MAKER BETWEEN INDIANS AND WHITES.
BECAME RICH AS A FUR TRADER IN AMERICA'S NORTH WEST TERRITORIES
MARRIED A SQUAW. HAD TWO CHILDREN. DIED 1804, PEORIA, ILL.

MARCH 27, 1943

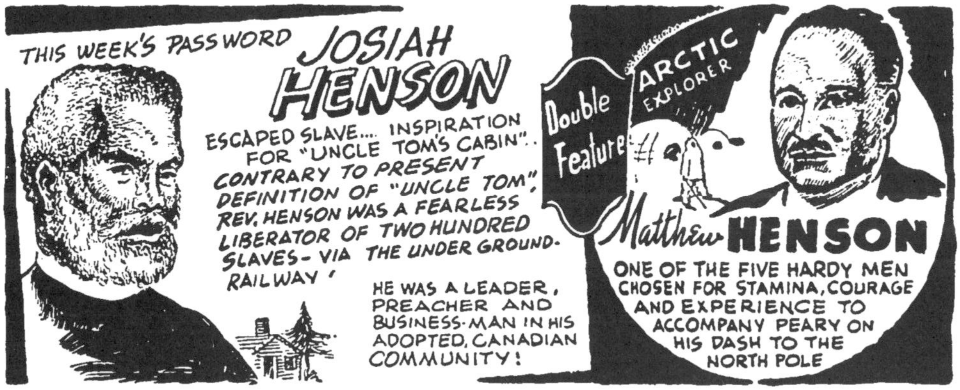
THIS WEEK'S PASSWORD
JOSIAH HENSON
ESCAPED SLAVE.... INSPIRATION FOR "UNCLE TOM'S CABIN". CONTRARY TO PRESENT DEFINITION OF "UNCLE TOM", REV. HENSON WAS A FEARLESS LIBERATOR OF TWO HUNDRED SLAVES - VIA THE UNDER GROUND-RAILWAY '
HE WAS A LEADER, PREACHER AND BUSINESS-MAN IN HIS ADOPTED, CANADIAN COMMUNITY!
Double Feature
ARCTIC EXPLORER
Matthew HENSON
ONE OF THE FIVE HARDY MEN CHOSEN FOR STAMINA, COURAGE AND EXPERIENCE TO ACCOMPANY PEARY ON HIS DASH TO THE NORTH POLE

APRIL 3, 1943

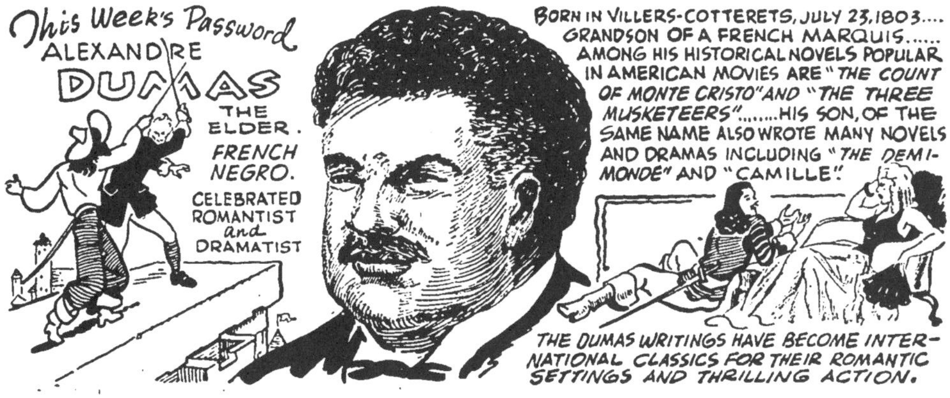
This Week's Password
ALEXANDRE DUMAS
THE ELDER.
FRENCH NEGRO.
CELEBRATED ROMANTIST and DRAMATIST
BORN IN VILLERS-COTTERETS, JULY 23, 1803.... GRANDSON OF A FRENCH MARQUIS...... AMONG HIS HISTORICAL NOVELS POPULAR IN AMERICAN MOVIES ARE "THE COUNT OF MONTE CRISTO" AND "THE THREE MUSKETEERS"........HIS SON, OF THE SAME NAME ALSO WROTE MANY NOVELS AND DRAMAS INCLUDING "THE DEMI-MONDE" AND "CAMILLE".
THE DUMAS WRITINGS HAVE BECOME INTERNATIONAL CLASSICS FOR THEIR ROMANTIC SETTINGS AND THRILLING ACTION.

APRIL 10, 1943

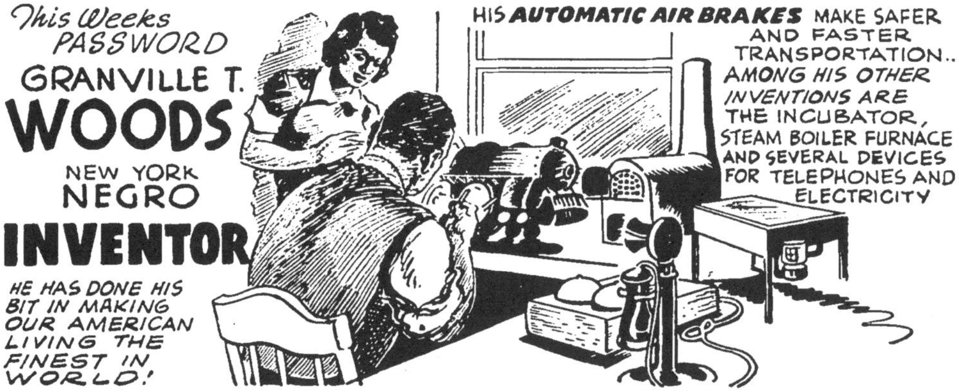
This Weeks PASSWORD
GRANVILLE T. WOODS
NEW YORK NEGRO INVENTOR
HE HAS DONE HIS BIT IN MAKING OUR AMERICAN LIVING THE FINEST IN WORLD!
HIS AUTOMATIC AIR BRAKES MAKE SAFER AND FASTER TRANSPORTATION..
AMONG HIS OTHER INVENTIONS ARE THE INCUBATOR, STEAM BOILER FURNACE AND SEVERAL DEVICES FOR TELEPHONES AND ELECTRICITY

APRIL 17, 1943

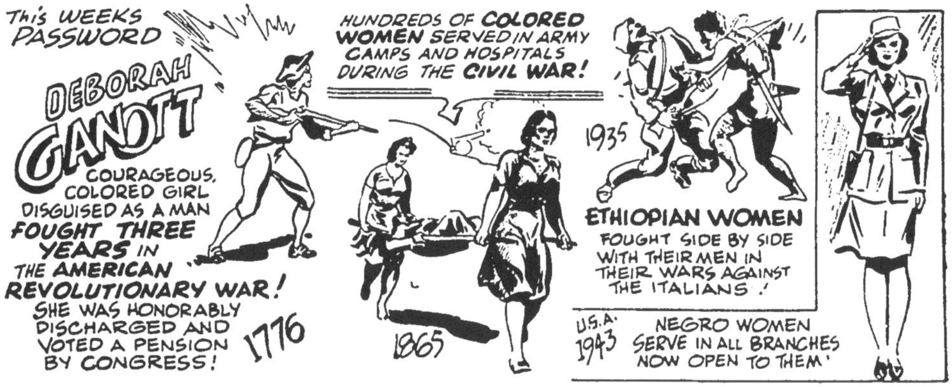
This WEEKS PASSWORD
DEBORAH GANOTT
COURAGEOUS, COLORED GIRL DISGUISED AS A MAN FOUGHT THREE YEARS IN THE AMERICAN REVOLUTIONARY WAR!
SHE WAS HONORABLY DISCHARGED AND VOTED A PENSION BY CONGRESS!
1776
HUNDREDS OF COLORED WOMEN SERVED IN ARMY CAMPS AND HOSPITALS DURING THE CIVIL WAR!
1865
1935
ETHIOPIAN WOMEN FOUGHT SIDE BY SIDE WITH THEIR MEN IN THEIR WARS AGAINST THE ITALIANS!
U.S.A. 1943
NEGRO WOMEN SERVE IN ALL BRANCHES NOW OPEN TO THEM'

APRIL 24, 1943

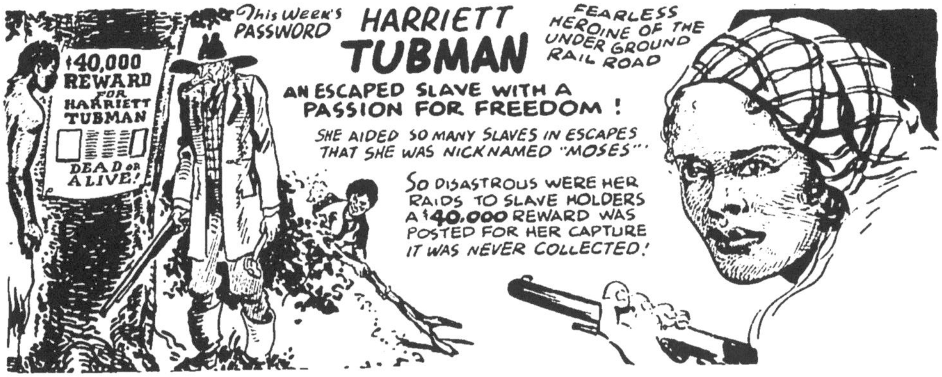
This Week's PASSWORD
HARRIETT TUBMAN
FEARLESS HEROINE OF THE UNDER GROUND RAIL ROAD
$40,000 REWARD FOR HARRIETT TUBMAN
DEAD OR ALIVE!
AN ESCAPED SLAVE WITH A PASSION FOR FREEDOM!
SHE AIDED SO MANY SLAVES IN ESCAPES THAT SHE WAS NICKNAMED "MOSES"
SO DISASTROUS WERE HER RAIDS TO SLAVE HOLDERS A $40,000 REWARD WAS POSTED FOR HER CAPTURE IT WAS NEVER COLLECTED!

MAY 1, 1943

This Week's Password

Carter Goodwin WOODSON

AN OUTSTANDING HISTORIAN OF THE PRESENT TIME

COMPILER AND PUBLISHER OF MANY VOLUMES OF FACTS ABOUT NEGROES OF THE WORLD AND THE PART THEY HAVE PLAYED AND ARE PLAYING IN HISTORY.........

ALSO FOUNDER OF THE ASSOCIATION FOR THE STUDY OF NEGRO LIFE AND HISTORY....

THE NEGRO A PROUD COURAGEOUS RACE...... AS PRESENTED by CARTER G. WOODSON

LEARNING THE THRILLING AND INTERESTING *FACTS* OF OUR RACE AS PRESENTED BY ABLE HISTORIANS LIKE CARTER G. WOODSON IS ONE OF THE BEST MORALE BUILDERS FOR AN OFTEN ABUSED PEOPLE

MAY 8, 1943

THIS WEEK'S PASSWORD

Dr. John Henry HALE M.D.,

HONORED BY NATIONAL MEDICAL ASSOCIATION IN 1938 FOR OUTSTANDING WORK

HAS PERFORMED OVER

17,000 OPERATIONS!

MAY 15, 1943

This Week's Password

JACK L. COOPER

FIRST NEGRO RADIO ANNOUNCER

STARTED IN WASHINGTON, D.C. 1925....... BROADCASTING REGULARLY OVER A CHICAGO STATION SINCE 1928.'

FORMER PRODUCER AND ACTOR IN HIS OWN ROAD-SHOW THAT TOURED THE COUNTRY IN THE EARLY TWENTIES...

MRS. JACK L. COOPER ANNOUNCER AND MUSICIAN

DANCER, DRUMMER, VENTRILOQUIST!

EX-BOXER AND BASEBALL STAR! RECEIVED *TWO* TITLES IN U.S. AND CUBA!

ONE TIME NEWS PAPER WRITER!

ELECTRICAL ENGINEER!!

MAY 22, 1943

THIS WEEKS PASSWORD

Alexander HAMILTON

BORN IN NEVIS. W.I. JAN. 11, 1757. EDUCATED IN U.S.A. ATTORNEY IN NEW YORK.... MEMBER OF CONGRESS, ELECTED TO STATE LEGISLATURE....... LIEUTENANT COLONEL UNDER GEORGE WASHINGTON!

KILLED IN A DUEL WITH AARON BURR WHOM HE CAUSED TO BE DEFEATED IN AN ELECTION FOR GOVERNOR OF NEW YORK

IF ALEXANDER HAMILTON WERE ALIVE TODAY HE WOULD BE SUBJECTED TO ALL THE INDIGNITIES SUFFERED BY THE RACE BECAUSE BY PRESENT DEFINITIONS HE WAS A NEGRO!

ALEXANDER HAMILTON WAS ONE OF THE FRAMERS OF THE AMERICAN CONSTITUTION.... THE FIRST SECRETARY OF THE TREASURY...... LEADER OF THE FEDERALIST PARTY...... HE RANKED WITH WASHINGTON, FRANKLIN AND JEFFERSON AS ONE OF THE FOUR GREAT MEN OF HIS TIME!

MEMBER AND PRESIDENT OF POWERFUL ANTI-SLAVERY SOCIETIES!

MAY 29, 1943

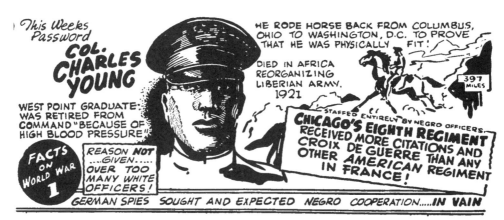

This Weeks Password

COL. CHARLES YOUNG

WEST POINT GRADUATE- WAS RETIRED FROM COMMAND "BECAUSE OF HIGH BLOOD PRESSURE"

FACTS ON WORLD WAR 1

REASON NOT ...GIVEN..... OVER TOO MANY WHITE OFFICERS!

HE RODE HORSE BACK FROM COLUMBUS, OHIO TO WASHINGTON, D.C. TO PROVE THAT HE WAS PHYSICALLY FIT!

DIED IN AFRICA REORGANIZING LIBERIAN ARMY. 1921

397 MILES

STAFFED ENTIRELY BY NEGRO OFFICERS. CHICAGO'S EIGHTH REGIMENT RECEIVED MORE CITATIONS AND CROIX DE GUERRE THAN ANY OTHER AMERICAN REGIMENT IN FRANCE!

GERMAN SPIES SOUGHT AND EXPECTED NEGRO COOPERATION.....IN VAIN

JUNE 5, 1943

This Week's Password

BENJAMIN BANNEKER

FIRST AMERICAN TO PRESENT AN INTERNATIONAL PEACE PLAN!

MANY IDEAS SUGGESTED BY MR. BANNEKER WERE USED 125 YEARS LATER BY PRESIDENT WOODROW WILSON IN HIS LEAGUE OF NATIONS!

SOME OF HIS OTHER ACCOMPLISMENTS

.... BUILT AMERICA'S FIRST CLOCK

.... ASSISTED IN LAYING OUT THE NATION'S CAPITOL....WASHINGTON.

.... PUBLISHED ALMANACS

.... HE WAS ONE OF THE MOST NOTED MATHAMATICIANS AND ASTRONOMERS OF HIS TIME

JUNE 12, 1943

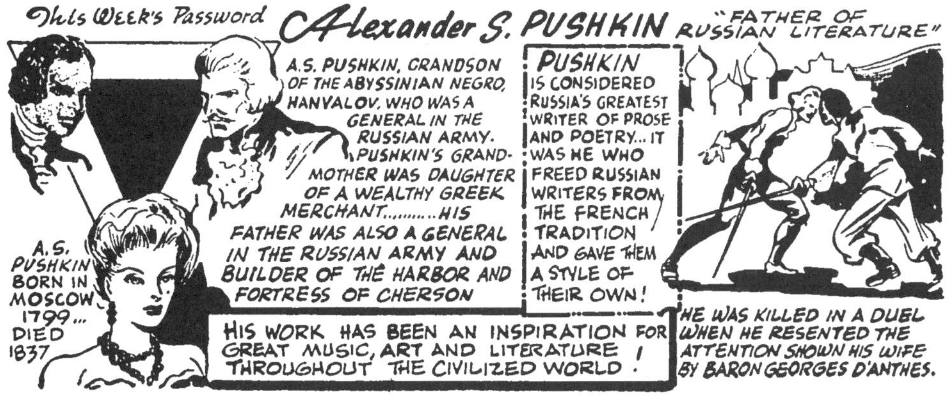
This Week's Password
Alexander S. PUSHKIN
"FATHER OF RUSSIAN LITERATURE"
A.S. PUSHKIN, GRANDSON OF THE ABYSSINIAN NEGRO, HANVALOV, WHO WAS A GENERAL IN THE RUSSIAN ARMY. PUSHKIN'S GRAND-MOTHER WAS DAUGHTER OF A WEALTHY GREEK MERCHANT..........HIS FATHER WAS ALSO A GENERAL IN THE RUSSIAN ARMY AND BUILDER OF THE HARBOR AND FORTRESS OF CHERSON
PUSHKIN IS CONSIDERED RUSSIA'S GREATEST WRITER OF PROSE AND POETRY... IT WAS HE WHO FREED RUSSIAN WRITERS FROM THE FRENCH TRADITION AND GAVE THEM A STYLE OF THEIR OWN!
A.S. PUSHKIN BORN IN MOSCOW 1799... DIED 1837
HIS WORK HAS BEEN AN INSPIRATION FOR GREAT MUSIC, ART AND LITERATURE THROUGHOUT THE CIVILIZED WORLD!
HE WAS KILLED IN A DUEL WHEN HE RESENTED THE ATTENTION SHOWN HIS WIFE BY BARON GEORGES D'ANTHES.

JUNE 19, 1943

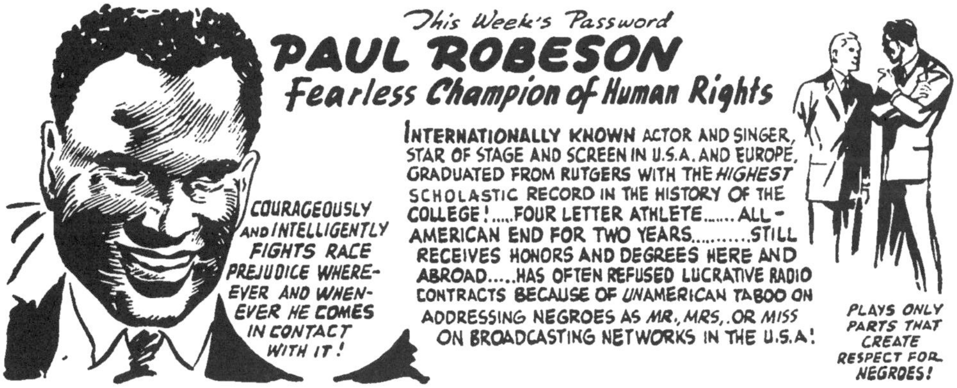
This Week's Password
PAUL ROBESON
Fearless Champion of Human Rights
INTERNATIONALLY KNOWN ACTOR AND SINGER, STAR OF STAGE AND SCREEN IN U.S.A. AND EUROPE, GRADUATED FROM RUTGERS WITH THE HIGHEST SCHOLASTIC RECORD IN THE HISTORY OF THE COLLEGE!.....FOUR LETTER ATHLETE.......ALL-AMERICAN END FOR TWO YEARS..........STILL RECEIVES HONORS AND DEGREES HERE AND ABROAD.....HAS OFTEN REFUSED LUCRATIVE RADIO CONTRACTS BECAUSE OF UNAMERICAN TABOO ON ADDRESSING NEGROES AS MR., MRS., OR MISS ON BROADCASTING NETWORKS IN THE U.S.A!
COURAGEOUSLY AND INTELLIGENTLY FIGHTS RACE PREJUDICE WHEREEVER AND WHENEVER HE COMES IN CONTACT WITH IT!
PLAYS ONLY PARTS THAT CREATE RESPECT FOR NEGROES!

JUNE 26, 1943

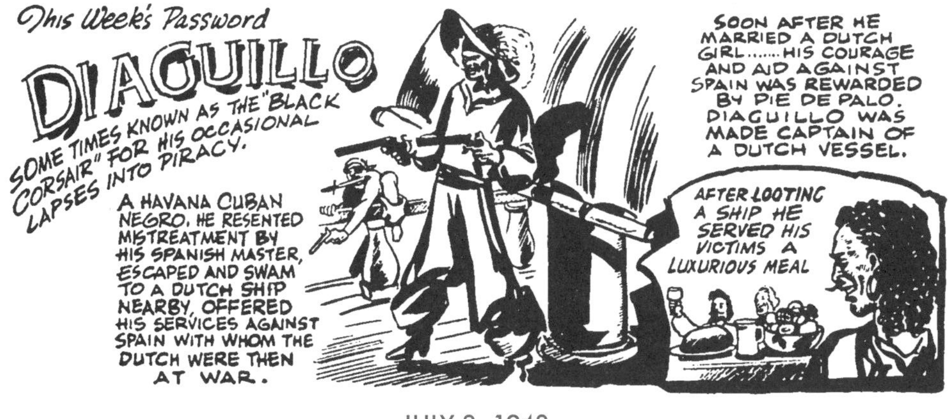
This Week's Password
DIAGUILLO
SOME TIMES KNOWN AS THE "BLACK CORSAIR" FOR HIS OCCASIONAL LAPSES INTO PIRACY.
A HAVANA CUBAN NEGRO, HE RESENTED MISTREATMENT BY HIS SPANISH MASTER, ESCAPED AND SWAM TO A DUTCH SHIP NEARBY, OFFERED HIS SERVICES AGAINST SPAIN WITH WHOM THE DUTCH WERE THEN AT WAR.
SOON AFTER HE MARRIED A DUTCH GIRL.......HIS COURAGE AND AID AGAINST SPAIN WAS REWARDED BY PIE DE PALO. DIAGUILLO WAS MADE CAPTAIN OF A DUTCH VESSEL.
AFTER LOOTING A SHIP HE SERVED HIS VICTIMS A LUXURIOUS MEAL

JULY 3, 1943

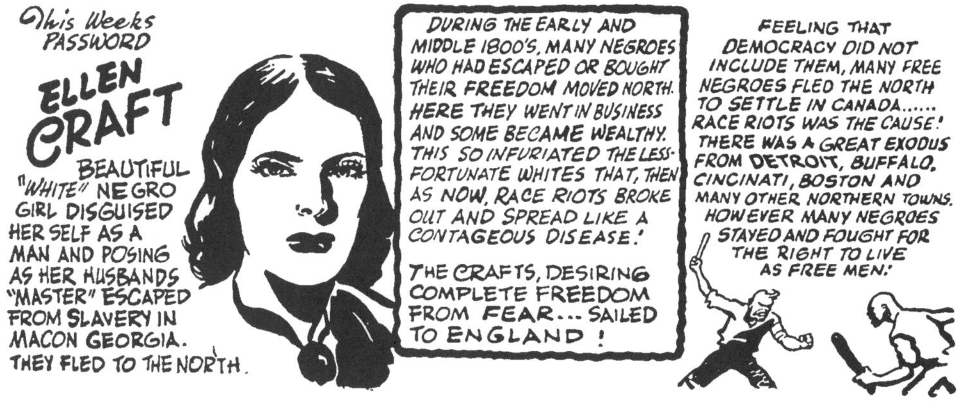
This Weeks Password
ELLEN CRAFT
BEAUTIFUL "WHITE" NEGRO GIRL DISGUISED HER SELF AS A MAN AND POSING AS HER HUSBANDS "MASTER" ESCAPED FROM SLAVERY IN MACON GEORGIA. THEY FLED TO THE NORTH.
DURING THE EARLY AND MIDDLE 1800'S, MANY NEGROES WHO HAD ESCAPED OR BOUGHT THEIR FREEDOM MOVED NORTH. HERE THEY WENT IN BUSINESS AND SOME BECAME WEALTHY. THIS SO INFURIATED THE LESS-FORTUNATE WHITES THAT, THEN AS NOW, RACE RIOTS BROKE OUT AND SPREAD LIKE A CONTAGEOUS DISEASE.'
THE CRAFTS, DESIRING COMPLETE FREEDOM FROM FEAR... SAILED TO ENGLAND!
FEELING THAT DEMOCRACY DID NOT INCLUDE THEM, MANY FREE NEGROES FLED THE NORTH TO SETTLE IN CANADA...... RACE RIOTS WAS THE CAUSE.' THERE WAS A GREAT EXODUS FROM DETROIT, BUFFALO, CINCINATI, BOSTON AND MANY OTHER NORTHERN TOWNS. HOW EVER MANY NEGROES STAYED AND FOUGHT FOR THE RIGHT TO LIVE AS FREE MEN.'

JULY 10, 1943

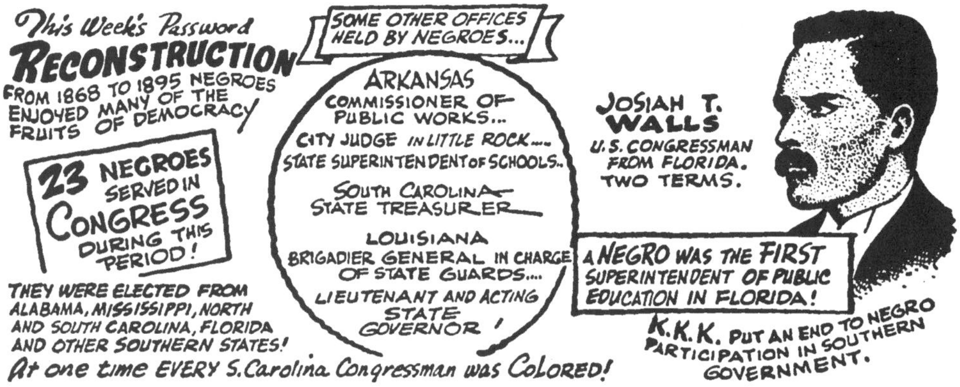
This Week's Password
RECONSTRUCTION
FROM 1868 TO 1895 NEGROES ENJOYED MANY OF THE FRUITS OF DEMOCRACY
23 NEGROES SERVED IN CONGRESS DURING THIS PERIOD!
THEY WERE ELECTED FROM ALABAMA, MISSISSIPPI, NORTH AND SOUTH CAROLINA, FLORIDA AND OTHER SOUTHERN STATES!
At one time EVERY S.Carolina Congressman was COLORED!
SOME OTHER OFFICES HELD BY NEGROES...
ARKANSAS
COMMISSIONER OF PUBLIC WORKS...
CITY JUDGE IN LITTLE ROCK....
STATE SUPERINTENDENT OF SCHOOLS..
SOUTH CAROLINA
STATE TREASURER
LOUISIANA
BRIGADIER GENERAL IN CHARGE OF STATE GUARDS....
LIEUTENANT AND ACTING STATE GOVERNOR!
JOSIAH T. WALLS
U.S. CONGRESSMAN FROM FLORIDA. TWO TERMS.
A NEGRO WAS THE FIRST SUPERINTENDENT OF PUBLIC EDUCATION IN FLORIDA!
K.K.K. PUT AN END TO NEGRO PARTICIPATION IN SOUTHERN GOVERNMENT.

JULY 17, 1943

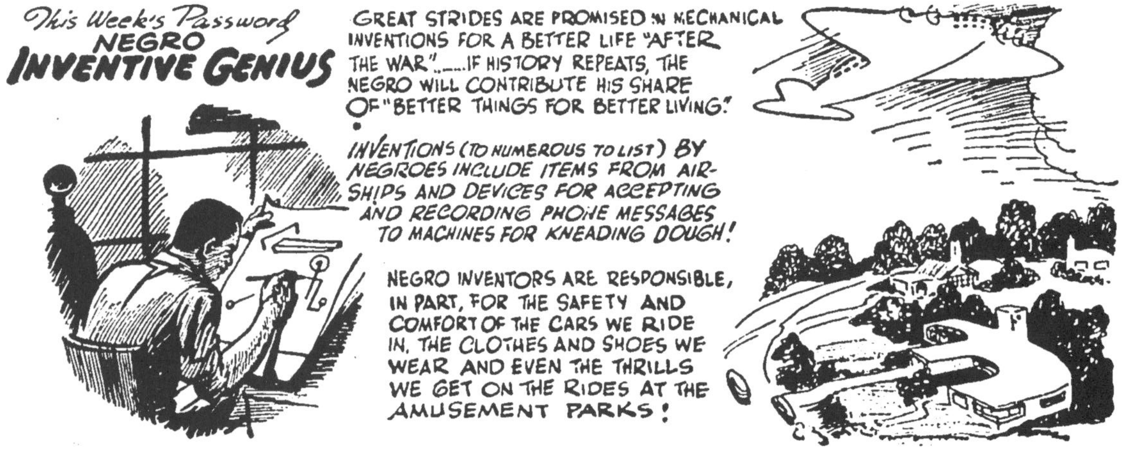
This Week's Password
NEGRO INVENTIVE GENIUS
GREAT STRIDES ARE PROMISED IN MECHANICAL INVENTIONS FOR A BETTER LIFE "AFTER THE WAR".....IF HISTORY REPEATS, THE NEGRO WILL CONTRIBUTE HIS SHARE OF "BETTER THINGS FOR BETTER LIVING."
INVENTIONS (TO NUMEROUS TO LIST) BY NEGROES INCLUDE ITEMS FROM AIR-SHIPS AND DEVICES FOR ACCEPTING AND RECORDING PHONE MESSAGES TO MACHINES FOR KNEADING DOUGH!
NEGRO INVENTORS ARE RESPONSIBLE, IN PART, FOR THE SAFETY AND COMFORT OF THE CARS WE RIDE IN, THE CLOTHES AND SHOES WE WEAR AND EVEN THE THRILLS WE GET ON THE RIDES AT THE AMUSEMENT PARKS!

JULY 24, 1943

This Week's Password

NEFERTARI
NEGRO
QUEEN OF EGYPT
1700 B.C.

CREDITED WITH FOUNDING THE EIGHTEENTH DYNASTY.

MANY MONUMENTS WERE ERECTED IN HER HONOR AND AS A TRIBUTE TO HER GREAT BEAUTY ..... SHE WAS SO LOVED BY HER SUBJECTS THAT THEY CONSIDERED HER ALMOST A GODDESS AND REFERRED TO HER AS WIFE OF THE GOD AMMON!

JULY 31, 1943

This Week's Password

Leonard Royd HARMON

MRS. NAUNITA HARMON CARROLL WAS DESIGNATED AS SPONSOR FOR THE DESTROYER ESCORT VESSEL U.S.S. HARMON NAMED FOR HER LATE SON, 26 YEAR OLD MESS ATTENDANT FIRST CLASS.... HE LOST HIS LIFE AT THE BATTLE OF GUADALCANAL SERVING ON U.S.S. SANFRANCISCO.

HE WAS GIVEN THE NAVY CROSS POSTHUMOUSLY FOR "EXTRAORDINARY HEROISM AND UNUSUAL LOYALTY."

THE U.S.S. HARMON IS THE FIRST NAVY VESSEL TO BE NAMED FOR A NEGRO.

HARMON WAS KILLED WHEN HE DELIBERATELY EXPOSED HIM SELF TO HOSTILE GUNFIRE TO PROTECT HIS SHIPMATES!!

AUGUST 7, 1943

This Week's Password
Lemuel HAYNES

NEGRO SON OF A WHITE MOTHER.

PREJUDICE DIRECTED TOWARD HIS YOUNG MOTHER CAUSED HER TO GIVE HIM TO SOME OF HER WHITE FRIENDS WHILE HE WAS QUITE YOUNG.

BEFORE HIS EDUCATION WAS COMPLETED IN THE SCHOOLS OF GRANVILLE, MASS., AMERICA WAS ENGAGED IN HER FIRST FIGHT FOR FREEDOM.

YOUNG HAYNES ENLISTED AND FOUGHT WITH VALOR THRU OUT THE REVOLUTIONARY WAR!

ON HIS RETURN TO CIVILIAN LIFE, HE BECAME A MINISTER

AFTER A PERIOD OF SURPRISE, CURIOSITY, RESENTMENT AND ANGER AT HAVING A NEGRO PASTOR, THE WHITE CONGREGATIONS BECAME ACCUSTOMED. THEN RESPECTED AND FINALLY LOVED AND REVERED HIM

HE PREACHED THRU OUT THE NEW ENGLAND STATES AND PART OF NEW YORK

AUGUST 14, 1943

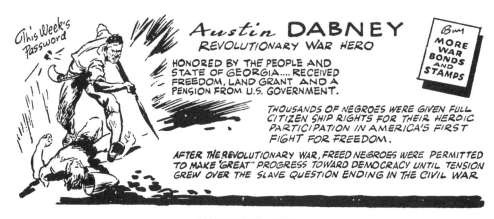

Austin DABNEY
REVOLUTIONARY WAR HERO

This Week's Password

HONORED BY THE PEOPLE AND STATE OF GEORGIA.....RECEIVED FREEDOM, LAND GRANT AND A PENSION FROM U.S. GOVERNMENT.

MORE WAR BONDS AND STAMPS

THOUSANDS OF NEGROES WERE GIVEN FULL CITIZEN SHIP RIGHTS FOR THEIR HEROIC PARTICIPATION IN AMERICA'S FIRST FIGHT FOR FREEDOM.

AFTER THE REVOLUTIONARY WAR, FREED NEGROES WERE PERMITTED TO MAKE "GREAT" PROGRESS TOWARD DEMOCRACY UNTIL TENSION GREW OVER THE SLAVE QUESTION ENDING IN THE CIVIL WAR

AUGUST 21, 1943

This Week's Password

JOHN B. RUSSWURM

GRADUATE OF BOWDOIN COLLEGE.. 1826 FIRST NEGRO IN U.S.A TO RECEIVE A COLLEGE DEGREE......EDITOR AND PUBLISHER OF FIRST NEGRO NEWSPAPER.... "FREEDOM'S JOURNAL" HE ALSO PUBLISHED "THE RIGHTS OF ALL"

FOUGHT CONSTANTLY AGAINST SLAVERY.

DESIRING MORE FREEDOM THAN IT WAS POSSIBLE FOR EVEN A "FREE" NEGRO TO ATTAIN IN AMERICA, HE JOINED WITH OTHER COLONISTS AND WENT TO AFRICA WHERE HE BECAME AN EDUCATOR AND A GOVERNOR OF A LIBERIAN PROVINCE

AUGUST 28, 1943

This Week's Password

PRINCE HALL
Father of Negro Fraternal Organizations In America

BORN SEPT 12, 1748. BARBADOS, B.W.I CAME TO U.S.A AT THE AGE OF SEVENTEEN....BECAME A METHODIST PREACHER IN CAMBRIDGE, MASS AT 27..... ALTHO HE FOUGHT BRAVELY DURING THE AMERICAN REVOLUTION, HE WAS FORCED TO GET A CHARTER FROM ENGLAND IN ORDER TO ORGANIZE A MASONIC LODGE FOR NEGROES.

THE RISE OF FREE MASONRY AMONG NEGROES WAS SOON FOLLOWED BY PETER OGDEN'S ORGANIZATION OF "THE GRAND ORDER OF (NEGRO) ODD FELLOWS"

HE, TOO, HAD TO OBTAIN A CHARTER FROM ENGLAND AFTER A REFUSAL BY AMERICANS.

Peter OGDEN

SEPTEMBER 4, 1943

THIS WEEK'S PASSWORD
ESTEVANICO,
A NEGRO
LED THE EXPLORATION of ARIZONA and NEW MEXICO
IN 1528

AFTER PAMFILO DE NARVAEZ AND 396 OF HIS SPANISH CREW HAD DIED OR BEEN KILLED BY INDIANS WHO REFUSED TO BE ROBBED, ESTEVANICO LED THE REMAINING THREE ON AN EXPLORATION TRIP THRU AMERICA'S SOUTH WEST IN SEARCH OF LOOT. HE FOUND A RICH INDIAN CITY BUT WAS MURDERED BY THE SUSPICIOUS NATIVES.

SEPTEMBER 11, 1943

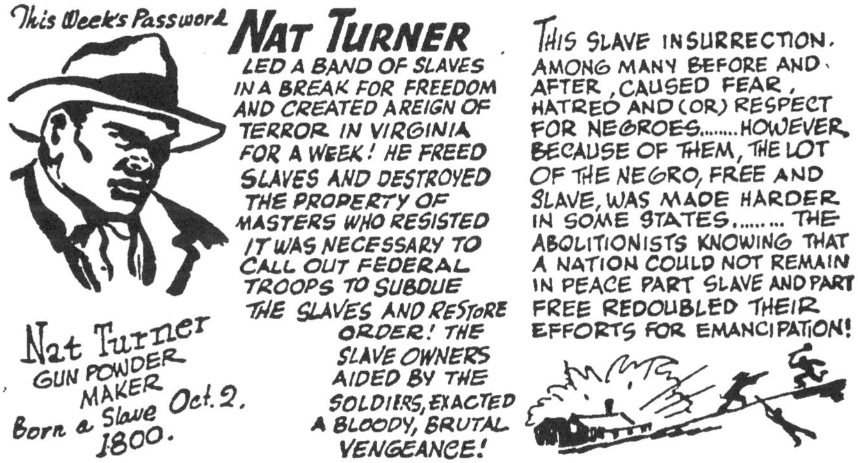

This Week's Password
NAT TURNER
LED A BAND OF SLAVES IN A BREAK FOR FREEDOM AND CREATED A REIGN OF TERROR IN VIRGINIA FOR A WEEK! HE FREED SLAVES AND DESTROYED THE PROPERTY OF MASTERS WHO RESISTED IT WAS NECESSARY TO CALL OUT FEDERAL TROOPS TO SUBDUE THE SLAVES AND RESTORE ORDER! THE SLAVE OWNERS AIDED BY THE SOLDIERS, EXACTED A BLOODY, BRUTAL VENGEANCE!

Nat Turner
GUN POWDER MAKER
Born a Slave Oct. 2. 1800.

THIS SLAVE INSURRECTION, AMONG MANY BEFORE AND AFTER, CAUSED FEAR, HATRED AND (OR) RESPECT FOR NEGROES........ HOWEVER, BECAUSE OF THEM, THE LOT OF THE NEGRO, FREE AND SLAVE, WAS MADE HARDER IN SOME STATES......... THE ABOLITIONISTS KNOWING THAT A NATION COULD NOT REMAIN IN PEACE PART SLAVE AND PART FREE REDOUBLED THEIR EFFORTS FOR EMANCIPATION!

SEPTEMBER 18, 1943

ROBERT RUSSA
MOTON

SUCCEEDED BOOKER T. WASHINGTON AS PRESIDENT OF TUSKEGEE IN 1915... U.S PRESIDENTIAL CONSULTANT ON NEGRO AFFAIRS..... SERVED ON MANY GOVERNMENT COMMISSIONS...AWARDED SPINGARN MEDAL AND HARMON PRIZE FOR PROMOTING INTERRACIAL GOOD- WILL AND RACE CULTURE.....WROTE A SYNDICATED COLUMN AND MANY BOOKS HIS BOOKS INCLUDE "RACIAL GOOD WILL" AND "WHAT A NEGRO THINKS"

SEPTEMBER 25, 1943

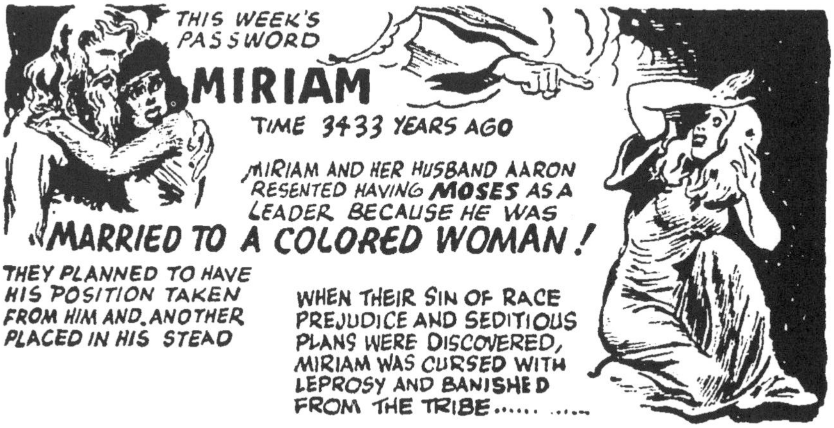
THIS WEEK'S PASSWORD
MIRIAM
TIME 3433 YEARS AGO
MIRIAM AND HER HUSBAND AARON RESENTED HAVING MOSES AS A LEADER BECAUSE HE WAS
MARRIED TO A COLORED WOMAN!
THEY PLANNED TO HAVE HIS POSITION TAKEN FROM HIM AND ANOTHER PLACED IN HIS STEAD
WHEN THEIR SIN OF RACE PREJUDICE AND SEDITIOUS PLANS WERE DISCOVERED, MIRIAM WAS CURSED WITH LEPROSY AND BANISHED FROM THE TRIBE...... .....

OCTOBER 2, 1943

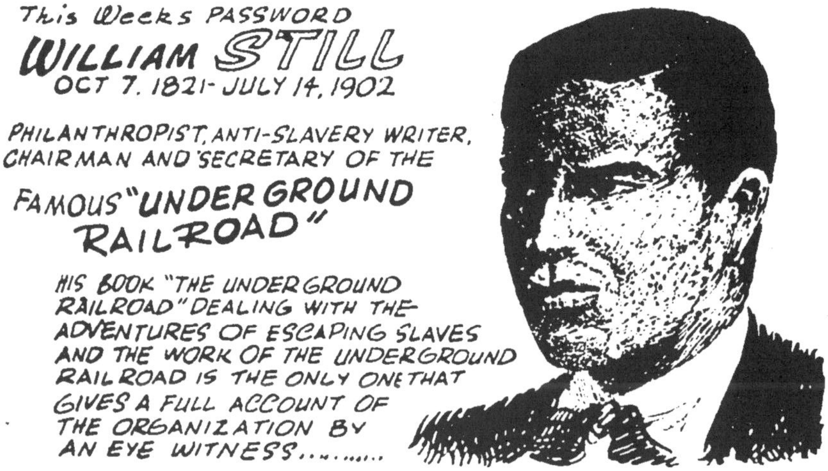
This Weeks PASSWORD
WILLIAM STILL
OCT 7. 1821- JULY 14, 1902
PHILANTHROPIST, ANTI-SLAVERY WRITER, CHAIRMAN AND SECRETARY OF THE
FAMOUS "UNDERGROUND RAILROAD"
HIS BOOK "THE UNDERGROUND RAILROAD" DEALING WITH THE ADVENTURES OF ESCAPING SLAVES AND THE WORK OF THE UNDERGROUND RAILROAD IS THE ONLY ONE THAT GIVES A FULL ACCOUNT OF THE ORGANIZATION BY AN EYE WITNESS..........

OCTOBER 9, 1943

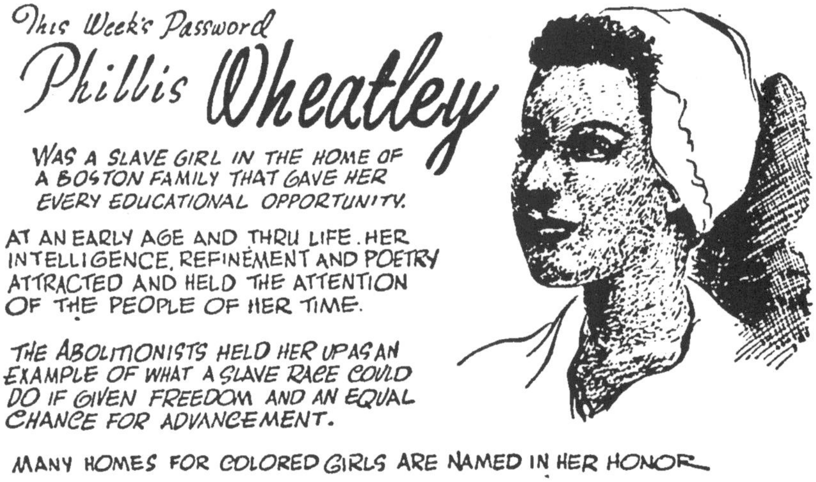
This Week's Password
Phillis Wheatley
WAS A SLAVE GIRL IN THE HOME OF A BOSTON FAMILY THAT GAVE HER EVERY EDUCATIONAL OPPORTUNITY.
AT AN EARLY AGE AND THRU LIFE. HER INTELLIGENCE, REFINEMENT AND POETRY ATTRACTED AND HELD THE ATTENTION OF THE PEOPLE OF HER TIME.
THE ABOLITIONISTS HELD HER UP AS AN EXAMPLE OF WHAT A SLAVE RACE COULD DO IF GIVEN FREEDOM AND AN EQUAL CHANCE FOR ADVANCEMENT.
MANY HOMES FOR COLORED GIRLS ARE NAMED IN HER HONOR

OCTOBER 16, 1943

THIS WEEK'S PASSWORD
MADISON WASHINGTON

A SLAVE, ESCAPED TO CANADA IN 1840 BUT RETURNED TO VIRGINIA TO RESCUE HIS WIFE

HE WAS CAPTURED AND SHIPPED SOUTH WITH 134 OTHER SLAVES EN ROUTE, THEY OVERPOWERED THE CREW AND FORCED THEM TO SAIL TO NASSAU B.W.I

THE AMERICAN GOVERNMENT DEMANDED THEIR RETURN.. THE BRITISH REFUSED!

AFTER A LONG COURT BATTLE, ENGLAND PAID THE UNITED STATES $110,000.00 FOR THE SLAVE'S FREEDOM!

OCTOBER 23, 1943

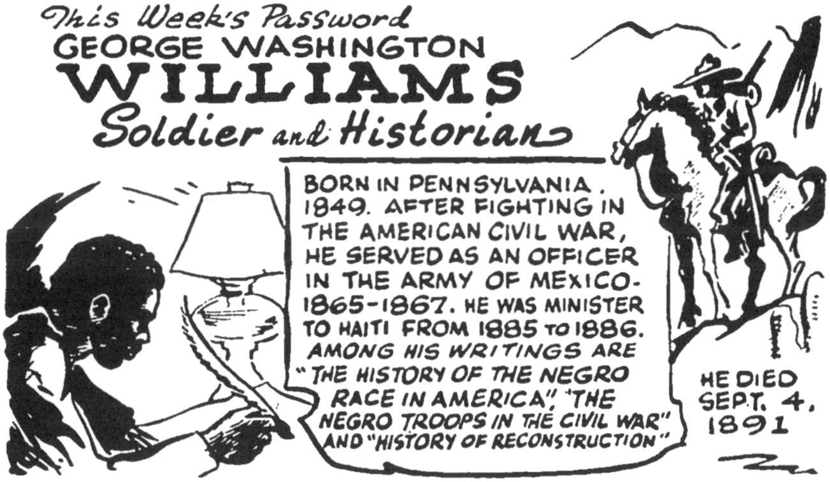

This Week's Password
GEORGE WASHINGTON WILLIAMS
Soldier and Historian

BORN IN PENNSYLVANIA, 1849. AFTER FIGHTING IN THE AMERICAN CIVIL WAR, HE SERVED AS AN OFFICER IN THE ARMY OF MEXICO-1865-1867. HE WAS MINISTER TO HAITI FROM 1885 TO 1886. AMONG HIS WRITINGS ARE "THE HISTORY OF THE NEGRO RACE IN AMERICA", "THE NEGRO TROOPS IN THE CIVIL WAR" AND "HISTORY OF RECONSTRUCTION"

HE DIED SEPT. 4, 1891

OCTOBER 30, 1943

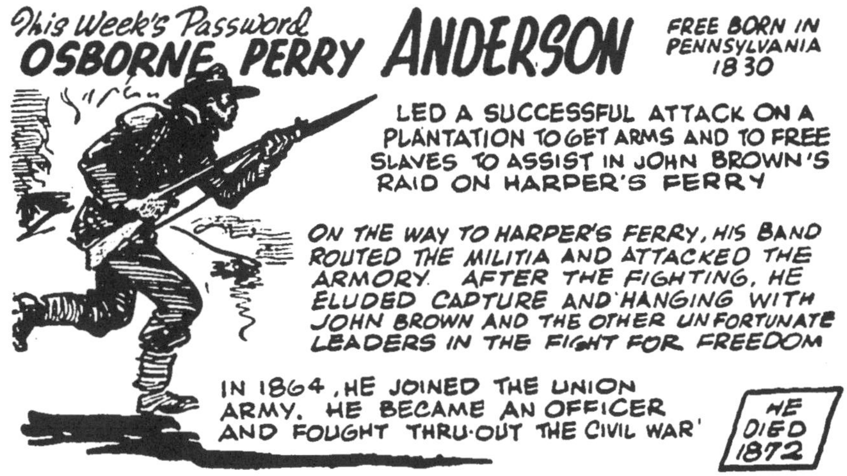

This Week's Password
OSBORNE PERRY ANDERSON

FREE BORN IN PENNSYLVANIA 1830

LED A SUCCESSFUL ATTACK ON A PLANTATION TO GET ARMS AND TO FREE SLAVES TO ASSIST IN JOHN BROWN'S RAID ON HARPER'S FERRY

ON THE WAY TO HARPER'S FERRY, HIS BAND ROUTED THE MILITIA AND ATTACKED THE ARMORY. AFTER THE FIGHTING, HE ELUDED CAPTURE AND HANGING WITH JOHN BROWN AND THE OTHER UNFORTUNATE LEADERS IN THE FIGHT FOR FREEDOM

IN 1864, HE JOINED THE UNION ARMY. HE BECAME AN OFFICER AND FOUGHT THRU-OUT THE CIVIL WAR'

HE DIED 1872

NOVEMBER 6, 1943

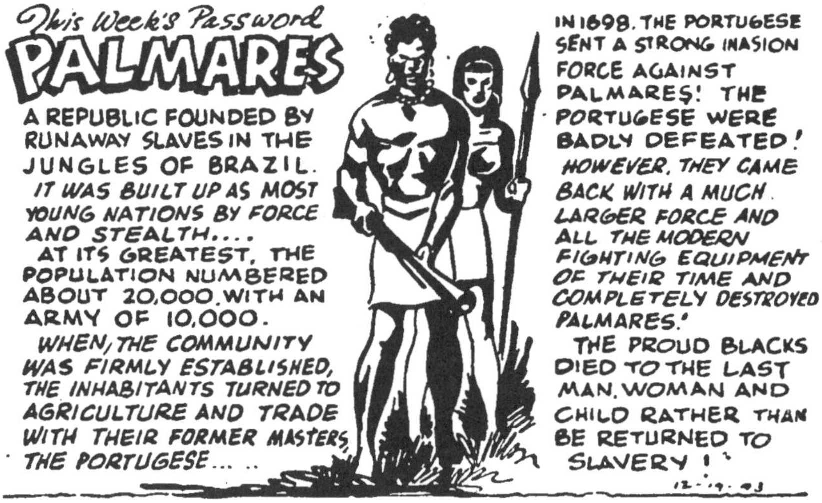
This Week's Password
PALMARES
A REPUBLIC FOUNDED BY RUNAWAY SLAVES IN THE JUNGLES OF BRAZIL.
IT WAS BUILT UP AS MOST YOUNG NATIONS BY FORCE AND STEALTH....
AT ITS GREATEST, THE POPULATION NUMBERED ABOUT 20,000, WITH AN ARMY OF 10,000.
WHEN, THE COMMUNITY WAS FIRMLY ESTABLISHED, THE INHABITANTS TURNED TO AGRICULTURE AND TRADE WITH THEIR FORMER MASTERS, THE PORTUGESE.....
IN 1698, THE PORTUGESE SENT A STRONG INASION FORCE AGAINST PALMARES! THE PORTUGESE WERE BADLY DEFEATED!
HOWEVER, THEY CAME BACK WITH A MUCH LARGER FORCE AND ALL THE MODERN FIGHTING EQUIPMENT OF THEIR TIME AND COMPLETELY DESTROYED PALMARES!
THE PROUD BLACKS DIED TO THE LAST MAN, WOMAN AND CHILD RATHER THAN BE RETURNED TO SLAVERY!
12-19-43

NOVEMBER 13, 1943

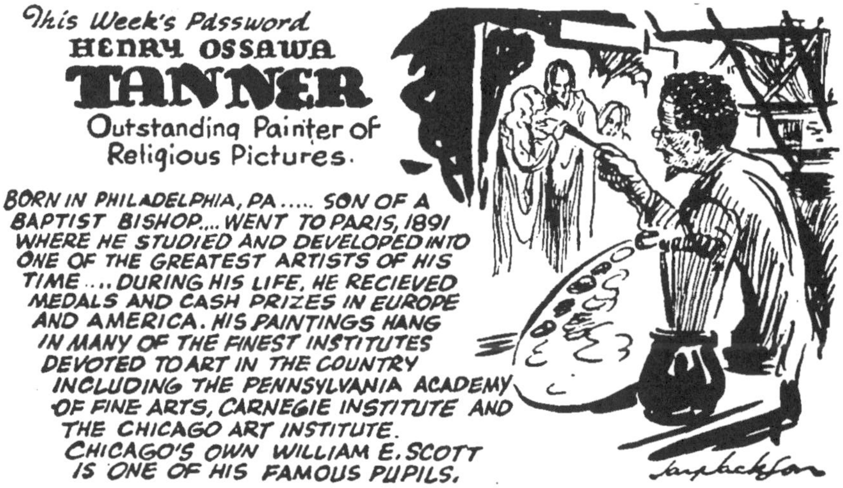
This Week's Password
HENRY OSSAWA
TANNER
Outstanding Painter of Religious Pictures.
BORN IN PHILADELPHIA, PA..... SON OF A BAPTIST BISHOP.... WENT TO PARIS, 1891 WHERE HE STUDIED AND DEVELOPED INTO ONE OF THE GREATEST ARTISTS OF HIS TIME.... DURING HIS LIFE, HE RECIEVED MEDALS AND CASH PRIZES IN EUROPE AND AMERICA. HIS PAINTINGS HANG IN MANY OF THE FINEST INSTITUTES DEVOTED TO ART IN THE COUNTRY INCLUDING THE PENNSYLVANIA ACADEMY OF FINE ARTS, CARNEGIE INSTITUTE AND THE CHICAGO ART INSTITUTE.
CHICAGO'S OWN WILLIAM E. SCOTT IS ONE OF HIS FAMOUS PUPILS.
Jay Jackson

NOVEMBER 20, 1943

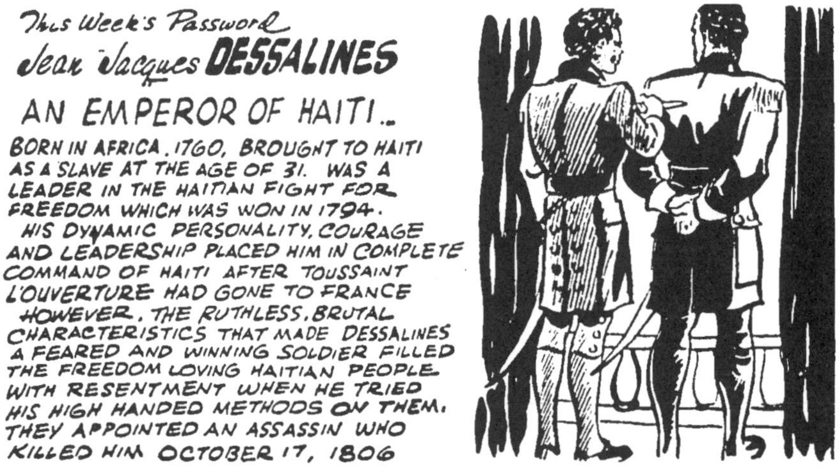
This Week's Password
Jean Jacques DESSALINES
AN EMPEROR OF HAITI..
BORN IN AFRICA, 1760, BROUGHT TO HAITI AS A SLAVE AT THE AGE OF 31. WAS A LEADER IN THE HAITIAN FIGHT FOR FREEDOM WHICH WAS WON IN 1794.
HIS DYNAMIC PERSONALITY, COURAGE AND LEADERSHIP PLACED HIM IN COMPLETE COMMAND OF HAITI AFTER TOUSSAINT L'OUVERTURE HAD GONE TO FRANCE
HOWEVER, THE RUTHLESS, BRUTAL CHARACTERISTICS THAT MADE DESSALINES A FEARED AND WINNING SOLDIER FILLED THE FREEDOM LOVING HAITIAN PEOPLE WITH RESENTMENT WHEN HE TRIED HIS HIGH HANDED METHODS ON THEM. THEY APPOINTED AN ASSASSIN WHO KILLED HIM OCTOBER 17, 1806

NOVEMBER 27, 1943

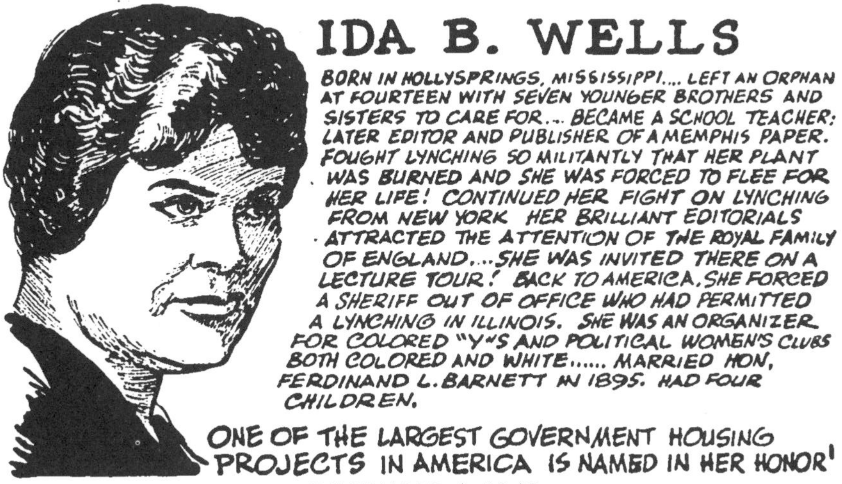
IDA B. WELLS
BORN IN HOLLYSPRINGS, MISSISSIPPI.... LEFT AN ORPHAN AT FOURTEEN WITH SEVEN YOUNGER BROTHERS AND SISTERS TO CARE FOR.... BECAME A SCHOOL TEACHER: LATER EDITOR AND PUBLISHER OF A MEMPHIS PAPER. FOUGHT LYNCHING SO MILITANTLY THAT HER PLANT WAS BURNED AND SHE WAS FORCED TO FLEE FOR HER LIFE! CONTINUED HER FIGHT ON LYNCHING FROM NEW YORK HER BRILLIANT EDITORIALS ATTRACTED THE ATTENTION OF THE ROYAL FAMILY OF ENGLAND.... SHE WAS INVITED THERE ON A LECTURE TOUR! BACK TO AMERICA, SHE FORCED A SHERIFF OUT OF OFFICE WHO HAD PERMITTED A LYNCHING IN ILLINOIS. SHE WAS AN ORGANIZER FOR COLORED "Y"S AND POLITICAL WOMEN'S CLUBS BOTH COLORED AND WHITE...... MARRIED HON. FERDINAND L. BARNETT IN 1895. HAD FOUR CHILDREN.
ONE OF THE LARGEST GOVERNMENT HOUSING PROJECTS IN AMERICA IS NAMED IN HER HONOR!

DECEMBER 4, 1943

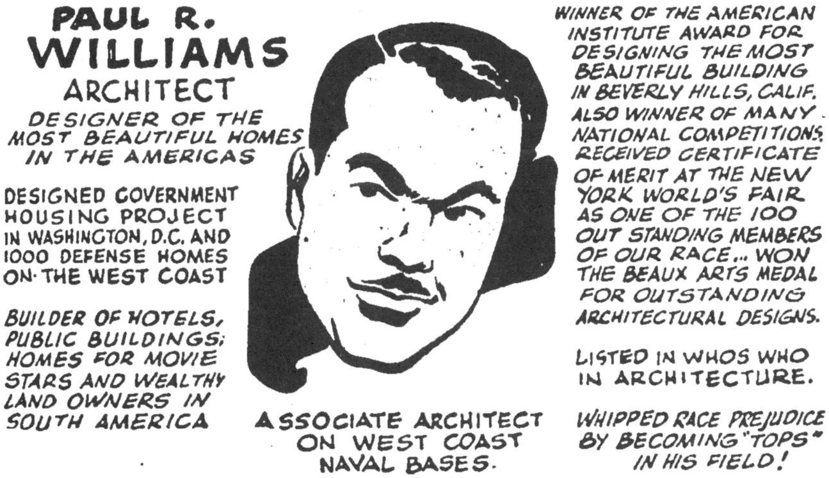
PAUL R. WILLIAMS
ARCHITECT
DESIGNER OF THE MOST BEAUTIFUL HOMES IN THE AMERICAS
DESIGNED GOVERNMENT HOUSING PROJECT IN WASHINGTON, D.C. AND 1000 DEFENSE HOMES ON THE WEST COAST
BUILDER OF HOTELS, PUBLIC BUILDINGS; HOMES FOR MOVIE STARS AND WEALTHY LAND OWNERS IN SOUTH AMERICA
ASSOCIATE ARCHITECT ON WEST COAST NAVAL BASES.
WINNER OF THE AMERICAN INSTITUTE AWARD FOR DESIGNING THE MOST BEAUTIFUL BUILDING IN BEVERLY HILLS, CALIF. ALSO WINNER OF MANY NATIONAL COMPETITIONS. RECEIVED CERTIFICATE OF MERIT AT THE NEW YORK WORLD'S FAIR AS ONE OF THE 100 OUT STANDING MEMBERS OF OUR RACE... WON THE BEAUX ARTS MEDAL FOR OUTSTANDING ARCHITECTURAL DESIGNS.
LISTED IN WHOS WHO IN ARCHITECTURE.
WHIPPED RACE PREJUDICE BY BECOMING "TOPS" IN HIS FIELD!

DECEMBER 11, 1943

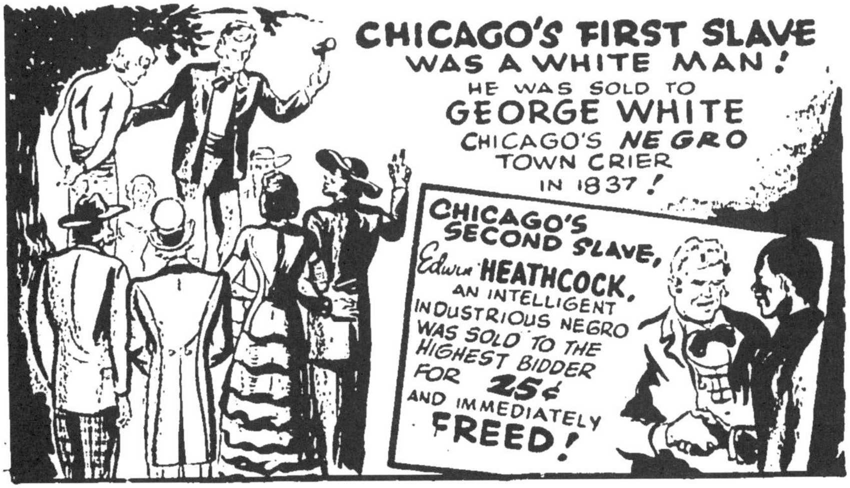
CHICAGO'S FIRST SLAVE WAS A WHITE MAN!
HE WAS SOLD TO GEORGE WHITE CHICAGO'S NEGRO TOWN CRIER IN 1837!
CHICAGO'S SECOND SLAVE, Edwin HEATHCOCK, AN INTELLIGENT INDUSTRIOUS NEGRO WAS SOLD TO THE HIGHEST BIDDER FOR 25¢ AND IMMEDIATELY FREED!

DECEMBER 18, 1943

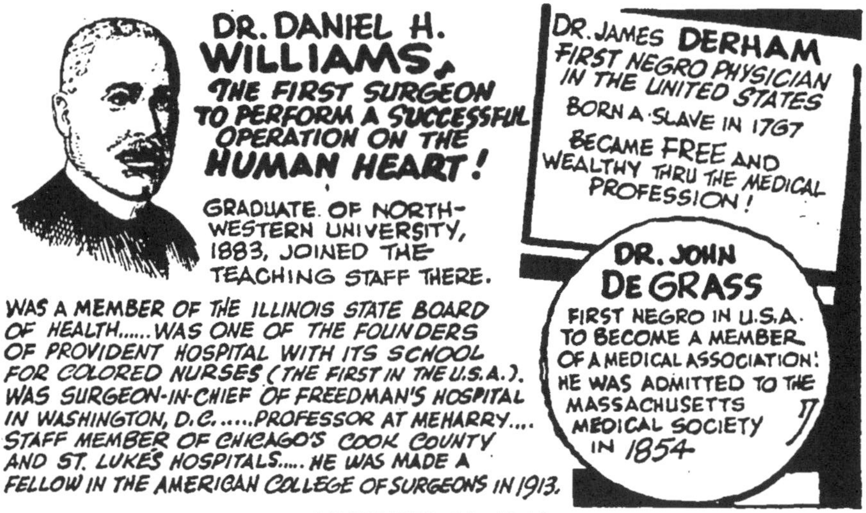
DR. DANIEL H. WILLIAMS, THE FIRST SURGEON TO PERFORM A SUCCESSFUL OPERATION ON THE HUMAN HEART!
GRADUATE OF NORTH-WESTERN UNIVERSITY, 1883, JOINED THE TEACHING STAFF THERE.
WAS A MEMBER OF THE ILLINOIS STATE BOARD OF HEALTH......WAS ONE OF THE FOUNDERS OF PROVIDENT HOSPITAL WITH ITS SCHOOL FOR COLORED NURSES (THE FIRST IN THE U.S.A.). WAS SURGEON-IN-CHIEF OF FREEDMAN'S HOSPITAL IN WASHINGTON, D.C.....PROFESSOR AT MEHARRY.... STAFF MEMBER OF CHICAGO'S COOK COUNTY AND ST. LUKE'S HOSPITALS..... HE WAS MADE A FELLOW IN THE AMERICAN COLLEGE OF SURGEONS IN 1913.
DR. JAMES DERHAM FIRST NEGRO PHYSICIAN IN THE UNITED STATES
BORN A SLAVE IN 1767
BECAME FREE AND WEALTHY THRU THE MEDICAL PROFESSION!
DR. JOHN DE GRASS
FIRST NEGRO IN U.S.A. TO BECOME A MEMBER OF A MEDICAL ASSOCIATION! HE WAS ADMITTED TO THE MASSACHUSETTS MEDICAL SOCIETY IN 1854

DECEMBER 25, 1943

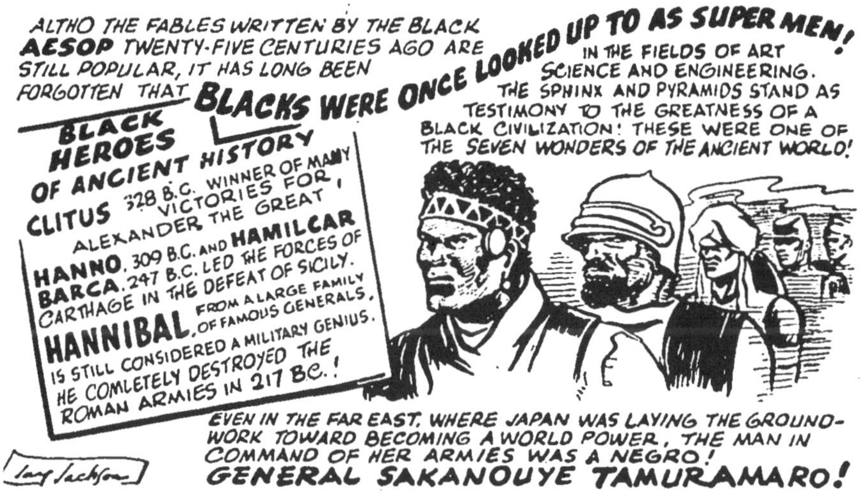
ALTHO THE FABLES WRITTEN BY THE BLACK AESOP TWENTY-FIVE CENTURIES AGO ARE STILL POPULAR, IT HAS LONG BEEN FORGOTTEN THAT BLACKS WERE ONCE LOOKED UP TO AS SUPER MEN! IN THE FIELDS OF ART SCIENCE AND ENGINEERING.
THE SPHINX AND PYRAMIDS STAND AS TESTIMONY TO THE GREATNESS OF A BLACK CIVILIZATION! THESE WERE ONE OF THE SEVEN WONDERS OF THE ANCIENT WORLD!
BLACK HEROES OF ANCIENT HISTORY
CLITUS 328 B.C. WINNER OF MANY VICTORIES FOR, ALEXANDER THE GREAT
HANNO, 309 B.C. AND HAMILCAR BARCA, 247 B.C. LED THE FORCES OF CARTHAGE IN THE DEFEAT OF SICILY.
HANNIBAL, FROM A LARGE FAMILY OF FAMOUS GENERALS, IS STILL CONSIDERED A MILITARY GENIUS. HE COMLETELY DESTROYED THE ROMAN ARMIES IN 217 BC.!
EVEN IN THE FAR EAST, WHERE JAPAN WAS LAYING THE GROUND-WORK TOWARD BECOMING A WORLD POWER, THE MAN IN COMMAND OF HER ARMIES WAS A NEGRO! GENERAL SAKANOUYE TAMURAMARO!

JANUARY 1, 1944

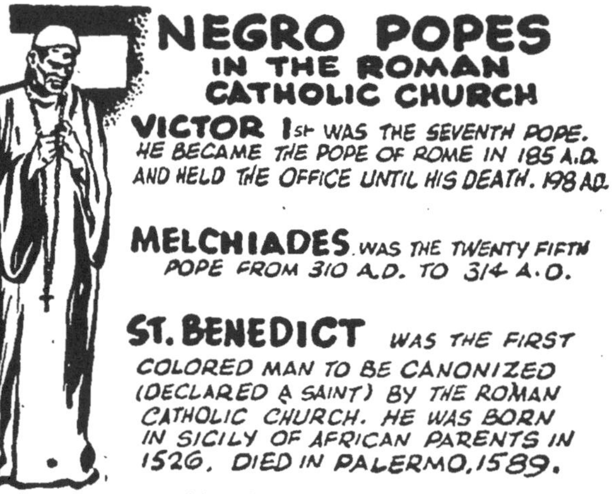
NEGRO POPES IN THE ROMAN CATHOLIC CHURCH
VICTOR 1st WAS THE SEVENTH POPE. HE BECAME THE POPE OF ROME IN 185 A.D. AND HELD THE OFFICE UNTIL HIS DEATH. 198 A.D.
MELCHIADES WAS THE TWENTY FIFTH POPE FROM 310 A.D. TO 314 A.D.
ST. BENEDICT WAS THE FIRST COLORED MAN TO BE CANONIZED (DECLARED A SAINT) BY THE ROMAN CATHOLIC CHURCH. HE WAS BORN IN SICILY OF AFRICAN PARENTS IN 1526. DIED IN PALERMO, 1589.

JANUARY 8, 1944

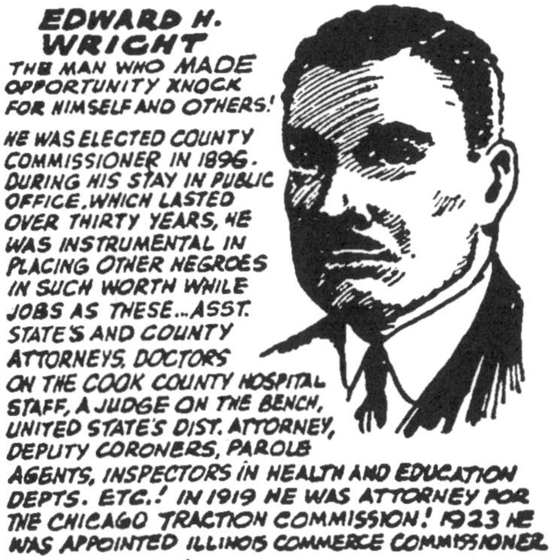
EDWARD H. WRIGHT
THE MAN WHO MADE OPPORTUNITY KNOCK FOR HIMSELF AND OTHERS!
HE WAS ELECTED COUNTY COMMISSIONER IN 1896. DURING HIS STAY IN PUBLIC OFFICE, WHICH LASTED OVER THIRTY YEARS, HE WAS INSTRUMENTAL IN PLACING OTHER NEGROES IN SUCH WORTH WHILE JOBS AS THESE...ASST. STATE'S AND COUNTY ATTORNEYS, DOCTORS ON THE COOK COUNTY HOSPITAL STAFF, A JUDGE ON THE BENCH, UNITED STATE'S DIST. ATTORNEY, DEPUTY CORONERS, PAROLE AGENTS, INSPECTORS IN HEALTH AND EDUCATION DEPTS. ETC.! IN 1919 HE WAS ATTORNEY FOR THE CHICAGO TRACTION COMMISSION! 1923 HE WAS APPOINTED ILLINOIS COMMERCE COMMISSIONER

JANUARY 15, 1944

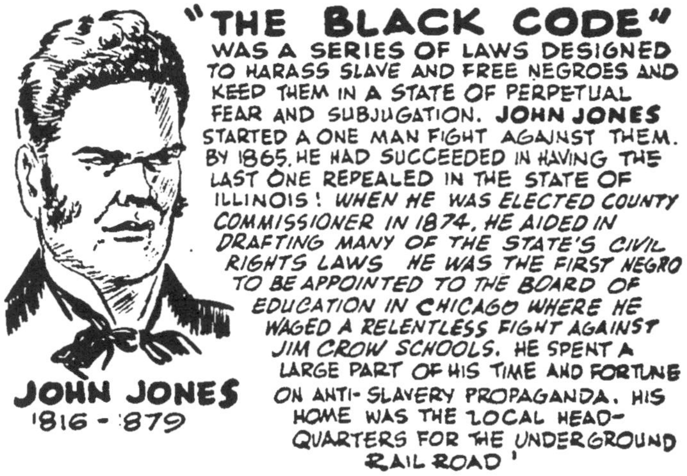
"THE BLACK CODE"
WAS A SERIES OF LAWS DESIGNED TO HARASS SLAVE AND FREE NEGROES AND KEEP THEM IN A STATE OF PERPETUAL FEAR AND SUBJUGATION. JOHN JONES STARTED A ONE MAN FIGHT AGAINST THEM. BY 1865. HE HAD SUCCEEDED IN HAVING THE LAST ONE REPEALED IN THE STATE OF ILLINOIS! WHEN HE WAS ELECTED COUNTY COMMISSIONER IN 1874, HE AIDED IN DRAFTING MANY OF THE STATE'S CIVIL RIGHTS LAWS HE WAS THE FIRST NEGRO TO BE APPOINTED TO THE BOARD OF EDUCATION IN CHICAGO WHERE HE WAGED A RELENTLESS FIGHT AGAINST JIM CROW SCHOOLS. HE SPENT A LARGE PART OF HIS TIME AND FORTUNE ON ANTI-SLAVERY PROPAGANDA. HIS HOME WAS THE LOCAL HEAD-QUARTERS FOR THE UNDERGROUND RAIL ROAD'
JOHN JONES
1816 - 1879

JANUARY 22, 1944

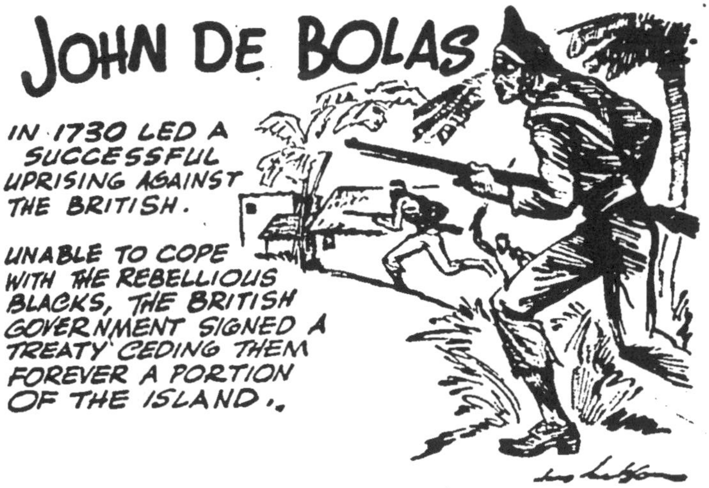
JOHN DE BOLAS
IN 1730 LED A SUCCESSFUL UPRISING AGAINST THE BRITISH.
UNABLE TO COPE WITH THE REBELLIOUS BLACKS, THE BRITISH GOVERNMENT SIGNED A TREATY CEDING THEM FOREVER A PORTION OF THE ISLAND.

JANUARY 29, 1944

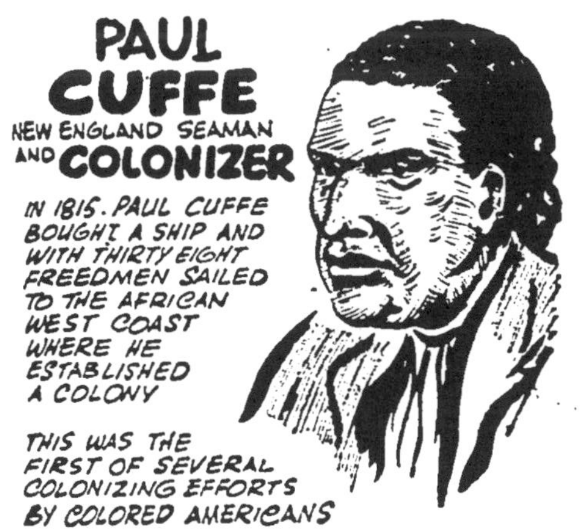
PAUL CUFFE
NEW ENGLAND SEAMAN AND COLONIZER
IN 1815. PAUL CUFFE BOUGHT A SHIP AND WITH THIRTY EIGHT FREEDMEN SAILED TO THE AFRICAN WEST COAST WHERE HE ESTABLISHED A COLONY
THIS WAS THE FIRST OF SEVERAL COLONIZING EFFORTS BY COLORED AMERICANS

FEBRUARY 5, 1944

Champion War Mother
MRS. OLIVIA JONES!

"DISCOVERED" BY A NATION WIDE, FOUR MONTH NEWSPAPER POLL, MRS. JONES HAS SEVENTEEN CHILDREN! NINE ARE IN THE ARMED FORCES!

SHE WAS CROWNED "CHAMPION WAR MOTHER" IN MEMPHIS, TENN. BY BISHOP R.R. WRIGHT!

FEBRUARY 12, 1944

WAR BONDS

Buy Another WAR BOND!

PRICE COLLINS
OFFICIALLY THE FIRST WAR BOND BUYER IN EVERY DRIVE SPONSORED BY OUR GOVERNMENT!

FEBRUARY 19, 1944

Louis Mathiew

BORN 1817 IN THE FRENCH COLONY OF GUADELOUPE.

HE WAS THE FIRST NEGRO TO BE ELECTED REPRESENTATIVE TO THE FRENCH NATIONAL ASSEMBLY!

HE RECEIVED THIS HONOR AT THE AGE OF THIRTY-ONE.

FEBRUARY 26, 1944

A NEGRO NAMED
YORK

ACCOMPANIED THE LEWIS AND CLARK EXPEDITION ON THE EXPLORATION OF AMERICA'S NORTH WEST...

HIS PLEASING PERSONALITY HELPED ALLAY THE SUSPICIONS OF INDIANS TOWARD WHITES AND AIDED IN OBTAINING THE RED MEN'S COOPERATION!

MARCH 4, 1944

Steven **LANDRUM**
OF LOUISVILLE, KY.

HE COULD NEITHER
READ NOR WRITE!

ALTHO, HE AMASSED
A FORTUNE IN
REAL ESTATE —

**INCOME TAX
PROBLEMS NEVER
BOTHERED HIM!**

HE WAS A
MATHAMATICAL GENIUS

HE COULD DO INTRICATE
PROBLEMS IN HIS HEAD
QUICKER THAN A TAX
EXPERT COULD DO THEM
ON AN ADDING MACHINE!

DIED, AUG. 30,
1923 AT
ABOUT 90
YEARS OLD!

SATURDAY, MARCH 11, 1944

Bessie Coleman

**PIONEER
AVIATRIX**

AVIATION TEACHER AND
STUNT FLYER

SHE GAVE EXHIBITION
FLIGHTS IN EUROPE
AND AMERICA ...

SHE WAS KILLED
WHEN HER PLANE
CRASHED AT
JACKSONVILLE, FLORIDA.

MARCH 18, 1944

**PETRO
ALONZA**
NEGRO
NAVIGATOR
WITH
**CHRISTOPHER
COLUMBUS**
WHEN HE
DISCOVERED
AMERICA.

*COLUMBUS WAS THE FIRST TO
CURSE AMERICA WITH SLAVERY!*
HE CONFISCATED THE LANDS OF THE NATIVES
AND FORCED THEM TO LABOR FOR THE
COLONISTS WHO WERE EX-CONVICTS FROM SPAIN!

MARCH 25, 1944

ILLITERATE
AFRICAN NEGRO
"SAVAGES" + A FEW MONTHS
TRAINING IN MODERN
MILITARY SCIENCE =

WORLD'S
BEST
JUNGLE
FIGHTERS!

THESE AFRICAN NEGROES ALSO
MASTERED THE MOST EXACTING
MECHANICAL AND MEDICAL SKILL
IN A SURPRISINGLY SHORT TIME

STIMSON →
NEGROES
CAN'T LEARN
ET?

TAKEN FROM A REPORT
OF THE BRITISH INFORMA-
TION SERVICE TO THE
O.W.I USA •

APRIL 1, 1944

ROBERT S. ABBOTT

LATE FOUNDER, EDITOR AND PUBLISHER OF "THE *CHICAGO DEFENDER*" HAS BEEN **HONORED BY** THE **UNITED STATES** GOVERNMENT.

THE LIBERTY SHIP "ROBERT S. ABBOTT," NAMED IN TRIBUTE TO THIS OUTSTANDING MAN, IS BEING BUILT IN RICHMOND, CALIF.

MR. ABBOTT HAS ALSO BEEN HONORED BY THE GOVERNMENTS OF FRANCE AND BRAZIL! HE WAS ACTIVE IN MANY CIVIC ENTERPRISES AND THE AUTHOR OF TWO BOOKS.

APRIL 8, 1944

SIMON

POWERFUL, GIANT BLACK FROM CYRENE...

ATTEMPTED TO SHAME THE MOB OUT OF CRUCIFYING CHRIST......
CARRIED THE CROSS, WHICH HAD BECOME TOO HEAVY FOR SEVERAL ROMAN SOLDIERS, UP THE LONG HILL TO CALVARY!

APRIL 15, 1944

JEAN BAPTISTE JULES **BERNADOTTE,**

A FRENCH NEGRO BORN JAN. 26, 1764.

HE WAS RAISED FROM GENERAL IN THE FRENCH ARMY TO THE **THRONE** OF **SWEDEN!**

AFTER HIS DEATH IN 1844, HIS SON OSCAR BECAME KING OF SWEDEN!

APRIL 22, 1944

General Benjamin Franklin **BUTLER**

BORN DEERFIELD, N.H. NOV. 5, 1818. SON OF A NEGRO BARBER.

RAN FOR GOVERNOR OF MASSACHUSETTS, 1860. DEFEATED MAINLY BECAUSE HE FAVORED THE PRO-SLAVERY BRECKENRIDGE FOR PRESIDENT. ALSO RAN IN 1877 AND 1879. LATER HE WAS A CANDIDATE FOR PRESIDENT OF THE UNITED STATES.

DURING THE CIVIL WAR HE WAS A GENERAL IN THE UNION ARMY AND A HERO IN THE BATTLE OF NEW ORLEANS.

HE GAINED PROMINENCE FOR HIS ADMINISTRATIVE WORK IN OCCUPIED AREAS!

APRIL 29, 1944

IN 1822, DOM ANTONIO JOSÉ D'ALCANTARA

PEDRO 1

SON OF JOHN VI, KING OF PORTUGAL AND NEPHEW OF FERDINAND VII, KING OF SPAIN, BECAME THE FIRST

EMPEROR OF BRAZIL

AT THE AGE OF 24!
ON HIS FATHER'S DEATH HE BECAME

KING OF PORTUGAL!

HE PLACED HIS DAUGHTER, DONNA MARIA ON THE THRONE OF PORTUGAL AND HIS SON, PEDRO II, FOLLOWED HIM AS RULER OF BRAZIL. HE WAS BROTHER-IN-LAW OF NAPOLEON! PEDRO II ABOLISHED SLAVERY IN BRAZIL IN 1888. THE PEDROS WERE OF AFRICAN DESCENT!

MAY 6, 1944

JOHN TYLER

OF VIRGINIA
PRESIDENT OF THE UNITED STATES, 1840-44

SOLD HIS DAUGHTER INTO SLAVERY FOR 'ELOPING WITH A NEGRO!

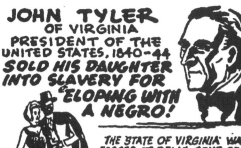

THE STATE OF VIRGINIA WAS FORCED TO RELAX SOME OF ITS SAVAGE "RACE PURITY" LAWS WHEN IT LEARNED THAT MANY OF ITS "FIRST CITIZENS" WERE PART NEGRO INCLUDING THREE U.S. PRESIDENTS, SENATORS, CONGRESSMEN, GOVERNORS, GENERALS, NAVAL OFFICERS ETC.!

MAY 13, 1944

BARON DE VASTEY

MULATTO "MINISTER OF PROPAGANDA" FOR KING CHRISTOPHE OF HAITI.

BARON DE VASTEY WAS EDUCATED IN THE COURTS OF EUROPE. HE RETURNED TO HAITI TO INSTALL ALL THE POMP AND GLAMOR INTO THE BEAUTIFUL PALACE AT SANS SOUCI.

HAITIAN STYLES OF 1817

EVEN THO' THE HAITIAN BLACKS HAD WON THEIR FREEDOM BY DEFEATING THE BEST TROOPS THAT SPAIN, ENGLAND AND EVEN THE GREAT NAPOLEON HAD SENT AGAINST THEM, KING CHRISTOPHE FELT THAT THEY STILL MIGHT FEEL INFERIOR BECAUSE THEY WERE COLORED AND FORMER SLAVES.

SO HE COMMISSIONED BARON DE VASTEY TO WRITE BOOKS ON AFRICAN HISTORY AND NEGRO ACHIEVEMENT WHICH WERE PRINTED ON THE ROYAL PRESS! BARON DE VASTEY WAS ALSO TUTOR TO THE PRINCE AND HE EMPLOYED WHITE LADIES FROM THE U.S.A. TO INSTRUCT THE PRINCESS IN THE SOCIAL GRACES AND RACIAL EQUALITY!

THE PALACE RUINS

MAY 20, 1944

ISAAC MURPHY, Jockey

THREE TIME WINNER OF THE KENTUCKY DERBY!
1884, 1890 AND 1891!

ISAAC MURPHY WAS BORN IN LEXINGTON, KENTUCKY, JANUARY 1st. 1861.

WILLIAM WALKER, NEGRO JOCKEY,

WON THE KENTUCKY DERBY IN 1877. HE ALSO WON AT CHURCHILL DOWNS JULY 4th 1878!

NEGROES ARE NO LONGER PERMITTED TO RIDE IN THE DERBY!

MAY 27, 1944

REV. ROSS D. BROWN, TABLOID HISTORIAN..

REVEREND BROWN COMPILED AN OUTLINE OF NEGRO HISTORY FROM THE BUILDING OF THE PYRAMIDS THRU 1943.

INCLUDED IN HIS BOOK IS A CHAPTER LISTING OUTSTANDING NEGROES AND EVENTS OF INTEREST TO OUR RACE FOR EACH DAY OF THE YEAR AND FOR EACH LETTER OF THE ALPHABET!

JUNE 3, 1944

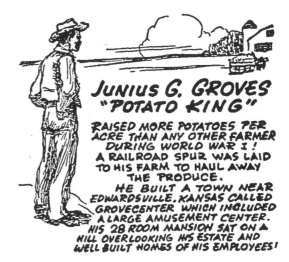

JUNIUS G. GROVES "POTATO KING"

RAISED MORE POTATOES PER ACRE THAN ANY OTHER FARMER DURING WORLD WAR I ! A RAILROAD SPUR WAS LAID TO HIS FARM TO HAUL AWAY THE PRODUCE.
HE BUILT A TOWN NEAR EDWARDSVILLE, KANSAS CALLED GROVECENTER WHICH INCLUDED A LARGE AMUSEMENT CENTER. HIS 28 ROOM MANSION SAT ON A HILL OVERLOOKING HIS ESTATE AND WELL BUILT HOMES OF HIS EMPLOYEES!

JUNE 10, 1944

Ludwig Van BEETHOVEN

CONSIDERED ONE OF THE GREATEST MUSICAL COMPOSERS OF MODERN TIME!

BORN, 1770 OF NEGRO EXTRACTION!

HIS COMPOSITIONS WERE VERY NUMEROUS AND IN EVERY VARIETY OF STYLE.

ALTHO' HE BECAME TOTALLY DEAF AT THE AGE OF FORTY, MUCH OF HIS BEST WORK WAS DONE AFTER THAT TIME.
HE DIED IN 1827. HIS STATUE, ERECTED IN BONNE, GERMANY, HIS BIRTH PLACE, WAS DESTROYED WITH HIS WORK BY RACE HATING NAZIS.

JUNE 17, 1944

ÆMILIANUS C. JULIUS, COLORED LABORER,

WORKED HIS WAY UP TO BECOME **EMPEROR OF ROME !**

HIS REIGN LASTED BUT FOUR MONTHS WHEN HE WAS KILLED BY HIS OWN SOLDIERS AT THE AGE OF 46 !

THE GREAT **JULIUS CAESAR** HIMSELF, COULD TRACE HIS ANCESTRY BACK TO AN AFRICAN GRANDMOTHER!

IN AMERICA TODAY HE WOULD BE A NEGRO!

JUNE 24, 1944

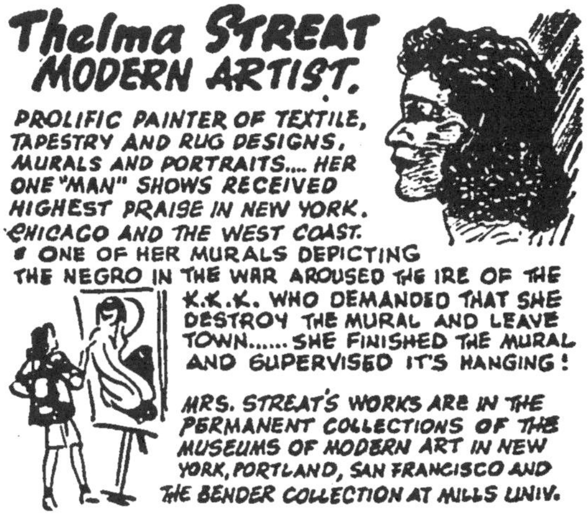
Thelma STREAT
MODERN ARTIST.
PROLIFIC PAINTER OF TEXTILE, TAPESTRY AND RUG DESIGNS, MURALS AND PORTRAITS.... HER ONE "MAN" SHOWS RECEIVED HIGHEST PRAISE IN NEW YORK, CHICAGO AND THE WEST COAST.
ONE OF HER MURALS DEPICTING THE NEGRO IN THE WAR AROUSED THE IRE OF THE K.K.K. WHO DEMANDED THAT SHE DESTROY THE MURAL AND LEAVE TOWN...... SHE FINISHED THE MURAL AND SUPERVISED IT'S HANGING!
MRS. STREAT'S WORKS ARE IN THE PERMANENT COLLECTIONS OF THE MUSEUMS OF MODERN ART IN NEW YORK, PORTLAND, SAN FRANCISCO AND THE BENDER COLLECTION AT MILLS UNIV.

JULY 1, 1944

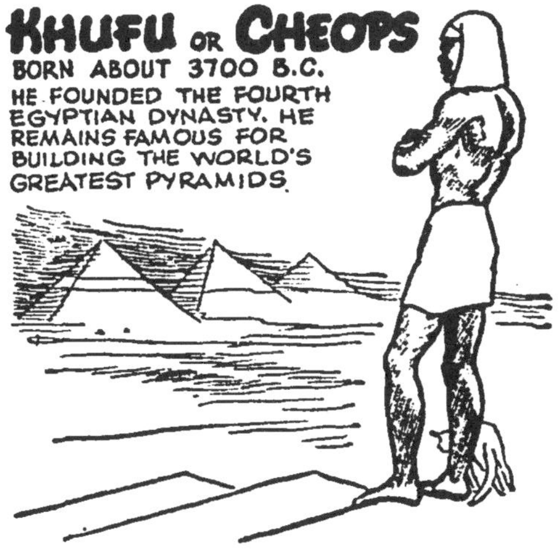
KHUFU OR CHEOPS
BORN ABOUT 3700 B.C.
HE FOUNDED THE FOURTH EGYPTIAN DYNASTY. HE REMAINS FAMOUS FOR BUILDING THE WORLD'S GREATEST PYRAMIDS.

JULY 8, 1944

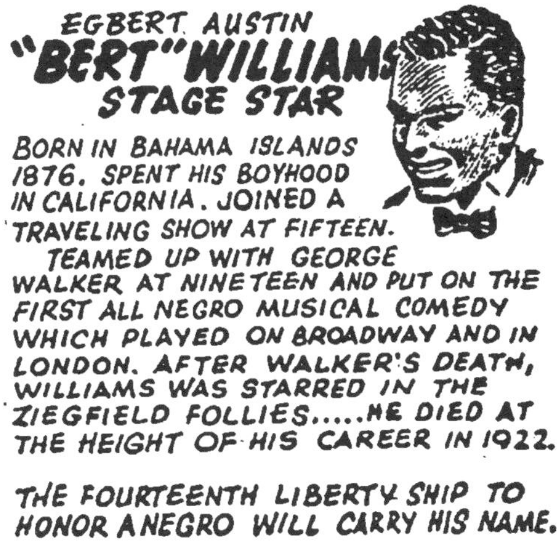
EGBERT AUSTIN
"BERT" WILLIAMS
STAGE STAR
BORN IN BAHAMA ISLANDS 1876. SPENT HIS BOYHOOD IN CALIFORNIA. JOINED A TRAVELING SHOW AT FIFTEEN.
TEAMED UP WITH GEORGE WALKER AT NINETEEN AND PUT ON THE FIRST ALL NEGRO MUSICAL COMEDY WHICH PLAYED ON BROADWAY AND IN LONDON. AFTER WALKER'S DEATH, WILLIAMS WAS STARRED IN THE ZIEGFIELD FOLLIES.....HE DIED AT THE HEIGHT OF HIS CAREER IN 1922.
THE FOURTEENTH LIBERTY SHIP TO HONOR A NEGRO WILL CARRY HIS NAME.

JULY 15, 1944

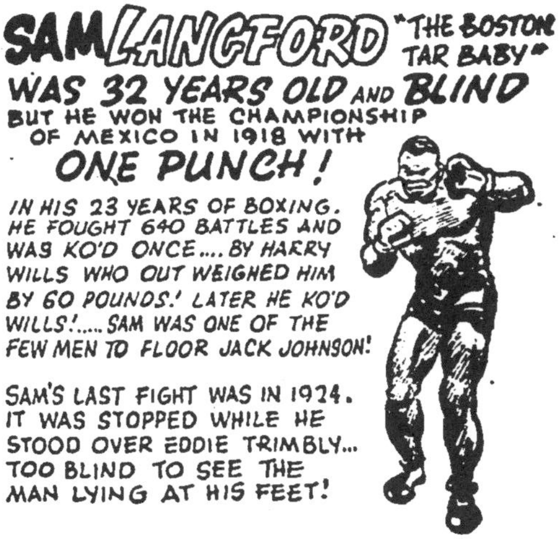
SAM LANGFORD
"THE BOSTON TAR BABY"
WAS 32 YEARS OLD AND BLIND
BUT HE WON THE CHAMPIONSHIP OF MEXICO IN 1918 WITH
ONE PUNCH!
IN HIS 23 YEARS OF BOXING. HE FOUGHT 640 BATTLES AND WAS KO'D ONCE.... BY HARRY WILLS WHO OUT WEIGHED HIM BY 60 POUNDS! LATER HE KO'D WILLS!..... SAM WAS ONE OF THE FEW MEN TO FLOOR JACK JOHNSON!
SAM'S LAST FIGHT WAS IN 1924. IT WAS STOPPED WHILE HE STOOD OVER EDDIE TRIMBLY... TOO BLIND TO SEE THE MAN LYING AT HIS FEET!

JULY 22, 1944

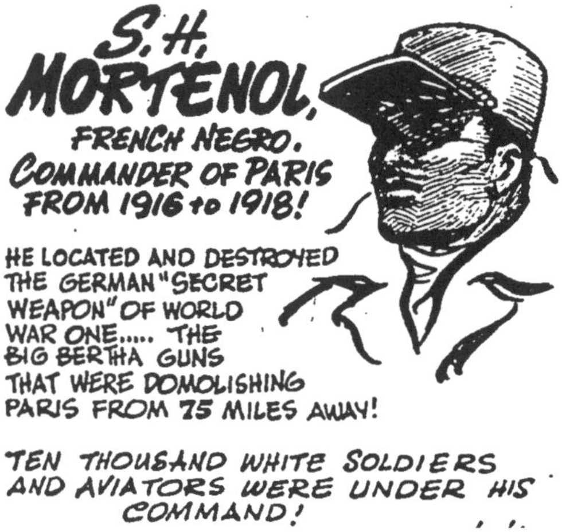
S. H. MORTENOL,
FRENCH NEGRO. COMMANDER OF PARIS FROM 1916 to 1918!
HE LOCATED AND DESTROYED THE GERMAN "SECRET WEAPON" OF WORLD WAR ONE..... THE BIG BERTHA GUNS THAT WERE DOMOLISHING PARIS FROM 75 MILES AWAY!
TEN THOUSAND WHITE SOLDIERS AND AVIATORS WERE UNDER HIS COMMAND!

JULY 29, 1944

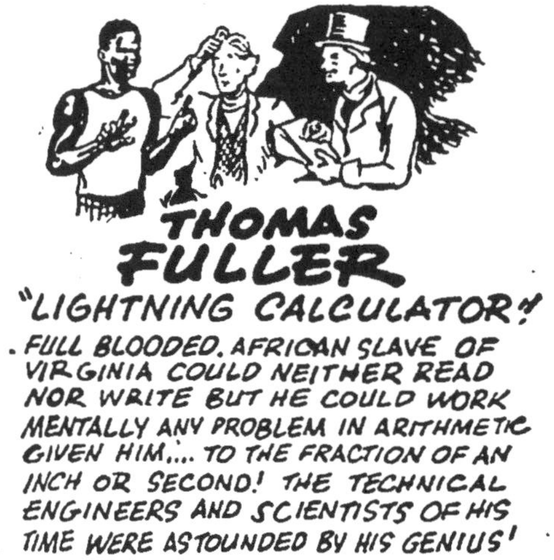
THOMAS FULLER
"LIGHTNING CALCULATOR!"
FULL BLOODED. AFRICAN SLAVE OF VIRGINIA COULD NEITHER READ NOR WRITE BUT HE COULD WORK MENTALLY ANY PROBLEM IN ARITHMETIC GIVEN HIM.... TO THE FRACTION OF AN INCH OR SECOND! THE TECHNICAL ENGINEERS AND SCIENTISTS OF HIS TIME WERE ASTOUNDED BY HIS GENIUS!

AUGUST 5, 1944

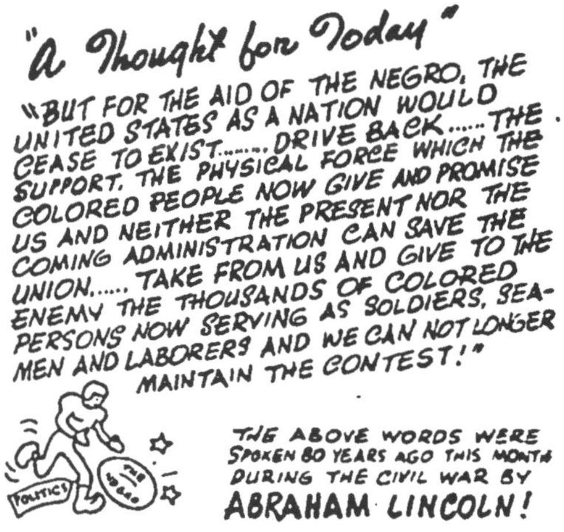
"A Thought for Today"
"BUT FOR THE AID OF THE NEGRO, THE UNITED STATES AS A NATION WOULD CEASE TO EXIST........DRIVE BACK......THE SUPPORT, THE PHYSICAL FORCE WHICH THE COLORED PEOPLE NOW GIVE AND PROMISE US AND NEITHER THE PRESENT NOR THE COMING ADMINISTRATION CAN SAVE THE UNION...... TAKE FROM US AND GIVE TO THE ENEMY THE THOUSANDS OF COLORED PERSONS NOW SERVING AS SOLDIERS, SEA-MEN AND LABORERS AND WE CAN NOT LONGER MAINTAIN THE CONTEST!"
POLITICS
THE NEGRO
THE ABOVE WORDS WERE SPOKEN 80 YEARS AGO THIS MONTH DURING THE CIVIL WAR BY
ABRAHAM LINCOLN!

AUGUST 12, 1944

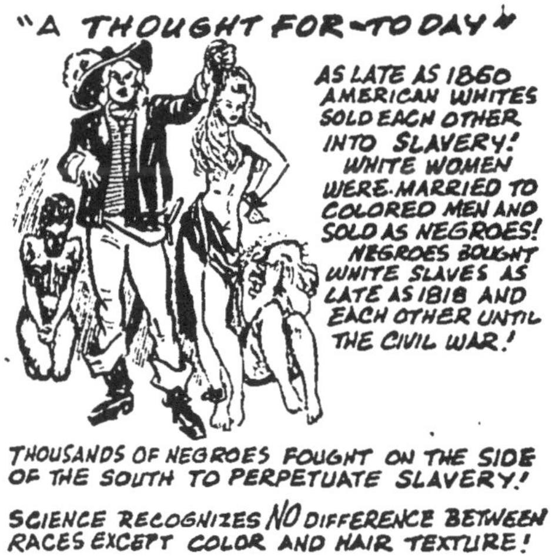
"A THOUGHT FOR-TODAY"
AS LATE AS 1860 AMERICAN WHITES SOLD EACH OTHER INTO SLAVERY! WHITE WOMEN WERE MARRIED TO COLORED MEN AND SOLD AS NEGROES! NEGROES BOUGHT WHITE SLAVES AS LATE AS 1818 AND EACH OTHER UNTIL THE CIVIL WAR!
THOUSANDS OF NEGROES FOUGHT ON THE SIDE OF THE SOUTH TO PERPETUATE SLAVERY!
SCIENCE RECOGNIZES NO DIFFERENCE BETWEEN RACES EXCEPT COLOR AND HAIR TEXTURE!

AUGUST 19, 1944

"A THOUGHT FOR TODAY"

NEGROES CROSSED THE ATLANTIC FROM AFRICA HUNDREDS OF YEARS BEFORE COLUMBUS!

THE FIRST WHITE MEN TO REACH AMERICA-FOUND NEGROES!

IN CENTRAL AMERICA THERE ARE NUMEROUS IDOLS CARVED FROM BLACK STONE WITH NEGROID FEATURES THAT STILL STAND AS AS LASTING PROOF THAT THE INDIAN NATIVES HAD NOT ONLY SEEN NEGROES BUT THOUGHT OF THEM AS GODS!

AUGUST 26, 1944

"A THOUGHT FOR TODAY"

HITLER, ONE OF THE WORST NEGRO HATERS OUTSIDE OF AMERICA, NEVER APPEARS IN PUBLIC WITHOUT AN ANCIENT NEGRO SIGN ON HIS ARMS CHEST AND CAP! THE SWASTIKA IS AN AFRICAN SYMBOL OF FERTILITY!

ST. MAURICE IS THE CELESTIAL SAINT OF GERMANY.... AS COMMANDER OF A ROMAN LEGION, HE GAVE HIS LIFE DEFENDING CHRISTIANS IN 287 A.D. HIS PICTURE BEARING THE GERMAN EAGLE GRACED MANY GERMAN CATHEDRALS.... HITLER OFTEN STRIKES A SIMILAR POSE FOR PHOTOGRAPHERS! ST. MAURICE WAS PURE NEGRO!

SEPTEMBER 2, 1944

"A THOUGHT FOR TODAY"

TO SOLVE THE COLOR PROBLEM IN HAITI,

NAPOLEON TRIED TO MAKE IT LEGAL FOR A MAN TO TAKE TWO WIVES! ONE WHITE, ONE NEGRO!

ALTHO SOME THEOLOGIANS WERE WILLING, THE POPE WOULD NOT GIVE THE FINAL CONSENT.

SEPTEMBER 9, 1944

"A THOUGHT FOR TODAY"

ADMIRAL: TITLE OF THE HIGHEST RANKING OFFICER IN THE ENGLISH, FRENCH AND U.S. NAVIES WAS SO NAMED BY ENGLAND OUT OF "RESPECT" FOR A BAND OF NEGRO SEA ROVERS!

IN THE EARLY 19th CENTURY, AMIR-AL BAHR (LORD OF THE SEAS), NEGRO, WAS COMMANDER OF A FLEET THAT TERRORIZED THE EUROPEAN COAST, ATLANTIC AND MEDITERRANEAN SHIPPING!

IN 1815 THE UNITED STATES SENT A FLEET TO AFRICA TO FREE WHITE AMERICANS HE HAD ENSLAVED!

SEPTEMBER 16, 1944

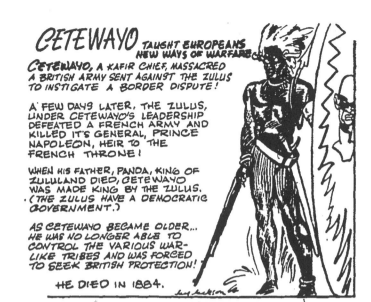

CETEWAYO TAUGHT EUROPEANS NEW WAYS OF WARFARE!

CETEWAYO, A KAFIR CHIEF, MASSACRED A BRITISH ARMY SENT AGAINST THE ZULUS TO INSTIGATE A BORDER DISPUTE!

A FEW DAYS LATER, THE ZULUS, UNDER CETEWAYO'S LEADERSHIP DEFEATED A FRENCH ARMY AND KILLED IT'S GENERAL, PRINCE NAPOLEON, HEIR TO THE FRENCH THRONE!

WHEN HIS FATHER, PANDA, KING OF ZULULAND DIED, CETEWAYO WAS MADE KING BY THE ZULUS. (THE ZULUS HAVE A DEMOCRATIC GOVERNMENT.)

AS CETEWAYO BECAME OLDER... HE WAS NO LONGER ABLE TO CONTROL THE VARIOUS WARLIKE TRIBES AND WAS FORCED TO SEEK BRITISH PROTECTION!

HE DIED IN 1884.

SEPTEMBER 23, 1944

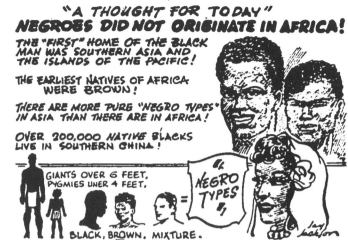

"A THOUGHT FOR TODAY"
NEGROES DID NOT ORIGINATE IN AFRICA!

THE "FIRST" HOME OF THE BLACK MAN WAS SOUTHERN ASIA AND THE ISLANDS OF THE PACIFIC!

THE EARLIEST NATIVES OF AFRICA WERE BROWN!

THERE ARE MORE PURE "NEGRO TYPES" IN ASIA THAN THERE ARE IN AFRICA!

OVER 200,000 NATIVE BLACKS LIVE IN SOUTHERN CHINA!

GIANTS OVER 6 FEET. PYGMIES UNDER 4 FEET.

BLACK, BROWN, MIXTURE. "NEGRO TYPES"

SEPTEMBER 30, 1944

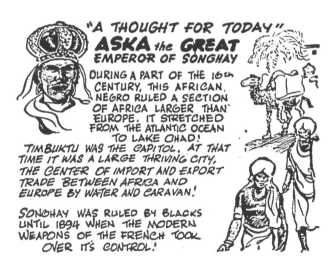

"A THOUGHT FOR TODAY"
ASKA the GREAT
EMPEROR OF SONGHAY

DURING A PART OF THE 16th CENTURY, THIS AFRICAN NEGRO RULED A SECTION OF AFRICA LARGER THAN EUROPE. IT STRETCHED FROM THE ATLANTIC OCEAN TO LAKE CHAD!

TIMBUKTU WAS THE CAPITOL. AT THAT TIME IT WAS A LARGE THRIVING CITY, THE CENTER OF IMPORT AND EXPORT TRADE BETWEEN AFRICA AND EUROPE BY WATER AND CARAVAN!

SONGHAY WAS RULED BY BLACKS UNTIL 1894 WHEN THE MODERN WEAPONS OF THE FRENCH TOOK OVER IT'S CONTROL!

OCTOBER 7, 1944

"A THOUGHT FOR TODAY"
"PRINCE ANTONIO APACHE"

TALL, HANDSOME INDIAN FROM ARIZONA, WAS WELCOMED INTO THE EXCLUSIVE SOCIETY OF NEW YORK'S "400"! HE WAS FETED IN THE GOLDEN HORSE SHOE AT THE METROPOLITAN OPERA AND LAVISHLY ENTERTAINED BY THE MILLIONAIRE BLUE BLOODS INCLUDING THE JOHN JACOB ASTORS!

PRESIDENT THEODORE ROOSEVELT CONSULTED HIM OFTEN ON INDIAN AFFAIRS!

"PRINCE ANTONIO APACHE" LAUGHED LONG AND HEARTILLY IN THE PRIVACY OF HIS SWANKY HOTEL ROOM FOR IN REALITY HE WAS TONY SIMPSON... A POOR YOUNG MAN FROM LOUISIANA WEARING A STRAIGHT, BLACK WIG TO PUT HIS HOAX OVER! FOR TONY WAS A....
..... NEGRO!

OCTOBER 14, 1944

"A THOUGHT FOR TODAY"
GIBRALTAR,
THE GIANT ROCK THAT GUARDS THE ENTRANCE TO THE MEDITERRANEAN SEA.... GIBRALTAR, THE SYMBOL OF PERMANENCE AND RELIABILITY IS NAMED FOR GEBAL-TARIK!

GEBAL-TARIK CAPTURED THE ROCK, THEN CALLED "CALPE" IN 711 A.D. FROM THERE HE MOVED HIS MOORISH ARMY INTO SPAIN WHICH WAS SUBDUED AND RULED BY THE BLACK SKINNED MOORS FOR SEVEN CENTURIES!

GEBAL-TARIK WAS AN EX SLAVE AND A NEGRO!

OCTOBER 21, 1944

"A THOUGHT FOR TODAY"
.....NEGRO ART.....
NEGROES HAVE INFLUENCED THE ART IN ALL THE CONTINENTS SINCE THE DAWN OF CREATION TO MODERN TIMES!

THE OLDEST PAINTINGS AND CARVINGS ON RECORD WERE EXECUTED BY NEGROES OVER 15000 YEARS AGO!

ASIATIC AND EUROPEAN MASTERS GIVE CREDIT FOR THEIR USE OF STRONG COLOR AND DESIGN TO THEIR ASSOCIATION WITH NEGRO ARTISTS!

THE "MODERN" ART AND MUSIC OF TODAY IS DEFINITELY OF AFRICAN NEGRO ORIGIN!

THE OLDEST DISCOVERED FIGURE CARVING IS OF A NEGRO WOMAN: SCIENTISTS SET ITS AGE AT ABOUT 12000 YEARS!

OCTOBER 28, 1944

"A THOUGHT FOR TODAY"
"QUEEN" LYBONN,
ENGLISH WOMAN WHO
"WENT NATIVE"

IN THE 1850'S. MRS. LYBONN WAS THE UNCROWNED QUEEN OF WEST AFRICAN SLAVE TRADERS!

ALTHO SHE WAS A DEALER IN "BLACK IVORY", SHE FELL IN LOVE WITH A NEGRO!

BOTH OF HER MULATTO DAUGHTERS MARRIED WEALTHY WHITES....ONE A BRITISH CONSUL!

NOVEMBER 4, 1944

"A THOUGHT FOR TODAY"
CUSH,
SON OF HAM, DIED ABOUT 2300 B.C. BUT HE STILL HAS LIVING DECENDANTS!

EMPEROR HAILE SELASSIE CAN TRACE HIS ANCESTRY BACK TO KING SOLOMON AND QUEEN OF SHEBA WHO MET 992 B.C.!

THE ETHIOPIAN ROYAL FAMILY IS THE OLDEST IN THE WORLD!

FROM THERE HIS DIRECT LINEAGE GOES BACK 1358 YEARS TO CUSH!

CUSH WAS NOAH'S GRANDSON!

NOVEMBER 11, 1944

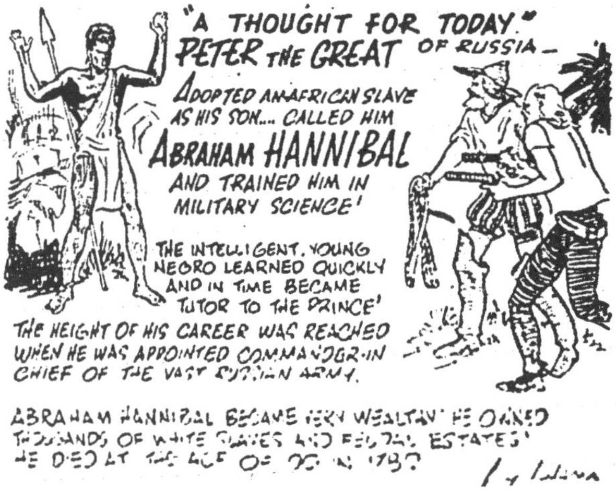
"A THOUGHT FOR TODAY"
PETER THE GREAT OF RUSSIA–
ADOPTED AN AFRICAN SLAVE AS HIS SON... CALLED HIM
ABRAHAM HANNIBAL
AND TRAINED HIM IN MILITARY SCIENCE'
THE INTELLIGENT. YOUNG NEGRO LEARNED QUICKLY AND IN TIME BECAME TUTOR TO THE PRINCE'
THE HEIGHT OF HIS CAREER WAS REACHED WHEN HE WAS APPOINTED COMMANDER-IN CHIEF OF THE VAST RUSSIAN ARMY.
ABRAHAM HANNIBAL BECAME VERY WEALTHY HE OWNED THOUSANDS OF WHITE SLAVES AND FEUDAL ESTATES'
HE DIED AT THE AGE OF

NOVEMBER 18, 1944

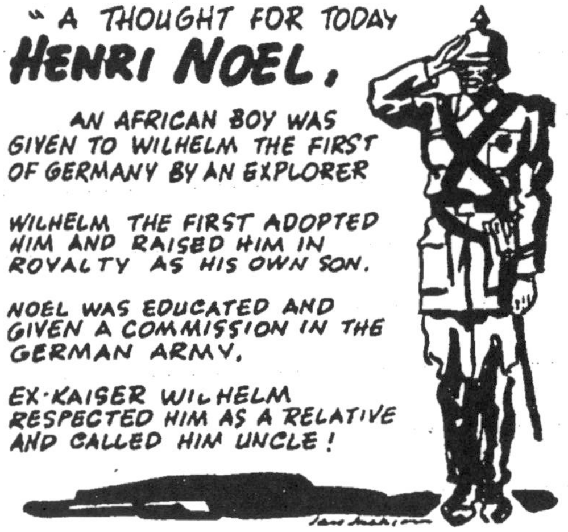
" A THOUGHT FOR TODAY
HENRI NOEL,
AN AFRICAN BOY WAS GIVEN TO WILHELM THE FIRST OF GERMANY BY AN EXPLORER
WILHELM THE FIRST ADOPTED HIM AND RAISED HIM IN ROYALTY AS HIS OWN SON.
NOEL WAS EDUCATED AND GIVEN A COMMISSION IN THE GERMAN ARMY.
EX-KAISER WILHELM RESPECTED HIM AS A RELATIVE AND CALLED HIM UNCLE!

NOVEMBER 25, 1944

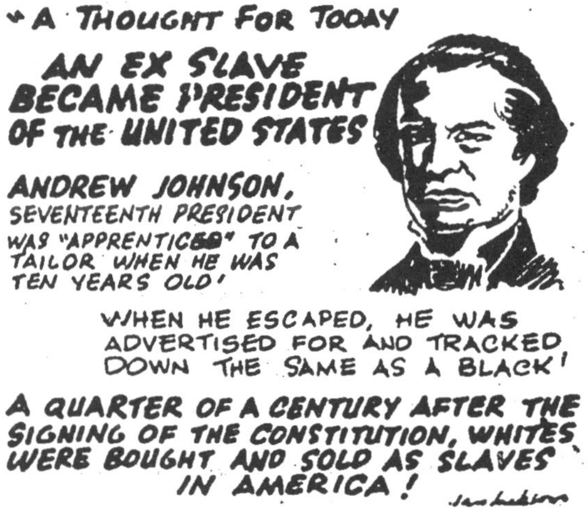
" A THOUGHT FOR TODAY
AN EX SLAVE BECAME PRESIDENT OF THE UNITED STATES
ANDREW JOHNSON, SEVENTEENTH PRESIDENT WAS "APPRENTICED" TO A TAILOR WHEN HE WAS TEN YEARS OLD'
WHEN HE ESCAPED, HE WAS ADVERTISED FOR AND TRACKED DOWN THE SAME AS A BLACK!
A QUARTER OF A CENTURY AFTER THE SIGNING OF THE CONSTITUTION, WHITES WERE BOUGHT AND SOLD AS SLAVES IN AMERICA!
Jay Jackson

DECEMBER 2, 1944

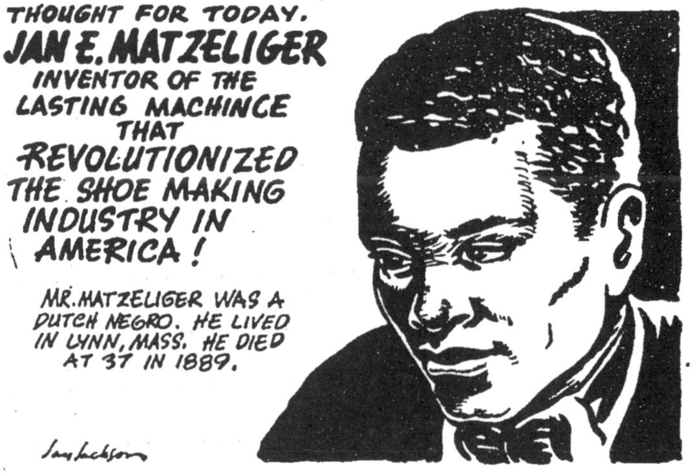
THOUGHT FOR TODAY.
JAN E. MATZELIGER
INVENTOR OF THE LASTING MACHINCE THAT REVOLUTIONIZED THE SHOE MAKING INDUSTRY IN AMERICA!
MR. MATZELIGER WAS A DUTCH NEGRO. HE LIVED IN LYNN, MASS. HE DIED AT 37 IN 1889.
Jay Jackson

DECEMBER 9, 1944

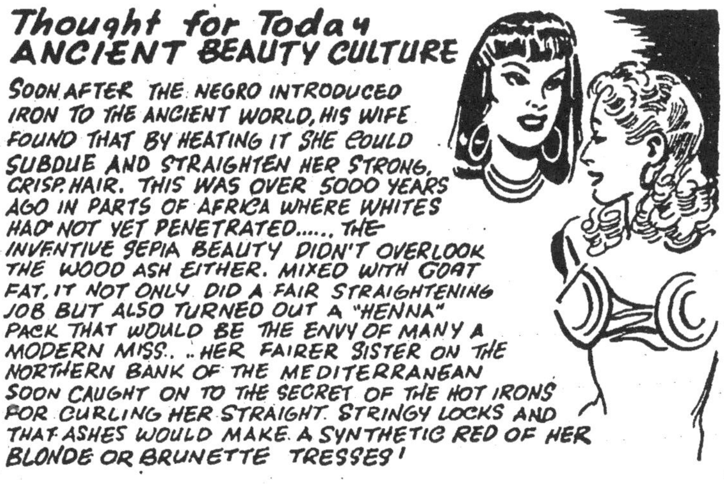
Thought for Today
ANCIENT BEAUTY CULTURE
SOON AFTER THE NEGRO INTRODUCED IRON TO THE ANCIENT WORLD, HIS WIFE FOUND THAT BY HEATING IT SHE COULD SUBDUE AND STRAIGHTEN HER STRONG, CRISP HAIR. THIS WAS OVER 5000 YEARS AGO IN PARTS OF AFRICA WHERE WHITES HAD NOT YET PENETRATED..... THE INVENTIVE SEPIA BEAUTY DIDN'T OVERLOOK THE WOOD ASH EITHER. MIXED WITH GOAT FAT, IT NOT ONLY DID A FAIR STRAIGHTENING JOB BUT ALSO TURNED OUT A "HENNA" PACK THAT WOULD BE THE ENVY OF MANY A MODERN MISS.. ..HER FAIRER SISTER ON THE NORTHERN BANK OF THE MEDITERRANEAN SOON CAUGHT ON TO THE SECRET OF THE HOT IRONS FOR CURLING HER STRAIGHT STRINGY LOCKS AND THAT ASHES WOULD MAKE A SYNTHETIC RED OF HER BLONDE OR BRUNETTE TRESSES!

DECEMBER 16, 1944

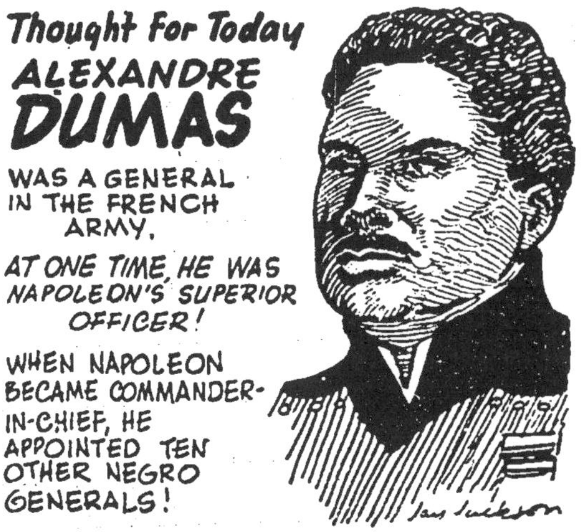
Thought for Today
ALEXANDRE DUMAS
WAS A GENERAL IN THE FRENCH ARMY.
AT ONE TIME, HE WAS NAPOLEON'S SUPERIOR OFFICER!
WHEN NAPOLEON BECAME COMMANDER-IN-CHIEF, HE APPOINTED TEN OTHER NEGRO GENERALS!

DECEMBER 23, 1944

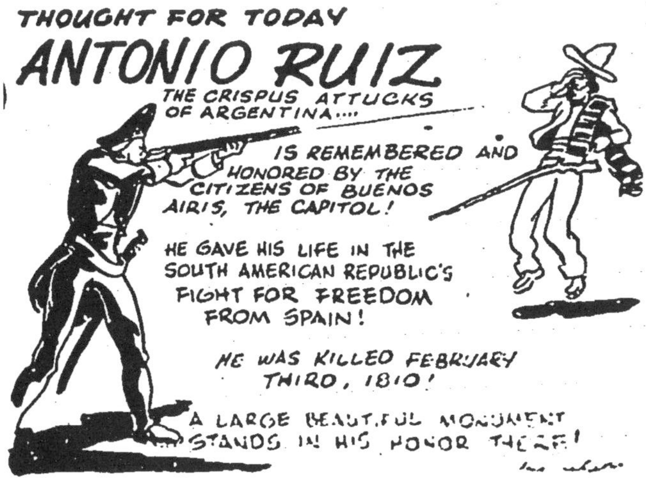
THOUGHT FOR TODAY
ANTONIO RUIZ
THE CRISPUS ATTUCKS OF ARGENTINA....
IS REMEMBERED AND HONORED BY THE CITIZENS OF BUENOS AIRIS, THE CAPITOL!
HE GAVE HIS LIFE IN THE SOUTH AMERICAN REPUBLIC'S FIGHT FOR FREEDOM FROM SPAIN!
HE WAS KILLED FEBRUARY THIRD, 1810!
A LARGE BEAUTIFUL MONUMENT STANDS IN HIS HONOR THERE!

DECEMBER 30, 1944

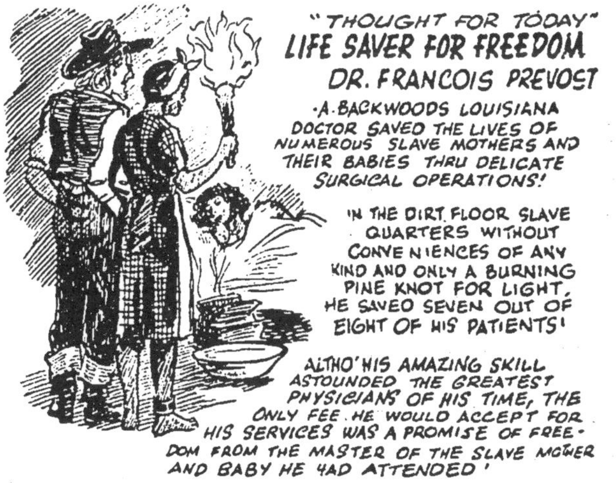
"THOUGHT FOR TODAY"
LIFE SAVER FOR FREEDOM
DR. FRANCOIS PREVOST
-A BACKWOODS LOUISIANA DOCTOR SAVED THE LIVES OF NUMEROUS SLAVE MOTHERS AND THEIR BABIES THRU DELICATE SURGICAL OPERATIONS!
IN THE DIRT FLOOR SLAVE QUARTERS WITHOUT CONVENIENCES OF ANY KIND AND ONLY A BURNING PINE KNOT FOR LIGHT, HE SAVED SEVEN OUT OF EIGHT OF HIS PATIENTS!
ALTHO' HIS AMAZING SKILL ASTOUNDED THE GREATEST PHYSICIANS OF HIS TIME, THE ONLY FEE HE WOULD ACCEPT FOR HIS SERVICES WAS A PROMISE OF FREE-DOM FROM THE MASTER OF THE SLAVE MOTHER AND BABY HE HAD ATTENDED!

JANUARY 6, 1945

ALSO AVAILABLE FROM NEW YORK REVIEW COMICS

YELLOW NEGROES AND OTHER
IMAGINARY CREATURES
Yvan Alagbé

PIERO
Edmond Baudoin

ALMOST COMPLETELY BAXTER
Glen Baxter

AGONY
Mark Beyer

MITCHUM
Blutch

PEPLUM
Blutch

THE GREEN HAND AND
OTHER STORIES
Nicole Claveloux

WHAT AM I DOING HERE?
Abner Dean

THE TENDERNESS OF STONES
Marion Fayolle

TROTS AND BONNIE
Shary Flenniken

LETTER TO SURVIVORS
Gébé

PRETENDING IS LYING
Dominique Goblet

VOICES IN THE DARK
Ulli Lust

ALAY-OOP
William Gropper

ELEPHANT *AND*
THE PROJECTOR
Martin Vaughn James

ALL YOUR RACIAL PROBLEMS
WILL SOON END
Charles Johnson

JIMBO: ADVENTURES IN PARADISE
Gary Panter

FATHER AND SON
E.O. Plauen

SOFT CITY
Pushwagner

THE NEW WORLD
Chris Reynolds

PITTSBURGH
Frank Santoro

DISCIPLINE
Dash Shaw

MACDOODLE ST.
Mark Alan Stamaty

SLUM WOLF
Tadao Tsuge

THE MAN WITHOUT TALENT
Yoshiharu Tsuge

RETURN TO ROMANCE
Ogden Whitney

W THE WHORE
Katrin de Vries and
Anke Feuchtenberger